THROUGH THE GOSPELS
TO JESUS

By Dwight Marion Beck

PROFESSOR OF BIBLE, SYRACUSE UNIVERSITY

Harper & Brothers Publishers New York

Library of Congress catalog card number: 54-5847

Preface

THIS BOOK is intended for any reader who desires to know how scholars study the Gospels and what are the results especially in recent years. It is also intended as a beginning textbook for college study for those who have no knowledge of biblical languages or of the technical terms of theology. Its references are limited to works available in English but are chosen to present various Protestant, Roman Catholic and Jewish viewpoints. It presupposes that the reader will have the text of the Gospels before him. Its purpose is a general study of Jesus, founder of the Christian faith, as set forth in the Gospels and as interpreted by scholars past and present. It undertakes: (1) to present a rapid historical survey of the world in which Jesus lived; (2) to summarize traditional and modern views about the origins of the Gospels; (3) to present briefly the sources for the study of Jesus and to introduce Mark, Matthew, Luke and John; (4) to explain at some length these Gospels, primarily in the light of their authors' original intent, and to explore their age-old, yet ever new, meanings for us today. This constitutes the main part of the work. The method is historical, the viewpoint is liberal, the attitude is open-minded reverence, the aim is to understand the most important books in Christendom and to lay hold on the truth as it is in Jesus.

> Let not my mind be blinder by more light
> Nor faith, by reason added, lose her sight.[1]

DWIGHT MARION BECK

Syracuse University

---

[1] John Donne.

Acknowledgments

My INDEBTEDNESS to many scholars is everywhere evident. In particular I wish to thank Professor Henry J. Cadbury and his staff at the Andover-Harvard Theological Library for their generous and courteous assistance which greatly aided my work. I appreciate the critical reading of parts of the manuscript by Professor Lindsey P. Pherigo of Scarritt College. My colleagues, Professor H. Neil Richardson and Professor John F. Olson, have carried some of my regular duties that I might have freedom to write when Syracuse University granted me a year's leave. Unnumbered students have quickened my thought by their questions and comments about Jesus and the Gospels. My greatest debt is to my wife, Jean. Her clerical work on the manuscript, her candid comments and her constant aid on a lengthy literary journey verify the scriptural proverb, "The heart of her husband doth safely trust in her."

Quotations from the American Standard Version and the Revised Standard Version are used by permission of the Division of Christian Education of the National Council of the Churches of Christ in the United States of America.

D.M.B.

Contents

PART V The Fourth Gospel

Contents

PART I

The World in Which Jesus Lived

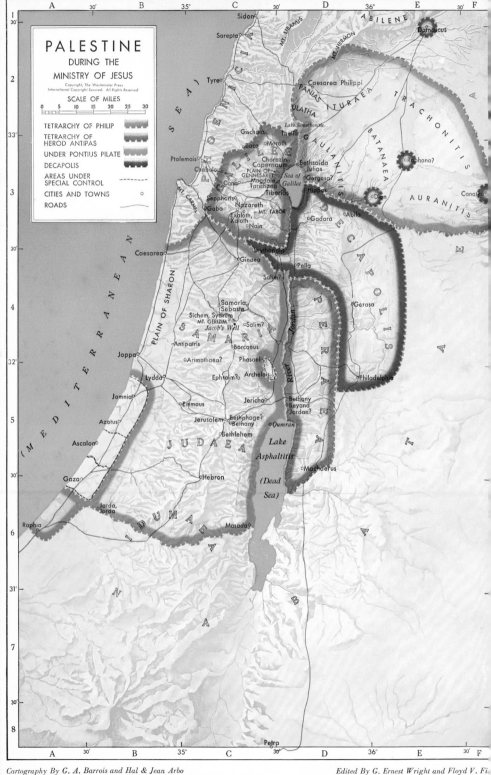

PALESTINE
DURING THE
MINISTRY OF JESUS

Copyright, The Westminster Press
International Copyright Secured. All Rights Reserved

SCALE OF MILES

0   5   10   15   20   25   30

TETRARCHY OF PHILIP
TETRARCHY OF
HEROD ANTIPAS
UNDER PONTIUS PILATE
DECAPOLIS
AREAS UNDER
SPECIAL CONTROL
CITIES AND TOWNS   o
ROADS

Sidon

Sarepta

ABILENE

Damascus

MT. LIBANUS

Tyre

MT. HERMON

Caesarea Philippi
PANIAS

ITURAEA

TRACHONITIS

ULATHA

Lake Semechonitis

Gischala

Thella

Baca

Meroth

GALILEE

GAULANITIS

BATANAEA

Ptolemais

Chorazin
Capernaum

Bethsaida
Julias

Raphana?

Chabulon

PLAIN OF
GENNESARET

Sea of
Galilee

Gergesa?

AURANITIS

Cana

Magdala
Tarichaea

Hippos

Dion

MT. CARMEL

Sepphoris

Tiberias

Canatha

Gaba

Nazareth

Abila

Exaloth,
Xaloth

MT. TABOR

Gadara

DECAPOLIS

Nain

Caesarea

Scythopolis

Pella

Ginaea

Salim?

Gerasa

Samaria,
Sebaste

PLAIN OF SHARON

Sichem, Sychem
MT. GERIZIM

Salim?

Jordan

PERAEA

Jacob's Well

Joppa

Antipatris

Borcaeus

Arimathaea?

Phasaelis

Philadelphia

Lydda

Ephraim?

Archelais

Jamnia

Jericho

Emmaus

Bethany
Beyand
Jordan?

Azotus

Jerusalem

Bethphage?
Bethany

Ascalon

Bethlehem

Qumran

Lake
Asphaltitis

JUDAEA

(Dead
Sea)

Gaza

Hebron

Machaerus

Jarda,
Jorda

IDUMAEA

Raphia

Masada

N

A

B

Petra

(MEDITERRANEAN   SEA)

(PHOENICIA)

Cartography By G. A. Barrois and Hal & Jean Arbo

Edited By G. Ernest Wright and Floyd V. Fi

1

The Country

THE HOMELAND of Jesus has had various names. In the days of his forefathers, as the Old Testament shows, it was the land of Canaan (Gen. 11:31). By a curious turn of history the well-known name of Palestine is not derived from Jews or Christians but from Philistines. These sea people, who probably came from the island of Crete and who settled in the thirteenth century B.C. on the coast of southwestern Canaan, left their name Philistia upon the region. In the fifth century Herodotus, the Greek historian, referred to the seacoast from Phoenicia to Egypt as Palaistine.[1] In the first century of the Christian era, Josephus, a Jewish historian, repeats this name which he applied to the area from Gaza to Egypt.[2] The Romans who ended Jewish independence in 63 B.C. called the country Palestina and often regarded it as part of the province to the north known as Syria. Though Palestine eventually became the name of the entire land, there was no single name for it in the first century. Separate names like Judea, Samaria, Galilee and Perea were applied to certain areas.

Palestine has often been called a bridge which aptly describes both its location and its shape. It stands between the two areas of great civilizations: the Nile and the Tigris-Euphrates valleys. Bounded on the west by the Mediterranean Sea and on the east by the vast desert of Arabia, Palestine stretches its 10,000 square miles from the gorge of the Litani River in the north to the rugged wilderness below Beersheba in the south. In size and contour it resembles New Hampshire. In a small area its amazing geographical diversities match the variety of its historical changes. This land bridge is most interesting for its scenery and for the march of events across it. No other country contains so much in so little space. Its length is about 150 miles, while its width progresses from thirty-five miles in the north to twice that distance in the south. Flying by plane from west to east one can easily distinguish four distinct parallel areas: (1) a narrow sandy coastal plain; (2) a wider central hilly region; (3) a deep river valley with

[1] *Hist.* VII.89
[2] *Ant.* I.vi.2.

two inland seas; (4) a high rough plateau that stretches eastward into the desert. Each of these areas needs further description.[3]

The coastal plain extends north and south with an unbroken sea line except where the range of Mount Carmel juts into the Mediterranean. Above Carmel the mountains soon come down to the sea and in the long line of foam where sea and land meet there is no welcoming break. It seems "as if the land were everywhere saying to the sea: 'I do not wish you, I do not need you!' "[4] Though the plain occasionally is four or five miles wide in other places, the hills march down to the sea as at the Ladder of Tyre where the road had to be cut in the face of a steep cliff to provide passageway. Below Carmel the coast widens ten miles into the Plain of Sharon and still farther south it expands twenty miles into the Plain of Philistia. These plains traversed by stream beds which slope westward from the steep hills are fertile, well-watered and adapted to agriculture except for drifting sand areas near the sea. They may have been partly forested in biblical days.

The central hilly area with its many valleys rises rapidly from the plain to an altitude which often reaches one half mile. This is a rocky country in which gray limestone outcrops everywhere amid small upland fields. From Mount Hermon in the north this wide rough ridge extends like a backbone to Idumea and the desert in the south (Negeb). North of Palestine two ranges of mountains, Lebanon on the west and Anti-Lebanon on the east, enclose a valley known as Coele (Hollow) Syria. Mount Hermon in the Anti-Lebanon range pushes snow-clad shoulders up to 9,100 feet. It is visible from much of upper Palestine. The foothills of the Lebanons slope down into Galilee where rolling hills diminish to the great Plain of Esdraelon (Jezreel). This is the only lowland which breaks the main central ridge. Its triangular level area reaches from Carmel in the west to Mount Tabor in the northeast and toward Mount Gilboa on

[3] G. A. Smith, *Historical Geography of the Holy Land* (4th ed. New York, n.d.), 45–104; W. J. Phythian-Adams in *A New Commentary on Holy Scripture* (New York, 1928), Pt.I, 634–46; E. E. Voigt in *The Abingdon Bible Commentary* (New York, 1929), 52–59; J. M. Adams, *Biblical Backgrounds* (Nashville, 1934), 139–86; G. Dalman, *Sacred Sites and Ways* (New York, 1935), 1–14; J. N. Schofield, *Historical Background of the Bible* (London, 1938), 3–29; J. E. Steinmueller, *A Companion to Bible Studies* (New York, 1941), I, 357–89; M. S. and J. L. Miller, *Encyclopedia of Bible Life* (New York, 1944), 22–232; G. E. Wright and F. V. Filson, *The Westminster Historical Atlas to the Bible* (Philadelphia, 1945), 17–21; F. Prat, *Jesus Christ* (Milwaukee, 1950), I, 445–53; E. W. K. Mould, *Essentials of Bible History* (rev. ed. New York, 1951), 8–19.

[4] G. A. Smith, *op. cit.*, 131.

the southeast. It has been famous as the breadbasket and the battlefield of Palestine. The hills of Samaria continue southward from Esdraelon with two central peaks, Mount Gerizim and Mount Ebal which tower upward about 3,000 feet. Still southward from Samaria the highlands of Judea extend in broken hills until they descend below Jerusalem and Hebron into the desert. To the westward an undulating region, cut by many valleys, steps down to the maritime plain. The eastern side drops so steeply toward the great rift of the Jordan that its arid, bleak and broken region is known as the Wilderness of Judea. From Jerusalem in the hill country at an altitude nearly 2,600 feet above sea level to the Dead Sea 1,275 feet below sea level there is a drop of 3,850 feet in fifteen miles. This whole central section of Palestine is described by Josephus.[5] He saw Galilee with soil universally rich and cultivated, Samaria with fruitful trees on hills and valleys, Perea with planted plains and Judea with excellent grasslands, each "very full of people."

A great geological fault created the valley in which flows one of the most remarkable rivers in the world. "Its role in history has been great beyond all rational measurement."[6] Man's story can be traced for 100,000 years in the Jordan valley. The Jordan, "the Down-Comer," rises from four smaller streams which drain snow and rain from the Lebanons. It flows through swampy stretches and soon reaches a small shallow lake, Semechonitis (Huleh) which lies near sea level. Beyond this lake the Jordan soon tumbles for ten miles in rapid descent into the fresh waters of the Lake of Galilee which is nearly 700 feet below sea level. This harp-shaped lake, thirteen miles long and eight wide, was famed for its fish. In the first century it was also named the Sea of Tiberias and Lake of Gennesaret. High hills descend near to the lake shore except for a small fertile plain on the northwest side. At Tiberias on the west side hot springs flow at which curative baths were built in Roman days.

Southward from the Lake of Galilee the Jordan continues for sixty-five miles through a valley three to fourteen miles wide until it empties into the salty Dead Sea. But the Jordan winds in serpentine coils so that its total course is about three times the airline distance from Galilee to the Sea. Many streams enlarge the Jordan from the eastern and the western highlands. The Jordan is a rapid, muddy stream about 100 feet wide and three to fifteen feet deep. There are two levels in the valley. First, a narrow, winding depression, the

[5] *Wars* III.3.
[6] N. Glueck, *The River Jordan* (Philadelphia, 1946), 62.

"Jungle of the Jordan," "through which the Jordan knifes its way, is tropical in character and, for the most part, lush green in color. Its vegetation is rank and thorn and thistle grow shoulder high. It is covered with dense and at times impenetrable thickets of oleander, cane, tangled bushes, vines, willows, poplars and twisted tamarisks. From the air it looms like a slimy green snake, standing out all the more startlingly because of the desert white and dirty gray of its surroundings." [7] Second, the broad upper floor of the valley which rises 150 feet above the river is a mass of broken marl hills. These steep, bare peaks and jagged valleys riffle the surface into an eroded desert-like area. The river meanders finally into the Dead Sea which was also known as the Sea of Salt and Lake Asphaltitis. It extends almost fifty miles southward between grim mountain heights which rise 4,000 feet above the sea. The width of the Sea is about ten miles. There is no outlet but hot winds and sun cause a remarkable evaporation which leaves its gray-blue, bitter waters with 25 per cent salt, magnesium chloride and other minerals. Like the Great Salt Lake of Utah its specific gravity is high enough to support readily any swimmer who lies down upon its surface. No fish live in this oily Sea and the whole surrounding area has a lifeless forbidding appearance. Below the Sea lie the desert stretches known in the first century as Nabatea.

The east Jordan highlands, cut by numerous canyons, rise rapidly from the valley. The gorges of three important rivers trisect the plateau. The Yarmuk enters the Jordan below Galilee, the Jabbok flows in at a point nearly midway to the Sea and the Arnon cuts its way at the middle of the Dead Sea. North of the Yarmuk black basalt rocks, extinct volcanoes and rich red soil stretch into a great upland plain. South of the Yarmuk limestone replaces the basalt and the rolling hills reach southward alternating with valleys until the desert takes over the area. The whole plateau region, east of the Jordan, is noted for both agricultural and pastoral use until it merges eastward into the desert of Arabia where lack of rainfall reduces its advantages for man. In the first century the area along the upper half of the Dead Sea and the lower Jordan was known as Perea and in earlier days as Moab and Ammon. North and east lay the region known as Decapolis, a general term which referred to Ten Cities. In Old Testament days Gilead was its name. Northeast of Galilee there was no single name for the region in the days of Jesus. Parts of it were known as

[7] Glueck, *op. cit.,* 63.

Gaulanitis, Batanea and Auranitis which bore Old Testament names of Bashan and Hauran.

The climate of Palestine varies from temperate to semitropical while its altitudes and seasons produce some unusual features. The maritime plain and the deep Jordan valley have hot summers and mild winters. The highlands are comfortable in summer and cold in winter, with occasional frost and snow. Rainfall, which averages twenty-six inches annually, comes in winter months, most heavily from December through March. From mid-May through October the skies are almost cloudless and rainless. The southwesterly winds of winter bring moisture off the sea. In summer the northwesterlies produce heavy dews and the northerlies cool the land. The dry east winds are rare in summer. The south or southeast winds are warm or burning hot and blow notably in spring or fall. The climate is healthy though there are great ranges in temperature, even in a single day, especially in the plateaus. There are extremes in climate from the icy slopes of Hermon to the unbearable heat around the Dead Sea.

The geographical aspects and climate of Palestine have not changed since Bible days. Tacitus, the Roman historian of the first century, described Judea as a country with a dry and sultry climate and a rich and fertile soil.[8] One modern traveler, while granting exceptions, has concluded, "The thoughtful visitor soon makes up his mind that nothing in Palestine under a roof is much worth seeing and nothing in Palestine out of doors is not worth seeing."[9] To a visitor the Holy Land, apart from its religious associations, displays unforgettable scenery. The country is tiny but immensely diversified. On a summer day a tourist can cross the entire land from west to east by automobile in two hours, but the constant changes delight the eyes and linger in memory. The incredible deep blue of the Mediterranean lightens into foaming waves upon a sandy shore. A fertile plain abounds in grain fields and orchards. Stately palm trees, silvery olive trees, dark green fig trees and climbing vineyards lead up through a rapid ascent toward the horizon of hills. The citrus fruit orchards of today are an importation later than Bible days. Rocky, bare ridges, interspersed with small patches of cultivated fields, stand out in the hills. Stones lie everywhere and are often used to terrace the hillsides. The limestone backbone of the country reaches north and south. Caves can be readily found in it. Not waiting at the medieval walls of old Jerusalem, the road enters the broken barren wilderness which

[8] *Hist.* V.6.
[9] H. E. Fosdick, *A Pilgrimage to Palestine* (New York, 1927), 20.

drops steeply toward the depths of the Jordan with its lunar land-
scape and its green bed of the river coiling toward its final sea. Beyond the gigantic trench the towering ramparts of the eastern plateau
are split by many gorges. Over all these varied scenes the sun, out of
a bright blue sky, spreads its dazzling light. When evening comes,
the softened sun, as it sinks into the western sea, sweeps golden
gleams across the hills. Then eastward across the deep valley before
darkness falls, amethystine shadows beautify mountains and sky with
brief indescribable splendor. The placidly clear or fantastically shad-
owed face of Palestine under a full moon, brightening the land beyond anything known in cloudy northern latitudes, remains a silvered
memory to those who have watched it through a summer night.

Though the attempt has often been made, there is little use in trying to trace the travels of Jesus geographically in a complete and orderly sequence because there is no exact information to connect the
references to journeys and places. The interest of the gospel writers
was not so much in where Jesus went but in who he was and what
he did and said. The Gospels contain some general information about
the travels of Jesus. Luke reports that the parents of Jesus, who lived
in Galilee, journeyed to Judea where Jesus was born in Bethlehem.
Matthew notes that the family fled to Egypt to escape Herod's deadly
orders for the massacre of infants. Jesus grew up in Nazareth, but
before he began his public ministry, he went down to the Jordan valley where John baptized him. He was tempted in the Judean wilderness. His public life centered in the countryside around the north end
of the Lake of Galilee. There are brief mentions of a trip into Gentile
territory in the region of Tyre and Sidon in Phoenicia. Also he withdrew northward into the country around Caesarea Philippi near
Mount Hermon. He visited the region of Decapolis on the east side
of the Lake of Galilee. He passed through Samaria on his southward
way to Jerusalem. He stopped at Jericho in the Jordan valley before
he climbed up the steep road to Jerusalem for the final week of his
life. The reports of the Gospels indicate that except for the extreme
south Jesus traveled through much of his small country. Its remarkable geography and unique religious history provide a fitting setting
for his incomparable life.

2

The Government

ROME RULED the world in which Jesus lived.[1] Her domain reached from Britain to the Euphrates. All the lands and the peoples bordering the Mediterranean and much of their hinterland were bound into an orderly peaceful international realm under her mighty hand. In 63 B.C. Pompey ended a century of Maccabean independence for which the Jews had started to fight against the Syrian Seleucid ruler, Antiochus IV (175–164 B.C.). Antiochus had undertaken to unify his kingdom, which included Judea. When he ordered all people to renounce the particular practices of their religions and when he commanded death for all who resisted, the Jews flared into revolt. Their heroic defense and successful fight is vividly described in I Maccabees. After religious freedom the Jews achieved political independence (141 B.C.) under Simon, one of the Hasmonean or Maccabean rulers. His son, John Hyrcanus (135–104 B.C.), enlarged Judean power when he subdued Transjordan to the east, Samaria to the north and Idumea to the south. His successors maintained this widened kingdom for a time but eventually weaker kings lost territory and quarreled about the throne. Their civil war invited Roman intervention. At Damascus each of rival Jewish kings, Hyrcanus II and Aristobulus II, besought the support of Pompey while a delegation from the Jewish people asked for an end to the Hasmonean kings and for a restoration of the traditional high priest for their ruler. After Pompey

[1] Josephus, *Ant.* XIV–XIX; *Wars* I–II; E. Schürer, *The History of the Jewish People in the Time of Jesus Christ* (New York, 1891), Div. I, I, 370–99; 416–39; II, 1–87; F. J. Foakes Jackson and K. Lake, *The Beginnings of Christianity* (New York, 1920), I, 1–34; G. W. Wade, *New Testament History* (London, 1922), 43–60; J. Klausner, *Jesus of Nazareth* (New York, 1926), 135–73; F. J. Foakes Jackson, *Josephus and the Jews* (New York, 1930), 95–169; S. Mathews, *New Testament Times in Palestine* (rev. ed. New York, 1933), 115–83; 258–81; G. H. C. MacGregor and A. C. Purdy, *Jew and Greek* (New York, 1936), 11–40; T. R. Glover, *The World of the New Testament* (Cambridge, 1937), 107–34; H. Lietzmann, *The Beginnings of the Christian Church* (New York, 1937), 17–26; J. N. Schofield, *The Historical Background of the Bible* (New York, 1938), 256–304; C. Guignebert, *The Jewish World in the Time of Jesus* (New York, 1939), 30–42; H. O. Mason in *The Story of the Bible* (New York, 1947), II, 1093–1117; G. Ricciotti, *The Life of Christ* (Milwaukee, 1947), 10–28; R. H. Pfeiffer, *History of New Testament Times* (New York, 1949), 5–45.

marched to Jerusalem, his troops fought three months to subdue the fortified Temple area. Pompey spared the Temple treasures but he outraged the Jewish sense of the sacred when he entered the Holy of Holies, God's dwelling place in the Temple, which only the high priest could enter. Thousands of Jews were shipped as slaves to Rome and the west. Aristobulus was taken to be exhibited in Pompey's triumph in Rome. Hyrcanus was set up as high priest and ethnarch. The kingship was abolished and Jewish dominion reduced to Judea, Idumea, Galilee and Perea. The Jews never forgot their lost independence (63 B.C.) nor the remembrance that their land belonged to the Lord rather than to pagan conquerors. In the next two centuries they battered themselves repeatedly into bloody impotence against the imperial power of Rome.

It is an ironical turn of history that the Jews under John Hyrcanus, who had conquered and Judaized Idumea, should in turn be largely ruled for almost a century by an Idumean family, the famous Herodians. A wealthy, powerful Idumean governor, Antipater, husband of a Jewish wife, adviser to the Hasmoneans, co-operator with Rome, arose to political leadership beside Hyrcanus, the high priest. When a rival poisoned Antipater, his sons, Phasael and Herod, continued as governors in Judea and Galilee respectively. Julius Caesar had aided Antipater and extended favors for the Jewish religion. After Caesar's assassination (44 B.C.), Cassius, one of the assassins, controlled Syria. Phasael and Herod gave him allegiance. Mark Antony and Octavianus Caesar, nephew of Julius, defeated Cassius and his fellow conspirators at Philippi. Though compromised by his previous support of Cassius, Herod by shrewd use of money and personal persuasion, won Antony's friendly aid to maintain power in Judea. But Antigonus, son of Aristobulus, supported by Parthian armies came to Jerusalem. He cut off the ears of Hyrcanus to disqualify him to continue as high priest. A priest had to be unblemished (Lev. 21:21). Phasael was killed and Herod fled eventually to Rome for help. Since the Parthians were dangerous rivals to Rome in the East, the Roman Senate made Herod king of Judea (40 B.C.) and vigorously supported him. Herod had to fight three years to establish his kingly position in Judea. Though he was one half Jewish and took a wife, Mariamne, from the royal Hasmonean family, he was not welcomed by the Jews. Entrenched in power, Herod made the high priest an appointee at his pleasure to the distaste of the Jewish people.

Herod the Great (40–4 B.C.) is famous as the ruler under whom Jesus was born. His long rule was marked by outstanding success as a Roman vassal. He was diplomatically skillful. He had to change his support from Antony to Octavianus after the latter defeated Antony at Actium (31 B.C.). After Octavianus became emperor Augustus (27 B.C.), Herod's kingdom was enlarged to include all of Palestine so that he ruled both Gentile and Jewish areas. Herod became a patron of Greek culture as well as of Jewish religion. He rebuilt old cities and founded new ones. Samaria was reconstructed as Sebaste. The seaport at Strato's Tower became magnificent Caesarea. The names of both cities honored Augustus. Herod constructed public buildings, palaces, fortresses and temples. His best-known structure was the Temple begun in 20 B.C. in Jerusalem, in which he desired to rival Solomon by enlarging the sacred place until its splendid stones, adorned with gold and surrounded by courts and porticoes, became the pride of Jewish pilgrims who admired it as the most beautiful sight in the world. One of Jesus' disciples exclaimed, "Look, Teacher, what wonderful stones and what wonderful buildings!" (Mk. 13:1).

Herod's last years were darkened by disease, jealousy, intrigues and family mistrust. A monarch who could execute his best-beloved wife and three sons could order the massacre of infants in Bethlehem after the birth of Jesus as reported in Matthew. Herod's long and successful reign gave him fame which has been variously estimated. His barbarity, polygamy and tyrannical severity were noted by Josephus, the Jewish historian, who used the now lost history of Nicholas of Damascus, secretary and friend of Herod. But Herod loyally supported his part in the vast Roman empire, maintained peace, promoted the arts and ruled his kingdom with a competent though heavy hand. From a political point of view he deserves his title, "Herod the Great."

When Herod died miserably, Augustus continued the policy of Rome which utilized local rulers for conquered countries. If legions were needed to protect the frontiers, as in Syria, the emperor kept such an area as a "province of Caesar" to which he appointed a propraetor who held office at the emperor's will. In lesser districts like Palestine cohorts garrisoned the country and Caesar selected a local leader like Herod or a Roman procurator like Pilate. In a safer region like the province of Asia the ruler was a proconsul appointed annually to the "province of the people" by the Senate. Rome was not a harsh mistress as long as her laws were observed, the peace kept, taxes paid and highways of land and sea kept safe for commerce. Rome had much tolerance toward the culture, the customs and the religion of her subject peoples as long as they violated no public morality.

Herod left his domain to three sons. Philip (4 B.C.–A.D. 34) was tetrarch over the area northeast of the Lake of Galilee which Luke (3:1) named Iturea and Trachonitis. He was well liked by his people, who were mainly Gentiles whom he ruled kindly and justly until his death. For his capital he rebuilt Banias and named it Caesarea to which Philippi was added to distinguish it from the coast city. Jesus visited this area in which Peter set forth his momentous declaration of Jesus as the Christ. Bethsaida on the Jordan near its entrance into the Lake of Galilee, a city frequented by Jesus, was rebuilt and named Julias by Philip. At his death his territory was united with Syria, then in A.D. 37 the emperor Caligula gave it to Agrippa I, grandson of Herod the Great, who ruled it until his sudden death in A.D. 44.

Herod Antipas (4 B.C.–A.D. 39) was made tetrarch over Galilee and Perea which is east of the Jordan. Jesus grew up and began his public life under the threatening rule of Antipas, whom he called "that fox" (Lk. 13:32). Antipas questioned Jesus to no avail the night before his crucifixion (Lk. 23:9) and he beheaded John the Baptist because he denounced the marriage of Antipas to Herodias, his brother's wife (Mk. 6:17–18), or according to Josephus because he feared John's popularity.[2] Antipas built a new Hellenistic capital on the west coast of Galilee and named it Tiberias in honor of the emperor. Jews avoided the Gentile city partly built over a cemetery which was believed to cause defilement. This city, not mentioned in the Gospels, is the only one now remaining on Galilean shores. Antipas' worst troubles came from his dealings with his wives. His first one was a Nabatean princess, daughter of Aretas IV. The Nabateans were a vigorous Arab people south of Idumea who had a marvelous rock-hewn capital at Petra, "a rose-red city half as old as time." When Antipas became interested in Herodias, his Nabatean princess fled home to Aretas, who later severely defeated Antipas in battle. When Herodias pestered her husband to seek from the emperor a kingly title, like that of his nephew Agrippa I, the latter sent accusations against Antipas and Caligula banished him and gave his domain to Agrippa.

Archelaus (4 B.C.–A.D. 6), as ethnarch, received Idumea, Judea and Samaria. His people disliked him and revolted when he left for Rome. Varus, the Syrian governor, subdued them. In a few years, the Jews charged Archelaus with misgovernment and Augustus ban-

[2] *Ant.* XVIII, 5.2.

ished him to Gaul. Judea was put under a succession of procurators of whom the most famous is Pontius Pilate (A.D. 26–36). The procurators made Caesarea their capital and came to Jerusalem mainly for the great festivals when insurrections might occur. They were supported by Roman cohorts, each composed of 500–600 soldiers recruited from non-Jewish cities. Jews resented Roman garrisons, taxes and foreign rule over a land which they believed belonged only to the Lord. Pilate was governor over a troublesome people longer and more successfully than his predecessors but he faced clashes which grew from religious roots. His troops offended the Jews when they carried standards bearing the emperor's image into Jerusalem. When threatened with death, the Jews bared their necks willingly rather than break the divine commandment which forbade images. Bloodshed followed Pilate's expenditure of some Temple money for a needed aqueduct. He massacred some Galilean pilgrims at their sacrifices (Lk. 13:1) and eventually his ruthless attack on credulous crowds of Samaritans gathered at Mount Gerizim, expecting to discover some sacred utensils, led to his recall to Rome and dismissal from office. Eusebius states that "he was compelled to become his own murderer and execute himself with his own hand." [3] Procurators ruled Judea until A.D. 41 when the emperor Claudius added it to the kingdom of Agrippa I who reigned until A.D. 44 when procurators again took charge until the great rebellion (A.D. 66–70) which Vespasian and Titus suppressed with complete destruction of Jerusalem, with slavery and terrible loss of life for many of its inhabitants and with ruin for Judea.

In accordance with Roman policy, procurators allowed local rule to the Jews. They had a Sanhedrin, a court composed of aristocratic priests, scribes and elders who administered the Law. Jews regarded their Law as God-given through Moses and as regulatory for all phases of life. The high priest presided over the seventy members of the Sanhedrin. Its only limitation appears to have been with the penalty of death which required also the sanction of the governor. It was partly some members of the Sanhedrin and partly Pilate who put Jesus to his cross. The country was divided into eleven areas over which a local Sanhedrin or council of seven to twenty-three members had authority. There were many details about the choice of members and procedures of the Sanhedrin as well as its relationship to Roman authority which are not clearly known. The procurator appointed or deposed the high priest and doled out to him the official robes for

---

[3] *Eccles. Hist.* II.7.

use at the festivals. Thus the sacred office became a political plum, tossed about by Roman favoritism. Most Jews felt galled by the Roman yoke and there were many malcontents. Some nurtured a spirit of violent revolt which often broke out in armed rebellion. Others separated themselves from political connections and nourished a life devoted to the Law. Others looked for some miraculous future intervention to defeat the oppressors of Israel. Others acquiesced in their situation because they guarded their wealth and valued their political powers granted by Rome.

3

Economic and Social Life

IN JESUS' day Palestine was basically an agricultural country though there were numerous craftsmen, tradesmen, priests and government officials. Direct taxes were paid to officials of Rome but the collection and the payment of customs were farmed out to men known as publicans who agreed to pay the required amount to the government and who then profited by any sums that they could collect above the agreed amount. These tax collectors were doubly despised since they worked for a foreign power and made excessive demands for money. There were poll taxes, tolls on highways and bridges and assessments on imports and on produce grown in the soil.

The Jews faced not only government taxes but also heavy religious dues. Priests held their positions by inheritance and handled all the rich revenues brought by many worshipers to the Temple. This center of worship also served as a national bank. Many priests possessed both wealth and power and sought always to maintain their status as well as to serve the Lord. The average loyal Jew faced considerable expense. There were tithes of the crops, payments for the first-born child and animal, for the first fruits and the best fruits of fields and trees. Some wool at shearing and certain parts of animals at slaughtering were exacted. The Temple required a half shekel from each man annually. There were offerings for sins, thanksgiving and vows, for the poor, the synagogues and the rabbis. The total tax to support both civil and religious institutions bore heavily upon everyone. It has been estimated to equal 30 to 40 per cent of income and "it may have been higher still." [1]

The craftsmen like carpenters, masons, potters, dyers, weavers, tailors, tanners, shoemakers, smiths and glassmakers supplied the skilled handwork needed in home and village. Certain towns gained fame for a particular craft, like the weavers in Sepphoris. Jesus was a carpenter in Nazareth (Mk. 6:3). Fishermen abounded in Galilee and along the Mediterranean. Their fish were salted and sold throughout the whole land. Salt and pitch came from the Dead Sea

[1] F. C. Grant, *The Economic Background of the Gospels* (Oxford, 1926), 105.

15

region. Many of the artisans sold their services and goods by barter directly to the consumer. Both the peasant and the shopkeeper in his small bazaar profited by two market days a week, Monday and Thursday, which stimulated trade. The great religious festivals with multitudes of pilgrims increased business especially in Jerusalem. Certain streets lined with stalls and booths were known for displays of meat, bread, wine and vegetables. Donkeys and camels transported goods in caravans which followed four main roads north and south which skirted the coast or followed the central plateau, the Jordan valley or the eastern highlands. East and west there were important routes from Jerusalem and from Sebaste. Westward highways led from Tiberias to the coast and from Caesarea Philippi to Tyre. Commerce created some wealthy men, while moneylenders and exchangers built fortunes, especially when their victims lost their land and liberty through failure to pay debts.

The soil provided the largest support for the people of Palestine. The land was cultivated skillfully by middle-class workers like peasants who lived in many villages. An occasional large estate of a wealthy man was managed by the owner or his steward. Many fruits were cultivated. Grapes were eaten fresh, dried into raisins and crushed by foot to make wine. Olives were famous for their oil. Dates, figs, pomegranates, plums, apricots and mulberries were grown. Vegetables like cucumbers, beans, peas, lentils, onions, garlic, cabbages, carrots and melons were favored by a climate conducive to long periods of growth in the fields. Such fruits and vegetables together with grains like barley, wheat and millet were staple foods for the workers on the land. Sheep, goats, cattle and poultry supplied meat or milk products. The farming was done mainly by the peasants, supplemented by the help of slaves. Jewish slaves were required by law to be freed the seventh year but Gentile slaves had no rights. The margin of subsistence was narrow for the farmers and a drought was a calamity leading to starvation. Landless laborers hired out by the day and sometimes waited in vain for employment. The hours were long; heavy work of all kinds was done by hand in the heat of lengthy summers. The people of the land faced a laborious skimpy existence, uncertain about daily bread.

The Gospels were written to tell the story of Jesus, not to describe social conditions, but his words are vivid with scenes from the countryside and the village life rather than the city. He knew the birds of the air, the fox in his hole, the scavenging dog, the scorpion and the snake, the gathering eagles, the mothering hen, the crowing cock, the skinny kid and the fatted calf, the wandering sheep amid dangerous wolves, the gray donkey and the supercilious camel. He mentions the lilies in their beauty, the field grass used for kindling fire, the vine and its abundant grapes, thorns, thistles, weeds, the walking sower, the sprouting seed and the busy harvest. He tells of children playing in the market place, of women grinding meal or carrying water, of builders who build on rock or sand, of laborers in the ripening fields, of the bridegroom, the father who divides his property to his sons and of the wealthy farmer who builds bigger barns. He knew the fishermen, the pearl merchant, the physician, the rich publicans, harlots, robbers, pious Pharisees, questioning Sadducees, priests, Levites and the learned scribes, hungry crowds, some demented and demon-haunted, some sick and weary.

Many of the actual details about dwellings, clothing, food and daily customs cannot be gathered from the Gospels and Josephus and it is difficult to sort out of the Mishnah the materials which refer to the time of Jesus. It is probable that Palestine had a population between 600,000–750,000. The average family lived much outdoors but made its home in a one-story house of stone, bricks or clay, accessible by a courtyard. The house had one door, a few small windows and an outside staircase which led to a flat roof, safeguarded by a parapet. In the warm, dry season the roof was used for living quarters. Within the house not much furniture was needed. The floor of packed earth or stone was spread with bright colored rugs, mats and cushions. Beds were like mattresses, easily rolled out on the floor at night and bundled up for the day. A small, low lamp of clay with an opening in the top for a wick held enough oil for light at night. Clay jars of many sizes and shapes served for storage of foods and of water which had to be carried from a common well. This well served also as a place of public news especially for the women who carried the water in clay jars perched on their heads. Cisterns conserved stagnant water during the long dry season. Food was cooked in a preheated oven outdoors or over a charcoal brazier. It might be served on a wooden platter, metal tray or clay container about which the eaters gathered to serve themselves with their fingers after a blessing was invoked. Two meals sufficed for the day's food. Special occasions like weddings or festivals were joyous feasts when meat was prepared but the average family could not afford it daily.

Not much is known of the actual materials used for clothing. Probably garments were made of leather or handwoven from wool, goat's hair or linen. Heads were protected by a square of cloth. Long shirts were held in at the waist by a broad sashlike girdle made of leather or woven hair in which tools, weapons or purses could be carried. A long outer cloak was worn when needed. Sandals completed the costume. These descriptions of habitations and clothing apply to the common people among whom Jesus lived. There were great palaces where the few rich and powerful people feasted sumptuously, appareled gorgeously in soft raiment of purple and fine linen. Indifferent to the crying needs of those whom Jesus called "the lost sheep of the house of Israel," they lived in luxury supported and served by many slaves.

Family life was believed to have been instituted by God. Normally all Jewish young men and women were married in their early teens. Mosaic Law prohibited marriage within certain degrees of kinship. Monogamy was general but polygamy was also practiced as the Herods prove. Betrothal and marriage were arranged by the bridegroom and his family with the family of the bride to whom a price was paid. The bride was brought to the home of the bridegroom in a wedding procession. After a wedding supper the bride was given by her parents to her husband. No formal ceremony before a religious leader was required. The household was paternal, with the husband in command over wife and children. The husband alone had the power of divorce, though the loss of the dowry was a deterrent. Life was sacred because God created it. Children were blessings from God. They were to be disciplined and taught reverence for the Lord. The father was obligated to teach the Law to his children, especially the sons. The boys were sent to school to the scribe to learn to recite and to read the Law. Each boy was also taught a trade or occupation by his father. The mother gave practical instruction to the daughter in all the crafts and the arts of the household as well as in the care of children.

The gray hairs of age were honored. When death broke the family circle, the care of the dead was a religious duty. The body was washed, anointed, properly clothed and buried the day of death or the next day. There was no embalming, no cremation, no coffin. Hired mourners wailed over the dead. Funeral orations were given but there was no formal religious service. Entombment was in the ground or in a cave. When they could afford it, a family had a rock-cut sepulcher with a door and niches on either side of the entry to receive the bodies. Since a corpse or a grave caused religious defilement for seven days, sepulchers were whitened to warn passersby of their presence.

4

The Heritage of Judaism

WHEN JESUS was born, Judaism was an old and renowned religion.[1] Moses had established its foundations thirteen centuries earlier and there were traditions reaching to Abraham several centuries before Moses. Its long development had resulted in important diversities within a larger unity. These diversities must be recognized but a part must not be mistaken for the whole. Two main developments can be distinguished: Judaism in Palestine and Judaism in the Dispersion or Diaspora which refers to Jews scattered throughout the world outside their homeland. Jesus lived within Palestinian Judaism but the Gospels not only tell of Jesus but they reflect at times a background of Hellenistic Judaism and of the Gentile world.

Judaism underwent tremendous changes after the fall of the nation to Rome (A.D. 70) and it eventually crystallized into the form known as rabbinical Judaism which is largely the continuation of Pharisaism, the major aspect which survived national destruction. "The Pharisees disappeared as an organized society in the third century of the Christian Era but their influence on western spiritual thought still sur-

[1] E. Schürer, *A History of the Jewish People in the Time of Jesus Christ* (New York, 1891), Div. II, I, 10-43; 207-379; W. O. E. Oesterley and G. H. Box, *The Religion and Worship of the Synagogue* (2nd ed. London, 1911), 27-142; Jackson and Lake, *The Beginnings of Christianity,* I, 34-168; G. W. Wade, *New Testament History* (London, 1922), 90-105; J. Klausner, *Jesus of Nazareth* (New York, 1926), 193-228; G. F. Moore, *Judaism* (Cambridge, 1927), I, 29-121; L. DeGrandmaison, *Jesus Christ* (New York, 1930), 262-300; T. H. Bindley, *Religious Thought in Palestine in the Time of Christ* (London, 1931), 1-105; S. Mathews, *New Testament Times in Palestine* (rev. ed. New York, 1933), 203-33; G. H. C. MacGregor and A. C. Purdy, *Jew and Greek* (New York, 1936), 43-158; K. and S. Lake, *Introduction to the New Testament* (New York, 1937), 187-208; H. Lietzmann, *The Beginnings of the Christian Church* (New York, 1937), 27-46; 95-134; M. S. Enslin, *Christian Beginnings* (New York, 1937), 78-143; H. K. Booth, *The World of Jesus* (New York, 1939), 23-75; C. Guignebert, *The Jewish World in the Time of Jesus* (New York, 1939), 59-171; 206-10; W. O. E. Oesterley, *The Jews and Judaism in the Greek Period* (London, 1941), 93-301; C. T. Craig, *The Beginning of Christianity* (New York, 1943), 38-52; G. Ricciotti, *Life of Christ* (Milwaukee, 1947), 29-77; R. H. Pfeiffer, *History of New Testament Times* (New York, 1949), 46-59; 166-96; N. H. Snaith, *The Jews from Herod to Rome* (Wallington, 1949), 62-203; M. Schoen, *The Man Jesus Was* (New York, 1950), 61-162; T. W. Manson, *The Servant-Messiah* (Cambridge, 1953), 1-35.

vives." [2] Prior to A.D. 70, Judaism had various religious leaders and writers described as kings, prophets, priests, historians, wisemen, scribes and apocalyptists. Their records are best known in the late Old Testament books, the Apocrypha, the Pseudepigrapha, the Gospels and in parts of Josephus and of the Mishnah.

Judaism of the first century can be surveyed in three main aspects: (1) beliefs and practices common to all Jews; (2) small particular groups which added distinctive beliefs and customs; (3) larger divisions distinguished by variations from the ideals of traditional Judaism. First, all Jews adhered to belief in one God alone. He was accepted as living, personal spirit, creator of the heavens, the world and man. He was holy, righteous, merciful and the just determiner of destiny for all men. His will for his chosen people Israel had been primarily revealed through Moses in the Torah or holy Law which had to be learned and obeyed. To keep the Law meant salvation, prosperity and security in God's sight. To disobey it brought divine judgment upon the offender. This Law, written basically in the first five books of scripture, though the other holy books also revealed God's will, ruled all of life. It covered everything, great or small, that a Jew did. It gave instructions about birth, education, marriage, death and all civil and criminal affairs. It taught high ethics like the Ten Commandments and minor matters like the growth of locks of hair. It required separation from all "unclean" contacts with certain foods, objects and idolatrous Gentiles. It made covenants like circumcision. It set holy days like the joyful Sabbath rest, festivals like Passover, Pentecost, Tabernacles, New Year and the somber Day of Atonement. It taught worship, prayer, almsgiving, repentance and peace. It fostered a national religion bound to a holy God-given land but also a universal faith to be observed in all other lands and even to be a light to which Gentiles could come and believe. It was a revelation of God's just dealings in mighty signs and wonders in aid of his people. It guided them toward a golden future when his holy purposes would be accomplished by himself or by his Messiah appointed to do God's work. All Jews looked to the one Temple in Jerusalem as the national shrine for sacrificial worship conducted by priests. They looked also to the ubiquitous synagogues for instruction by men learned in the Law or from hearing it read by one another.

Second, the particular groups can be subdivided into those who were professional leaders with special functions such as priests and scribes and those adherents to groups, characterized by beliefs such

[2] L. Finkelstein, *The Pharisees* (2nd ed. Philadelphia, 1940), xxix.

as Pharisees, Sadducees and Essenes. A priest or a scribe could belong to any of these groups or to none. In the long history of Israel great authorities in religion arose, flourished and disappeared.[3] Kings were ended by the Babylonian conquest (586 B.C.) except for a brief revival in the Maccabean period in the second century. At this latter time prophets were believed to have ceased though their influence continued. Priests flourished until Rome destroyed them and their Temple (A.D. 70). In the Maccabean age John Hyrcanus, who came from a family of priests, first combined kingship and high priesthood. The office of high priest was hereditary and lifelong but the Herods and the Romans soon separated the functions of king and high priest and made the latter a political tool to help rule the Jews. The entire priestly class, traditionally descended from the sons of Aaron, brother of Moses, formed a caste which had great power. They took pride in their genealogies. Under rigid regulations they were consecrated as holy leaders for the temple services. They were aided by a lesser religious order, the Levites, who were assistants at the Temple and musicians, guards and porters. The life of the priests centered in the Temple which was a place of peculiar sanctity linking all Jews to Jerusalem and to God. This Temple stood facing east in an area of about twenty-five acres, marked off from the rest of Jerusalem by porticoes and gates and by chambers for priests' living and for treasures and gifts. An outer court was open to Gentiles but Greek signs warned them not to enter the inner courts on penalty of death. The high white marble sanctuary contained sections, each progressively holy. Beyond the eastern entrance with its impressive pillars stood the Court of Women, then westward the Court of Men open to laymen, then the Court of Priests where they offered the daily sacrifices morning and evening, then a Holy Place, open only to priests, then beyond a veil, the Holy of Holies, which contained only God's invisible glory and which the high priest entered once a year on the Day of Atonement. The whole area and the sacred building, like a mountain of snow with its dazzling gold plates, have been impressively described by Josephus.[4] The priests and the staff numbered 20,000 who were divided into twenty-four "courses" whose duties were rotated a week at a time. When free of temple duties the priests followed other employments. Their duties at the killing and the burning of animals for both public and private sacrifices involved long ceremonials and detailed ritual. While lay worshipers could pray and

---

[3] J. Pedersen, *Israel* (London, 1940), II, 33–197; H. W. Robinson, *Inspiration and Revelation in the Old Testament* (Oxford, 1946), 122–261.

[4] *Ant.* XV.11; *Wars* V.5.

bring gifts, the cult activities were in the hands of the priests. The sacrifices were essential gifts of life to maintain holiness as an acceptable condition of man before God. Only holy priests could offer them in one holy place. All this elaborate work of priests at the Temple was based on the holy Law which was believed to have come directly from God.

But the priest was nearing his end. The future lay with the scribe, the doctor of the Law, the learned man, whose origins are connected with Ezra (Ez. 7:6, 11) 400 years earlier than Jesus. The scribe, in the person of his successor, the rabbi, is the authority in Judaism who has persisted across the centuries. Since the Law came from God, the scribe's main functions were to study it, to teach it and to administer it as jury and judge. He also knew how to copy the Law when new rolls were needed. He formed a school and taught unpaid while he supported himself in some other work or profession. There were both elementary schools for children and advanced ones for a lifelong learning in the Law. Directions for the scribe, traditionally dated from Ezra's contemporaries, specified three things: "Be deliberate in judgment, raise up many disciples and make a fence about the Law." [5] The delights, the inspiration, the treasures and the boundless blessings of the Lord which enrich the man who studies the Law are the theme of the longest Psalm (119) and of the sage, Ben-Sira (Ecclus. 39:1–11). The two greatest teachers just before the Christian Era were Shammai and Hillel. The former, a native Judean, was very strict and the latter who came to Judea from Babylon was lenient in the interpretation of the Law.

The scribes' school and the synagogue have had incalculable influence upon Judaism. The two were intimately related and both are expressions of the dominant idea that the Sacred Scriptures must be read, taught and obeyed. Synagogue was a term applied both to an assembly and to the place of assembly. Its institutional origins are obscure but it is thought to have arisen during the sixth-century Exile as a needed gathering of Jews to sustain a common faith and life far from their homeland. It is scarcely mentioned in the Old Testament but by the time of Jesus it was everywhere though its actual conditions are not fully known in the first century. Luke gives the only contemporary account of a synagogue service but it is incidental to a story about Jesus (Lk. 4:16–21).

The synagogue was a gathering of the people for instruction in the truths of Judaism primarily though not exclusively by the scribes.

---

[5] *Pirke Aboth* 1:1, H. Danby, *The Mishnah* (London, 1933), 446.

Judaism owes the preservation of its existence more than anything else to the synagogue.[6] It became a democratic community center for praise and prayer to God, for schooling, for legal decisions and for discussions. The synagogue was in charge of a "ruler" who was one of the elders of the community. There was a paid "attendant" who took care of the building and the sacred rolls. Sometimes he served as schoolmaster. The synagogue was open daily but obligation to attend was limited to Sabbath and other holy days. The building was probably a plain hall with a platform on which was an ark or a chest containing the rolls of the Law and the prophets. There was a lectern for reading the holy word. The people sat on benches facing the ark. Opposite to them were the chief seats of the scribes who sat while they taught. Nearest the ark was Moses' seat, the seat of honor. In a Sabbath service there were prayer, reading from the scripture and a kind of sermon or homily. Possibly there was singing, since Paul mentions singing psalms in the early church, the daughter of the synagogue (Col. 3:16). Each Jew was expected to recite the Shema (Hear) (Dt. 6:4-9; 11:13-21; Num. 15:37-41) twice daily. A notable teacher, Simeon, from the third century B.C., declared that the world was maintained by the Law, by worship and by deeds of mutual kindness.[7] On the Sabbath the people in the synagogue recited the Shema and followed it with prayers which became known as the Eighteen Benedictions (Shemoneh Esreh) during which, if a priest was present, the priestly blessing (Num. 6:24-26) was given. Regular sections from the Law and from the prophets were read in Hebrew and translated into Aramaic by an interpreter who was not the reader. Both reader and interpreter stood for this part of the service. Scripture reading was open to any adult male member of the congregation. The sermon was not limited to a certain individual though the scribe was best able to expound the lesson and to quote appropriate scriptures. The sermon was spoken in the native tongue and a brief prayer followed.

Judaism had a number of parties of which the Pharisees and the Sadducees were most prominent. They had much in common as Jews but each had distinctive traits. The origin of the Pharisees is not clearly known, but in the Maccabean age there is mention of a group, the Hasidim or Saints, who were zealous for the Law. They may have been the forerunners of the Pharisees, well described as

---

[6] Moore, op. cit., II, 281–307.
[7] Pirke Aboth 1:2.

Separatists who found joy in the Law which hallowed everything.[8] They insisted on separation from everything and everyone unclean in order to live holy lives of undivided loyalty to the Law of God. They were noted for their study and rigid adherence not only to the written Law but to the "tradition of the elders" which was the oral interpretation and application of the written codes. For example, the Law commanded the Sabbath to be kept holy and the tradition might list all kinds of forbidden work or prescribe the length of a Sabbath-day journey. These oral additions opened the way for progress in Judaism though they were not regarded as new since God's Law was held to be perfect, final and complete, though it had to be adapted to changing circumstances. Many scholars interpreted the Law orally especially from 400 B.C. to A.D. 200. At last, the great bulk of the tradition which consisted of running commentaries and sermons (Midrash) about separate books of scripture and of topical discussions and rules or "orders" (Mishnah) was gradually reduced to writing in the third to fifth centuries of the Christian Era. The Mishnah was further studied, interpreted and added to until it became the "ocean" of the Talmud. The scribal Pharisee is a kind of ancestral father of the Talmud which to this day is decisively important in teaching Judaism.

The Pharisee believed that obedience to God's Law meant joy and life for man and that repentance for disobedience could restore his happy relationship to God. He believed in angels and in demons, in the resurrection and in the coming of the Messiah. But his religion was expressed more in what he did than in what he said. As much as possible he lived aloof from political and economic contacts with those who did not observe the Law. He said his daily prayers, attended synagogue and Temple, fasted, tithed, ate "clean" food from "clean" dishes after ritual washings, observed Sabbaths and holy days, wore his phylacteries (prayer-bands) and tassels on his mantle to remind him of the commandments. These actions and many others akin to them sometimes led the Pharisee into hypocrisy, formalism and legalism, but his intent was to live a life entirely hallowed by doing God's will in everything. The Pharisees appear frequently in the Gospels, often though not always in opposition to Jesus. Some, but not all of the Pharisaic leaders, deserved his condemnation. As a whole they represented the best elements in Judaism and the survival of their successors is evidence of their fidelity to their faith. It is probable that some of the Pharisees developed into a liberty-loving left-wing faction, founded in A.D. 6 in a revolt against taxation. Josephus

[8] H. Loewe in *Judaism and Christianity*, W. O. E. Oesterley, ed. (London, 1937), I, 105–90.

named them a "fourth philosophical sect" and reported that they called no man lord nor feared any kind of death. This faction is to be distinguished from the revolutionary movement in A.D. 66 known as Zealots who constituted another of the numerous violent uprisings against Rome.

In contrast to the Pharisees, who were progressive middle-class townsmen and laymen, stood the Sadducees, who were conservative countrymen and aristocratic priests. They seem to have originated like the Pharisees in the first century B.C. Their name may have come from Zadokites, a priestly family, established by Solomon (I Kgs. 2:35) or from a Hebrew word of similar sound, which meant righteous. They were mainly concerned with the service of the Temple and with the practical administration of public national affairs. They differed from the Pharisees in that they accepted only the five books of Moses as obligatory and rejected the "tradition of the elders." They denied the resurrection, immortality of the soul, the existence of angels and spirits. They appear infrequently in the Gospels and never in friendly contacts with Jesus. They soon disappear from history after the destruction of Jerusalem and the Temple.

Another group, not mentioned in the Gospels, the Essenes, a "third philosophical sect," is known from Jewish writers, especially Josephus.[9] The meaning of the name, Essene, is not established. The Essenes lived like farmer-monks in communal disciplined brotherhoods where their houses were not open to strangers. Prayer and work filled their days. They were known for their stoical stamina, continence, silent ritualistic meals, purificatory baths and ablutions, white garments, possessions in common and strictest Sabbath observance. They rejected slavery, marriage though not absolutely, the use of oil and sacrifices at the Temple. They required members to pass through periods of preparation for three years before they attained full rank. They seem to have adapted some customs and beliefs from Oriental and Greek sources since they prayed toward the eastern sun and believed that their immortal souls were united to their bodies as in prison until freed by death when the good souls rejoiced in a blessed region and the wicked ones were allotted a dark den full of punishments. Speculation has linked both Jesus and John the Baptist with the Essenes but without any valid evidence. Other ascetic groups are known like the Therapeutae, a contemplative order in Egypt, and the Covenanters of Damascus who tried to reproduce the

---

[9] *Ant.* XVIII.1.5; *Wars* II.8.2–13; cf. W. O. E. Oesterley, *The Jews and Judaism in the Greek Period*, 255–65.

early life of Israel in Moses' day, but they are unimportant except as witnesses to the diversities in Judaism. These religious parties probably constituted less than 10 per cent of the total Jewish population in Palestine.

Third, some larger groupings can be characterized by their modifications from the ideals of Judaism. The common people did not belong to any religious parties because their way of life and ignorance of the Law prevented it. These "people of the land" often failed to maintain ceremonial purity though probably many lived good lives. Their laxity affected the ceremonial purity of the food which they supplied to more careful Jews. Hillel thought these ignorant people could not be pious. They are among the ones called "sinners" in the Gospels (Mk. 2:15-17), whom priests and Pharisees contemptuously described as an accursed crowd who did not know the Law (John 7:49). It appears that Jesus and his disciples belonged among these masses since they did not follow all the traditions about the Sabbath or the ritual washings.

Apocalypses are revelations which bring into sight that which is hidden and unseen. The books of Daniel and Revelation are best known among many lesser works. The apocalyptists have been called a party but not properly so because their visionary beliefs might have been held by any Jew in Jesus' day. Their ideas are like a swirling eddy in the broad stream of Judaism. The apocalyptists were successors to some aspects of the prophets. The idea of interpreting world history was important to the Jews. This world had been created by God and he had a goal for it. The prophets had proclaimed a Day of the Lord, defeat of evil foes, a new covenant, a peerless Jerusalem, an ideal restoration of Israel and the coming of the Messiah. But these things had not come to pass in the present world. The apocalyptist, wearied by centuries of foreign oppression, looked in fantastic visions into a supernatural future world. He received divine revelations from God through angels about the fate of individuals, nations and the world. He wrote these visions usually in the name of some ancient man of God to help validate them. He arranged cryptic systems of chronology as he envisioned a climax to the course of earthly history. Cosmic and human woes would warn of the coming End. Then would follow an ideal age usually under the reign of the Messiah with peace and prosperity for his people. Next would come final and terrible strife between the hosts of God and of the devil with complete defeat for evil. Then would come the resurrection of the dead, a final judgment to settle the fate of the good and the evil; then

God would put an End to the present age and inaugurate a new age or world to come.

The most decisive of these imaginative ideas was that the cata-strophic End was coming soon. It was the prelude to the new order, the coming age, the rule of God. Any orderly presentation of apoc-alyptic ideas is apt to be misleading because the future was unknown, the language highly figurative, the concepts strangely varied and the patterns of thought amazingly diverse. By the end of the second cen-tury A.D. the apocalyptists had surrendered much of their influence to the rabbis who concentrated on the Law. However, Jesus lived at the height of interest in apocalyptic fancies and the Gospels reflect some of their ideas which have continued through the centuries to influence thoughts about the future.

The Jews of the Dispersion, scattered from Babylonia to Spain, did not have many contacts with Jesus who never traveled among them. Some of them were always coming to Jerusalem for worship at the Temple. Many of the same transforming influences, mainly Hellen-istic, which worked on the Jews abroad, had been known in Palestine since Alexander conquered it (332 B.C.). There may have been more than two million Jews spread throughout the world or twice as many as in their homeland. The largest settlements were in Babylon and in Egypt. They shared the scriptures, the synagogue, the Sabbath and festivals, the many Jewish customs and beliefs and the fierce loyalty for the national homeland.

The distinctive developments in the Dispersion center in the scrip-tures, in proselyting and in cultural interests. The Jews abroad lived under the laws of the cities where they dwelt but they followed their own scriptural Law and had their own courts wherever possible. But they did not tend to develop the multiplied oral traditions as did the Pharisee at home in Jerusalem. Moreover, the constant use of a for-eign tongue had its effect on the scriptures because the Hebrew Bible was translated into Greek for the first time in Egypt about 250 B.C. The name, Septuagint, came from the supposed seventy-two trans-lators. "The translation known as the Septuagint was one of the mo-mentous events in history." [10] It gave to Jew and to Gentile his Bible in the universal language of the day. It met the need of the Jew to have his scriptures easily accessible to his children who grew up more familiar with Greek than with Hebrew. It was soon widely known and used. Since it included several books not acceptable as part of the Hebrew Bible in Palestine, it introduced history, stories and wisdom

[10] Jackson and Lake, *op. cit.*, I, 153.

literature with a wider scope than found among Palestinian teachers of the scriptures. The gospel writers knew the Septuagint and used it. Since the Gospels were written in Greek, some of the Old Testament quotations of Jesus appear in the Greek form of the Septuagint. When Christians soon collected their New Testament into a canon, they added them to the Septuagint. The Jews eventually retained the Hebrew Bible as scripture and refused the additions found in the Greek Bible.

The Gentile world was attracted to Judaism because of its unswerving monotheism, its democratic worship without idols, its ancient scripture, its Sabbath rest and its noble ethical ideals. It was repelled by circumcision and by its uncosmopolitan attitudes. But proselytism was well known. Jesus stated that scribes and Pharisees traveled sea and land to make one proselyte (Mt. 23:15). This missionary zeal was fostered among Hellenistic Jews by writings like Isaiah 40–66 which idealized the Jew among foreigners as a light to the Gentiles and Jerusalem as a united nations religious center. The Jews faced some ridicule, unfriendly criticism and even occasional attacks. Well-educated Gentiles like Cicero and Tacitus maligned them but they continued to seek proselytes. These converts had to meet rigid requirements in circumcision for males, a ceremonial bath and a sacrifice at the Temple. They had to learn to give undivided allegiance to God whose commands had to be accepted because they were divinely revealed truth. They became not only members of a religious cult but also of the Jewish nation. Consequently there were many adherents, "fearers of God," who would not accept conversion but who continued a relationship to Judaism. Women especially were largely numbered among these adherents. Zeal to convert Gentiles changed under later forbidding imperial edicts and the Jews ceased to be a missionary people. But in the first century the Dispersion was a fertile seed plot for the gospel.

The Jew in foreign lands formed a democratic community of his own people governed by a council of elders. He paid his temple tax annually and felt obligated to visit Jerusalem for festivals and worship. He remained a member of the Jewish nation with special civic privileges due to the requirements of his faith about food and Sabbath. But he was affected culturally. He adopted the languages of the Gentiles. He saw their public festivals and amusements, he entered business, formed guilds for workers, learned something of Greek philosophy and literature and of Roman law. He wrote an extensive religious literature in Greek. Inevitably he modified somewhat the rigid separatism of Palestinian Judaism. When he traveled to his homeland, he brought a broadening influence into strait-laced Jerusalem. Some Jews adopted Gentile ways and life but most of them remained like an island in a sea of Hellenism. Where the land and the sea met, there began a mingling well exemplified in the apocryphal Wisdom of Solomon and in Philo, born about 10 B.C. This famed philosopher of Alexandria was perhaps the most remarkable Jew of the Dispersion. His influential writings proclaimed his familiarity with Greek thought as with fidelity to his ancestral faith he built a bridge of thought to connect Hebraism and Hellenism.

There was one final large group, the Samaritans, who might be described as half-breed Jews. They were the descendants of the foreign settlers imported into Palestine at the Assyrian conquest of the land in the eighth century B.C. who mingled with the native Hebrews. Their notable break with Judaism came in the fourth century when Nehemiah excluded them from participation in the life of Jerusalem. They were conquered by John Hyrcanus who destroyed their city and Temple. Herod rebuilt it magnificently as Sebaste. The information about their beliefs and hostile dealings with the Jews is limited. They represented an arrested development of Judaism whose beliefs and practices they shared to a great extent. They exalted Moses, accepted only his books, the Pentateuch, as scripture, regarded Mount Gerizim, not Jerusalem, as the place for a temple with its high priest, its ritual, its sacrifices and festivals. Like the Sadducees they rejected the resurrection. They looked for a coming prophet or Messiah to restore ideal conditions. The Gospel of Luke refers to the Samaritans more frequently and favorably than the other Gospels.

Into this complex world of Judaism with its ancient sacred lore and laws, its learned leaders, its patterned priests, its manifold parties and ideas, its legalists, conservatives, revolutionaries, visionaries and its laboring and heavy-laden masses came clear, fresh life from "God's Galilean." Jesus came with spiritual simplicity, deep ethical insight and elemental faith in God. The common people heard him gladly, felt his healing hands and marked his single-minded devotion to the rule of God. They listened to his simple and selective fulfillment of the Law, they remembered his pictorial parables of everyday life under the light of God. They never forgot his stark suffering in death. His appearances after resurrection aroused everlasting hopes in them and increased their confidence that God's life, power, mercy and love were uniquely manifested in him. They spoke their faith and soon wrote it in the Gospels.

PART II

The Origins of the Gospel

5

Internal and External Evidence

FOR NINETEEN centuries men have read the Gospels according to Matthew, Mark, Luke and John. These four small books arouse an endless interest because they tell good news about Jesus whose presence among men made them marvel and caused them eventually to change their calendars and to date all time before and after his coming. His continuing influence widens across the centuries like expanding waves from a mighty stone dropped into his Galilean lake. Since Jesus wrote nothing himself, we are dependent upon records written by his friends. The study of these records centers upon literary and historical problems rather than upon Jesus, though the results of our inquiry inevitably affect our views about Jesus. It is important to distinguish a book, even one held to be holy, from a person. Pages are not people. The Gospels are not Jesus though they provide indispensable information about him. Inquiries about the beginnings of the Declaration of Independence are not identical with loyalty to the United States though there may be a relationship. A reliable effort to discover the origins of the Gospels employs methods comparable to those used in the study of any ancient book. The focus of attention is on the makers of the Gospels and their documents, not upon Jesus himself. The issue, therefore, is literary and historical rather than religious.

If we are eager to enter every avenue of knowledge about Jesus, there is no satisfaction in the one-sided though important assumption that "every scripture is inspired of God" (II Tim. 3:16) and that therefore no further inquiry is needed since divine authorship is sufficient for any believer. Man also made the Scriptures. "This is the disciple that . . . wrote these things" (John 21:24). Hence we examine the disciple and what he wrote. To look at the Bible from its own angle is to see it as God's word through man. Our present interest is to discover man's part. Who wrote the Gospels? How many? When? Where? Why? To whom? What sources? How written? How reliable? What language?

Evidence concerning the Gospels falls in two kinds known as *internal* and *external*. *Internal evidence* arises from the documents themselves, such as the author's statements, style, use of sources, historical references, arrangement of materials, religious emphasis, in short anything which can be discovered from the pages of the Gospels. There is little direct internal evidence from the Gospels themselves about their origins. Most of the internal evidence arises from cumulative detailed studies which result in inferences which are not always accepted uniformly among scholars. Much laborious study and dispute would have been avoided if the Gospels had been given a title page and a preface to explain all facts about their origin. But the wine of present-day methods in bookmaking cannot be poured into the old wineskins of ancient documents. The Bible frequently shows anonymous writings. These writings belonged to their hearers. There was no private ownership such as a copyright implies. The message from the Lord was for his people and outweighed any messenger. The value of the writings did not depend on incidental facts about the name of the writer, his materials, methods or sources. The value arose from experiences that persuaded men that God had "visited and redeemed his people." The writers of Mark and Matthew do not give any specific statements about the origin of their books. Near the close of his work the writer of the Fourth Gospel states that his purpose is to provide belief about Jesus and life in his name (20:30-31). There are two postscripts at the end (21:24-25) of which the first declares the writer is a true witness and the second that there are many things which could still be written. This kind of information tantalizes more than it satisfies curiosity. Luke is the only writer, who following the vogue of his Hellenistic age, provides a preface (1:1-4). While he does not name the author nor the time and the place of writing, he does give invaluable aid at certain points. His work, like many others, dealt with "fulfilled" or accomplished things, his information came from firsthand participants, his methods undertook an orderly account. He had "followed all things closely for some time past." His purpose was to help Theophilus know the truth of which he had been informed. Such internal evidence is usually taken today to outweigh the external because the writers are nearer to their recorded events and the authors historically take precedence over later men who read them. This modern viewpoint of many scholars differs from the older one in which the declarations of an authoritative church about the Gospels were accepted as valid above any individual investigation of the documents themselves.

External evidence refers to what has been discovered or written about the Gospels by other writers especially early ones who quote or explain or repeat traditions or add their own views. Consider first the external evidence in which are set forth the most important passages to show clearly the *traditional view*. It is clear that the other twenty-three books of the New Testament, more or less contemporary with the Gospels, do not deal with them as books though the writer of Acts, Luke (Acts 1:1–5), refers to his former treatise about the deeds and the teachings of Jesus. All these other New Testament books presuppose the contents of the Gospels.[1]

[1] On the basis of fifty passages G. Ricciotti reconstructs an orderly extragospel life of Jesus. *Life of Christ* (Milwaukee, 1947), 91. Cf. M. Goguel, *Life of Jesus* (New York, 1933), 119–33.

6

The Traditional View of the Church Fathers

THE EARLIEST external evidence is debatable as so often happens in dealing with beginnings. Since the seventeenth century certain documents and writers who immediately follow the original apostles of Jesus have been known as "The Apostolic Fathers." [1] "The New Testament in the Apostolic Fathers" (Oxford, 1905) was thoroughly studied by a Committee of the Oxford Society of Historical Theology. [2] They examined Barnabas, Didache, I Clement, Ignatius, Polycarp, Hermas, II Clement and prove that these writings contain many parallels to the contents of the Gospels. However, these parallels may be taken to come from written Gospels, or from current traditions oral and written similar to those which preceded the present Gospels. Yet there is lack of agreement among scholars concerning the earliest clearest statement of the evidence. The Didache (Teaching of the Twelve Apostles) is a kind of early church manual which tells of the two Ways of Life and of Death and provides directions for church concerns like fasts, prayer, baptism, Eucharist and prophets. The Lord's Prayer is to be said three times daily and it is quoted entire with this statement, "Pray as the Lord commanded in his gospel" (8:2). The Oxford Committee holds that "the gospel" "apparently means the Message itself rather than any special record." Kleist and Goodspeed state that the reference is to Matthew or possibly to the Four Gospels (Kleist). The issue remains unsettled, though the weight of opinion inclines to hold the references mean the written Gospels. [3] Evidently the ideas of the Gospels were well known and quoted in the first half of the second century but whether known from oral statements or from written sources antecedent to the Four Gospels cannot be determined. The mists of the past hide the early

[1] K. Lake, *Apostolic Fathers* (London, 1912); J. Kleist, *Ancient Christian Writers* (Westminster, No. 1, 1946; No. 6, 1948); E. J. Goodspeed, *The Apostolic Fathers* (New York, 1950).

[2] Cf. W. Sanday, *The Gospels in the Second Century* (London, 1876).

[3] "The earliest mention of a written gospel," A. Souter, *Text and Canon of the New Testament* (New York, 1913), 160; E. C. Moore, *New Testament in the Christian Church* (New York, 1904), 76.

history of the Gospels. They existed as separate books in various churches. Copies must have been made and circulated. They were doubtless read at Christian meetings and increasingly treasured but we know nothing until after the middle of the second century when the Gospels begin to emerge into daylight.

During this period the church decided on four Gospels chosen out of many narratives (Lk. 1:1). The decision was not unanimous since it was forced by a powerful religious reformer, Marcion of Pontus and Rome, who undertook as one of his aims to purge Christianity of its Judaism and its scriptures and to establish a fixed list of Christian books limited to the Gospel of Luke and ten writings of Paul. He aroused much opposition and the church had to select the writings among those in use which were apostolic, inspired, authentic and authoritative. These had to meet the need for teaching believers, for missionary purposes and for meeting unfriendly criticism. This was the beginning of the Christian canon which followed a pattern already known in the use of the Hebrew Scriptures which were held as holy books. The Christian books were a continuation of God's revelation from the past into the present. "The acceptance of the four gospels and a collection of Paul's epistles was probably almost automatic."[4] The Gospels exist because the community of believers, a new Israel, produced, verified and perpetuated them as the revelation of God. Placed first in the Christian scripture, they were books of the church, for the church, by the church or by the people who believed and lived in fulfillment of God's purposes, known in Christ.

Justin Martyr, born about A.D. 100, a Palestinian philosopher, became a Christian through the advice of some unnamed one who urged him to know the prophets and the friends of Christ. He traveled widely in his blanketlike philosopher's robe, and died a martyr in Rome about A.D. 165. Among his writings are two *Apologies* intended to defend his faith before high Roman officials and a *Dialogue with Trypho* in which he debates with an informed Jew the interpretation of the Hebrew Scriptures. Justin and Trypho tried to convert each other, but their efforts ended in a draw. In the *Dialogue* there is mention thirteen times of *Memoirs;* for example,

The *Memoirs* which I say were composed by his [Jesus'] disciples and them that followed them [ciii:7]. Finding him [Jesus] written down in the *Memoirs* of his apostles as Son of God and calling him Son we have understood that he is so. . . . We are told that he [Jesus] changed the

---

[4] E. Blackman, *Marcion and His Influence* (London, 1948), 36, 126; J. Knox, *Marcion and the New Testament* (Chicago, 1942), 31.

name of one of the apostles to Peter and we find it recorded in his *Memoirs* that this took place [cv:3].

In the *Apology* (I, 66) there is similar mention, "For the Apostles in memoirs composed by them, which are called Gospels, had thus delivered unto us what was enjoined upon them." [5] "It is generally accepted that Justin means by the phrase (Memoirs of Apostles) the Synoptic Gospels and probably also the Fourth Gospel." [6] Justin knew the story of Jesus and interpreted the Jewish Scriptures in its light. He reinforced the view that Christ fulfilled the Scriptures. Thus Justin aided in their acceptance as part of the Bible for Christians. This was one of the important steps, which Christians took to maintain the relationship of their religion with its mother Judaism.

The next evidence comes from Papias, bishop of Hierapolis (now in western Turkey), of whose life little is known. He wrote about A.D. 140 five books called *Explanations* (or *Interpretations*) *of the Lord's Sayings*. These books are lost, though known in part by references and quotations of later writers. The most information comes through Eusebius, who wrote his famous *Ecclesiastical History* in ten books, A.D. 311–325. He was Bishop of Caesarea (seaport of Palestine), where he had access to a large library of a noted scholar, Pamphilus. "Eusebius of Caesarea was the first writer to conceive the idea of presenting to the world a history of the Christian church as a unit standing by itself." [7] There are no early church historians to compare with Luke in the first century and Eusebius in the fourth. Eusebius planned his writing to cover the span from Jesus to his own day. He set forth "successions from the holy apostles," important affairs and leaders, disasters and martyrdoms. A hard-working, honest man of singular genius, he undertook to keep his history and philosophy separate, but he was biased and uncritical. While much of his history is tedious, he does give about 250 quotations from earlier sources. These constitute the most valuable part of his work. His quotations from Papias about the Gospels have occasioned much study and comment. He quotes Papias but little, probably because he disliked the fancies of Papias about the future. Scholars wish he had quoted much more, even if he did think Papias a man of small intelligence. The quotations from Papias about the Gospels follow:

So then Matthew compiled the oracles (Logia) in the Hebrew language but everyone interpreted them as he was able.

[5] *Ante-Nicene Fathers,* A. Roberts and J. Donaldson (New York, 1896), I, 185.

[6] A. L. Williams, *Justin Martyr* (London, 1930), 209 (note).

[7] Eusebius, *Eccl. Hist.* II, 28 (Lawlor and Oulton, London, 1927).

This also the elder used to say. Mark indeed having been the interpreter of Peter, wrote accurately, howbeit not in order, all that he recalled of what was either said or done by the Lord. For he neither heard the Lord, nor was he a follower of His, but, at a later date (as I said) of Peter; who used to adapt his instructions to the needs (of the moment), but not with a view to putting together the Dominical [Lord's] oracles in orderly fashion so that Mark did no wrong in thus writing some things as he recalled them for he kept a single aim in view; not to omit anything of what he heard, nor to state anything therein falsely.

This next quotation does not refer specifically to the Gospels but contains important evidence about Papias' attitudes and methods and sources.

But I will not hesitate also to set down for thy benefit, along with the interpretations, all that ever I carefully learnt and carefully recalled from the elders, guaranteeing its truth. For I did not take delight as most men do, in those who have much to say, but in those who teach what is true; not in those who recall foreign commandments but in those who recall the commandments given by the Lord to faith, and reaching us from the truth itself. And if anyone chanced to come who had actually been of the elders, I would inquire as to the discourses of the elders, what Andrew or what Peter *said,* or what Philip, or what Thomas or James, or what *John* or Matthew or any other Lord's disciples; and the things which Aristion and *John the elder,* disciples of the Lord, *say.* For I supposed that things out of books did not profit me so much as the utterances of a voice which liveth and abideth.[8]

These brief and puzzling extracts have been much studied with no unanimous decisions and little additional light. The reference to the Hebrew language of Matthew is usually taken to mean Aramaic (cf. Acts 21:40), since it had supplanted Hebrew in current use. "Oracles" may mean sayings or accounts, including sayings. It is a well-known word in the Old Testament for utterances of the Lord. Does it refer to the Gospel of Matthew or to a collection of sayings used by Matthew? How literal and how loose was the interpretation and in what languages? The longer section on Mark shows that he aimed to include all he heard and to tell the truth. Though he wrote accurately of all he remembered that the Lord said or did, why did he not recall more of Jesus' sayings, since Matthew and Luke give many more? Does his lack of order indicate a literary or chronological shortcoming or is he defending Mark as against larger orderly gospels? Mark knew the Lord's oracles from Peter's oral instructions

[8] *Ibid.* III, 39:16, 15, 3–4.

which were fitted to needs of hearers. Mark translated for Peter but he himself was not a hearer or first follower of Jesus. If Papias is correct about Peter as the basis for this Gospel, why was Mark's Gospel soon less authoritative than the others? Why is Peter put in an unfavorable light? Whether Peter was alive or dead and where Mark wrote we are not told. Papias credits his truthful information carefully learned and remembered to the Elder (John) or to elders who had been followers of the Lord's disciples. Is his evidence second or third hand? Some of his evidence comes from disciples whose words had been spoken. Others were still speaking. He preferred "as a man of primitive times" a living voice to the contents of books. What books were at hand? Did he rightly follow a well-known historical distinction that there is a valid viewpoint *within* history of a participant which is not the same as a viewpoint *outside* the historical events? "I was there" states an experience different from "I read about it." Why are there no references from Papias about Luke? These questions are asked to indicate that our earliest sources fail often to provide all the information desired about the Gospels by a later reader.

Theophilus (c.115–c.180), a bishop of Antioch, wrote three small books to Autolycus to defend Christianity. In a discussion of Genesis he quoted one of the "holy writings" and named John as the author. The quotation is the first verse of the Gospel of John.[9]

Irenaeus, "one of the greatest figures of the first ages of the church,"[10] is known as Bishop of Lyons in Gaul in the latter quarter of the second century. Born somewhere in the East (Asia Minor), known in Rome, he worked in the west as a true Catholic leader and missionary priest and bishop. About A.D. 180 he wrote a large and a notable five-volume book *Against Heresies*. In this work he shows his many-sided genius with a theological yet practical mind as he undertakes to discredit heretics and establish believers in the gospel and the church. His numerous citations of Scripture show that he sees Christians as worshipers of the same God as the Jews. The Scripture, whether Old or New, had the same source and authority in God. Christians worship in a new fashion and follow a new Christ under the guidance of the church or new Israel, which guarantees the rule of truth. In his most famous statement about the Gospels, "pillar and ground of the church," Irenaeus insists the gospel was first preached by the apostles invested with power and the gift of the Holy Spirit

---

[9] *Ad Autolycum*, II:22, in Roberts and Donaldson, *op. cit.* II, 103.
[10] J. Lawson, *Biblical Theology of Saint Irenaeus* (London, 1938), 5.

and with perfect knowledge. After the oral proclamation of the gospel,

> Matthew also issued a written gospel among the Hebrews in their own dialect, while Peter and Paul were preaching at Rome and laying the foundations of the church. After their departure, Mark, the disciple and interpreter of Peter, did also hand down to us in writing what had been preached by Peter. Luke also, the companion of Paul, recorded in a book, the gospel preached by him. Afterwards, John, the disciple of the Lord, who also had leaned upon his breast, did himself publish a gospel during his residence at Ephesus in Asia.[11]

The leading position of Irenaeus and the early date of his writing invest this statement with great importance. Like the statements of Papias this passage has had a long list of interpreters. Some accept its views as final, others look at its positive statements as gathered in the haze of a century when orthodoxy was more important than historicity. Where did Irenaeus secure his information? How trustworthy are his sources? Does he rely too much on tradition? Does not his strong assurance validate his truth which he finds backed by a venerable church with authoritative leaders? Since the Scriptures come from God, can they be doubted or their authorship questioned? It is important to recognize that Irenaeus holds to four Gospels only and sets forth the traditional view about them in his period of history. It is not important to hold with Irenaeus that there can only be four Gospels because there are four regions of the world and four principal winds.[12] Irenaeus allegorizes his scripture almost as constantly as he quotes it. However, he can vividly condemn the heretics who destroy the truth as they try to weave ropes of sand with scriptures or like tricky artists rearrange jewels so that a king looks like a dog or a fox.

A fragment of a catalogue of books accepted in the Church at Rome in the latter part of the second century was discovered by L. A. Muratori at Milan and published in 1740. Based on a Greek original, the mutilated fragment in poor Latin contains no reference to Matthew but opens with a statement usually taken to mention Mark,

at which however he was present and so set them down. The third book of the gospel, that according to *Luke,* was compiled in his own name in order by Luke, the physician, when after Christ's ascension Paul had taken

[11] W. W. Harvey, *Sancti Irenei* (Cambridge, 1857), II, 3–6; *Adv. Haer.* III.1.2, in Roberts and Donaldson, *op. cit.* I, 414.
[12] *Adv. Haer.* III.11.8.

him to be with him like a student at law. Yet he neither did see the Lord in the flesh; and he too, as he was able to ascertain (events, so set them down), so he began his story from the birth of John. The fourth of the gospels (was written by) *John* one of the disciples. When exhorted by his fellow-disciples and bishops he said, "Fast with me this day for three days; and what may be revealed to any of us, let us relate it to one another." The same night it was revealed to Andrew, one of the apostles, that John was to write all things in his own name and they were all to certify.[13]

This unknown writer speaks with authority for the church and mentions other works which are not to be received any more than gall is to be mixed with honey. His details about Luke and John as authors represent current tradition in his day and are largely inferential from the Gospels.

Tertullian, born about A.D. 160 in the Roman province of Africa, son of a Roman centurion, was well educated in science, law, philosophy and literature. When converted to Christianity at mid-life, he became a powerful fighting foe of paganism and heresy and flaming advocate of his faith. He wrote about thirty books which establish his lasting fame as a creator of ecclesiastical Latin and one of the founders of theology for western Christianity. In his work *Against Marcion* (A.D. 208–211), the "Pontic mouse" who gnawed the Gospels to pieces, Tertullian defends the Gospels against Marcion's single mutilated edition of Luke.

Even the wasps make combs; so also these Marcionites make churches. The same authority of the apostolic churches will afford evidence to the other gospels also which we possess equally through their means and according to their usage—I mean the gospels of John and Matthew—whilst that which Mark published may be affirmed to be Peter's whose interpreter Mark was. For even Luke's form of the gospel men usually ascribe to Paul. And it may well seem that the works which disciples publish belong to their masters.[14]

Tertullian also stresses the position that the "evangelical testament" has apostles for authors who were assigned by the Lord himself the office of publishing of the gospel. As far as the facts go, he does, however, not seem to add any new facts to the earlier tradition.

Clement of Alexandria (c.150–c.215), a most learned teacher, writer and theologian, used Greek philosophy to interpret the gospel of Jesus. Long and late he read the scriptures in which he believed the

[13] H. M. Gwatkin, *Selections from Early Writers* (London, 1893), 79; G. Milligan, *New Testament Documents* (London, 1913), 289.

[14] Tertullian, *Anti-Marcion* IV, 5, in Roberts and Donaldson, *op. cit.,* III, 350.

voice of God had spoken a divine plan for the world's education. These scriptures should be studied for literal, moral and mystical or spiritual meanings. He set forth his allegorical comments on scripture in an eight-volume work, *Hypotyposes* (outlines or sketches), parts of which have been preserved. Concerning the order of the Gospels Eusebius reports Clement as follows:

He said that those gospels were first written which included the genealogies, but that the gospel according to Mark came into being in this manner: When Peter had publicly preached the word at Rome and by the Spirit had proclaimed the gospel, that those present, who were many, exhorted Mark, as one who had followed him for a long time and remembered what had been spoken to make a record of what was said; and that he did this and distributed the gospel among those that asked him. And that when the matter came to Peter's knowledge he neither strongly forbade it nor urged it forward. But that John, last of all, conscious that the outward (lit. bodily) facts had been set forth in the gospels, was urged on by his disciples and divinely moved by the Spirit composed a spiritual gospel.[15]

Clement not only gives an order for the Gospels but he locates Mark as writing at Rome during Peter's lifetime though Peter was noncommittal about the book. Like John in the Muratorian fragment, Mark is urged to his task by friends. The spirit moved Peter's preaching and prompted John's spiritual Gospel.

Origen (c.185–c.203), Clement's most famous pupil, known also as Adamantius (man of iron, due to his powerful reasoning or to his voluminous writings, 2,000) became the foremost biblical theologian of the early church. With prodigious knowledge and endless curiosity he studied and wrote in Alexandria and Caesarea. In a catalogue of the scriptures he accepted only the same fourfold gospel in the same order as Clement but provided no new information about authors and books.[16]

Scholars have long known that many old Latin manuscripts contain prefaces or Prologues about various books of the New Testament which give information about author, place of origin, purpose and occasion of writing. Since 1928 there has been an increased interest in an early dating of some of these prefaces known by a new title, *Anti-Marcionite Gospel Prologues*. Prominent scholars have accepted a date from the latter part of the second century. Of these early Prologues none exist for Matthew but Mark and John have brief ones in

[15] *Eccl. Hist.* VI.14:6, 7 (Lawlor and Oulton).
[16] *Ibid.* VI.25:4, 5, 6.

Latin, translated from Greek, and Luke has a longer one in Greek. *Mark's Prologue* reports that he was "stump-fingered," that he was an interpreter for Peter and wrote in Italy after Peter's death. *About Luke* it is said that Luke was a Syrian from Antioch, a doctor, a disciple of apostles including Paul. He served the Lord faithfully, remained unmarried, died aged eighty-four in Boeotia, full of the Holy Spirit. After Matthew had recorded his Gospel in Judea and Mark in Italy, Luke moved by the Holy Spirit composed his Gospel in Achaia (Roman province in Greece) for Gentiles so that the faithful might be guarded with an accurate narrative of the ministry as against Jewish myths of divisive, vain fabrications. A "prophet among the Twelve" provides the recollection. Afterward Luke wrote the Acts; John, the Apostle, one of the Twelve, wrote the Revelation in the island of Patmos and later the Gospel. *John's Prologue* states that his gospel, as Papias declared, was written in John's lifetime but Papias had taken it in dictation. Marcion, the heretic, was rebuked and was cast off by John though he brought a letter from brethren in Pontus.[17] The statements about Mark and Luke appear early and reliable. The statement about John has caused debate and denial, since obviously the Apostle John did not live to face Marcion.

The external evidence about the Gospels has been reported for a period covering 100–150 years. Later writers provide no additional information, except inferences from the Gospels or uncertain legends. During this time the great concern was to distinguish apostolic from unauthentic writings. The apostolic writings, like the Old Testament, were verified as from God. The Gospels inspired by the Holy Spirit gave the true report of God's purposes fulfilled in Christ and in the equally authoritative sayings of Jesus. Eventually the church with its claim of divine sanction took the developed view that it produced both the Gospels and a tradition about them and its claims were final for long centuries. There was little departure from these views until the eighteenth and nineteenth centuries when some scholars turned from acceptance of ancient external testimony to firsthand evidence in the Gospels. Their move had been prepared in the twelfth century when Bible study passed from cloisters to universities and in the sixteenth when Protestantism stressed direct relationship of believer and Bible, rather than traditions of the church.

In general the traditional viewpoint assumes that the gospel under the influence of the Holy Spirit was first spoken, then written; in other words life precedes literature. Its truth was guaranteed by the apostles who were appointed by Jesus. There was only the fourfold Gospel. All other attempts were rejected as unapostolic, unfit for church use and for holy scripture. The four were accepted as written in the traditional order, though the order of Matthew, John, Luke, Mark also appears in some versions. *Matthew,* the earliest and most favored, was written by the tax collector (Mt. 9:9; Mk. 2:14; Lk. 5:27) who was one of Jesus' original disciples. He wrote before the Fall of Jerusalem (A.D. 70) in Hebrew (Aramaic) for Jewish Christians in Palestine in order to prove Jesus was the Messiah. He wrote from his own experience. His book was early and reliably translated into Greek since the Church Fathers quote the Greek text. The second Gospel was written by a man with a double name *John Mark,* a Jerusalemite (Acts 12:12, 25; 13:5, 13; 15:37, 39; Col. 4:10; Philem. 24; II Tim. 4:11; I Pet. 5:13), companion of Paul and Peter. He wrote in Greek for Roman Christians in order to prove Jesus is the Son of God. His Gospel was written before A.D. 70 before the death of Peter whose memoirs he preserves, though the publication may have been after Peter died, A.D. 67. *Luke's Gospel* was written by a Greek doctor (Col. 4:14) who was converted at Antioch and traveled much with Paul (II Tim. 4:11) as his other book, Acts, shows since he uses the first person pronoun frequently in the latter part. Where he wrote is uncertain but his Gospel for Greek Christians follows the teaching of Paul. It is dated probably before Paul's death and the Fall of Jerusalem. As his preface shows, he aimed at an orderly account to aid the understanding of Theophilus who needed certainty about his faith. *John* was a fisherman, one of the Twelve (Mt. 4:21; Mk. 1:19; Lk. 5:10), usually identified with the Beloved Disciple (John 13:23; 19:26; 20:2; 21:20). He wrote near the end of the first century at Ephesus for Gentile Christians. His purpose (20:31) was to make sure his readers believed that Jesus was the Christ, the Son of God, and thereby received life in his name.

The first manuscripts (autographs) of the Gospels disappeared early. When the church verified the Four Gospels in the second century and made copies, probably titles were added for identification, e.g., "According to Matthew." Then symbols were added as early as Irenaeus,[18] who found in Scripture four living creatures (Rev. 4:7; cf. Ezek. 1:10) which he took to forecast aspects of Christ in the Four

---

[18] *Adv. Haer.* III.11, 8

Gospels. Later writers disagreed with Irenaeus on his assignment of symbols and the choice of Ambrose and Jerome (Eusebius Hieronymous) became the commonly accepted identification which finds expression in church windows and sculpture and architecture on which one may speculate if the sermon does not percolate. A table will illustrate the symbols.

	MATTHEW	MARK	LUKE	JOHN
Irenaeus	man	eagle	calf	lion
Jerome	man	lion	ox	eagle

7

The Synoptic Problem and
Its Suggested Solutions

THE WELL-ESTABLISHED traditional view of the origin of the Gospels continued undisturbed until many upsetting changes laid the foundations for our modern world. The revival of classical learning, the art of printing, the revolt against the Roman Church, the translation of the Bible from international Latin into national, living languages, the widened horizons of newly discovered lands, the development of commerce, the beginnings of modern science, the trust in man's reason as well as in divine revelation, the individual independence of judgment, the challenge by nations of the rule of the Pope, the authority of the Bible as against the hierarchy of the church, all these and more, have moved western man to positions far from his medieval days.

Prominent among these important changes was the fact that men could read the Bible again in Greek and Hebrew as well as in their native languages. No longer did they know the life and the teachings of their Christ by the mummeries of dramatic plays often fantastically imagined, or by the mystery of the sacrificial mass, or by the monkish imitations of holy men, or by the acute and extensive theologies of the Scholastics, or by the storied windows and the sculptured saints of the cathedrals, or by the glorious artistry of the Holy Family, or by the soaring hymns of Ambrose, or by somber Gregorian chants, or by the long strings of quotations (catenae) taken from commentaries on the scripture by Latin and Greek church fathers. The Bible provided a direct approach to the historical realities of their faith.

Another of these important changes arose when men began to question some long-established viewpoints, and when they sought *internal* evidence from the Gospels and trusted it more than external evidence. Hitherto, the Gospels had been paraphrased and harmonized, their authority unquestioned, their teachings equated with later church doctrines, their historical accuracy taken for granted, their inerrancy axiomatic, their miracles certified, their inspiration divinely guaranteed. All these points came under scrutiny and questioning as scholars began to study the Gospels afresh with historical criticism instead of dogmatic ideas. They began to ask questions about the Bible as they would in the literary study of any book of antiquity. Men started to examine the life of Jesus, depending more on their own judgments than upon the dictates of past authorities. Hence they tended to make Jesus a modern man. Long detailed studies of texts, languages, sources and historical conditions were often combined with philosophical speculations and psychological guesses. The result has been that for 200 years the world of biblical scholarship has been flooded with a sea of ideas about the Gospels and Jesus. The great divide between the modern view and the traditional one lies in the stress on critical historical study as contrasted with dogmatic theological study. These two can never be entirely separated, since every theologian finds a historical rooting and meaning in the story of Jesus and every historian works from certain philosophical and religious viewpoints in the background of his mind. The long detailed story of modern research in the life of Jesus has been chronologically traced (1771–1901) in Schweitzer's epoch-making book, *The Quest of the Historical Jesus,* which was published in 1906 in German under the title *Von Reimarus zu Wrede* and later editions *Geschichte der Leben-Jesu-Forschung* (*History of Research in the Life of Jesus*). A survey of the research since Schweitzer (1900–1940) is given by McCown, *The Search for the Real Jesus.*

"We have ample evidence that within a very few years after Papias wrote differences between St. John and the Synoptic Gospels had begun to attract attention," [1] but when modern historical investigation of the Gospels began in the eighteenth century, John, the "spiritual Gospel," was again recognized as different in language, order of events, style and thought from the other three Gospels. These three had similar words and order of events and many parallel passages. Varying explanations were sought for these similarities. They were striking enough to produce a special title for Matthew, Mark and Luke as the "Synoptic Gospels" since they were "looking together" at the same subject and thus presented a common view. These Synoptics were evidently related to each other or to forerunners. Every permutation and combination was suggested. These fall into three main forms. The Gospels depended upon: (1) oral tradition; or (2) upon documents; or (3) upon both.

[1] J. Lightfoot, *Essays on Supernatural Religion* (London, 1889), 207.

The Gospels were once held to be alike because they had a com-mon *oral* Aramaic source which had been retold so often it acquired a fixed form. This hypothesis has been severely named "asylum ignorantiae" and "asylum orthodoxiae" by Schmiedel in a famous article on the Gospels.[2] This oral Aramaic theory fails because: (1) it does not adequately explain the amazing Greek likenesses of the three Gospels; (2) it does not account for the large amount of the teachings of Jesus omitted by Mark but present in Matthew and Luke; (3) it does not explain the differences though it helps with some of the similarities. However, this theory contains some truth. It explains the existence of Aramaic material which later appears in the Synoptic Gospels though it does not account for the Greek form. This theory tells something of the manner in which the gospel was first known by word of mouth, informally and by public preaching. In the book of Acts the first followers of Jesus ceased not to teach and preach as witnesses. They were not interested in producing literature but in converting their fellow man. They knew the example Jesus had set not in writing but in teaching. They expected a New Age soon to transform this present one. But the fact that these first Christians produced an oral Aramaic tradition must be kept separate from the theory that our written Gospels are directly dependent only upon it. A variation of this *oral* Aramaic gospel was paralleled with the idea that there was a written Aramaic gospel but it faces the same criticism as the oral theory plus the absence of satisfactory evidence for its existence. There is almost unanimous agreement among scholars to drop the oral theory as an adequate explanation of the relationships among the Synoptics though it has had staunch defenders like Gieseler, Westcott, Wright and Lattey. However, interest in the oral gospel arose again in the study known as Form Criticism as will be shown later.

The second main theory is known as *documentary dependence,* which may mean either that the Gospels were formed from earlier documents or that they were copied from each other. Again, every possible combination has been proposed: (1) Mark wrote first, then Matthew and Luke copied; (2) Matthew was repeated by Mark and Luke; (3) Luke was copied by Matthew and Mark. These variants departed from the early order of Augustine, who standardized the sequence of Matthew, Mark, Luke with Mark as an abbreviator of Matthew and Luke as one who used both Mark and Matthew.[3] But

[2] *Ency. Bib.* (New York, 1899–1903), Cols. 1845–46.

[3] *De Cons. Ev.* I.ii.4 (Works of Aurelius Augustine, M. Dods, Edinburgh, 1871–76), VIII, 142.

the simple suggestion of one of two sources for the Synoptics did not explain the complexities and the differences between the Gospels. Hence additional theories arose. Earlier fragments or short written narratives were suggested as the bond of connection for the Gospels, though their existence was hard to prove. The recognition of interdependence between the Synoptics (Griesbach, 1745–1812) led to wideranging results which still command no universal consent. The great bulk of books, the articles in professional journals, the long list of scholars would require volumes if they were fully set forth. Some variations of these documentary theories remain as most acceptable to scholars today. This literary investigation can be divided historically into theories which are designated as: (1) one document; (2) two documents; (3) four documents; (4) multiple documents. These are followed by an attempt to penetrate into the oral period prior to the writing of documents. This last method has been known as "Form Criticism" or "Formgeschichte" as used by its German exponents. Each of these theories will be briefly explained and evaluated.

These theories are attempts to solve the "Synoptic Problem." This problem arises out of the need to account for the likenesses and the differences of the first three Gospels. Both the harmony and the variety must be explained from a literary and a historical standpoint. The *one-document* theory, which holds that there was one original Gospel, in Hebrew or Aramaic, can be dropped as oversimple and as lacking historical evidence. This theory can be diagrammed thus:

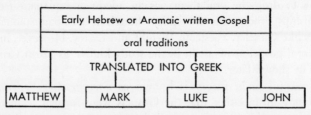

The *two-document* theory has commanded wide assent to the present day, though not with Roman Catholic scholars, since the Pontifical Biblical Commission (June 26, 1912) denied the theory as lacking any witness of tradition or any historical argument.[4] The theory was developed mainly from 1850–1925. Its acceptance as a fundamental solution rests on internal evidence since it departs at certain points from the traditional view. Since this theory has ac-

---

[4] J. Steinmueller, *Companion to Bible Studies* (New York, 1941–44), III, 110–29.

quired a position somewhat like that of evolution in science, there is need to see its merits.[5] It stands on two feet. One is that Mark is the Gospel first written, the other that there was a second written Source or Q. This symbol usually is taken to stand for the German word *Quelle* (source) as used by Wellhausen, but its origin in the latter nineteenth century is claimed in England also when J. A. Robinson used Q as the next letter in the alphabet to distinguish sayings from narrative designated P which came from Peter.[6] These two sources, Mark and Q, were used by Matthew and Luke. To these points in the theory must be added the common agreements that: (1) the Synoptics are connected by Greek sources; (2) oral tradition cannot explain relations; (3) Matthew and Luke did not use each other's Gospel. The clearest way to see the Synoptic relationships is found in Barr's "Diagram" in which on a single large sheet the Gospels are shown in columns, drawn to scale, with appropriate colors to show the parallel or individual passages and with lines to indicate the varying positions of the material found in each Gospel in relation to the others.

The reasons for the dependence of Matthew and Luke upon Mark and for the probable existence of Source Q need to be stated briefly. The conclusions came from careful scientific scrutiny of the three Greek Gospels. The idea that Mark was written first is not new, since Storr (1794) and Herder (1796) had declared Mark to be the oldest Gospel. "It was Holtzmann's *The Synoptic Gospels* written

[5] For earlier discussion of the Synoptic Problem see: B. F. Westcott, *Study of the Gospels* (4th ed. London, 1872), 161–208; A. Jülicher, *Introduction to the New Testament* (New York, 1904), 338–67; P. W. Schmiedel, *Ency. Biblica* (New York, 1904), cols. 1845–72; T. Zahn, *Introduction to the New Testament* (New York, 1909), II, 367–427.

For recent discussion see: F. C. Burkitt, *Earliest Sources for the Life of Jesus* (London, 1910), 32–46; J. Moffatt, *Introduction to the New Testament* (New York, 1911). 177–217; B. H. Streeter in *Peake's Commentary on the Bible* (London, 1920), 672–80; A. S. Peake, *Critical Introduction to the New Testament* (New York, 1921), 45–72; F. D. V. Narborough in *New Commentary on Holy Scripture* (London, 1928), 33–42; A. C. Deane, *How to Understand the Gospels* (New York, 1929), 1–42; B. S. Easton, *The Gospel before the Gospels* (New York, 1930), 3–27; E. C. Hoskyns and F. N. Davey, *The Riddle of the New Testament* (London, 1931), 102–10; J. H. Ropes, *The Synoptic Gospels* (Cambridge, 1934), 89–117; A. Barr, *Diagram of Synoptic Relationships* (Edinburgh, 1938); M. S. Enslin, *Christian Beginnings* (New York, 1938), 426–36; A. Richardson, *The Gospels in the Making* (London, 1938), 11–59; F. B. Clogg, *Introduction to the New Testament* (New York, 1943), 179–203; R. Heard, *An Introduction to the New Testament* (London, 1950), 30–52; A. M. Hunter, *Interpreting the New Testament* (Philadelphia, 1951), 34–48; T. Henshaw, *New Testament Literature* (London, 1952), 79–91; A. H. McNeile, *An Introduction to the Study of the New Testament* (2d ed. Oxford, 1953), 59–91.

[6] R. H. Lightfoot, *History and Interpretation in the Gospels* (New York, 1934), 27.

in 1863 that was most influential in establishing this basic fact [the priority of the Second Gospel] of Synoptic study." [7] But the evidence was cumulatively assembled by the hands of many scholars like B. Weiss, Loisy, J. Weiss, Wellhausen, Jülicher, Harnack, Allen, Stanton, Hawkins, Burkitt, Streeter and many others. This view reverses the traditional one of Augustine that Mark abbreviated Matthew. Augustine is later (fourth century) than the earlier Fathers who stated that Matthew was first written and who give Mark credit for a Gospel based on Peter's preaching.

The *two-document* theory is outlined thus:

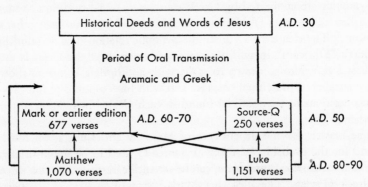

In actual fact Matthew usually abbreviates Mark where they report the same narrative. Hawkins shows that in nine similar stories Mark uses 1,840 words and Matthew 971 and Luke 1,476.[8] Streeter gives five main reasons which show Matthew and Luke as dependent on Mark. (1) They reproduce 90 per cent of Mark. (2) They follow Mark's outline. "Wherever Matthew departs from Mark's order Luke supports Mark and whenever Luke departs from Mark's order, Matthew agrees with Mark." They never agree together against Mark. (3) Mark's language is smoothed out and grammar improved and any of his passages which might cause offense or lessen the regard for Jesus and the disciples are toned down or removed. (4) The form of Mark's writing is more primitive and original. For example, Mark gives Aramaic words of Jesus eight times, Matthew once and Luke not at all. (5) The differing methods of Matthew and Luke in their use of Mark and non-Marcan material seem to indicate a single document like Mark.

The hypothesis of a Source-Q arises from a close comparison of

---

[7] Easton, *op. cit.*, 4.
[8] J. C. Hawkins, *Horae Synopticae* (Oxford, 1899), 127.

Matthew and Luke of those verses (200–250) which they share in common but which are not in Mark. They are mainly teaching. They follow a common order frequently. They sometimes have a double form which points to a written form. The exact extent of Q varies since the material common to Matthew and Luke is not always exactly alike in each Gospel. Moffatt summarizes sixteen of the leading scholars who have selected and printed the verses known as Q.[9] Since his time (1910) there are notable arrangements and discussions by Streeter, Cadbury, Grant and Manson.[10] There are questions not only about the identification of Q but also about its content and the use of the term. Is it composed of teachings only or does it contain narratives like the Temptation? Does Q stand for a historical document, prior to Matthew and Luke but not in Mark? Is it to be identified with the Matthean Hebrew oracles mentioned by Papias? What is its date? How is it quoted by Matthew and Luke? The main point to be noted is that there has been wide acceptance of the idea that Matthew and Luke not only used Mark but they also had a sizable written Greek source of sayings, composed within a generation of Jesus' death which each evangelist used in his own way, independent of the other's treatment. "It is certain that even in the earliest community men had recourse to the 'words of Jesus' as the highest court of appeal which shows that a collection of them was soon formed." [11] Luke's form of Q is usually held to be nearer the original pattern which disappeared early. Since Mark is known, independent of its use by the other two writers, its use by Matthew and Luke constitutes a valuable norm for judgment about their use of Q which can be discovered only in Matthew and Luke. The value of the Source-Q lies in its explanation of the remarkable parallels in Matthew and Luke and in its evidence as an early form of Jesus' teachings. The possible theory that Luke used Matthew and therefore the hypothesis of Q can be dropped has been carefully worked out but has not commanded the more common consent given to Q.[12]

It is a fact that Matthew and Luke each contain material not in Mark or Q. Each Gospel has some parts peculiar to itself. It was

[9] Moffatt, *op. cit.*, 197–202.

[10] B. H. Streeter, *The Four Gospels* (New York, 1924), 273–94; H. J. Cadbury, *The Making of Luke-Acts* (New York, 1927), 98–110; F. C. Grant, *The Growth of the Gospels* (New York, 1933), 74–81; H. D. A. Major, T. W. Manson, C. J. Wright, *The Mission and Message of Jesus* (New York, 1938), 331–440.

[11] A. Harnack, *Constitution and Law of the Church* (London, 1910), 345.

[12] E. W. Lummis, *How Luke Was Written* (Cambridge, 1915), vii, 114–115; B. G. Jameson, *The Origin of the Synoptic Gospels* (Oxford, 1922), 6; Ropes, *op. cit.*, 66–68, 93; Enslin, *op. cit.*, 431–34.

often thought that Matthew and Luke found this special material in oral or written form which was earlier or later than Mark and Q. The two-document theory fails to explain decisively about much of this material. It also limits too much the number of possible earlier documents. It does not answer enough questions about the relations of Mark and Q or the sources of Mark. The next step came in the recognition that there might be, not two, but four blocks of written tradition from an earlier date than Matthew and Luke. Mark and Q, the "Big Two," were accepted but there remained two other facts. Matthew and Luke had each recorded events and sayings, found only in each of them, and only four Gospels existed. Here the detailed research and amazing learning of Streeter created great interest and considerable acceptance as he worked through text, tradition and current theories to propose a *four-document* theory. He examined the special aspects of Matthew and Luke and decided that they represented documents. He stressed the life of some great church as the place of origin of each of the four Gospels. Mark reflected Roman tradition. Matthew's special source (M) came from Jerusalem and Luke's (L) from Caesarea while Q arose in Antioch. These four sources were collected and combined in the following pattern with a first edition of Luke (Proto-Luke) as an intermediate step.[13]

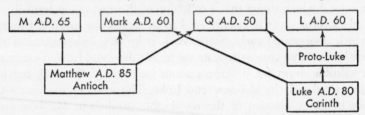

Streeter also studied afresh the way in which Matthew and Luke used Mark and decided that Matthew had followed Mark's narrative outline into which he had inserted five great blocks of teaching. Luke had formulated his own first edition and then later inserted Mark into his plan since he has many chapters, where he departs from Mark to use his own outline. Like Q, the hypothetical documents M, L and Proto-Luke cannot be proved beyond doubt though Streeter has excellent support for the last.[14]

From this stage the next step was to try to discover numerous documents which may have been used by the gospel writers, since "many had taken in hand to write" about Jesus when eyewitnesses were

13 Streeter, *op. cit.*, 150–81, 485–562.
14 V. Taylor, *Behind the Third Gospel* (Oxford, 1926), 182–213.

available (Lk. 1:2). How many actual written documents existed before the Four Gospels cannot be determined with certainty but the latest step can be labeled the *multiple-documents* theory. Grant mapped seven strands of tradition and sources. He listed them as Syrian, Roman, General (Traditional Petrine narrative), Palestinian-Syrian (Q), Palestinian-Caesarean (L), Palestinian-Judean (Special Passion narrative) and Judean (Lukan infancy narrative).[15] This theory helps to illustrate the final stage of research in which documents can be posited. Such efforts to find a variety of written sources, antecedent to the present Gospels, indicate an intensity of study but cannot be taken as beyond the field of possibilities. Since it is often hard to draw a line between the oral and the written sources which existed before the Gospels were written, it is probable that a limit has been reached in the search for written records behind the Gospels.

The results of much study of *written* sources which existed prior to our present Gospels may be arranged in a descending series of probability. "The Q hypothesis is reasonably but not absolutely certain; the arguments for the Marcan sayings-collection are strong but not irrefutable; the M hypothesis is cogent but speculative; the L hypothesis, in its documentary form, is doubtful." [16] These theories concern written sources but it is well to remember that the information about the life and the teachings of Jesus, whether written or oral, has its origin like the branches of a tree which reach out in various directions but which go back to a trunk shared by all.

Because the investigation of possible written sources seemed exhausted after a century of diligent research, attention has turned since 1919 to the oral period or the gospel before the Gospels.[17] It might be possible to penetrate to the actual beginnings of the Gospels or to the first circle of people who knew Jesus. Starting from the example of analysis of documents by Old Testament experts, scholars examined the way the Gospels were put together. They found short independent but connected literary forms like pearls on a string. These pearls could be sorted and graded according to various shapes and values. Their stages of growth could be detected. The pearls had

[15] Grant, *op. cit.*, 66.

[16] V. Taylor, *The Gospels* (5th ed. London, 1945), 34. The probable texts of Q, M and L with discussion of their nature and value are given in E. B. Redlich, *Students' Introduction to the Synoptic Gospels* (London, 1936), 51–109, 188–244. Cf. Streeter, *op. cit.*, 197–98; Grant, *op. cit.*, 74–95; A. M. Hunter, *Work and Words of Jesus* (London, 1950), 131–92.

[17] E. F. Scott, "New Criticism of the Gospels," *Harv. Theol. Rev.* XIX (1926), 143–63.

grown in the sea of the early Christian communities but the string had been manufactured by gospel writers. The pearls had been selected, polished and valued, even created at times, in the living environment of the church in the course of its preaching, controversy, teaching, persecution and worship.

This method of study which undertook to discover the forms of the gospel material in their early oral stages and to re-create the life of the first Christians who produced these gospel patterns is known as *Form Criticism* or Form history from the name established in Germany, *Formgeschichte*. The best-known writers on this subject are Dibelius, Schmidt, Bultmann, Easton, Taylor, Lightfoot, Grant and Redlich. Their studies are influential because they try: (1) to penetrate to hidden depths earlier than written records while they use the records as clues in their search; (2) to classify the original elements of the Gospels according to style and religious interests; (3) to evaluate historically each individual unit (pericope); (4) to show the immediate intentions of the people who under the influence of Jesus produced and applied the first stories and teachings about him to their daily living. "Whatever was told of Jesus' words and deeds was always a testimony of faith as formulated for preaching and exhortation in order to convert unbelievers and confirm the faithful." [18]

Form Critics have pointed out that it is probable that the first written element in the Gospels was the narrative of Jesus in his final days in Jerusalem. This story was the most important climax in all that was remembered about Jesus. From the first his followers distinguish between all that he "began to do and to teach" (Acts 1:1). Additional groups can be discovered such as stories told of miracles which do not stress his teachings, controversies, stories leading to a striking saying as the main point and stories about Jesus himself. His teachings such as parables, brief, ethical, prophetic sayings or forecasts about the future age were collected and soon put into written form for practical use, but the "form" of these units was determined by word-of-mouth repetition before they were written. Study of their style shows their purpose. For such originally separate elements the gospel writers provided a framework of continuity which resulted in

[18] Easton, *op. cit.,* 31–81; F. V. Filson, *Origins of the Gospel* (New York, 1930), 85–114; V. Taylor, *Formation of the Gospel Tradition* (New York, 1933), 1–43; F. C. Grant, tr. *Form Criticism* (Chicago, 1934); Lightfoot, *op. cit.,* 27–56; C. H. Dodd, *History and the Gospels* (New York, 1938), 77–110; E. B. Redlich, *Form Criticism* (New York, 1939), 9–80; D. W. Riddle, *The Gospels* (Chicago, 1939), 1–110; Richardson, *op. cit.,* 102–29; L. H. Marshall in *Studies in History and Religion,* ed. Payne (London, 1942); H. A. Guy, *The Study of the Gospels* (London, 1952), 1–16; McNeile, *op. cit.,* 46–58.

the Gospels. The needs of the church played a large part in selection and preservation of the materials used to aid in instruction, in conversation, in meeting enemies or in ritual. Therefore the Gospels do not present any primary interest in history or in biography or in mere storytelling. They report those essentials which concern a living faith in God's fulfillment of his purposes, revealed in Jesus Christ and accepted in faith by his followers. This stress on the faith of the community of believers has resulted in enlargement of interest in the religion of the early Christians but in diminution of confidence in the Gospels as records of Jesus. However, some Form Critics are confident that the tradition arose early when eye witnesses were still alive and its reliability is founded in actual events and teachings of Jesus.[19] Form Criticism, as a method of study, gives insight into problems and work of the gospel makers, assurance about the greatness and the trustworthiness of the evangelical tradition and ability to distinguish the authentic words of Jesus from later church formulations. "We see Jesus better for we behold him, not only in the final form which tradition assumes in the Gospels, but also in the lives, thoughts and desires of men throughout the formative period." [20] But Form Criticism has encountered more adverse opinion on its historical estimates than on its discovery of literary forms in the Gospels. Redlich lists seven contributions and thirteen limitations of this kind of study.[21] Its skepticism about the genuineness of many of Jesus' sayings and about the historicity of some of the records of Jesus' life has aroused opposition. Even its advocates acknowledge that its use requires great caution which they themselves do not always exercise. Some scholars hold that "Form Criticism is not historical criticism" while others believe "it is not primarily literary but philosophical and historical theory." [22] One of its staunchest exponents is also the least confident, not about the Gospels as records of a community but as historical reports about Jesus. "We must frankly confess that the character of Jesus as a human personality cannot be recovered. We can neither write a life of Jesus nor present an accurate picture of his personality." [23] The materials are not at hand for a life but the actual preaching and action of Jesus are at hand. But there is also historical

[19] M. Dibelius, *Gospel Criticism and Christology* (London, 1935), 84; F. C. Grant, "Form Criticism," *Relig. in Life* III (1934), 351–66; "Further Thoughts on Form Criticism," *ibid.,* V (1936), 532–43.

[20] Taylor, *op. cit.,* 189.

[21] Redlich, *op. cit.,* 77–80.

[22] R. H. Casey, *Quantulacumque* (London, 1938), 115; cf. Easton, *op. cit.,* 81.

[23] R. Bultmann, "A New Approach to the Synoptic Problem," *Jour. of Rel.* (1926), 359.

gain in the recognition that the gospel matter has had a history. "The material in the Gospels has been poured through many sieves and mixed in many crucibles." [24] "It becomes increasingly likely that the process by which oral tradition was reduced to writing and finally presented in the Gospels was a good deal more complicated than we usually think and that much of the material which was later incorporated in the Gospels was in written form at an earlier date than is commonly allowed." [25] The variety is evidence of faithful preservation and leads to confidence in the historicity of Jesus. Critics of Form Criticism usually admit or adopt some of its positions while they modify or reject others. Form Criticism assumes that the Gospels are historical records of the gospel message rather than of Jesus while the older view stresses confidence in the Gospels as records of historical facts concerning Jesus. But the gospel history and the gospel message are really at one since the history is the message in earlier form. This is due to the belief of the first Christians that history is the field where God acted to reveal himself in the reality of Jesus. The Gospels combine the two meanings of history as actual occurrence and as the record of it. They require the reader to decide about the truth of their amazing religious message but also to scrutinize them carefully as historical documents. Thus the investigation of Form Critics in the twilight time of beginnings of the Gospels continues with valuable and debatable results.

Parallel in time to the Form Critics but independent in procedure and viewpoint C. C. Torrey investigated for many years the origins of the Gospels and reached new positive conclusions in 1933 which depart from the "bankruptcy of modern criticism." [26] In his theory of *Semitic Gospels* he holds negatively that the study of origins has been at fault because of two false premises: (1) the Gospels were written in Greek; (2) they are dated late in the first century. Positively he insists that all the Gospels were written in Aramaic in Palestine before the mid-century. The Synoptics were soon translated into Greek, John somewhat later. Both the language and the thought of the Gospels are evidence for this Aramaic theory. The Greek Gospels contain not only Semitic coloring but mistranslations which can be understood when put back into Aramaic. The thought of the Gos-

---

[24] H. J. Cadbury, "Between Jesus and the Gospels," *Harv. Theol. Rev.* XVI (1923), 81.

[25] T. W. Manson, *Companion to the Bible* (New York, 1939), 99; cf. E. F. Scott, *The Purpose of the Gospels* (New York, 1949), 50–99.

[26] *Four Gospels* (New York, 1933), 237–86; *Our Translated Gospels* (New York, 1936), ix–lx; *Documents of the Primitive Church* (New York), 1–110.

pels is early and of one type, modeled according to Old Testament prophecies and intended to meet the need of Jewish Christians to prove that Jesus was the expected divine-human Messiah. To collections of scriptural proofs were added the teachings of Jesus. These written materials lie back of the present Gospels. Q is an unnecessary hypothesis and the Elder's report about Peter and Mark given by Papias is "fiction."

The view that John was written in Aramaic goes back to 1645 and a parallel view for the other Gospels to 1797. Torrey has modern fellow workers like C. F. Burney.[27] However, criticism of Torrey's theory raises questions about the existence of Aramaic Gospels since copies of them are unknown, about the interpretation of the Greek and the Aramaic languages, about the thought of the Gospels which may be both Palestinian and Hellenistic and about the complexity of literary relationships of the Greek Gospels which an Aramaic translation increases more than it explains.[28] This theory has the advantage that: (1) it stresses the great change of the message of the gospel from one language to another and it clears some puzzles in translation; (2) it emphasizes confidence in an early traditional date of writing the Gospels; (3) it keeps a strong continuity between mother Judaism and daughter Christianity. However, this theory lacks decisive authority since little is known of the hypothetical written Aramaic Gospels and of the translators who may have turned them into Greek. According to G. A. Barton, "It is a hypothesis resting on unproved and unprovable hypotheses."

The external and internal evidence about the origins of the Gospels stands briefly summarized in the preceding pages. It is clear that the traditional view and the modern views of many scholars do not coincide at several points. The strictly conservative Protestant view of the Synoptic Problem was recently summarized by H. C. Thiessen,[29] who reviews the current theories about gospel origins and re-

---

[27] *Aramaic Origin of the Fourth Gospel* (Oxford, 1922).

[28] H. J. Cadbury, "Luke—Translator or Author?" *Amer. Jour. of Theol.* XXIV (1920), 436–55; D. W. Riddle, "Logic of the Theory of Translation Greek," *Jour. of Bib. Lit.* 51(1933), 13–30; "Aramaic Gospels and the Synoptic Problem," *Ibid.*, 54 (1935), 127–38; R. Marcus, "Torrey's Translation of the Gospels," *Harv. Theol. Rev.* XXVII (1934), 211–39; J. A. Montgomery, "Torrey's Aramaic Gospels," *Jour. of Bib. Lit.* 53 (1934), 78–99; M. Burrows, "Principles for Testing the Translation Hypothesis in the Gospels," *Ibid.*, 53 (1934), 13–20; G. A. Barton, "Professor Torrey's Theory of the Aramaic Origin of the Gospels," *Jour. Theol. Stud.* XXXVI (1935), 351–73; A. T. Olmstead, "Could an Aramaic Gospel be Written?" *Jour. Near East. Stud.* I (1942), 42–75; D. Daube, "Concerning Reconstruction of the Aramaic Gospels," *Bull. John Rylands Lib.* 29 (1945), 1–39.

[29] *Introduction to the New Testament* (Grand Rapids, 1943), 101–29.

jects all of them in favor of the traditional position that each author under inspiration of the Holy Spirit wrote an independent account, unrelated to any other Gospel, based on some direct knowledge, oral teachings and short written records. The historical order of the Gospels is Matthew, Luke, Mark, John. But there is equal confidence about the reliability of the records about Jesus in the conclusions of modern scholarship. In the words of the liberal and learned historian, H. Lietzmann,

> Facts have their own importance and demand their rights from serious science, they fight their way through and, in the end, hold the field. It may be granted that our sources containing Jesus' words and deeds have been moulded by the Christian Church: we can clearly perceive the work done on them by the earliest Christians, so clearly, indeed, that we can often find therein what is characteristic of the opinions and the hopes of this very community. But in spite of all the transformation effected by tradition, we see in every direction the genuine rock of reliable information upon which the historian can build—if only he will deal with the sources of primitive Christianity by the same methods as all other sources in this world.[30]

In order to arrive at any tentative conclusions there is first the obligation to know well the Gospels and then to master as far as possible the agelong efforts of learned men to discover all possible information about the Gospels. The historian then must decide to the best of his ability within the limits of his work but not as an arbiter of faith, agnosticism or unbelief. Any attempt to determine the divergent issues between the past and present viewpoints will meet both assent and dissent. It must be admitted at times that some desired answers are not obtainable today and some modern questioners go astray when they expect mere scientific satisfactions from gospel makers and writers whose original purposes and products were to be religiously reliable about some exciting good news from God through Christ. Two ventures in dealing with both internal and external evidence deserve notice.[31] The early Church Fathers depended upon Papias and had no independent knowledge beyond him and the Gospels. Hence when an issue arises, it lies largely between the accuracy of Papias and the evidence of the Gospels. The brevity and the uncertainty of meaning in Papias' statement about *Matthew* do not provide for a scholarly judgment about the authorship of the First

---

[30] *Beginnings of the Christian Church* (New York, 1937), I, 54–55.
[31] Hoskyns and Davey, *op. cit.,* 265–85; A. M. Perry, *The Interpreter's Bible* (New York, 1951), VII, 60–74.

Gospel or the Source Q if such a document existed. A study of *Mark* shows a carefully ordered narrative rather than disordered Petrine teaching, though the writer may have had information from an eyewitness. That *Luke* wrote the Gospel is a tradition and critical deduction rather than a certainty based on evidence within the Gospel. "The truth is that the Synoptic Gospels were written as anonymous and undated documents." "The *Fourth Gospel* like the first three, remains in respect to authorship and precise date an enigma." [32] The long story of the fascinating study of the origins of the Gospels yields many theories but few certainties. If the unflagging zeal of centuries of scholars arouses admiration, there is also caution about their conclusions. There must be recognition of unsolved problems even in the face of ceaseless efforts to discover the unknown. "The synoptic problem is a complicated one; it becomes more complicated the more one studies it, and no solution can claim to be complete in its scope or to be any more certain than is that particular hypothesis which is more probable than the alternatives." [33] "The unattainable ideal of Gospel criticism is first to reconstruct the process by which those memories and impressions of the first disciples were transformed and translated within the Christian society into narratives and discourses, and then to trace the process of literary consolidation which welded the traditional material into literary wholes." [34]

[32] Hoskyns and Davey, *op. cit.*, 281, 285.
[33] Cadbury, *The Making of Luke-Acts*, 64.
[34] J. M. Creed, *Gospel according to St. Luke* (London, 1930), liv.

8

Materials and Existing Copies of the Gospels

ONE ASPECT of the study of gospel origins deals with the actual materials, writing and transmission of the books themselves. The first books disappeared early. Handwritten copies were made and distributed in increasing numbers. A few copies of the Gospels, from the fourth, fifth and sixth centuries, are well known and later gospel manuscripts total about 1,500 with the passing of time and the growth of Christianity. The early copies were probably written in Greek with capital letters (uncials), without punctuation or separation of words, upon rolls of papyrus though the book form (codex) is now thought to reach back to the second century or earlier. The papyrus rolls were well known in gospel days and were used from distant antiquity to the seventh century of the Christian Era. The rolls were made from the triangular stem of a tall marsh plant which was split into thin strips which were placed in two layers at right angles to each other. These layers were glued, pressed, dried, polished and pasted into rolls when a longer space of writing was needed. The sheets could be made of varying sizes though usually smaller than typing paper of today and the rolls varied in length though they seldom exceeded thirty feet. The ink of soot, water and gum and the reed pen were readily at hand as the writer wrote in columns which stood the short way of the roll. The rainless sands of Egypt have preserved thousands of pieces of papyrus though it is not a durable substance. Papyrus was supplemented and later supplanted by parchment or vellum (a finer grade) which was made from skins of animals like sheep, goats, calves and antelopes. These skins were stretched, dried, scraped and chalked to provide thin, long-lasting sheets for books. Parchment replaced papyrus from the fourth century and in turn after the tenth century slowly gave way to paper.[1]

[1] A. Deissmann, *Light from the Ancient East,* (rev. ed. London, 1927), 24–50; C. R. Gregory, *Canon and Text of the New Testament* (New York, 1907), 299–326; F. C. Kenyon, *Handbook to Textual Criticism of the New Testament* (London, 1901), 17–38; J. Finegan, *Light from the Ancient Past* (Princeton, 1946), 307–31; B. M. Metzger, "Recently Published Greek Papyri of the New Testament," *Bib. Arch.* X (1947), 26–44.

Since a span of two hundred fifty years stretches between the first Gospels and the existing manuscripts and since different copies made by hand contain variations, the work of textual or lower criticism is "to recover so far as possible the actual words written by the writer." [2] The existing text of the Gospels is known: (1) from the study of earlier vellum and papyri Greek manuscripts; (2) from the quotations in the Church Fathers and in service books of the church; (3) and from early translations or versions of the Gospels. The original language of the Gospels is designated as common (Koine) Greek to distinguish it from the classical Greek known in writers like Plato or Euripides who flourished three centuries earlier. Classical and common Greek could be distinguished roughly in the same way that the English of the Authorized or King James Bible (1611) is readily recognized as alike and different from twentieth-century English. The Greek of the Gospels shows the strong influence of its Semitic predecessors such as the Aramaic spoken by Jesus and his fellow Jews and the Hebrew Scriptures and their Greek translation, known as the Septuagint. This influential first translation of the Scriptures had been known and used first by Jews in Egypt whence it had spread widely for three centuries before the writing of the Gospels.

The life history of a Gospel, like a human being, has hidden beginnings. The actual first writing is not known. But since the words and the deeds of Jesus were highly treasured, copies were soon made of each Gospel. These copies circulated separately, then were united into the well-known fourfold form plus the book of Acts as Christianity spread. Copies were quickly required in large numbers though there was no organized book trade for the distribution of authenticated copies.

For the first hundred years and to a great extent for the first two hundred or two hundred and fifty years, copies of the New Testament books must have been produced locally by local scribes as private individuals. We can imagine a local church or congregation borrowing a copy of a Gospel or an Epistle from its neighbor and making its own transcript without much care for precise accuracy. These were not works of literary art, they were books necessary for salvation in which the substance was what mattered, not the precise words or arrangement of them.[3]

Scribes made mistakes, comparison with other copies was often diffi-

[2] K. Lake, *The Text of the New Testament* (6th ed. London, 1943), 1.

[3] F. C. Kenyon, *Recent Developments in the Textual Criticism of the Greek Bible* (Oxford, 1933), 76; Kenyon, *The Story of the Bible* (New York, 1937), 133–44; C. C. McCown, "The Earliest Christian Books," *Bib. Arch.* VI (1943), 21–31.

cult and the best copies for use in worship were sometimes destroyed in persecution. A revised copy is called a "recension."

The earliest fragments of a Greek gospel date from the middle of the second century.[4] These fragments consist of three leaves from a codex and are mostly like the Gospel of John. They were found in 1920 and published in 1935 (Egerton papyrus 2). The early part of the third century is represented by Chester Beatty papyri, famous for their codex form and for their many parts of the Bible including small sections from each of the Gospels. They were found in Egypt about 1930. The earliest, large, nearly complete vellum manuscripts are known as Codex Sinaiticus (Aleph), Codex Alexandrinus (A), which are at the British Museum, Codex Vaticanus (B) which is at the Vatican, and the Freer Gospels (W) at Washington. These uncials date from the fourth and the fifth centuries. About one hundred uncials are known and designated by letters. The uncials were succeeded by those manuscripts written in a flowing style and known as cursives or minuscules. These Gospels date from the ninth century to the beginning of printing in the fifteenth century and their number totals about 1,400.

Many quotations from the Gospels or in a form resembling the Gospels are found in Greek writers like the Apostolic Fathers, Justin Martyr, Marcion, Tatian, Clement of Alexandria, Origen, Eusebius, Athanasius and Chrysostom and in Latin authors like Tertullian, Cyprian, Jerome and Augustine. Since they often depended on memory, the study of their scriptural echoes poses many problems. These men who wrote before the fifth century are most important. The church also made gospel readings for use in public worship known as lectionaries of which 1,500 are known. Some of these systems of reading the scripture reach into great antiquity. Lectionaries are used for comparative study by textual critics but their readings have not added any weighty information beyond the gospel manuscripts. Totaling uncials, cursives and lectionaries, there exist about 4,500 manuscripts of the New Testament which make it by far the "best preserved ancient document in the world." [5]

The gospel was first spoken in Aramaic, then written; Greek books appeared and as Christianity spread rapidly, the Gospels were soon

---

[4] H. I. Bell and T. C. Skeat, *Fragments of an Unknown Gospel* (London, 1935), 1–7; Bell, *Recent Discoveries of Biblical Papyri* (Oxford, 1937), 3–30; Kenyon, *Our Bible and the Ancient Manuscripts* (London, 1931), 124–28; C. H. Dodd, "A New Gospel," *Bull. John Rylands Lib.* 20:1 (Jan. 1936), reprint.

[5] I. M. Price, *The Ancestry of Our English Bible* (2nd rev. ed. by Irwin and Wikgren, New York, 1949), 161.

translated. The many early translations can be grouped into three main headings, Syriac, Latin and Egyptian. In the Syrian Church, Tatian's harmony of the Gospels (Diatessaron; i.e., through four) in the second century gave way by the fifth to a dominant translation known as Peshitto (Simple). In the Latin Church, likewise early translations fell behind the famed Vulgate by Jerome in the fourth century who labored long in Bethlehem where his reputed underground cell below the Church of the Nativity is still pointed out to Holy Land pilgrims. The Vulgate gradually gained such a leading position for 1,000 years in west Europe that the Roman Catholic Church decreed at the Council of Trent (1546) that this translation must be received by its members as "sacred and canonical." This Vulgate lies back of present-day Catholic English Bibles such as the Rheims-Douay (1609) and its successors. With the Renaissance Greek came again to prominence in European study and there was a return from the Latin to the Greek Gospels. The first printed and published Greek and Latin New Testament was the work of Erasmus (1516). In 1514 Cardinal Ximenes of Toledo printed a Greek Testament, not published until 1522, along with an Old Testament in columns containing the Septuagint, Vulgate and Hebrew. This edition in these various languages is known as a polyglot and is named Complutensian from the Latin name of a university town near Madrid. From these two printed Greek texts and their successors produced by the editor-printers Stephanus, Beza and especially Elzevir came the "Received Text" (1550). This text attained wide acceptance and stands back of the classic Protestant English translation known as Authorized or King James (1611). Its revisions in England (1881) and in America (1901, 1946, 1952) reach into our present time. The Received Text was eventually displaced by the work of Lachmann, Westcott and Hort, with others who established a Greek text of the Gospels which is more accurate and selective in its readings.

The study required by these manuscripts, quotations and versions is highly technical but it is basic to all knowledge of the Gospels because their text must be the starting point for further historical study.[6] The textual critic is a kind of genealogist as he works among manuscripts which fan out from early days. He studies each copy of the Gospels, compares and notes each variation from other copies.

---

[6] A. Souter, *The Text and Canon of the New Testament* (London, 1912), 111–38; Streeter, *op. cit.,* 3–148; Kenyon, *Our Bible and the Ancient Manuscripts,* 98–179; Enslin, *op. cit.,* 475–509; W. H. P. Hatch, *The Principal Uncial Manuscripts of the New Testament* (Chicago, 1939), 3–25; Lake, *op. cit.,* 1–10.

These variations may be accidental or intentional when a scribe tried to correct an apparent error. He establishes families or main groups and their descendants. He compares these families and attempts a reconstruction nearest to the lost original text. If mistakes are evident, he will conjecture a possible wording which appears to be more correct though change is always conjectural. These studies result not in loss of confidence about the actual words of the Gospels but in increasing certitude that in the large number of Bible manuscripts the authentic records remain, not in exact identical words since the Aramaic disappeared quickly but in essential truth which was safeguarded by devoted witnesses.

PART III

Sources for the Study of Jesus

9

Roman and Jewish Sources

HISTORICAL STUDY of Jesus is almost wholly dependent for source material upon the New Testament, especially the Gospels. In view of the extraordinary importance of Jesus as seen by men of later ages, wonder may arise that there are only scanty references to him outside of Christian circles for a century after his death and that very little survives as a record of his deeds and words. The extravagant supposition that if all the things that Jesus did were written "even the world itself would not contain the books that should be written" (John 21:25) shows an early and ardent estimate of the deeds of Jesus and foreshadows his increasing importance. "Nothing is more remarkable in our time than the endless procession of Lives of Jesus." [1] But there is almost no evidence among non-Christians that Jesus made an impression upon them. Christ crucified was to the Jews a stumbling block and to the Gentiles foolishness, though he was the power and the wisdom of God to those who answered his call (I Cor. 1:23). The references to Jesus in non-Christian writers near to Jesus' day can be canvassed quickly.

Three Roman writers give scanty but valuable information, since it comes from those who had no concern for Christianity. *Pliny,* called *the Younger* to distinguish him from his uncle who is famous for his *Natural History,* was a wealthy nobleman appointed governor of the province of Bithynia (North Central Turkey today) by Emperor Trajan where he administered public affairs (A.D. 111–115) which are known from his letters to Trajan. Pliny asked advice from his emperor as he reported his methods at the trials of Christians who were so numerous as to create a problem. Renegade Christians "all worshiped your statue and the images of the gods and cursed Christ" and were pardoned. Faithful Christians were executed unless they were Roman citizens whose death penalty was reserved for the Emperor's decision. Even the torture of two slave women called deaconesses revealed nothing further of their guilt or of "this depraved and excessive superstition."

[1] E. F. Scott, "Recent Lives of Jesus," *Harv. Theol. Rev.* XXVII (1934), 1.

They were in the habit of meeting on a certain fixed day before it was light when they sang in alternate verses a hymn to Christ, as to a god, and bound themselves by a solemn oath, not to do any wicked deeds, but never to commit any fraud, theft or adultery, never to falsify their word, nor deny a trust when they should be called upon to deliver it up; after which it was their custom to separate and then reassemble to partake of food—but food of any ordinary and innocent kind.[2]

Tacitus, the aristocratic historian, tersely told the facts of his age, and interpreted them often with contempt, in his great *Histories* and *Annals* of Rome during the first century of the Christian era. In the Annals published about A.D. 116, he described the terrible fire in Rome (A.D. 64) and discussed its possible origin at the Emperor's order.

Therefore to scotch the rumor Nero substituted as culprits and punished with the utmost refinements of cruelty, a class of men, loathed for their vices whom the crowd styled Christians. Christus, the founder of the name, had undergone the death penalty in the reign of Tiberius, by the sentence of the procurator Pontius Pilate, and the pernicious superstition was checked for a moment, only to break out once more, not merely in Judea, the home of the disease, but in the capital itself, where all things horrible or shameful in the world collect and find a vogue.[3]

Suetonius, the friend of Pliny, biographer and reporter, published his *Lives of the Caesars* in A.D. 120. In his record of the reign of Claudius (A.D. 41–54) Suetonius reports in a single sentence that "since the Jews constantly made disturbances at the instigation of Chrestus, he expelled them from Rome." [4] The spelling of Chrestus raises difficulty and the sentence reads as if Chrestus were present in Rome. Possibly the name may refer to some unknown Jewish agitator but more probably in view of the reference to Christus by Tacitus and the custom of Christians to refer to Christ's presence among them, the word is simply another spelling of Christus. This expulsion of Jews which caused Aquila and Priscilla to move to Corinth where they became friends of Paul is also reported by Luke (Acts 18:2).

The Jewish evidence about Jesus appears in Josephus and in the Talmud. Josephus (A.D. 38–95?) was born of a priestly family in Jerusalem; highly educated, he became a Pharisee; he shrewdly survived the terrific war in Palestine (A.D. 66–70), first as a participant on the Jewish, then on the Roman side. Then he retired on a pension to

---

[2] *Letters* X.96, tr. Malmuth, II, 401–5, Loeb Class. Lib.
[3] *Annals,* XV.44, tr. Jackson, IV, 283, Loeb Class. Lib.
[4] *Lives of the Caesars,* V.26, tr. Rolfe, II, 53, Loeb. Class. Lib.

Rome and attained lasting fame as a historian. His best-known books are *The Jewish War,* which covers about a century from Herod the Great to the Roman destruction of Jerusalem, and *The Antiquities of the Jews,* which tells the old and glorious story of his people for the benefit of Greco-Roman readers. Josephus gave little space to Jesus since he wished to please his own people and to present them favorably to the Gentile public. The brief references to Jesus probably contain some Christian additions though there has been much dispute about what Josephus actually wrote.[5] The probable additions are herewith set in italics:

Now about this time [Pilate's governorship] lived Jesus, a wise man, *if indeed it be lawful to call him a man.* For he was a doer of wonderful works, a teacher of men who receive the truth with pleasure; and he drew to him many of the Jews and many of the Gentiles. *He was the Christ.* And when Pilate, at the information of the leading men among us, had condemned him to the cross, those who had loved him at first did not cease to do so. *For he appeared to them alive again the third day as the divine prophets had foretold this and ten thousand other wonderful things concerning him.* And the tribe of Christians so named from him are not extinct at this day.

*   *   *

He [Ananus, Jewish high priest] assembled the Sanhedrin of judges and brought before them the brother of Jesus who was called the Christ, whose name was James, and some others, and having accused them as breakers of the law, he delivered them over to be stoned.[6]

Only the oldest parts of the *Talmud* contain any evidence of value about Jesus and all the evidence is not agreed upon by scholars. The teachers from the time of Jesus to the completion of the Mishnah (A.D. 220), which is the oldest part of the Talmud, are known as Tannaim (Traditioners). There are no direct references to Jesus in the Mishnah, but there is mention of Jesus in the Baraitha and the Tosefta, which contain certain quotations and compilations from the teachers of the Tannaitic period. J. Klausner has reported these early statements about Jesus and has distinguished both the untrustworthy ones and the increasingly unfavorable later views. The unreliable list includes the charges that Jesus was born of an adulteress and a father named Pandera, sometimes identified as a Roman soldier; that his

[5] Among many discussions of this tangled issue one of the most judicious is given by H. St. J. Thackeray, *Josephus* (New York, 1929), 124–49.

[6] *Ant.* XVIII.3.3; XX.9.1; Whiston's tr. revised by A. R. Shilleto, III, 274–75, 405, Bohn Standard Lib.

death was preceded forty days by a herald who proclaimed it; that there is doubt about Jesus' share in the world to come. The accepted list states that Jesus of Nazareth practiced sorcery (miracles), led Israel astray, mocked at the words of the wise, expounded Scripture like a Pharisee, had five disciples, said he had not come to take away or add to the Law, was hanged (crucified) as a false teacher on the eve of Passover and his disciples healed in his name.[7] This scanty and hostile evidence from the Talmud indicates that only the unusual was remembered about Jesus since Jewish teachers preserved positive teachings for their own people and omitted viewpoints held to be erratic or false like those of apocalyptic writers or Jesus. Also the awful events of the Jewish revolt against Rome have drawn a curtain of destruction over the era before A.D. 70. After the revolt the Sadducees disappeared while the Pharisees survived. Their rivalry to Christianity led to increasing antipathy to Jesus. With their devotion to the written Scriptures and with their oral tradition which for two centuries after Jesus was forbidden to be written for any public use, the result is uncertainty about reports from the time of Jesus. It has been pointed out that the common element about Jesus found in both Roman and Jewish tradition is that he was a crucified false-teacher.

---

[7] *Jesus of Nazareth* (New York, 1926), 46–47; M. Goguel, *Life of Jesus* (New York, 1933), 70–104; C. Guignebert, *Jesus* (New York, 1935), 12–22; M. Goldstein, *Jesus in Jewish Tradition* (New York, 1950), 22; The passages relating to Jesus were collected by R. T. Herford, *Christianity in Talmud and Midrash* (London, 1903), 35–96.

10

Christian Sources: Extracanonical and Canonical

THE CHRISTIAN sources for the study of Jesus are divided into those found outside the New Testament and those within it. The first group called *noncanonical* provides little reliable information and much discussion. These writings consist of fragments of early gospels like the *Gospel according to the Hebrews* or *According to the Egyptians* or lost heretical books like the *Birth of Mary* which are known largely from quotations by early church writers. There are several Infancy Gospels, like the *Book of James* or *Protevangelium*, which tell stories of Mary's parentage and of her childhood, or the *Gospel of Thomas* with its fanciful miracles wrought by Jesus in his childhood when he turned clay sparrows into flying, chirping birds or when he dazzled his teacher in his first day at school as he took a book and taught the Law with beauty and fluency to a great multitude quickly gathered. Another group consists of stories of the Passion, like the *Gospel of Peter* which gives the death cry of Jesus as "My power, my power, why hast thou forsaken me?" or the *Gospel of Nicodemus* (Acts of Pilate) with its fantastic details of the "Descent into Hell."

There are also some materials known as "Agrapha" (unwritten things) which have no known source but which relate sayings and traditions of Christ unknown in the Gospels, such as "It is more blessed to give than to receive" (Acts 20:35) or "Be ye approved moneychangers."[1] These appear mostly as quotations in the Church Fathers.

Finally there are some recently discovered gospel fragments, of which those dated in the third century like the Oxyrhynchus sayings of Jesus repeat the canonical gospels and add new sayings like "If ye fast not from the world, ye shall not find the Kingdom of God." M. R. James, who gives the best summary of noncanonical literature, rightly observes that these noncanonical writings as a whole exclude

---

[1] M. R. James, *The Apocryphal New Testament* (Oxford, 1924), 35. Cf. J. R. Ropes, "Agrapha," in *Hast. Bib. Dict.* V, 343–52; A. F. Findlay, *Byways in Early Christian Literature* (Edinburgh, 1923), 1–178.

themselves from the Bible because they are far inferior.[2] They provide interesting historical information about the imaginations and the theology of the men who wrote them in the early Christian centuries. They have had wide influence in later religious thought, literature and art but they have no established place as history or religion or eyewitness evidence for the life and the teaching of Jesus such as they often claim. Here it is important to distinguish historical evidence found for the time in which men write but not for the earlier time for which they wished to increase both religion and history. No certain decisions can be made except as these later records conform or fail to measure to standards known in the Gospels.

There are many kinds of stories, whether grotesque or theological, but they must be called fictional rather than historical. The sayings of Jesus were striking enough to etch themselves into men's memories and it is possible that some genuine sayings were handed on outside the Gospels. There are some which would not sound amiss in the Gospels, as when Jesus is reported to have said to a Sabbath worker, "Man, if thou knowest what thou doest, thou art blessed, but if not, thou art accursed and a transgressor of the Law." But when the apocryphal gospels are completely surveyed, they show interests in Jesus far out of balance with the canonical Gospels. In 1919 Walter Bauer collected all the apocryphal records and composed a life of Jesus from them.[3] He found these writers greatly concerned about the beginning and the ending in the same manner as the Apostles' Creed jumps from "born of the Virgin Mary" to "suffered under Pontius Pilate." There was comparatively little mention of the public ministry of Jesus, either of words or works. The apocryphal evidence must be read critically. Such reading does not generate confidence in added knowledge of Jesus in his own day but these writings show the ever widening influence of Jesus and constitute a valuable part of the tradition about him. Many of these noncanonical parallels have been collected and conveniently arranged in their proper position relative to the Gospels in a synopsis entitled *Gospel Parallels* in which the text is the Revised Standard Version.[4]

In the *canonical Christian sources* the earliest, most important evidence about Jesus comes from Paul, the educated Pharisee, a contemporary of Jesus, who changed from an active persecutor of Christians to a zealous preacher and missionary for Christ shortly after

[2] James, *op. cit.* xii–xxvii.
[3] *Das Leben Jesu im Zeitalter der neutestamentlichen Apokryphen* (Tübingen, 1909).
[4] New York, Nelson, 1946.

Jesus' death and resurrection. His letters date approximately in the decade A.D. 50–60. They were written primarily to people of Christian churches to aid their understanding of their faith and to insist on its application in actual life. They were not written as scripture nor with an eye to a distant future church but rather for immediate situations where Paul believed he could apply "the power of God unto salvation" (Rom. 1:16). Probably he never knew Jesus personally but at his conversion he received a revelation of the risen Christ and a commission to be his apostle to the Gentiles (Gal. 1:15–16). He knew the first disciples of Jesus like Peter and John in Jerusalem (Gal. 2:9) and reported that his apostleship received the right hand of fellowship of these apostles as well as validation through Jesus Christ and God. Paul's purposes in his letters were religious and practical not biographical and he does not attempt to recount the activities and the teachings of Jesus. He centered attention on the crucifixion and the resurrection and saw these events as parts of God's purposes to save believing men from their sins and to energize them with the indwelling Christ.

Paul's references to Jesus, written about twenty-five years after his death, provide invaluable evidence which was given in the presence of those who knew Jesus. Paul assumed that the contents of the Gospels had been preached and believed prior to the arrival of his letters. Paul's evidence is not uniformly interpreted since scholars do not agree on the genuineness of the thirteen letters which bear his name. From a traditional standpoint G. Ricciotti has collected twenty passages from Paul from which he constructs an orderly extragospel life of Jesus.[5] From a historical standpoint Goguel discusses the Pauline evidence which is scattered and fragmentary though it gives clear proof about the historical tradition concerning Jesus while the other New Testament writers verify the same fact.[6] Out of a multitude of references to Jesus in the genuine letters of Paul there is evidence of a group of people who knew him and gave witness especially about his death and his resurrection. The minimum evidence establishes Jesus as a historical man. "Concerning the flesh" he was a Jew (Rom. 9:5), a descendant of Abraham and David (Gal. 3:14; Rom. 1:3), born of a woman and subject to Jewish Law (Gal. 4:4). He lived as a man (Phil. 2:7–8), he had apostles like Peter and John and brothers of whom one was named James (I Cor. 9:5; Gal. 1:19). He was made a minister to his own people (Rom. 15:8). His teachings are cited as

---

[5] *Life of Christ* (Milwaukee, 1947), 91.
[6] *Op. cit.*, 105–33.

authority for marriage (I Cor. 7:10), for support of ministers of the gospel (I Cor. 9:14) and for the observance of the Supper since on the betrayal night he commanded the action and the remembrance with the shared bread and wine as his body and blood (I Cor. 11: 23–25). He was reproached and his own countrymen were responsible for his death (I Thess. 2:15). He was obedient to the death on the cross (Phil. 2:8) which was placarded before the eyes of men (Gal. 3:1). Numerous references confirm his death (Rom. 5:8, 6:10; I Cor. 15:3; Gal. 2:21). He was raised and appeared six times to his followers (I Cor. 15:4–8; I Thess. 4:14; Rom. 1:4). Paul knew of the humility (Phil. 2:7–8), the gentleness (II Cor. 10:1) and the unselfishness of Jesus (Rom. 15:3). Paul's allusions to the words of Jesus indicate a tradition commonly known among Christians.

The other New Testament writers repeat and confirm the same stress on the sufferings, the death and the resurrection of Jesus. The writer of Hebrews had information from those who had heard the Lord (2:3). He reports that Jesus came from the tribe of Judah (7:14). He knew of his temptations (2:18; 4:15), of his nature as man (2:14), of his faithfulness (3:2), of his prayers and obedience to suffering (2:10, 18; 5:7–8) and adds the detail that it occurred "outside the gate" (13:12). God brought Jesus, the Great Shepherd, from the dead (13:20). Luke, the first historian of the church, refers to Jesus as "a man approved of God" by mighty works (Acts 2:22), who went about doing good, preaching good tidings of peace and healing all who were oppressed of the devil (10:36, 38). He was denied and crucified by lawless men but witnesses to his resurrection gave their testimony (2:23; 3:14–15; 5:30). Jesus made a good confession before Pontius Pilate (I Tim. 6:13). I Peter reports that Jesus did not revile nor threaten but committed himself to God (2:23). John knew of the "Lamb that had been slain" (Rev. 5:6), who was dead and alive again (1:18; 2:8). The latest writer repeats part of the Transfiguration scene (II Pet. 1:16–18) but this may be based on the Gospels rather than independent evidence. These references are samples of the constant acceptance everywhere in the New Testament of Jesus as living among men and also bearing witness to a divine life beyond men.

In addition to this minimum historical witness all the writers in the New Testament give many important explanations about Jesus which rest primarily upon their faith as it interpreted the facts. These authors saw the same divine purpose at work earlier in Israel's history and later in Jesus. As God gave the Law with its full directions after he had freed his people, Israel, from slavery in Egypt so he had redeemed his people, the new Israel, in sending his Son of Davidic descent. He had spoken and acted in this Son whose life, teachings, death and resurrection provide both a fulfillment of the past and a new revelation, available at once but looking toward a new heaven and earth. Salvation comes to those who repent, believe and act upon God's revelation in Christ. The church is the answer to the gospel which proclaims God's supreme act in Christ. Not much is given in the first preaching, reported in Acts, about the ministry of Jesus since the gospel is good news, not good advice, nor a good example of a great man. Christianity from its beginning was religion not reminiscence but it also never ignored the story of Jesus as an event which remained on a historical basis. The New Testament makes sense out of the Gospel Story "only by recognizing in it the entry into history of a reality from beyond history. Thus history becomes 'sacred' history." [7] The origin and the existence of the church also make sense only if it is seen to have a historic founder in Jesus.

A strong trend against the liberal "bare-fact" study of the Gospels has resulted in a return to reading the records in the light of their primary religious rather than historical interests. A cleavage has appeared between scholars who continue to attempt the recovery of actual circumstances and those biblical theologians who hold that there is an "Apostolic Gospel" which was witnessed and proclaimed from the first days by followers of Jesus. This gospel can best be discovered in outline in the sermons of Acts though it is confirmed by Paul and the rest of the New Testament. This gospel inevitably blended fact and faith. Thus it is held that any historical study must begin with the evidence of this gospel with its more than human claims. It proclaimed a fulfillment of God's purposes, prepared for by the prophets and scripture, made known through Jesus Christ who will come again. Therefore, men must believe the gospel and be ready for the end of this age and the coming of a new age.

The work of the student must be first to discover what the writers of the New Testament themselves believed and taught rather than to attempt to find all the answers to the puzzling problems of today. Yet the Gospels bear a timeliness and a relevance for readers of every age which make it impossible to see them only as remote outdated documents. But the modern cart must not be put before the historical

[7] C. H. Dodd, *History and the Gospel* (New York, 1938), 181.

horse. Some think that the cart and the horse cannot be distinguished but there are elements in the study of Jesus which are properly subject to the methods of historical research. A balanced, historical view must take account of both fact and faith, events and explanations, memory and creative imagination, actual religious experience and reflective reconstructions.

11

Six Viewpoints in the Study of Jesus

ONE OF THE results of modern study of the Gospels has been a stronger reliance on the Synoptics for historical information than upon John. But the gap between the two has been lessened lately. All the Gospels are seen to be religious interpretations of certain historical facts. Since the first three are earlier and have much in common in origin and outlook, they still provide the most satisfactory medium. For the study of Jesus it is often better to add John later than to attempt a simultaneous study of all four. There are certain discernible schools of thought which can be distinguished by the manner in which they deal with the Gospels.

1. There are the traditional studies which blend all four Gospels into one account on the assumption that all are equally reliable and sacred as God's word. They are written from a faith that stresses supernatural aspects and everything is accepted on the simple assurance that all things are possible with God. If differences or difficulties arise, they are explained or harmonized as far as possible and if inexplainable, they are assigned to the area of God-given faith which operates on a higher level than any human reason. Fidelity to the viewpoints of past Christian writers, especially to the early ones or to the authoritative teaching of the church, is stressed. Often the purpose of study is to lead to acceptance of dogma or to induce belief in the reader or to apply the ideals of Jesus to the problems of the present. Frequently a practical devotional interest dominates this endless flow from the printing presses or patterns of thought are imposed on the Gospels which move far from the original forms and meanings. Sometimes Jesus becomes the source for all the claims of orthodoxy. Notable illustrations can be found in the works of Protestants like Edersheim, *Life and Times of Jesus the Messiah* (1883); D. Smith, *Days of His Flesh* (1905) and Fahling, *Life of Jesus* (1936) or of Roman Catholics like Lagrange, *Gospel of Jesus Christ* (1934); Lebreton, *Life and Teaching of Jesus* (1934); Ricciotti, *Life of Christ* (1940) and Prat, *Jesus Christ* (1950).

2. Liberal scholars in the nineteenth century undertook historical studies which sought to discover the actual facts in the Gospels. They thought the skin of beliefs could be peeled like that of an onion and a center of factual certainty reached. These attempts often induced weeping and painful protests in orthodox believers. An overconfidence led to the belief in the amount of truth capturable by scientific methods. But a vast amount of additional information was accumulated about Near Eastern civilizations, about contemporary Greco-Roman religions, about rabbinical Judaism, about linguistics and manuscripts, about analyses of the Gospels and their possible sources. The two-document hypothesis gained ground. Mark seemed to provide a reliable historical base for events and Q was equally reliable for teachings. The other Gospels gave more or less historical proofs according to their evidence and the decision of the investigator. Confident comprehensive reconstructions of the life of Jesus which conformed to modern historical standards filled library shelves. Such studies were made by O. Holtzmann, *Life of Jesus* (1904); Harnack, *What Is Christianity?* (1901); by the Jewish scholar, Klausner, *Jesus of Nazareth* (1926); by Case, *Jesus* (1927); Mackinnon, *The Historic Jesus* (1931); Guignebert, *Jesus* (1935) and Goguel, *Life of Jesus* (1932), which is often regarded as the best historical study of Jesus. There is no single result but Jesus often emerged from this kind of study as a superlative ethical teacher who was made divine by men like Paul.

3. Sometimes the amount of knowledge taken from the Gospels was radically reduced or changed. This resulted in a flurry of mythical interpretations about 1910–1920 from men like J. M. Robertson, W. B. Smith, Drews and Couchoud. The Gospels were viewed as finespun speculations in which Jesus disappeared from history in a fog of fancies. These theories date back to the prime mythmaker, D. F. Strauss (1836), and scarcely deserve mention except for their revival among uninformed people whose ignorance is exploited by occasional radicals. Few facts of ancient history are better established than the fact of a historical Jesus. This point has been well verified by Case, *Historicity of Jesus* (1912); Goguel, *Jesus the Nazarene, Myth or History* (1926) and Wood, *Did Jesus Really Live?* (1938).

4. Shortly after the beginning of the twentieth century the liberal students of the Gospels were doubly shocked by the far-reaching investigations of Wrede in *Das Messiasgeheimniss in den Evangelien* (*The Messianic Secret in the Gospels*), who upset confidence in Mark's historical framework. Wrede also stressed the secret Mes-

sianic character of Jesus as due to Mark's own theory which he imposed upon his Gospel. Then Schweitzer, following J. Weiss, emphasized *The Mystery of the Kingdom of God* (1901) and the serious shortcomings of the liberal study of Jesus in *The Quest of the Historical Jesus* (1906). In his theory, known as "thorough-going eschatology," he argued that the Gospels show an enigmatic Son of Man, an unknown Figure haloed in wonder. Jesus looked for the End of the world soon. He can only be seen as he faced a cataclysmic future in which even his ethics are intended for the brief interim before the End comes. The real first-century Gospels cannot be transformed into modern rational writings nor can Jesus be other than an "ineffable mystery," a visionary who sees a divine event at hand when a new Era is soon to appear. However, Christ can be spiritually resurrected within his followers.

5. The ebbing tide of the nineteenth-century liberalism was also countered by the incoming tide of Form Criticism which maintained that the study of the pregospel period made it impossible to write a life of Jesus. Hence Form Criticism spends its energies on ingenious reconstructions and regroupings of the present gospel materials so that the problems, beliefs and trends of the early church could be confidently recovered with occasional far-off glimpses of the actual days before the crucifixion. Whether the first traditions arose out of actual historical conditions or whether the Spirit-led imagination of the early community created them is still debated. The actual life of the church was complex but from earliest times it bore witness that in recent history an act and an appearance of God has been made known in human flesh. Bultmann in his *Jesus* (1926) sets forth the teaching of Jesus about the Kingdom, the will of God and his nature and acts with considerable historical confidence. Dibelius shows much greater confidence in the limited knowledge of the history of Jesus. His book *Jesus* (1939) distinguishes various levels of certainty in the Gospels but accents the decisive character of faith which cannot be proved by history.

6. There are scholars, mainly English, who still maintain confidence in a middle-road position which takes account of extreme viewpoints but retains assurance that a clear and convincing portrait of Jesus emerges from historical study. They admit that a biography of Jesus is impossible in a full sense due to lack of available materials and uncertainty about the reliability of some accounts and their present order. This is due to the original authors whose interest was in good news more than in history. But the historian is in a better posi-

tion than ever before to use both the New Testament and the knowledge of its background and civilization. He can use to advantage the
previous attempts of scholars, granting that some questions can never
be adequately answered. He refuses to stop at the witness of the
apostles in his search for the Jesus of history. He knows that religious,
not historical, motives dominate the records and that interpretations
outweigh factual interests. But since Christianity was founded on the
confidence that God acted on the scene of history, then historical examination of the existing records is essential. Such examination made
with a love of truth, with the use of a historian's tools in a critical
study of the documents, with a readiness to recognize and evaluate
the reality of God's part in men's affairs will result in some confidence
in the main outlines of the features of a "real Personality and a real
Career." This claim was established earlier by F. C. Burkitt in *Jesus
Christ* (1932). It has been verified in an outstanding study by Major,
Manson and Wright entitled *Mission and Message of Jesus* (1938)
which aimed at a competent untechnical study of Jesus for the average reader. In like manner there are readable, popular yet scholarly
studies by C. J. Cadoux, *Life of Jesus* (1948), H. E. Fosdick, *The
Man from Nazareth* (1949), E. J. Goodspeed, *Life of Jesus* (1950)
and A. M. Hunter, *Work and Words of Jesus* (1950), among many
which might be named.

What we can hope to prove is that in the fourth decade of the first century the Christian Church grew up around a central tradition which however it is expressed—in preaching, in story, in teaching and in liturgical
practice—yields a coherent picture of Jesus Christ, what he was, what he
stood for, what he said, did and suffered. The step beyond that will probably be taken by something more akin to faith than to objective historical
judgment.[1]

----

[1] Dodd, *op. cit.*, 110.

12

The Gospel of Mark

THE STUDY of the *first three Gospels* requires not only an investigation into the meaning of the contents but also the discovery as far as possible of everything about each writing. Parts of the answers have been discussed in the chapter on the origins. Here there is need to survey the Roman Mark, the Jewish Matthew and the Greek Luke in order to get a preview of each book as one might look at a tree in a grove before minute examination of bark, leaves or microscopic cells. For the beginner the study of the Gospels themselves proceeds in two general directions; first by use of separate studies of each Gospel, such as commentaries, and second by the use of harmonies or synopses which present the Synoptic Gospels in parallel columns for comparative purposes. These harmonies show all that is at hand about Jesus and so produce a total picture. The commentaries which introduce and explain the text sharpen the panel view of each separate Gospel. It is essential not to have a blurred view which blends everything about Jesus into a general sameness. It is equally essential to avoid a partial view which rests on one book instead of four.

Mark, the least popular Gospel in the ancient Christian world, has in modern study fulfilled one of Jesus' sayings that the last shall be first.[1] It has been widely held that the main points of the traditional view are historically acceptable. John Mark had lived first as a Jew, then as a Christian, in Jerusalem with his mother whose home was a place of prayer in the first days of the church. He was a missionary companion with Paul in some of his journeys and jails and acted as a son and an interpreter for Peter. Shortly after the death of Peter and Paul in Nero's persecution Mark wrote in Rome (A.D. 64–

---

[1] A. Menzies, *The Earliest Gospel* (London, 1901), 1–54; A. Plummer, *St. Mark* (Cambridge, 1915), x–xlviii; B. W. Bacon, *The Gospel of Mark* (New Haven, 1925), 316–34; A. E. J. Rawlinson, *The Gospel of Mark* (London, 1925), xi–lx; H. J. Cadbury, *The Making of Luke-Acts* (New York, 1927), 76–96; A. W. F. Blunt, *The Gospel according to St. Mark* (Oxford, 1929), 11–81; J. H. Ropes, *The Synoptic Gospels* (Cambridge, 1933), 3–32; B. H. Branscomb, *The Gospel of Mark* (New York, 1937), xiii–xxxviii; E. B. Redlich, *St. Mark's Gospel* (London, 1948), 9–65; F. C. Grant, in *The Interpreter's Bible* (New York, 1951), VII, 629–47; V. Taylor, *Gospel according to St. Mark* (London, 1952), 1–140.

70) the first connected account of the public career of Jesus. Since he himself did not know Jesus, he depended upon Peter's instructions. He wrote in Greek an accurate, true, complete but not orderly record of what he had heard. He wrote for Roman Christians who faced possible martyrdom in a hostile world of Gentiles and Jews. These Christians needed strength and understanding from the good news of Jesus Christ who preached the gospel of God, proclaimed his rule, called followers, worked miracles to defeat disease and demons, faced his foes, forecast a future to be fulfilled in God's time, suffered innocently at the hands of Jews and Romans, died on the cross and arose from the dead. Mark's narrative showed a brief, public, popular ministry in Galilee, a withdrawal northward in the face of rising opposition and then a more detailed account of the few final days in Jerusalem. Through his career Jesus moved as one with a great mission from God as the scriptures proved. He uses the title "Son of man." He was a teacher, a prophet and Son of God. As Messiah his recognition, limited first to demons and disciples, reached its open climax and rejection in Jerusalem before the Jewish Council. But the impressions Jesus left upon those who heard and saw him reflect intense interest, wonder, awe, fear and astonishment from the first great day in the synagogue at Capernaum to the last day when the Roman centurion saw him die and declared, "This man was a Son of God."

Mark had a framework of actual events, based on Peter as eyewitness, in which he arranged shorter reports on specific activities and teachings of Jesus. His Gospel moves swiftly, graphically and dramatically to its denouement. "He writes colloquial Greek in an uncultured style for purposes primarily religious." [2] His favorite word is "straightway." He uses the present tense 151 times in sixteen chapters. In his Greek he could choose for past events the imperfect tense (incomplete action) or the aorist (completed action) and he strongly favors the imperfect. The difference in these tenses is not always evident since a literal translation is not good style. His vivid language arrests the reader. The Spirit drives Jesus, his followers hunt him out, he sighs deeply. The demoniac hacks himself, the blind man leaps up, the great crowd jostles Jesus or sits like garden plots on the green grass. Everyday details of Palestinian life pass as rapidly and realistically as a movie film: the fisher and his flung net; the little boat and its pillow; working people like the hired men, the slave, the

[2] Bacon, *op. cit.*, 320; cf. M. S. Enslin, "Artistry of Mark," *Jour. Bib. Lit.* LXVI (1947), 385–99.

porter, the farmer; the grainfields, sickle and harvest time, vineyard and watchtower; clothing like the tunic and the leather belt, sandal and thong, cloak and fringe, long robes, linen and purple; daily life in the home with its door, guest chamber, porch, bed, lamp and lampstand, basket, pot, pitcher, cup, millstone; food like bread, honey, fish, yeast; animals like camels, swine, dogs, a colt; religious observances for Sabbath, synagogue, Passover, blessing at meals, washing, fasting, the great Temple with burnt offerings and money boxes.

Mark is the shortest of the Gospels with sixteen chapters compared with twenty-eight in Matthew, twenty-four in Luke and twenty-one in John. It is the most filled with action. Jesus is the strong Son of God whose eighteen miracles almost equal the twenty each in Matthew and Luke and far outnumber seven in John. He meets crowds, gathers disciples, challenges opponents and travels frequently. He teaches in synagogues, homes and at the lakeside often using parables but while Mark reports many of his words, he lacks other famous parables and teachings found in the other Gospels. Jesus looks searchingly at people, sits with disciples, puts his arm round a child, touches a leper, takes the hand of the little maid in death. He hungers, tires, wonders, angers, pities, groans, greatly fears, prays, holds silence before Pilate, cries and dies, expectant of resurrection.

Mark's *motives and plan* must be inferred from his book. His motives appear simple and devout. He tells a continuous story of Jesus' public activities and shows how he was unjustly brought to his doom. But in and through this story runs a "Gospel of God" which Jesus not only preached but which these events declared. Mark's book is like a portrait set in effective lighting. There are two kinds of thought, one which deals with a real man, powerful and purposeful, yet kind and humble and another which sees a mysterious Figure with an austere and awesome secret whose life, death and resurrection were unfolding God's rule and purpose for all who have faith. Mark's plan appears from the proportions of his work. He divides his book almost in half to give first many loosely connected stories, mostly of mighty acts in public life in Galilee and then the tightly strung tragedy in Jerusalem. By comparison Matthew and Luke give about one quarter of their books to the Jerusalem story. With minor variations all four gospel writers in recording the Jerusalem ministry share a common order of events. This fact indicates both a reflection of actual events and a tradition about them which had crystallized before it was put into writing. The death of Jesus dominates this section as he knowingly accepted his fate as God's will when his enemies killed him. The events and the teachings in the earlier part of Jesus' career in Galilee show variations in which the writers exhibit freedom to arrange their accounts as appeared best to them. The arrangement is sometimes chronological, sometimes geographical and often topical which sets forth a report about Jesus which met the religious needs of the readers.

Plan of Mark

1. The Beginnings of the Gospel .... 1:1–13.
2. The Mission of Jesus in and near Galilee .... 1:14–9:50.
3. The Story of Jesus in Judea and Jerusalem .... 10:1–16:8.
4. A Later Addition .... 16:9–20.

The *beginnings* show John Baptist as a forerunner to Jesus and relate the baptism and the temptation of Jesus. The *mission in Galilee* has many short sections which set forth the power of Jesus in preaching and healing, in gathering followers; controversies with Jewish leaders; withdrawal northward from Galilee; repeated forecasts of a fatal future. The *story of the last days* presents Jesus teaching on his way to Judea, his entry into Jerusalem, the Temple cleansed, further conflicts, the Last Supper, arrest, trials, crucifixion, burial and empty tomb. The *addition* is taken except by traditionalists [3] as not a part of Mark since it is lacking in the two earliest fourth-century manuscripts, a fact which is also reported by early Church Fathers. Also some manuscripts have a different conclusion or give both conclusions. Another writer, Ariston, is also credited with the addition. He might be Aristion, named by Papias as a disciple of the Lord. Both ideas and vocabulary show striking differences from Mark. The abrupt ending at verse eight is possible for a sentence or paragraph but not probable for a whole book.[4] A good guess is that the final sheet was lost or worn out before copies were made and the needed ending was soon supplied since it is known from the fifth century. But it is also possible that Mark completed his Gospel as it stands with awesome fear at the wonder of the resurrection of Jesus.

The foregoing summary about Mark faces some outstanding dis-

---

[3] J. Steinmueller, *Companion to Scripture* (New York, 1944), III, 86–89, in view of the Pontifical Biblical Commission which holds that Mark wrote these verses, suggests that Mark for some unknown reason was interrupted and some copies distributed before he wrote his conclusion.

[4] Streeter, *op. cit.*, 336–60; W. Knox, "The Ending of St. Mark's Gospel," *Harv. Theol. Rev.* XXXV (1942), 13–23; R. H. Lightfoot, *Locality and Doctrine in the Gospels* (New York, 1938), 1–48, and *The Gospel Message of St. Mark* (Oxford, 1949), 80–97.

sents in view of recent study which has tried to penetrate Mark's sources, methods and purposes. Some writers center attention on two or three strata in Mark which they have discovered.[5] Others question the traditional date or author and discover interests which determined the choice and the kind of tradition in Mark as they emphasize his meaning for his first readers.[6] Any outline must be based not on chronological and geographical references but upon theological topics. Written by a Roman Christian but anonymous from the start, the book reflects not Peter alone but various strands of tradition from both Palestine and Rome. There was perhaps a major plan centering in two sacraments, baptism and holy supper. This meant repentance as set forth in the first half of the Gospel and the doctrine of the cross in the second half. Or there were other motives at work. The Messiahship of Jesus as a fulfillment of all men's hopes, yet long a secret, was the chief theme but his death had to be explained in its relation to Jewish leaders, Roman officials and the will of God. For his public life, certain aspects had to be selected such as his acts of power, his stress on faith, his teachings, his conflicts, his private teachings to disciples, his return to power. Since Peter appears seldom in a favorable light and since there are some unfamiliar or mistaken geographical references (7:31) and explanations historically unsuitable for Palestine (10:12), the conclusion is drawn that Papias was reporting hearsay and therefore the actual author can no longer be historically identified. Such dissent deserves notice because of the learning of its advocates but it remains a minority view.

Mark's sources are variously discovered by investigators who do not reach common conclusions. It is possible to discover certain kinds of sources: (1) Peter whose information shows in 1:16–39; 2:13–19; 4:35–5:43; 6:7–13, 30–56; 8:14–9:48; 10:32–52; 11:1–33; 13:3, 4, 32–37; 14:17–50, 53–54, 66–72; (2) the story of the Passion which included and exceeded Peter's participation, 14:1–15:8; (3) a collection of sayings, parables and teachings to disciples somewhat like Q, 1:7–13; 3:22–30; 4:21–25, 30–32; 6:7–11; 8:12, 34b, 38; 9:42–50; 10:11–12, 42–44; 11:23; 12:38–40; (4) a series of conflicts between Jesus and opponents as in 2:13–3:6; (5) some legendary stories like the death of

---

[5] J. M. C. Crum, *St. Mark's Gospel* (London, 1927); A. T. Cadoux, *Sources of the Second Gospel* (London, 1935).

[6] F. C. Grant, *The Growth of the Gospels* (New York, 1933), 96–150 and *The Earliest Gospel* (New York, 1943), 34–57; R. H. Lightfoot, *History and Interpretation in the Gospels* (New York, 1934), 97–115; J. Weiss, *The History of Primitive Christianity* (New York, 1936), 687–703; Redlich, *op. cit.*, 9–41; C. C. Torrey, *Documents of the Primitive Church* (New York, 1941), 1–40.

John Baptist, 6:14–29; (6) the "Little Apocalypse" (13:1–37) which evidently was read before Mark used it. Some scholars accept this Form Criticism of Mark because it provides wider early bases for information besides Peter and yet at the same time they accept the traditional date and author or even suggest an earlier date.[7]

Mark's Gospel well deserves its symbol of the lion. This is a bold and courageous book about a triumphant Hero whose brief and swiftly darkened career was guided by a voice out of the clouds. Unconcerned about style, Mark told his earthly-divine story with vivid realism, with tremendous dramatic force and with an objective loyalty to the events as he knew them and to the records as he had received them. His book is the briefest but fullest in details. His interest was in Jesus set forth in living fashion so his readers could be assured in their faith and guided in their conduct. He wrote as a confident believer in his Gospel but he did not state his private opinions because he gave the accounts as they were known and used in public worship. He had no similar complete book before him but he had shorter sections at hand and he knew the narratives of Hebrew scriptures. With great skill and judgment he arranged the first part of his story in loosely connected but coherent scenes, followed by a tense dramatic climax. Writing in utter simplicity he created a new kind of book, a Gospel, whose charm and power are in its lifelike portrayal of a fascinating Figure who walks with both men and God. The reader is like one who stops before a striking shopwindow scene and forgets the strong clear plate glass through which he looks until some reflection reminds him of the glass as well as of the scene. This story of tragedy transfigured by boundless faith deserves to be read, not piecemeal, but in its entirety from its abrupt beginning to its striking ending. Then the Advent Sunday Collect about the Holy Scriptures in the Book of Common Prayer might be uncommonly capitalized, "Read Mark and inwardly digest." Those who know Mark well will agree with Grant's high estimate, "As a creative achievement in the history of literature and in the history of the Christian Church it is impossible to rate too highly this severely limited and incomplete and far from perfect writing of some Roman Christian, put together in the strenuous days of the later sixties."[8] On the basis of recent most intensive study Taylor concludes that here is a writing of first-rate historical importance. "In sum we may

---

[7] T. W. Manson, "The Gospel of Mark," *Bull. John Rylands Lib.* 28 (1944), 119–36.

[8] *The Growth of the Gospels*, 156, 157.

say that in Mark we have an authority of first rank for our knowledge of the Story of Jesus. Separated at the time of writing by little more than a generation from the death of Jesus, its contents carry us back farther into the oral period before Mark wrote to the tradition first of the Palestinian community and subsequently that of the Gentile Church at Rome." [9] In Venice, St. Mark's Cathedral stands in mosaic splendor before its sunny square as it welcomes visitors. They soon see that the handiwork of Byzantine and Lombard artisans of different times did not always join perfectly. But the whole cathedral with its golden façade, glowing colors, decorations and costly altar shines unforgettably in the viewer's memory. So does Mark's book.

[9] *Op. cit.*, 148.

13

The Gospel of Matthew

SOON AFTER its writing, the *Gospel of Matthew* arose to the leading position among the Four Gospels and has maintained its predominance to the present. In a famous tribute Renan declared it to be the most important book that has ever been written.[1] It has always been the Gospel preferred for use in the church. This leadership was partly due to its prestige as the work of one of the original twelve apostles in Palestine and partly due to its excellent arrangement which made it the most usable for study, teaching and public reading. Early tradition claimed that it was apostolic, translated from Hebrew in Palestine. The verdict of competent judges today is that it is not the work of the apostle Matthew, not translated from Hebrew and not Palestinian.[2] The actual author is unknown by name. In 1946 G. D. Kilpatrick wrote, "Concerning authorship we are still much in the dark."[3] If it be asked how then did Matthew's name become attached to the book, the answer is not known though suggestions abound. All the Gospels were probably anonymous until titles were affixed some time early in the second century to insure some apostolic connection. It is possible, as Papias claimed, that the apostle Matthew made a collection of the words (oracles) of Jesus in Hebrew. These sayings translated into Greek could have become part of the larger, final Gospel which was then titled "according to Matthew" because of the earlier work but this is no certainty. A possible clue to authorship is sometimes seen in the change of the name *Levi* (Mk. 2:14) to *Matthew* (Mt. 9:9) and in the addition of

---

[1] *Les Évangiles* (2nd ed. Paris, 1877), 212, 213; A. Plummer, *An Exegetical Commentary on the Gospel according to St. Matthew* (London, 1915), vii–xxxiv; A. H. McNeile, *The Gospel according to St. Matthew* (London, 1915), xi–xxxii; P. A. Micklem, *St. Matthew* (London, 1917), ix–xxxvi; G. H. Box, *St. Matthew,* (Edinburgh, 1922), 3–61; T. H. Robinson, *The Gospel of Matthew* (London, 1928), ix–xx; B. W. Bacon, *Studies in Matthew* (New York, 1930), 3–142; B. T. D. Smith, *St. Matthew* (Cambridge, 1933), vi–xl; J. H. Ropes, *The Synoptic Gospels* (Cambridge, 1934), 33–58; F. W. Green, *The Gospel according to St. Matthew* (Oxford, 1936), 1–22; S. E. Johnson in *The Interpreter's Bible* (New York, 1951), VII, 231–50.

[2] Bacon, *op. cit,* 24.

[3] *Origins of the Gospel according to St. Matthew* (Oxford, 1946), 7.

"tax collector" after the name Matthew (Mt. 10:3) which Mark had omitted (Mk. 3:18). Such facts are taken as the hints which led to ascription of authorship to Matthew. Since it was literary custom among Jewish authors to assume notable names from the past when they wished to convey religious messages, Matthew's name might have been used by an unknown scribe.[4] The writer of the present Gospel depended on Mark for his narrative and added little to the story except legendary details. Scholars find it hard to believe an eye-witness like the tax collector, Matthew, would be so dependent on Mark who was not an apostle. Matthew added much to the teaching. He may have been a Jewish-Christian scribe who brought forth "out of his treasure things new and old" or a converted rabbi who stood staunchly for the power and the glory of Israel's faith in the past. As a Christian teacher he opposed not the ideals of Judaism but its Pharisaic form. He has been described as a tax collector, an apostle, a scribe, a Christian Hellenist and a Grecian Jew but his actual identity remains in doubt. He was concerned not to write about himself but about Jesus, the lawgiver, even greater than Moses.

Where he lived can be suggested but not proved. This Greek book fits better in a Jewish Hellenistic background than in Palestine. A popular view chooses Antioch in Syria, north of Palestine, where there was a strong early church which contained both Jews and Gentiles. This would help explain the ecclesiastical interests and the sometimes incompatible elements like the commands of Jesus to preach only to Israel and also to all nations. Since the author uses Mark (A.D. 65–70) and since Matthew was in turn quoted by Ignatius (A.D. 115), a plausible date is A.D. 85. If Matthew had given the year for his references "unto this day," he would have saved much later conjecture.

Matthew's *purposes, sources and characteristics* must be discovered largely by study of his great and impressive work. He wrote to prove Jesus was the Messiah long foretold in Hebrew prophecy, or to provide a revised gospel book for liturgical use, or to supplement Mark with an "ordered compend of the commandments of Jesus," [5] or to show Jesus was not only the Christ but also Son of David, or to defend the Christian faith against unbelieving Jews, or to prove Jesus established the Kingdom of Heaven (the Church), or to present a manual for Christian catechists, or to gain converts from Judaism.

He wrote not in Mark's rugged style nor with Luke's literary art

[4] *Ibid.*, 134–39.
[5] Bacon, *op. cit.*, 83.

but in clear, direct, dignified language which directs attention, not to itself, but to its incomparable subject. His words are easily memorized because of the balanced sentences, the repetition, the rounded phrasing, superbly adapted to public reading and hearing. Like hard ice that speeds a skater on to his enjoyment or destination Matthew provides a smooth, undistinguished foundation for the exaltation of One who excelled even the greatest Hebrew, Moses.

His written *sources* include Mark, a collection of teachings (Q), a list of Old Testament prophecies about the Messiah and other materials which may have been written or oral. These include sayings found only in Matthew which are labeled M, a genealogy of Jesus' ancestors and the nativity narrative. Matthew's use of these sources gives some insight into his characteristics. He had first a master plan which shows the scope of his well-organized mind as he faced the making of his book. Like a great architect he could design a massive cathedral, enshrine a glorious rose window and fix every tiny spire. This plan basically included the structure of Mark into which he inserted at intervals five large blocks of the teachings of Jesus, with an introduction about his birth and a conclusion about his sufferings, death, resurrection and great commission to his disciples. In the following outline the five blocks of teaching are in italics. The ending of each of these sections is marked by Matthew's formula, "And when Jesus had finished."

A. The Beginnings   The Nativity   1, 2

B. Christ's Life   Book   I (a) Baptism and Temptation   3, 4
    and New Law   (b) *Sermon on the Mount*   5–7

             Book   II (a) Nine Miracles   8, 9
                       (b) *Instructions to Disciples*   10

             Book   III (a) Questions and Controversies 11, 12
                       (b) *Seven Parables of the*
                           Kingdom   13:1–52

             Book   IV (a) Various miracles, teachings for
                       disciples   13:52–17:27
                       (b) *Offenders and Forgiveness*   18

             Book   V (a) Teachings and Events in Judea
                       and Jerusalem   19–22
                       (b) *The Future*   23–25

C. The Endings   The Last Days in Jerusalem 26–28

Matthew's *use of Mark* shows him as an editor though his whole book is a great literary religious creation rather than a compilation. "Scientific study of the Synoptic Gospels has established clearly enough what Matthew is: it is a revised and enlarged edition of Mark." [6] Matthew reproduces eleven twelfths of Mark but he does not hesitate to correct or abbreviate Mark. When Mark incorrectly credits Isaiah with a quotation from Malachi, Matthew omits it. When Mark writes of a woman who may divorce her husband, Matthew drops out the statement since this was possible with Romans but not in Judaism. Mark takes 325 words to tell of the Gadarene demoniac but Matthew relates it in 135 words. Matthew omits details from Mark like the indignation of Jesus at his disciples who hindered the coming of children to him or the fact that Jesus took a child into his arms or that he loved the rich young man who refused to follow him. Sometimes Matthew adds explanations to Mark which state that Elijah was to come and Matthew identifies him as John the Baptist. Jesus warns about the leaven of the Pharisees and Sadducees in Mark and Matthew says that this leaven is their teaching. Matthew emphasizes the miraculous more than Mark who wrote that *all* the sick were brought to Jesus and he healed *many* which Matthew revises to read that *all* were healed. "From that hour" in Matthew shows that immediate results occur in miracles while Mark has no such note of time.

Matthew has greater interest in the *Words of Jesus* than any other gospel writer. Expressed in mathematics Matthew has 644 verses out of 1,068 which contain sayings attributed to Jesus or three fifths of his total. Luke which is parallel to Matthew in many ways has 1,149 verses of which 586 or one half give words of Jesus. In contrast Mark has 661 verses of which 285 or three sevenths record sayings.[7] "He taught" them meant much to Matthew who skillfully collected parables, discourses, brief pointed sentences, denunciations and instructions so that the message of Jesus shines in verbal splendor. It is this Gospel which has set into the minds of its many readers certain phrases and words like "the Kingdom of Heaven" and "Father" as a name for God, which are now a common part of our speech. "Father" as applied to God appears in Matthew forty-six times, in Luke seventeen times and in Mark five times. Luke and Mark use "the Kingdom of God" since their Gentile readers were not bound by a reverence which required a synonym for God. However, Matthew also uses this term occasionally.

Matthew has a strong interest in the relationship between the *He-*

[6] T. W. Manson, "The Gospel according to St. Matthew," *Bull. John Rylands Lib.* 29 (1946), 410.

[7] W. G. Scroggie, *A Guide to the Gospels* (London, 1948), 193.

brew Scriptures and Jesus. He knows the Old Testament so well that he refers to it about 130 times in quotations and allusions, most of which are given in the words of Jesus.[8] He thinks of this record as a source book of promises which had been brought to pass in Jesus. Twelve times he cites the proof from scripture with the same formula, "that it might be fulfilled," as was spoken through some prophet or psalmist. He quotes often from the Septuagint and occasionally from the Hebrew Bible. He revises Mark to make it conform to prophetic statements. In Mark Judas was promised money for betrayal but in Matthew the thirty pieces are paid and later flung down by Judas whose suicide thus left the money for the potter's field as foretold in Jeremiah. Often Matthew adapts an account to meet Old Testament language without using his formula of fulfillment. At crucifixion Jesus refused wine and myrrh in Mark but in Matthew the wine and the gall are like the psalmist's words. Another aspect of this relationship shows Jesus in fulfillment of the Law which will not pass away until everything is accomplished. Jesus did not come to destroy Judaism but to complete it. As Moses spoke the Law in the past, so Jesus likewise said, "I say unto you," and thus he does not set aside but sets forth God's perfect Law.

Matthew is the *most Jewish* of the gospel writers. His knowledge of scripture, his plan for the new gospel modeled on the five books of Moses, his interest in the fulfillment of prophecy, the coming of the Messiah, the unending importance of the Law, the customs of alms, prayer, fasting, his apocalyptic hope, his Jewish vocabulary, his warnings about scribes and Pharisees, his avoidance of the sacred name of God, his emphasis on Jesus as a true observer of his inherited faith, his concern for ethical regulations and "good works," his dislike of lawlessness—all these indicate a time and a writer who lived when Christianity was still within the fold of Judaism though taking its first steps toward the new Israel that was to "make disciples of all nations." G. F. Moore has shown that the Synoptic Gospels witness to the prevailing Jewish teaching of their time and that "Matthew is, of the three, the most important source of Judaism, not only for its contents but for its attitude; it is at once the most conservatively Jewish of the Gospels and the most violently anti-Pharisaic."[9] It is a Jewish yet catholic Gospel which combines aspects which face two ways, toward the mighty doings and commandments of God for Israel and

[8] *Ibid.,* 270.
[9] *Judaism* (Cambridge, 1927), I, 183, 186; cf. W. C. Allen, *The Gospel according to St. Matthew* (New York, 1907), 309–20.

toward the extension through Christ of these divine revelations for a "light to the Gentiles."

Peter and the Church stand out in Matthew. Grant called Matthew "the ecclesiastical Gospel" and Harnack and Kilpatrick believed that it is a liturgical book prepared for and used in worship. It is the only Gospel which mentions the church though this name occurs but thrice. But there are other directions and problems of the disciples which imply the church. Peter occupies a special position since Matthew only tells of Jesus' promises, "Thou art Peter and upon this rock I will build my church" and "I will give thee the keys of the kingdom of heaven," though his power to bind and loose is bestowed later on all the disciples. Only Matthew tells of Peter trying to walk on the water or receiving directions to go fishing to find a half shekel to pay the temple tax for Jesus and himself.

There is an increasing *reverence of Jesus and a regard for the disciples* which show that Matthew had to safeguard them against attacks. The birth of Jesus is not told but the incidents connected with it defend Jesus. His ancestry relates him to Abraham and David while the story of the Magi shows that the Messiah had been forced to live away from his native Bethlehem. Mark reports that Jesus asked the man who ran and knelt to him, "Why do you call me good?" but Matthew changes the question to, "Why do you ask me about what is good?" Matthew omits Mark's questions by Jesus which might imply ignorance as well as references to his anger, amazement, sighs and grief. According to Mark, James and John steal a march on the other ten disciples in their request to Jesus for preferred positions in the coming hour of glory but in Matthew it is the mother of the disciples who makes the forehanded request for her two sons. Mark bluntly recounts the questions, the fear, the astonishment, the lack of understanding and the knowledge of disciples but Matthew chooses to omit these shortcomings.

Matthew shows a disciplined mind which requires *orderly arrangements* in his writing. He likes to present his discourses and events in groups of three, five and occasionally seven. His pages march with triads. Events and parables occur in threefold form; three temptations, three miracles (leprosy, palsy, fever), three denials by Peter, three parables about the future and three wonders at the crucifixion. Teachings and names abound in triplets: ask, seek, knock; alms, prayer, fasting; prophets, wisemen, scribes. There are five great discourses, five contrasts in the Sermon on the Mount between Mosaic Law and the teachings of Jesus which begin, "But I say unto you"; five important questions in one fateful day in Jerusalem. Seven parables appear in the thirteenth chapter. Matthew presents ideas in pairs; God and mammon, salt and light, mustard seed and leaven, just and unjust, wise and foolish virgins, sheep and goats. This use of likeness and contrast is found in all Gospels but markedly in Matthew.

Matthew wrote with a high anticipation of the *future* with its coming of the Son of Man and its reward for the righteous and its judgment on evildoers who will fall into "weeping and gnashing of teeth," a phrase six times repeated throughout the Gospel. A crisis is coming soon, "the end of the world." Matthew uses this expression with its sense of urgency, warning and apocalypse. He places three great parables in chapter twenty-five to illustrate the dramatic coming of the heavenly Son of Man. "The enhancement of interest in Matthew is more remarkable since in other Christian documents—whether earlier than Matthew, like the later epistles of Paul or later like the Fourth Gospel—the delay in the Second Coming was obviously causing less and less emphasis to be laid on this particular element in the early Christian belief." [10]

[10] Streeter, *The Four Gospels*, 522.

14

The Gospel of Luke

THE GOSPEL of Luke [1] stands out from the other Gospels because it is the only one written by a Gentile, because it has a formal preface and because it is volume one of a larger work now known as Luke-Acts. In his preface the author steps forth briefly but importantly with information about himself, his subject and his knowledge relative to it, his sources, methods and his purpose. Since his book does not bear his name and since Papias contains no mention of him, the earliest identification of Luke as author of the Third Gospel is by Irenaeus (A.D. 180) whose claim is repeated by many early writers. The evidence for Luke as author is based primarily on the preface, on Paul's references to Luke by name (Col. 4:14; Philem. 24; II Tim. 4:11) and on certain passages in Acts known as the "we-sections" (Acts 16: 10–17; 20:5–15; 21:1–18; 27:1–28) because the writer gave a first-person report of travels with Paul who refers to him as a beloved physician and fellow worker. Other commonly accepted views see Luke as a converted Greek, an accomplished historian, a highly skilled writer, a devoted Christian and a missionary traveler who knew the Mediterranean world from Jerusalem to Rome.

Actually the identification of Luke, the doctor companion of Paul, with the author of the Third Gospel has faced some upsetting studies during the last quarter century. In 1882 W. K. Hobart in his *Medical Language of St. Luke* examined Luke-Acts in detail with parallels from Greek sources and decided a medical tinge ran through it. His position verified tradition and was supported by the studies of notable

---

[1] A. Plummer, *The Gospel according to St. Luke* (New York, 1896), xi–lxxxv; W. F. Adeney, *St. Luke* (Edinburgh, 1922), 3–47; L. Ragg, *St. Luke* (London, 1922), xi–lii; B. S. Easton, *The Gospel according to St. Luke* (New York, 1926), ix–xxxvii; H. Balmforth, *The Gospel according to St. Luke* (Oxford, 1930), 1–30; J. M. Creed, *The Gospel according to St. Luke* (London, 1930), xi–lxxxix; W. Manson, *The Gospel of Luke* (London, 1930), xi–xxx; H. K. Luce, *The Gospel according to St. Luke* (Cambridge, 1933), ix–xxxii; J. H. Ropes, *The Synoptic Gospels* (Cambridge, 1933), 58–88; J. A. Findlay, *The Gospel according to St. Luke* (London, 1937), 1–30; T. W. Manson, "The Gospel of Luke," *Bull. John Rylands Lib.* 28 (1944), 382–403; S. M. Gilmour in *The Interpreter's Bible* (New York, 1952), VIII, 3–26.

scholars like Harnack and Moffatt. In 1920 Cadbury after most careful study of the subject concluded decisively that "the style of Luke bears no more evidence of medical training and interest than does the language of other writers who were not physicians." [2] His conclusion has been accepted by many scholars. Luke may have been a doctor, as tradition affirms, but his language will not prove the fact. A technical, medical language was not used in antiquity. Medical jargon is a modern development.

Another investigation, shared by several scholars, produced *The Beginnings of Christianity,* the most complete study in English of its subject.[3] The whole question about the identity of Luke as the author of Luke-Acts is explored but no decision is given. Doubt about Luke as author centers mostly on whether he is both the writer of the "we-sections" and the final editor and whether his accounts in Acts tally historically with Paul's letters which are earlier. One of the contributors to *The Beginnings of Christianity* continued his work in a valuable, informative volume on the material, the methods, the personality and the purpose of the author. On these points much can be learned but he concluded, "Modern scholarship cannot unanimously accept or reject the tradition of Luke's authorship." [4] If rejected, we have an anonymous book in no way impaired but, if accepted, we know little more than the book affords about the personal habits of mind which affect the reliability of the work. However, this noncommittal position does not agree with many writers of commentaries who still maintain the traditional authorship by Luke. It is clear that the relatively late identification of Luke by name could have arisen from an authentic historical report or from inferences based on New Testament writings. Since Luke was not an apostle and occupied no special position in the church and since no other name in ancient or modern times has risen in serious competition, it is reasonable to accept his authorship. Except for his dating, Manson represents a well-known position, "The external data seem to me to be satisfied if Luke-Acts was the work of Luke, a companion to Paul, written in Achaia, round about A.D. 70 as a public defense of the Christian church against the suspicion of being mixed up with rebellious Jews and a public assurance that the Christian gospel was no seditious propaganda but a message of universal peace and goodwill." [5] Street-

[2] *Style and Literary Method of Luke* (Cambridge, 1920), 50.
[3] Jackson and Lake, 5 vols. (London, 1920–1933), I, 207–357.
[4] H. J. Cadbury, *The Making of Luke-Acts,* 359.
[5] *Bull. John Rylands Lib.* 28 (1944), 403.

er's conclusion deserves its fame as a summary on authorship of the
Gospels. "The burden of proof is on those who would assert traditional authorship of Matthew and John and on those who would deny
it in case of Mark and Luke." [6]

Luke has not only written the longest Gospel but his whole work,
Luke-Acts, constitutes two sevenths of the New Testament which
makes him its largest contributor. His work is a mine for digging
much treasure. His purposes, sources, methods and characteristics
have been amply established but his date and place of writing cannot
be closely determined.

His *purposes* are multiple. In his preface he wrote that Theophilus
might know the truth of the things of which he had been informed.
Beyond this reference to a personal reader the great narration of the
Founder and the Faith unfolds. Luke is the first and irreplaceable
Christian historian. No other appears for three centuries until Eusebius. Luke wrote not for one church, not for Christians only to see
how God worked his wonders to perform, but also for a reading
Gentile public. His preface follows the form known in his day for a
work for general reading. He desired his readers to know the matchless story of Jesus whose Christly rule as Lord fulfilled God's gracious
purposes from the past and whose Spirit empowered his followers as
they moved everywhere with joy to share good tidings with all
people. This Gospel is nearest to a biography though Luke's purpose
is to relate fact to increase faith. He had followed all things closely
for some time past in order to write an orderly account that would
inform and confirm his fellow Christians and also show the Greek
reading public that their faith contained only good in which the
Roman government could find no fault and in which anyone could
share to his salvation.

For his *sources* Luke states that the matters of which he writes
came from "eyewitnesses and ministers of the word." Modern study
notes the parts he shares with Mark and with Matthew and the unusual amount of material found only in his Gospel. This amount constitutes about one third of his book while Matthew has about one
fifth not found elsewhere. Luke copied about one half of Mark. We
do not know why he omitted one considerable section (Mk. 6:44–
8:26). Perhaps his copy of Mark lacked the passage or his space was
limited, or more probably he thought he had his own materials
which covered the same topics. He quotes Mark's story in long sections, interspersed with other materials. He follows Mark's order

[6] *Op. cit.*, 562.

generally though he did not hesitate to place stories such as the return of Jesus for his first preaching at home in Nazareth in another spot. He copies the words of Jesus more accurately than he repeats other reports. He shortens Mark's stories, smooths his style, avoids repetitions, drops numerals and names and strange foreign words like "Hosanna." He changes Mark's historic presents into the past and compacts his sentences. Jewish terms are generalized. "Scribes" become "lawyers" and "Master" replaces "Rabbi." Luke has a particular interest like Mark in the final days at Jerusalem which are forecast early in his narrative (9:51). Something of the stark tragedy in Mark is softened into longer perspective which makes a more complete story with more added details like the specific charges against Jesus before Pilate. But there are also small omissions which reduce the idea of the death of Jesus as a sacrifice for sins. Like Matthew Luke displays more reverence for Jesus and a higher regard for the disciples. Luke omits the story that friends would seize Jesus, "For they said, 'He is beside himself,' " and also leaves out the account of the undue ambition of James and John for the chief seats in the future. He does not report that the disciples fled at the arrest and the crucifixion of Jesus.

Like Matthew Luke's second source was Q, the collection of sayings which can be identified where Matthew and Luke share material that is much alike. Since Luke's method with Mark is known, it can be accepted that he followed the same pattern with Q which he quotes in relative order and with little change of wording from the source. For this reason scholars prefer to follow Luke's version of Q rather than Matthew who mixes and transposes his sources into smaller, shorter quotations instead of the longer blocks found in Luke's method.

Streeter, reinforced by Taylor, rejected the older view that Luke re-edited Mark along with Q plus his own special sections. This is due to prolonged study of the special parts found only in Luke. Since Mark and Q compose less than one half of Luke and since these sources are arranged in long sections, Streeter held that Luke began a new gospel independent of Mark which he did not yet possess. He collected his own sources (L) for a life of Jesus since "many had written" as his preface states. He had Q and he combined it with L into an early Gospel (Proto-Luke). Then later he found Mark and inserted it in sections in his previous gospel. If these Marcan sections which make up 30 per cent of Luke were omitted, there would still be a readable Gospel though some disagree. Proto-Luke can be found thus: Luke 3–4:30; 5:1–11; 6:12–8:3; 9:51–18:14; 19:1–28, 37–44, 47, 48; 22:14–24. This theory can be put into an equation. Before Streeter Mk. + Q + L = Lk; after Streeter, Q + L (Proto-Luke) + Mk. = Lk. This theory has become influential but has not commanded general acceptance. It helps explain Luke's special section, 9:51–18:14, and his omissions of Mark and his alternate strips of Mark and non-Marcan elements.

The Infancy stories stand apart in Luke because of their unusual topic, their Semitic style, their Messianic hopes, their familiarity with Jewish customs and their poetic beauty and angels' appearances. Whether these narratives are translated from some Hebrew or Aramaic source or composed by Luke in septuagint style is debatable. The traditional explanation of their origin selects Mary as the ultimate source of information. Some writers suggest that Luke found people who could inform him during his two-year stay with Paul, the prisoner, in Caesarea (Acts 24:27). Nothing is certainly known about the origin of these stories beyond Luke but their distinctive aspects indicate them as one of his sources. His preface clearly shows that there were first eyewitnesses and teachers who delivered the "matters," then others who had written and finally Luke's own orderly information based on immediate touch with everything which resulted in his book. To determine written sources beyond Mark and Q and probably some parts of L is difficult but that Luke had firsthand contacts in which he found both oral and written reports about Jesus is established by his preface.

An outline of Luke helps to understand the way he used his sources and arranged his whole story. The italic sections in 1 and 2 are in Luke only. In 5 Luke has much of his own special material but shares some of his teachings with Q. This long section is often called a travel document from the setting which Luke gives to it. In 6 there are some verses which are only in Luke.

1. *Preface*	1:1–4
2. *Infancy and Youth of John Baptist and of Jesus*	1:5–2:52
3. Mission of John; Baptism and Temptation of Jesus	3–4:13
4. Teaching and Deeds of Jesus in Galilee	4:14–9:50
5. *Teaching during the Journey to Jerusalem*	9:51–19
6. Last Days in Jerusalem	20–24

The following sections are in Luke only:

Ch. 1–2	10:17–20	14:1–14	19:1–10
3:10–14	25–42	28–33	41–44

4:14–30	11:5–8	15:8–30	22:1–28
5:1–11	27–28	16:1–12	23:5–12
6:24–26	12:13–21	19–31	26–32
7:11–17	35–38	17:7–22	39–43
36–50	47–50	28–31	24:13–53
8:1–3	54–47	18:1–14	
9:51–56	13:1–17		
61–62	31–33		

Luke is known for attractive *characteristics* that portray him as the beauty-loving artist that later legend affirmed. He writes as a Christian with enthusiasm for Jesus. He nowhere is concerned about himself except for the formal bow in his opening verses. He works like an accomplished portrait painter with an entrancing subject and the artistic outcome is a combination not only of the essential subject but also unrivaled skill in portrayal. Beside the powerful Roman Mark and the instructive Jewish Matthew shines the happy Hellenism of Luke. Perhaps the sunny skies over Achaia reflected in the incredible blue of the Mediterranean brightened Luke's pages as he heralded God's good tidings from their beginnings in angelic voices over shepherd fields to their endings with great joy in the blessings of disciples at the Bethany ascension.

Luke has written the *most complete Gospel* both about the life and the teaching of Jesus and about the wide range of his interest in all kinds of people. Jesus from birth was the "Saviour who is Christ the Lord" for all mankind. His concern is not for the Jew alone but for Samaritans and Gentiles and especially the "sinners," a term Luke uses more than the other Gospels taken together. Jesus came to seek and save the lost. The repentant prostitute, the grafting Zaccheus, the criminal companion on the cross all found forgiveness. The poor, the outcast, the needy, the widow, the debtor, the prodigal, the publican, the fisherman Peter gained glad relief. More women and children pass in these pages than elsewhere in the Gospels. Women adorn the scenes of infancy and boyhood of John and Jesus, they provide out of their means for the travels of Jesus, they entertain him at home, they lament his way to the cross, they witness the crucifixion and share the resurrection appearances. The widow of Nain receives her only son back to life, the only daughter of Jairus revives, a widow pesters an indifferent judge and a woman receives release from a long crippled condition. No unfavorable light falls on woman in Luke's gallant leaves while a feminine charm frequently graces his famous stories.

Jesus shares in the *social life* with the "people," one of Luke's favorite words. He discusses the never-ending problems of poverty and wealth. There are domestic scenes where Jesus dines repeatedly with Pharisees and also with Mary and Martha, with Zaccheus and even after the resurrection at the village home in Emmaus. As Luke illustrates the importance of hospitality, he describes many aspects of home life. The poor have the gospel preached to them with blessings on their future. The rich fool, the rich ruler, the rich man who neglected Lazarus suffer sadly from their misuse of wealth. The strongest sayings of Jesus about riches, the "mammon of unrighteousness," are recorded by Luke who alone describes the Pharisees as "lovers of money."

It is Luke who sees Jesus as one who prays and teaches about *prayer*. From his baptism while at prayer to his last breath on the cross as he commits himself to his heavenly Father, Jesus is shown by Luke alone in prayer at seven important points of his life. It is Luke who reports the prayer parables about the midnight visitor, the unjust judge, the Pharisee and the publican. In parables Luke is supreme. He alone tells about fifteen of these incomparable stories of Jesus such as the Good Samaritan, the Prodigal Son and the Lost Coin.

It is Luke who stresses joy, cheerfulness, thanksgiving and praise to God arising from the Good News. The father makes merry when his lost son comes back as do the angels over repentant sinners. Laughter will replace weeping, joy will reward the persecuted. Like the sweet singer of Israel Luke is a Psalmist of the Nativity whose hymns are better known by later Latin titles than in his original Greek: Magnificat, Benedictus, Gloria, Nunc Dimittis (1:46-55, 68-79; 2:14, 29-32).

While Luke shares the common belief in *miracles* in his day with Matthew and Mark, he relates twenty miracles of which six are his alone. He is more distinctive in his fondness for angels whose appearances especially mark the arrivals in this world of John and Jesus, but the beat of angelic wings accompanies the Temptation, the Judgment, Lazarus to Abraham's bosom, Gethsemane and the Resurrection. Nowhere does the naturalness of Luke's supernatural show with greater effect than in his birth stories whose remarkable charm and simplicity have glorified God and his gift of peace in Christ. Much of Luke's thought of unusual events he explains by a reference to the Spirit. It is Luke who sees more rays fanning out from the full orb of Jesus than his fellow evangelists. As babe and boy, as Savior and Lord, as prophet and Christ, as physician and exorcist, as teacher

and traveler, as friend to all and foe to no man, as righteous martyr and mighty ascended One, "it seemed good" to Luke to write
about Jesus.

Luke had to tell the greatest story ever told but he also had the best
literary equipment among the writers of the New Testament. His
vocabulary in Luke-Acts runs to 2,697 words and only Paul approaches him with 2,446 words. By comparison, Matthew, almost as
long as Luke, has 1,542 words and Luke's vocabulary is one sixth
larger in the Gospel apart from Acts. Luke has 312 words peculiar
to himself while Matthew has 137.[7] Luke's capacity as a writer appears when he begins with a long single sentence, well balanced,
stocked with choice words in good, idiomatic Greek style. Then in
the rest of his two opening chapters his style is filled with Semitisms,
so that they read like Hebrew scriptures. Then he comes back to
Greek style, blended with septuagintal form to continue through the
rest of the book. He is a versatile author who can quote the Old Testament easily but not with Matthew's special interest in it. He can
tell an unsurpassed story or describe a Palestinian scene in picturesque
language or sketch his named or unnamed characters in living fashion. He can use dramatic contrasts most effectively as Pilate and
Herod, Jesus and Barabbas face their life and death decisions.

His writings show *datings* which set events in their time relationships with the contemporary world and its leaders. While the influence of Paul on Luke was stressed in older interpretations of Luke
and though they do share a considerable section of their vocabulary,
it is plain that Luke does not repeat or stress many of the essential
points in Paul's thought though the latter half of Acts is a biography
of Paul. Hence Luke is no longer called a Pauline Gospel. Perhaps
Luke had matured his own Christianity before he knew Paul.

The *date* and the *place* for Luke's Gospel remain without exact decisions. No study of the Gospel date can proceed without knowledge
of Acts which ends abruptly in Rome about A.D. 62–63. The simplest
reason for an ending which left Paul in prison, his fate undecided, is
that Luke wrote as far as events had occurred. Since the Gospel preceded Acts, a date near A.D. 60 has been often proposed. At the other
extreme is a date near A.D. 100 because it can be held that Luke used
the *Antiquities* of Josephus written in A.D. 94. This inference is questioned as lacking sufficient evidence. There remains a third possibility
which better satisfies the relationship of Luke and Mark who preceded Luke and also the more developed understanding about Jesus.

[7] Cadbury, *Style and Literary Method of Luke,* 1, 2.

Since Luke changed Mark's reference to "abomination of desolation" to "Jerusalem surrounded by armies" (Mk. 13:14; Lk. 21:20), it is thought that Luke knew of the siege of Jerusalem by Roman armies (A.D. 70). Hence a date parallel to Matthew (A.D. 85) is often selected. No place can be chosen by more than a possibility. Church writers from the second century suggested Achaia or Alexandria. Modern guesses include Caesarea, Ephesus and Rome. This is a case where there is no safety in numbers.

Since a study of the Synoptics often includes references to Q, though this hypothetical document has its skeptics, it is well to list the sections not in Mark which are much alike in Matthew and Luke since they, like their sections from Mark shared by Matthew and Luke, should be distinctively colored or checked in the text of the Gospels. Since the line of likeness in Matthew and Luke is not easily drawn for Q, there are listings which vary. This list given by V. Taylor distinguishes by parentheses the passages in Matthew for which there is doubt.[8]

RECONSTRUCTION OF Q

Luke	Matthew
3:7–9, 16–17	3:7–12
21–22	16–17
4:1–13	4:1–11
6:20–23	5:(3, 5–6, 11–12)
27–36	(39–48); 7:12
37–40	7:1–2; 15:14; 10:24–25
41–42	7:3–5
43–46	(12:33–35); 7:16–21
47–49	7:24–27
7:1–10	8:5–10, 13
18–35	11:2–11, 16–19
9:57–60	8:19–22
10:2–12	9:37–38; 10:9–15
13–15	11:21–23
21–24	25–27; 13:16–17
25–27	(22:34–39)
11:2–4	(6:9–13)
9–13	7:7–11
14–23	12:22–30
24–26	43–45
29–32	38–42

[8] *The Gospels* (5th ed. London, 1945), 27, 28.

33–35	5:15; 6:22–23
37–12:1	(23)
12:2–12	10:26–33; 12:32; 10:19
22–34	6:25–33; (6:19–21)
39–46	24:43–51
51–56	(10:34–36; 16:2–3)
57–59	5:25–26
13:18–21	13:31–33
23–30	(7:13–14; 25:10–12;)
	(7:22–23;8:11–12)
34–35	23:37–39
14:11 cf. 18:14	12
15–24	(22:1–10)
26–27, 34–35	(10:37–38; 5:13)
15:4–7, 10	(18:12–14)
16:13	6:24
16–18	(11:12–13; 5:18, 32)
17:1–6	18:6–7; (18:15, 21–22; 17:20)
22–27, 33–37	24:26–28, 37–41; 10:39
19:12–27	(24:14–30)
22:30	(19:28)

PART IV

The Synoptic Gospels

15

Introduction

ANY STUDENT of the Gospels soon discovers that these extraordinary books have had an amazing interest for an endless list of interpreters who vary greatly in their methods, understanding and explanations during centuries. "How difficult and delicate are the problems which beset the student of the Gospels; how cautious and patient he must be; and how resolutely he must decline to accept probabilities and possibilities as certainties." [1] He must first try to discover accurately the meaning of the Gospels when written. This involves most careful historical reconstruction of the world in which both Jesus and the gospel writers lived. To re-create this world of the long ago he needs often more primary sources than he possesses. He must determine not only what the gospel writer meant but how faithfully he reported the words and the works of Jesus. To know the historical Jesus the only approach must be made through his reporters. Hence arise the baffling questions about how much is the mind of Jesus and how much is the thought of his first followers. Also the student needs ample information about the ceaseless work of fellow workers in the past and the present. But he needs something beyond mere historical knowledge and objectivity because religion like art is best known by participation rather than by observation alone. He needs information about the continuing influence of these Gospels in the actual life of people and appreciation of the effects on those who apply the truth of the Gospels in human relations. Bunyan's famous pilgrim had to keep his way to the Celestial City in the face of both enticements and dangers. There is the lure of a life remote enough for scholarly escapism and the religious modernity blind to its historical heritage. The nature of the Gospels requires a proper balance between history and religion which are so blended in these books that the readers see them as one. The long centuries of Bible study make plain that the essentials for understanding and interpretation include both the literal meaning and the living meaning.

The Gospels have been read mainly for direct religious aid in

[1] R. H. Lightfoot, *The Gospel Message of Mark* (Oxford, 1950), 105.

which the dominant interest was a belief in Christ as one who made known to men the whole will of God and the right life with man. The test of twenty centuries indicates that such reading has a powerful effect upon the devotional reader both in mind and in conduct. This is the result to be expected from the original purposes of the writers who reflect a practical use of the gospel to foster a definite Christian outlook and life. These writers were sure that their books contained invaluable truth whose ultimate source was God. Its range reached beyond man's sight but it had come to a focus in the field of history in Jesus of Nazareth. This truth whose dimensions defied definition had been tested in actual living for a generation before it was written but when written, it was given a personal fixed form discoverable by any reader or hearer. The Gospels reflect historical happenings but their readers were expected to accept and use the good news in their present lives and thus assure their glorious future. Since the Gospels came from the church, it has fostered and directed the study and the practice of their contents. Modern advances in gospel study have often gone beyond church auspices. Special studies isolate historical, linguistic, literary and theological aspects which have been developed to a refined degree. But it must be kept in mind that the Gospels were written for the common reader, not for the specialist. They are like their own lucid Galilean lake; within a limited area they combine a remote past, an alluring beauty and a common-sense utility. Their antiquity engages the historian, their composition invites scientific scrutiny and literary criticism, their mystery attracts the religious wayfarer and in their waves and deeps the fisherman finds his food, quenches his thirst and sails and swims to his heart's content.

To acquire information in and about the Gospels is supremely important but it ought not to be divorced from practical purposes. The will to know the Gospels is the first step toward possession of their treasures. Methods of study vary widely. There is agreement among many scholars to read first the Synoptics taken together since they share a literary and a historical relationship. Since John presents its own approach it is often studied separately after the Synoptics. Another method extracts the sources within the Gospels and studies these elements as prior steps toward the completed records. There are still advocates of the method which places all four Gospels together for comparative study. There are many studies made of each Gospel alone or of some special phase of it but these studies are apt to contain references to the other Gospels. Assuming that the Synoptics are to be studied together, it is advisable to read Mark first not simply because it is the earliest written but because it deals only with those aspects of Jesus which were public knowledge and which were verified by the experiences of the disciples and later in the church. This explains the plan of this study which begins with Mark and places the birth narratives at a later point because the preaching of the gospel by Jesus and his first apostles did not include references to his special birth. With Mark as a center the Gospels of Matthew and Luke are to be carefully compared to discover where they agree with Mark and with each other and where they present their own special accounts. For the beginning student who lacks general knowledge of the Gospels it is wise first to read rapidly through each Gospel separately using both the classic King James version and a good modern translation. This rapid reading sets in mind the main outlines of the story of Jesus, it distinguishes somewhat the distinctive viewpoints of each writer, it follows the fact that the Gospels were written as individual books and helps to avoid getting lost later in the forest of detailed study.

The plan of this present study follows generally though not always the exact order of the Synoptics as they are arranged in *Gospel Parallels* (New York, 1949) with the text of the Revised Standard Version (1946). The Synoptics are divided into five main parts: (1) *The Galilean Story of Jesus,* Mt. 3–18; Mk. 1–9; Lk. 3–9:50; (2) *Luke's Special Section,* 9:51–18:14; (3) *Final Days of Jesus in Judea and Jerusalem,* Mt. 19–27; Mk. 10–15; Lk. 18:15–23; (4) *Reports of the Resurrection,* Mt. 28; Mk. 16:1–8; Lk. 24; (5) *Nativity Narratives,* Mt. 1–2; Lk. 1–2. In any attempted chronology of Jesus, the Infancy stories stand first and any reader may turn to this section first but chronology, except in most general terms, was not the interest of the gospel writers whose good news concerned the commonly shared public life and ministry of Jesus. When their experiences with Jesus, living and resurrected, had established his unique significance, two of the gospel writers added birth narratives to their earlier sources. These narratives are best read in historical study in the light of the earlier knowledge of Jesus rather than as the first approach to him.

In the plan of study outlined above, the first section requires some rearrangements of passages to avoid repetition since the Synoptics are not identical in order and contents. The general principle in this section recognizes a logical distinction between the doings and the teachings of Jesus. The readings from the Gospels follow mainly the order of activities in Mark with Matthew-Luke parallels until Jesus withdrew from Galilee northward before his final journey to Jerusalem (Mk. 8:27) except for the omission of his teaching in parables (Mk. 4:1–33). Then the readings center on the collections of teachings primarily, in parables first which are found in all Synoptics and then in the more general words such as the Sermon on the Mount. Since Matthew and Luke do not hesitate to place their parables in the middle or the latter part of their books, it is clear that they do not regard the order of the small sections of parables or incidents in Mark as one which they must rigidly follow though they do maintain the content of the teaching with little change. After the first section there is little change from the general plan of the Synoptics. These readings as outlined aim to make clear the whole plan of the synoptic account of Jesus, to follow distinctive sections in each Gospel and to study parallel accounts. The reading of the Gospels is best done in this plan by the use of *Gospel Parallels* with its wealth of arrangements, citations and references. The Revised Standard Version is used because it is an excellent translation in the language of today as the Greek of the Gospels was the current language of their day. The American Standard Version (1901) is a more literal translation and leads the reader in faithful fashion to the Greek. The King James or Authorized Version (1611), famous for its stately rhythms and reverential style, will remain as the best known though less accurate English translation. The notable modern translations by Moffatt and by Goodspeed and in the Roman Catholic Confraternity edition stand out among numerous versions of the New Testament.

16

The Beginnings of the Gospel

Mt. 3:1–12; Mk. 1:1–8; Lk. 3:1–20; Mt. 14:1–12; Mk. 6:17–29
(1–5, 110, 111)[1]

EACH WRITER of his Gospel started his story as he thought best. Mark is briefest with an incomplete sentence that reads like a title. It places the beginnings in well-known historical events. Matthew and Luke reach farther back into the circumstances of a unique birth. Matthew begins with a genealogy of Jesus and Luke with a formal Greek preface. John looks to the eternal aspect of a divine purpose, power and life known as the Word (Logos). All these Gospels associate John the Baptist with the coming of Jesus and all agree in relating Jesus to God. These various beginnings illustrate the fact that men wonder at their unexplained experiences with a marvelous man and hunt backward in his history to explain and complete his story.

Beginning of Mark. Like clear water whose depth is deceptive Mark's unique opening is plain until probed for its possible meanings. The "beginning" may arise from the prophetic message shown in the Old Testament or from John the Baptist's preaching and movement but it is best taken as a kind of title for the human-divine events which constitute the book. The "gospel" is a word of many meanings. Originally it referred to good news or to the reward paid for such tidings. It could mean the message spoken by Jesus but here it is the good news preached about him or a proclamation that God had done something for man in Christ. It included all that Jesus was and said and did. A century after Mark the "gospel" began to be applied to the four written records, still later the term meant a section of these books read in public worship. It is still widely used in Mark's sense as the salvation from God found in the words and the actions of Jesus Christ, the Son of God. "Jesus" is the common form of Joshua, a name well known in Hebrew history and scripture which meant "The Lord is salvation" (help). Mark simply gives the name as known with no need for identification or explanation of its signifi-

---

[1] Numbers in parentheses following the scripture readings refer to sections in *Gospel Parallels.*

cance as in Matthew (1:21). It was a name in ordinary use since it appears in Luke's list of the ancestors of Jesus, as part of the name of the insurgent, Barabbas, in reference to a magician in Acts and to a fellow worker of Paul. Mark adds "Christ" to Jesus as a surname rather than as a title. It means "The Anointed One" which was its first usage. He also later uses it as a title (8:29). As a surname it is a confession of faith that Mark puts in his first verse but seldom uses thereafter. It is not one of the more favored titles for Jesus like Teacher, Son of Man or Lord in any of the Gospels. This fact is noticeable in view of the later universal use of Christ which rests more upon Paul's popularization of it. Its meaning as a title, "The Anointed One," depends upon the ancient custom of dedication of the Hebrew king or high priest to his holy position as God's agent by the pouring of oil upon him. When Christianity moved outside Judaism to Greeks who did not know the custom, Christ (Messiah) became a name.

The "Son of God" may or may not have been part of Mark's own writing as the manuscripts variously indicate. Elsewhere in Mark this same title is bestowed on Jesus by demons who recognize him supernaturally and by the Roman centurion as a tribute for the manner of his death (3:11; 5:7; 15:39). The idea of Sonship is common in Mark who does not define it but illustrates it with a divine voice at the baptism and at the transfiguration and in a question of the high priest to Jesus (1:11; 9:7; 14:61). But Mark does not give the "Son" as a title used by the disciples or in the public teaching by Jesus. In Jewish thought, both Old Testament and post-biblical, "Son of God" was well known to express the relationship of the Lord: (1) to his people, "Israel is my first born son" (Ex. 4:22); (2) to a King; (3) to a righteous man, "Thou art my son; this day have I begotten thee" (Ps. 2:7); (4) to angels (Dan. 3:25); (5) less frequently to the Messiah, "My Son, the Messiah, shall be revealed, together with those who are with him and shall rejoice the survivors four hundred years" IV Ez. 7:28).[2] For Mark "Son of God" verified Jesus as Messiah, as chosen by God, as healer and as superhuman in death.

John, Baptizer, Preacher, Forerunner, Martyr.[3] John is one of the most prominent people in the New Testament. Only Jesus, Paul and Peter are more often mentioned. His importance was recognized later as the church made him a saint, appointed a feast day for him, col-

---

[2] R. H. Charles, *Apocrypha and Pseudepigrapha of the Old Testament* (Oxford, 1913), II, 582; V. Taylor, *The Names of Jesus* (New York, 1953), 52–65.

[3] There is but one up-to-date scholarly work in English on John the Baptist: C. H. Kraeling, *John the Baptist* (New York, 1951).

lected relics, pictured him in art and in the Orthodox Church placed him prominently on the iconostasis. All the Gospels connect John with Jesus. From a Christian view the sun soon dimmed the moon but both John and his movement had remarkable significance and even rivalry for beginning Christianity. As a part of the gospel John's coming was a forecast according to divine prophecy since he was a herald for Jesus, his greater successor. The Hebrew scriptures as the record of the words and the works of God were searched by the followers of Jesus for all possible forecasts about the coming of the Messiah. All the Synoptics quote the scriptures to show that the prophets foretold one crying in the wilderness to prepare the way of the Lord. Mark quotes from Malachi (3:1) and reflects the current view that Elijah, the mighty prophet of the ninth century, would be sent to turn the hearts of the people before the terrible day of the Lord (4:5-6) or before the Messiah came. He identifies John with the messenger from Malachi but Matthew and Luke omit Mark's quotation which is incorrectly attributed to Isaiah and use it later about John (Mt. 11:10; Lk. 7:27). Luke gives additional verses from Isaiah which culminate in a promise that all mankind shall see the salvation of God which accords with Luke's universalism.

In Mark John appears in the wilderness as the "Baptizer," in Matthew as the Baptist and in Luke as the son of Zechariah, a priest. Both Matthew and Luke identify the wilderness, the place of John's preaching, the former in the uninhabited countryside of Judea, the latter about the Jordan. In Luke John receives his message directly from God like the prophets of old. This is a revival from an earlier day since prophecy was believed to have ceased while the scribes repeated rather than created religious truth. John's arrival receives an elaborate dating in the fifteenth year of Tiberius (A.D. 28-29) and in the rule of five important civil and religious leaders. His appearance in the wilderness marked a new beginning as in past Hebrew history Moses had founded a new people in the wilderness. John's picturesque clothing and desert food, omitted by Luke, helped to prove his prophetic mission and resemblance to Elijah (Zech. 13:4; II Kgs. 1:8; 2:8). Four kinds of locusts were listed among the "clean" foods allowed by the Law, "ye may eat the locust after its kind" (Lev. 11:22) and these with honey were plentiful in the Jordan area. "Even today they are used for food by Bedouins, either cooked in salt water or roasted on coals, then dried, reduced to powder and eaten with salt." [4] Later words of Jesus show that John came neither eating nor drinking.

---

[4] G. Dalman, *Sacred Sites and Ways* (New York, 1935), 84.

Such asceticism made people think him a madman yet according to Jesus no one greater had been born.

John's preaching attracted great crowds who traveled far to hear him and join his movement. Luke reports that the people wondered whether he were the long-awaited Messiah. His preaching centered in: (1) *repentance of sins with baptism;* (2) *a mightier one coming.* Mark does not list the sins nor explain the repentance. Matthew and Luke (Q) give his rough warning to religious leaders and multitudes who trusted racial descent from Abraham more than lives fruitful in good deeds. A sharp contrast stands between the children of snakes and of Abraham. God can provide new followers of the righteous Abraham who was his friend. In the Aramaic, John's native tongue, there is a possible play on these "sons" who can rise even from "stones." The warning of a wrath to come, foretold by prophets and like an ax already cutting fruitless trees into firewood, reflects the expectation of the end of the age and the judgment soon to come on evildoers. Repentance required changed lives which turned from sin to God. Repentance in Hebrew thought meant a wholehearted active return to the Lord rather than a change of mind as the Greek word suggests (Acts 3:19).

Luke provides some samples of changed conduct. John's answers to those who asked what to do show his emphasis not on belief but on practice. The crowds must share clothes and food with the needy. Tax collectors, who honor him with the title "Teacher," must be honest in the face of easy graft; soldiers must not rob in violence nor be dissatisfied with their wages. Individual sins confessed in public led to the act of baptism. The exact form of baptism by John cannot be determined but it appears probable that the convert immersed himself in the Jordan as John observed and directed. Washing is a well-known rite in many religions but John's baptism arose in Palestinian Judaism as its Messianic results show. This baptism by John is not one of the many washings for ritual "uncleanness" required in the Law and applied in the Mishnah nor was it the same as the ceremonial bath taken by the proselyte when with circumcision and sacrifice he became a Jew. John was not concerned about the mode of baptism but preached a "baptism of repentance" or an inner purity for the individual such as the prophets had required for the nation. Isaiah gave the word of the Lord, "Wash you, make you clean; put away the evil of your doings before mine eyes" (1:16) and Ezekiel declared the Lord would cleanse Israel, "I will sprinkle clean water upon you, and you shall be clean" (36:25). This was a preparation for a new heart and spirit. The Psalmist prayed: "Wash me, and I shall be whiter than snow" (Ps. 51:7). John's baptism is nearer the prophetic ideals than the legal ceremonies. It was a new act symbolic of repentance and of submission to expected judgment.

John's baptism has significance in view of the fact that baptism became an all-important sacrament in Christianity. Its meaning is summarized by Marsh [5] in five points: (1) a preparation for a coming greater one whose judgment was imminent; (2) an immersion in the water of the Jordan, famous for changes due to divine action such as the cure of the Syrian general Naaman after obedience to Elisha's instruction to wash in it to cure his leprosy; (3) a baptism of repentance which required an outstanding return to God; (4) demands which all people must meet; (5) a rite probably not repeated as were Jewish ceremonial ablutions. To these points it may be added that John's baptism (6) made ready the recipients to enter and share the soon coming day of the Lord; (7) marked off John's disciples as a group; (8) used no formula of name, words or standardized form of washing nor any appeal to miracle; (9) required no witnesses as Jewish proselyte baptism did; (10) linked John and Jesus in their only recorded meeting; (11) influenced the establishment of Christian baptism.

John did not name the coming mightier one nor call him Messiah but in his own relative importance to this greater one he was like a slave unworthy to untie his sandals or carry them. This "one" was taken by the Evangelists to be Jesus but John may have thought only of some supernatural figure. This "one" will baptize with the Holy Spirit and Q adds "with fire" which produces an effect quite different from Mark's idea. The reference to fire is best understood in the light of the twofold traditional Hebrew conception of the Spirit which empowered men to fulfill God's purposes and which defeated the forces of evil. "It is possible to suggest that in the original saying of John which underlies the relevant New Testament material there was an allusion to the Spirit as a purgative and destructive force working through the Messiah." [6] Mark, however, sees in the forecast of the Holy Spirit the reception of power for a new life. This "one" will separate good and bad like the farmer who clears his floor with his fork after threshing his crop by throwing it into the air for the wind

---

[5] H. G. Marsh, *Origin and Significance of New Testament Baptism* (Manchester, 1941), 23–48; H. H. Rowley, "Jewish Proselyte Baptism and the Baptism of John," *Heb. Un. Coll. Ann.* XV (1940), 313–34; T. W. Manson, *The Servant-Messiah*, 36–49.

[6] Kraeling, *op. cit.*, 62.

to blow chaff aside as the wheat falls to the ground. The wheat is stored and the worthless chaff burned. This was another warning like the ax laid to the tree. Baptism with the Holy Spirit was a familiar idea in prophetic and apocalyptic writings. The Lord would pour out his Spirit upon all people with marvelous results (Joel 2:28) or the Messiah would bestow special favors. When the Gospels were written, the coming of the Spirit after Jesus' death was an experience reported as of great significance. The New Testament documents abound in references to the Spirit. But here John sees a baptism of the Spirit as an act that would parallel his water baptism but far transcend it as God's presence reached his followers through the coming age. The Synoptics see in John's forecast a reference to Jesus, as the sequence shows, but John's words when spoken may not have had any such exact identification for him. Many ideas about the coming Messiah were popular. John felt his part was to be the voice of preparation but his message did not name Jesus though the baptism of Jesus brought him soon upon the scene. Luke adds that John exhorted and evangelized the people. Later reports show that John's disciples fasted and were taught to pray (Mk. 2:18; Lk. 11:1). Matthew's report that John preached the kingdom of heaven was at hand looks like an editorial addition to parallel the preaching of Jesus (4:17). "Kingdom of heaven" is a specialty with Matthew who uses it thirty times to mean the lordship or rule of God which was soon to come and he believed that John preached it as well as Jesus. This is quite possible since the expectation flourished. Matthew uses "heaven" so as to avoid the sacred name of God which Mark and Luke do not hesitate to use for their Gentile readers.

The success of John's work is reflected (1) in Luke's report that all men wondered whether he were the expected Messiah; (2) in the fact that he had followers twenty-five years later in Ephesus (Acts 18:24-19:5); (3) in various groups who later claimed him as founder. His courage appears as Luke writes of his rebuke of Herod's evil doings, especially his marriage to his brother's wife, Herodias. Josephus also wrote that Herod had slain John, a good man who summoned the Jews to follow the way of righteousness, to deal justly with one another, to walk in piety before God and to come for baptism after their souls had been cleansed by righteousness. Fearing that John's great influence might lead the people to revolt, Herod took precaution to send him in chains to the fortress of Machaerus (on the east side of the Dead Sea), and there put him to death. There was public opinion that God punished Herod for John's death by the defeat he suffered in war with Aretas, King of the Nabateans. Aretas was father to Herod's wife who had been superseded by Herodias and Aretas fought to avenge this insult which came when Herod, visiting his half brother in Rome, fell in love with his sister-in-law Herodias, who soon agreed to divorce her husband. But Herod's wife learned of the intrigue and skipped home to her father, Aretas. This account by Josephus [7] is independent of the Gospels but there are parallels and omissions. Josephus does not connect John with any Messianic significance nor does he see in baptism more than washing of the body after the soul was cleansed. While Josephus interprets John's death as due to his potential leadership in revolution, Mark tells a popular story that the death was revenge for John's rebuke of the immorality of the Herods. John was jailed to please Herodias after he had declared that it was not lawful (Lev. 18:16) for Herod to take his brother's wife who was also his niece. Herodias held a grudge deep enough to kill John but Herod, nominally a Jew, had a fear about this holy man to whom he listened gladly but perplexedly. Dramatic shadows play across Mark's banquet scene on Herod's birthday when the daughter of Herodias, whose name, Salome, is given by Josephus, dances in to charm Herod to extravagance and then out and in again with her mother's gruesome demand for John's head to be served like a course at the feast table. Herod counted his hasty vow above the life of a courageous prophet who died at a woman's whim because he spoke God's word of rebuke. John had faithful disciples who cared for his body in proper burial as Jewish custom required. His meteoric career probably lasted a year, about A.D. 28.

How and where Mark secured his information is not known. Several points in his story are debated. Herod's title was not king but tetrarch as Matthew and Luke show. Herodias had been the wife of another Herod but not of the Philip who was tetrarch of the region northeast of the Sea of Galilee and who married Salome. Either there is confusion between a husband and a son-in-law of Herodias or else there were two brothers each named Philip. The relationships of the Herodian family are complicated. Herod's capital at Tiberias in Galilee seems to be the place of the banquet in Mark but Josephus claims Machaerus as the scene of death. Salome was probably not too old to charm Herod, but history can not determine her age beyond the general range of the twenties. A princess usually would not be such an

[7] *Ant.* XVIII.5.2.

entertainer though the Herods were loose morally. Mark placed this story of John's death where it foreshadowed the future of Jesus and he contrasted the unrighteous Herods with the righteous John. Luke omits the story. Matthew greatly shortens it, adding that Herod desired to kill John but feared his popularity with the people.

17

The Baptism of Jesus

Mt. 3:13–17; Mk. 1:9–11; Lk. 3:21–22 (6)

THE SYNOPTICS agree that John baptized Jesus and that this event was most decisive in the life of Jesus.[1] In Mark the baptism occurs when Jesus, identified by village and region, came to John at the Jordan. From Nazareth to the lower Jordan entailed sixty to seventy miles of travel. Mark tells the story as an experience of Jesus who, as he arose up out of the water, saw the heaven opened, the Spirit descending upon him and heard the heavenly voice with its famous assurances. Both Matthew and Luke add explanatory words, "of God" and "holy," to the "Spirit" and though it is like a dove, they give reality by their description of its "alighting" and its "bodily form." Matthew changes the words of the voice to the third person so that they become a witness to John though the vision of the Spirit belongs to Jesus. Luke omits the vision, mentions the crowds baptized with Jesus and places the Spirit and the voice during the prayer which followed baptism rather than at the moment of baptism. The message of the voice is a combination of lines from a Psalm (2:7) and the prophet Isaiah (42:1). Jesus is recognized as a beloved Son and as a delight. These accounts show that Jesus was interested in John, that he left his home to meet him, that he accepted baptism as John preached it, that he received a remarkable divine endowment and approval that changed his whole life. Baptism was the inner inaugural aspect which led soon to public teaching and activity.

[1] I. Abrahams, *Studies in Pharisaism and the Gospels* (Cambridge, 1917), I, 30–46; C. R. Bowen, "Prolegomena to New Study of John the Baptist," and E. W. Parsons, "John the Baptist and Jesus," in *Studies in Early Christianity*, ed. S. J. Case (New York, 1928), 129–47, 151–70; J. Moffatt, "John the Baptist," in *History of Christianity in Light of Modern Knowledge* (London, 1929), 185–97; A. E. J. Rawlinson, *St. Mark* (London, 1925), 251–56; D. Plooj, "The Baptism of Jesus," in *Amicitiae Corolla,* ed. H. G. Wood (London, 1933), 239–52; Marsh, *Origin and Significance of New Testament Baptism,* 101–8; J. W. Bowman, *The Intention of Jesus* (Philadelphia, 1943), 10–40; C. K. Barrett, *The Holy Spirit and Gospel Tradition* (London, 1947), 25–45; W. F. Flemington, *The New Testament Doctrine of Baptism* (London, 1948), 25–33.

But these vivid stories are far from simple. They are weighted with great meaning. They present important information about Jesus but they have made difficulties from the beginning to the present though not for Mark. Though his religious purpose is clear, Matthew's dialogue is often regarded as actually improbable since Mark and Luke report no special recognition of Jesus by John. John's later doubts about Jesus (Mt. 11:2–11) point to the same conclusion. Matthew reports a preliminary conversation where John feels his need to be baptized by Jesus. Yet John proceeds to baptize Jesus who had assured him that righteousness was thus fulfilled for them since Jesus had come with the purpose to be baptized. This act "to fulfill all righteousness" gives the reason for baptism and defends Jesus against attack as a sinner who had to be baptized like the others who came to John. It shows that Jesus decided the issue in his first spoken words in Matthew. He accepted his baptism as an obligation, shared with John, to obey fully the will of God. It is often held that Matthew reports the dialogue because he knew that John preached repentance, that baptism among Christians involved cleansing from sin as well as initiation into a new community, that Jesus was greater than John and that he was sinless. Faith in the sinlessness of Jesus is reflected in Christian claims that he was tempted in all points like as we are and that he did no sin (Heb. 4:15; I Pet. 2:22). This faith had its base in reflections on the life of Jesus as the holy and righteous one (Acts 3:14) who revealed God and whose death was a perfect sacrifice offered to God who raised him from the dead. That this faith faced problems beyond historical settlement is evident through Jerome's quotation from the Gospel of Hebrews which recorded that the mother and the brothers of Jesus suggested that since John baptized for the forgiveness of sins, "let us go and be baptized of him." Jesus said to them, "Wherein have I sinned that I should go and be baptized of him? Unless peradventure this very thing that I have said is a sin of ignorance." [2]

That Jesus came to be baptized as a sinner can be affirmed but it is abhorrent to Christian orthodoxy as well as an unwarranted speculation. "He would have sought no baptism for remission of sins had he not been conscious of sin." [3] That he came "as a sinless sin bearer who by submitting to baptism identified himself with his sinful and repentant people as later orthodoxy teaches" can be declared improb-

[2] M. R. James, *Apocryphal New Testament* (Oxford, 1924), 6.

[3] J. M. Murry, *Jesus, Man of Genius* (New York, 1926), 22; cf. Kraeling, *op. cit.*, 136.

able.[4] That we can reconstruct the mind of Jesus in the unknown years and as he came to the Jordan is scarcely possible on our present information beyond the clear indication that he "was concerned about the near approach of the kingdom of God and the ethical demands which its imminence made."[5] He accepted John as a prophet who declared God's purposes and his baptism was an endorsement of John and an obedience to God. Mark and Luke never mention any repentance for Jesus and Matthew is equally confident in the righteousness of Jesus. The dialogue that he reports between John and Jesus omits any reference to sin and is a defense of Jesus which shows that John recognized Jesus as superior and that Jesus desired baptism as a completion of religious duty. This dialogue represents not a verbatim report but important ideas about John and Jesus. There is a proper place for discussion of the sinlessness of Jesus but there is serious doubt whether this dialogue is the place for it or even presents the issue. "The question is not whether Jesus has or has not sins to confess but whether he is to obey the call of God which comes through the last and greatest of his prophets."[6]

The origin of the story of the baptism and the nature of the vision and the voice have occasioned much comment. Perhaps Jesus first told the story, or the disciples, or John or some mythologist who dramatized the sonship of Jesus. The event can be taken as substantially historical since it accounts for the relationship of John and Jesus and since it was the beginning of the Gospel (Acts 1:22; 10:37) and since it contained points which required Christian explanation and defense. The nature of the experience of Jesus at baptism is best understood in symbolical terms though some readers prefer to take the record literally and miraculously. His baptism produced results beyond the usual effects on John's followers. The heavens split, the Spirit coming like a dove, the voice speaking from heaven are graphic biblical ways to describe how God comes to man. To make the event more real Luke pictures the Spirit like a dove in bodily form and Matthew reports the voice as audible to others besides Jesus. But the essential point remains that God is spirit and spiritual things are spiritually discerned though a report of an inner world is often made in visible audible forms.

Messages from God came in different ways in the Hebrew religion. Dreams, sacred lots, miracles, angels and laws mediated his will. The

---

[4] H. D. A. Major in *Mission and Message of Jesus* (New York, 1938), 23.
[5] Barrett, *op. cit.*, 35.
[6] T. W. Manson in *Mission and Message of Jesus*, 442.

simple direct word came often to prophets as expressed in the phrase, "Thus saith the Lord." But the direct word of God was thought to have ceased with the prophets, Haggai, Zechariah and Malachi. Then arose the thought of a divine voice from heaven (Dan. 4:31) later literally called the "daughter of the voice" which was heard by rabbis as a kind of substitute for the Holy Spirit which had inspired the word of the Lord. This divine voice could sometimes be heard like the sound of a bird. One rabbi reported it in time of prayer as cooing like a dove, saying, "Woe to the children on account of whose sins I destroyed my house and burned my temple and exiled them among the nations of the world." Then Elijah had appeared to the rabbi and said, "Not in this moment alone does it exclaim but thrice each day does it exclaim thus" (Berachoth 3a). This story illustrates the symbol of the dove whose meaning is not easy to determine since it also may reflect the thought of the creative spirit of God brooding on the face of the waters at creation (Gen. 1:2).

The descent of the Holy Spirit upon Jesus is striking in view of the infrequent mention of the Spirit in the Synoptics. In the rest of the New Testament on the contrary there is overflowing evidence about the Spirit, from Peter's preaching that God anointed Jesus with the Holy Spirit and power (Acts 4:27; 10:38), through Paul's frequent stress of the Spirit of life in Christ Jesus (Rom. 8:2) to John, the Seer, who declared the "testimony of Jesus is the spirit of prophecy" (Rev. 19:10). The Old Testament basis for the Spirit is an ample one. There is the divine Spirit which is the breath of God, creative and life-giving (Gen. 1:2; 2:7), destructive as a storm (Ps. 18:15) and the cause of death (Job 4:9). The Spirit could empower a hero like Samson with incredible strength (Judg. 14:6, 19) or kindle Saul to overcome cruelty (I Sam. 11:6). It could create craftsmanship in gold and silver, stone or wood or make Joshua a leader to succeed Moses (Num. 11:16-17) or revive a dead people in captivity (Ezek. 37:1-14) or anoint the Servant to preach good tidings to the poor (Isa. 61:1). In the Apocrypha the Spirit and wisdom give knowledge (Wisd. 9:17) and the Spirit indwells all things (12:1) and created all things (Jth. 16:14).[7] In later Jewish literature the Spirit gives insight, understanding, might and righteousness (I Enoch 49:3; Pss. of Sol. 17:42). The basic thought through these writings is that the Spirit is God in action. How much of this broad current of the Spirit was

[7] E. F. Scott, *The Spirit in the New Testament* (New York, 1927), 11–60; D. C. Simpson in *The Spirit in Life and Thought* (London, 1927), 61–76; A. J. Macdonald, *The Interpreter Spirit and Human Life* (London, 1944), 9–64.

flowing in Mark's mind as he wrote of the descent of the Spirit on Jesus cannot be known but Mark wrote when the Spirit, both in Hebrew scriptures and Christian experiences, was believed to be everywhere manifested. For him the beginning of Jesus' ministry was understandable when Jesus accepted a place in John's mission and received a miraculous spiritual equipment for entrance upon his role as the mightier one. Matthew and Luke follow Mark here though each had written an earlier story of the work of the Spirit as the cause of the conception of Jesus. "It appears that the Messiahship, since it underlies the office of Jesus as the Servant of the Lord, his status as son of God and the descent upon him of the Spirit, is the key to the understanding of the baptism narrative and apart from it the whole event, as it is recorded in the Gospels, is meaningless." [8]

The study of this baptism of Jesus has fallen into varying forms. There are those who blend together all the information, biblical and extrabiblical, into one uncritical acceptance of all accounts which seeks to extract lessons for conventional Christian living. Others like the Church Fathers see the story as the institution of the all-important sacrament of baptism though later writers tended to locate this rite as established by Jesus in Judea (John 3:22). Others try to enter into the original religious experience of Jesus and speculate much on his response to John, his vision, his sonship, his call and his inner life. At the other extreme are those who reject the whole account with its religious motives as unhistorical.[9] Still others while recognizing that Jesus, like other prophets, had a remarkable initial call from the Lord find a primary interest in the gospel which proclaimed what God had done in Christ. Since Jesus was the Messiah, the baptism shows his divine appointment by water and Spirit. This is the essential point. This view lets the reader not so much into the mind of Jesus as into the secret of his Messiahship which was not known at first by those who were with him but is plain to the readers of the Gospel. It is often pointed out that the baptism is the first step in the secret unfolding Messiahship as Mark tells the story. The second step is the recognition of Jesus by the demons (1:24). The third is in the momentous declaration of Peter at Caesarea Philippi (8:29). The fourth is the symbolic ride into Jerusalem (11:9). The climax is in the open claim, "I am," before the high priest (14:62), and in the tribute of the centurion to his death (15:39). Whether Mark had this plan in mind or was simply reporting the sequence of events cannot be determined.

[8] Barrett, *op. cit.*, 44.
[9] C. Guignebert, *Life of Jesus* (New York, 1935), 155.

Not all these steps deal with the Messiah. Finally there is the view that Jesus' divine sonship is the vital point in the baptism. The emphasis is not on any inner experience of Jesus but upon the announcement that Jesus is already a unique Son. "There is no suggestion in Mark that Jesus' baptism marked the birth of his 'messianic consciousness.' " [10] "The story of the baptism, as we now have it, seems an attempt of the early Christians to pierce the mystery of the forces that lay behind Jesus' decision to begin his proclamation of the coming Kingdom of God." [11] One may reasonably think it rests on a real decisive event in the relationship of Jesus to God, adapted to religious instruction.

[10] F. C. Grant, *Interpreter's Bible* (New York, 1951), VII, 654.
[11] B. H. Branscomb, *Gospel of Mark* (New York, n.d.), 20.

18

The Temptation

Mt. 4:1–11; Mk. 1:12–13; Lk. 4:1–13 (8)

THE BREVITY of Mark's story of the temptation is matched by its singular description of the Spirit which drove Jesus to the lonely wilderness where he met Satan, wild beasts and angels and by its reticence about the content of the temptation. That the man of God faced a period of proving his faith was accepted in Jewish thought. Abraham, Noah, Joseph, Job and Daniel had demonstrated victory over evil and glory to God who allowed the trials that led to triumph. Empowered by the Spirit which had come at baptism, Jesus faced his adversary in solitude. The wilderness was not only the place where demons dwelt but historically it had been the scene of testing and training for Israel. The forty days were famous as the period that Moses spent in the Mount when he received the Ten Commandments. To escape Jezebel's vengeance Elijah had traveled forty days to the same sacred place. In biblical usage forty days refers to a considerable but not an exact period of time like the present use of the word "month." The driving of the Spirit meant some inner divine compulsion which impelled Jesus to face the evil one. Yet he was not alone since the Spirit was in him and messengers of the Lord aided him throughout the trials. The reference to wild beasts may indicate a simple natural fact or may suggest a contrast with the absence of human beings, or it may recall the hope that the Messiah would restore the friendly relations with animals as in the Garden of Eden, or it may look to the fulfillment of poetic prophecies when wild beasts would be changed or would harm no holy man (Isa. 11:6; Ezek. 34:25). "If ye work that which is good, my children, both man and angels shall bless you; and God shall be glorified among the Gentiles through you, and the devil shall flee from you, and the wild beasts shall fear you, and the Lord shall love you and the angels shall cleave to you" (Test. Naph. 8:4). Mark says nothing of fasting nor does he report a victory over Satan but he assumes it and soon tells of numerous defeats of demons by Jesus. Mark uses the older Semitic name, Satan, for the evil one and his story is independent of Q. He brings to the reader the more than human forces operating for and against Jesus who endured trials which qualified him for his new work immediately before him.

Matthew and Luke (Q) agree with Mark that the temptation was under the leadership of the Spirit for forty days but they stress the fast and give a dramatic dialogue between Jesus and the devil which sets forth the content of three temptations. The devil attacks with plausible suggestions and Jesus repulses him with the armor of scripture quotations. Matthew and Luke concur on the thought of the three temptations but not on the order in which the second and the third ones are presented. The original order in Q and the more logical climax are matters of dispute. Matthew states that angels came after the devil left Jesus and Luke writes that the devil departed until another convenient season.

Even though a historian like Goguel does not include the temptation in his *Life of Jesus* there are four aspects of the ordeal which require discussion: (1) fasting; (2) the devil; (3) the meaning of each temptation; (4) the nature of the narrative. Fasting is well known as a discipline to induce spiritual development. Judaism was not an ascetic religion but fasting was commonly observed at proper times such as the Day of Atonement (Lev. 16:29). The Pharisees fasted twice a week (Lk. 18:12). There were the renowned examples of Moses, reputed as one who neither ate nor drank for forty days in the holy mountain (Exod. 34:28) and of Elijah who went forty days on the strength of one meal (I Kgs. 19:8). These stories may have influenced the span of time in which Jesus fasted. There is the simple explanation that the region was mostly foodless or the psychological one that intensity of inner struggle overcame physical concerns but it is more probable that fasting was a religious action, preliminary to the first temptation.

The Satan appears seldom and late in time in the Old Testament. In Job (1:6–12) he is an adversary in the court of heaven who roams the earth and is allowed by the Lord to test man. In Chronicles (I, 21:1) he prompted David to take a census of Israel which was regarded as the cause of a plague. In an earlier record of the same event (II Sam. 21:1) the Lord was responsible for motivating David but more developed thought was reluctant to charge the Lord with evil. The contact of Judaism with Persian thought (538–333 B.C.) helped the growth of the idea of a secondary power or god of evil and darkness who opposed God who is good. Thus many of the calamities in nature and the evil impulses in man were explained as due to a supernatural evil being. By the days of the Gospels this Satan was thought to have his hosts of demons to aid him in his evil work. In the temptation he undertakes to defeat the Son of God before he begins his public work. This is a decisive battle because the whole future activity of Jesus depended on its outcome. The devil failed in his obstructive designs on the Spirit-led Jesus who is aided by angels. These heavenly messengers and the Lord were a good counterpart to the devil and his demonic legions. The lore of angels aided men to understand the good which attends men in the face of evils. These attendants of the Lord in earlier days constituted the court of the heavenly king and emphasized his majesty and glory. Seen and unseen, they brought messages to men, dreaming or awake. They guarded from danger, aided at death and defeated invisible evil adversaries. Later Jewish thought believed the Torah was given through them. In Daniel, leading angels are known by name, Gabriel and Michael (8:16; 12:1) and in Tobit it is Raphael who is the wonderworking guide (5:4). Sadducees refused to believe in angels but Pharisees accepted them. They appear but little in the teaching of Jesus but in this temptation they support and serve him. Luke who thinks of Jesus as filled with the Holy Spirit does not repeat with Matthew and Mark the part played by angels.

Temptation means a test of a person whether required by God or in reverse presumptuously by man of God. The devil begins two tests not with doubt but with a signal title as the basis for his misleading. "Son of God" is not a common designation for the Messiah in Jewish thought nor is it recorded in the Synoptics that Jesus ever used it for himself. After Christians used it much to describe the nature and the mission of Jesus, it may have been avoided by Jews. In this story "Son of God," which had a wider appeal than the Jewish "Messiah," corresponds to the title given at baptism. Most discussions assume that Son of God and Messiah are practically the same. The first temptation to make bread from the stones which abounded in the wilderness reflects the current belief that the age of the coming Messiah would include abundance of food when even manna would be supplied again. The devil suggests that the Son of God should be able to provide plenty to meet his own hunger or the constant hunger of the plundered poor. The need was imperative but Jesus met the challenge with an answer from Deuteronomy (8:3) which proved that God in his dealings with Israel in the wilderness allowed his people to hunger, then fed them with manna that he might teach them that man lives by more than bread. The final directions for the life of the Son of God must come from God not from the devil.

In the next test Matthew and Luke show almost complete agreement except that Matthew gives the Jewish name "holy city" for Jerusalem, a usage which has continued among Jews, Moslems and Christians to the present. When the devil put Jesus on a little wing of the Temple, the giddy height above the Kidron valley set the opportunity for the tempter to quote a Psalm to prove his point that Jesus, as Son of God, could trust God in a venturesome leap and his angels would save him. Since God had made a promise, he would fulfill his word. Jesus met this specious use of scripture with another verse from Deuteronomy (6:16), which reads like a commandment as quoted but it continues on to a historical reference, "as ye tempted him in Massah," which in turn depends on an incident (Ex. 17:7) in which Moses, facing stoning by a murmuring thirsty mob of his people, smote the rock with his rod at God's command to produce water. But as Moses named the place Massah (Proving), he reflected that the people had put God to test by questioning whether he was with them or not. They did not trust God but forced a miracle. The Son of God could not thrust such compulsion on to God in a needless risk either to assure himself of God's power or to attract public attention to it or to prove it by a miracle. There was a Jewish tradition that the King Messiah would reveal himself on the roof of the Temple with teachings from the prophets but it had no reference to a leap from the top.

For the final test Matthew states that the devil took Jesus up to a high mountain and showed him the whole world. This may reflect the outlook that Moses had from Mount Nebo (Dt. 34:1-3) from whence he saw the magnificent sweep of the Promised Land, westward beyond the depths of the Jordan valley. Matthew sets forth both the complete obeisance required by the devil and the vehement dismissal of Satan by Jesus. Luke gives no location for the world view but the vision is accomplished in a moment of time and he amplifies a most subtle appeal of the devil who promises all authority and glory of all kingdoms. It was common knowledge that the world was part of Satan's domain and he could deliver it at will. The one condition for Jesus to obtain the whole world was homage to the devil, a small act for a great reward. But the Son of God used again his trusted weapon from his well-learned chapter (Dt. 6:13). This quotation changed the word "fear" to "worship" and added "only" to the command but omitted the rest of the verse which required swearing by the name of the Lord. The promise was great but the cost was greater. The Son of God could not surrender loyalty to God or his sonship and service to him alone. All the world needed to be won for God but it could not be gained by the loss of his life with God at the behest of the evil one. A great and good goal was not gained by debasement.

The temptation narratives are set as a sequel to the baptism and they are important however they are interpreted. "It seems likely that the picture given in Q has been filled in by the imagination of the early church." [1] They are dramatic dialogues with facets like the pinnacle or a sight of the world which forbid a literal reading. One modernizing method of interpretation has been to look for instruction from the temptations with parallels in the experiences of other great religious leaders or of the reader who knows the drop in spirit that follows a high peak like baptism. It is possible to point out moral guidance for the hour of temptation in the dangerous drive of physical appetite, in the appeal of admiration for sensational achievements and in the universal desire for power even though it produces corruption. But there is little evidence of the use of these stories for teaching purposes in the rest of the New Testament. The early Christians did not re-enact these tests of Jesus. Another method has been to read these stories as autobiography. Their first narrator could only have been Jesus if they report his experiences. Hence it is supposed he told them first to his disciples to show his ideas of his Messianic mission. This often accepted explanation of their origin is quite possible, judged by their simplicity, use of scripture and picturesque details but the present form is far from autobiographical though not mere imagination or parable. They are stories about Jesus and if the core came from him as a vital attitude about his work and life with God, they have been wrapped in triple form with scriptural backing to teach the triumphant defeat of the devil by Jesus. "To understand our Gospels at all we must ever again remind ourselves that what we read is written there not because it was interesting or because it was a known item of the Master's biography but solely and only because it somehow enshrined the gospel." [2] In pictorial form the temptations show the Son of God equipped with power by the Spirit as he faced decisions about the use of his power. They show his use of the written Word as an arsenal for victory in controversy over the right course

[1] J. M. Creed, *Gospel according to St. Luke* (London, 1930), 62.
[2] C. R. Bowen, *Studies in Early Christianity*, ed. S. J. Case (New York, 1928), 146.

in problems of his Messiahship. They show his rejection of a faith founded on the astonishment of miracles as proof about himself or God. They show fidelity and obedience to God by the One who pleased him. They show that the Son of God was in no way exempted from the assaults of evil. "My son, if thou comest to serve the Lord, prepare thy soul for temptation" (Ecclus. 2:1). They show solitude and fasting as accepted in the example of Jesus. They show a verbal duel with the devil in the belief that the power of evil had a real focus in Satan who afflicted not only all men but even the Son of God. The reality of this adversary has long been maintained not only in orthodox circles but also in the vocabulary of the profane. However, this existence did not become an article in the Christian creed. The denial of his actuality has been achieved by taking him as poetic personification or by insistence that there can be no god of evil in a monotheistic universe or by reliance on man's own responsibility for his deviltry or by the paradox that the only good in the devil is in getting rid of him. Of late such denials have been beset with the secret fear that the devil flourished most by denials. Gigantic evils in the affairs of men have led to the resurrection of demonic forces by the theologians. However, modern man is much more wary than first-century man about easy acceptance of the devil who can enter humanity or cause the endless ills which afflict mankind. For those who ponder good and evil this drama of the testing of the Son of God stands as aloof, mysterious, fascinating as the traditional flat-topped Mount of Temptation west of the Jordan. But once the ascent is conquered the view is entrancing.

19

First Preaching, Teaching and Disciples in Galilee

Mt. 4:12–22; Mk. 1:14–20; Lk. 4:14–30 (9, 10, 11)

THE DAYS of preparation were over. Jesus was ready. Momentous beginnings center in the person, the place, the message and the disciples. How long after baptism and temptation until John's arrest is not known but Mark and Matthew agree that Jesus began his public work after John was imprisoned. All the Synoptics state that Galilee was the scene of first activity. Luke sets a genealogy of Jesus after the temptation and gives his own summary which is that Jesus moved into Galilee in the power of the Spirit as his fame spread widely while he taught with honor in the synagogues. This summary leads to a quite different account of a surprising visit to Nazareth. Matthew sees the beginnings as fulfillment of prophecy as Jesus left Nazareth and lived in Capernaum at the north end of the Sea of Galilee. Eight centuries earlier Isaiah in a renowned Messianic passage had written of a great light shining in Galilee (the Circle) of the Gentiles. This northern region of Hebrew people had been brought to darkness and death by Assyrian invaders under Tiglath-Pileser (II Kgs. 15:29) but Isaiah said restoration and relief were to come. Matthew found this light in the presence and the preaching of Jesus in Galilee. Capernaum was one of many towns which filled well-populated Galilee, a region famed for beauty, fertility and commerce which extended eastward to Decapolis.[1] There was a flourishing trade in fruit and fish which led to the tax office (Mk. 2:14). The center of community life was the synagogue, a gift of a Roman centurion (Lk. 7:5). The remains of an impressive synagogue have been dug up and partly replaced though this structure probably dates from a century or more after Jesus. No reasons are given for the selection of Capernaum as the hub of the Galilean ministry of Jesus. Probably he felt at home among people of his own area and level of life. They lived simply as farmers, fishers and traders. With its central location on level land, looking southward over the blue waters of the lake, the town had

[1] Dalman, *Sacred Sites and Ways*, 133–53.

133

easy access to neighboring villages where Jesus could reach many hearers. Peter had his home there and Jesus enjoyed his hospitality. Thus there were attractive opportunities for Jesus to begin his public appeal though Capernaum unfortunately failed to respond to his mighty works and faced a condemnation to Hades. It was not a region of the Gentiles as in its earlier days though it was near to non-Jewish territories and Gentiles were well known.

The Synoptics agree that the first and the most important activity of Jesus was preaching and teaching. Preaching meant not a formal religious discourse but a proclamation of God's reign and teaching was not in schools but in informal instruction. Mark gives far less of Jesus' teaching than the other two Gospels but his summary of Jesus' preaching is more complete. The gospel of God or "of the Kingdom of God," as many manuscripts state it, indicates that its content is good news from or about God. Mark reports the first preaching of Jesus in rhythmic fourfold form, which is a great introduction to the whole message of Jesus and about him in the rest of the book.

1. *"The time is fulfilled"* reflects the thought not of clock time but of destiny determined by God. The hour has struck for the completion of God's purposes. The dawn of a new day is breaking, the stroke of divine action is evident in the climax of the Kingdom.

2. *"The Kingdom of God"* or heaven is often misread with modern meanings which take it as a domain or society. It should be read as the reign or the rule of God. Its existence was long known but its nearness is the point in the preaching of Jesus. It is at the door. Jesus did not define or explain the reign of God. His mission was to proclaim that the time had come to prepare men for it by repentance and changed lives. The phrase, "the Kingdom of God," is not in the Old Testament and it is not frequent in the post-biblical writings. But the idea of God as King runs through Hebrew scriptures. "I am the Lord, your Holy One, the Creator of Israel, your King" (Isa. 43:15). "His kingdom ruleth over all" (Ps. 103:19). This Kingship reflects a divine purpose rather than a human plan. It means the sovereignty of God over all the earth as acknowledged by Israel when the Law was given at Mount Sinai. When an individual accepted the divine rule revealed in the Law (Torah), he took upon himself the yoke of the Kingdom. To recite the Shema ("Hear" Dt. 6:4–9; 11:13–21; Num. 15:37–41) was to take the same yoke. God's rule was manifested in the creation and in nature, in control over nations, in the Mosaic Law, in the history of Israel and in his daily providence over each person. God's nature is righteousness but man was created free

to obey God or to rebel and refuse his law. Therefore, God's kingly
rule was impeded but not destroyed even though there was a limited
rival ruler in Satan. These obstructions to the reign of God required
not only a battle against present evil but a forward look when divine
rule would be better realized. God's purposes had a coming fulfillment. Promises abound in the scriptures. "The saints of the Most
High shall receive the kingdom, and possess the kingdom for ever"
(Dan. 7:18). When God decided the issue, he would reward the
righteous, gain victory over all powers of evil, judge the evildoers
and establish his kingly rule. Prophetic hopes looked for this establishment on this earth with or without a Messiah to maintain God's
reign (Isa. 9:7; Zech. 14:9). This Golden Age would bless Israel in
physical, political and righteous fashion. Apocalyptic visions pictured
a new kind of world and a Coming Age, often with a supernatural
Messiah after the sudden destructive end of the present age which
God alone could miraculously accomplish. Rabbinical thought is reflected in part of the Kaddish (holy) which is a prayer as well known
in Judaism as the Lord's Prayer in Christianity. God created the
world according to his will and "may he establish his kingdom during your life and during your days and even more speedily and at a
near time." [2] God's reign will come when nations acknowledge him
as Israel does and in Israel when each Jew fulfills the requirements
of the Mosaic Law.

With this background the Kingdom of God is decisive in the teaching of Jesus. No other term appears as often on his lips. It is his great
theme. The whole reality of his religion centers in this phrase. The
truth he preached proclaims God's rule and man's opportunity to
accept it. His parables illustrated this message. He taught men to
pray "Thy kingdom come." He disclosed its powers in exorcism and
miracles. Its importance cannot be overstressed nor can its profound
truth be compressed into a definition. This ideal must be kept in
mind throughout all study of the gospel. No net of words can contain the whole truth for which Jesus preached, worked, lived, hoped,
died and lived again. Jesus nowhere defined the Kingdom. Consequently its nearness and its nature have had endless explanations. It
is a mystery made known to disciples according to Mark yet it is
publicly proclaimed by Jesus. His preaching had power because he
believed the Kingdom was near and in some sense realized in himself and in his work. It is near, it is here and it is to be completed in
God's time. It is God's gift and the eternal fact of his salvation. "The

[2] *Daily Prayer Book*, ed. J. H. Hertz (rev. ed. New York, 1948), 213.

correct understanding of what he [Jesus] meant by it is the key to an appreciation of the career of Jesus." [3]

3. Men are required to *repent*. Jesus shared a message of repentance with John the Baptizer who had urged men to turn to God lest they fall before the wrath to come, but Jesus invited men into the unending opportunities in God's reign, long awaited but now at hand. The doorway into the Kingdom was to renounce one's sins. A change must be made for something better. Repentance was not simply remorse for the past but a change in character. It was man's answer and action in response to a divine summons. This fundamental requirement was well known in the prophetic religion which Jesus inherited and advanced. He exempted no one in his call. Entrance into the Kingdom was by individual decision rather than by national action. Unlike John there was no requirement of baptism. Repentance meant a turn from any malign influences, either of man or of demons, and a turn to God so that God's forgiveness led to a new life.

4. *"Believe in the gospel"* can be better stated as "have faith in the gospel." This is an extraordinary statement since the New Testament usually directs such faith to God or Christ. Jesus taught faith rather than belief. He moved far beyond the mental assent which is often the meaning of belief. Faith meant acceptance of the gospel of God followed by trust and action in it. The coming rule of God must be met by an adventure in entering it. In view of the uncommon expression "believe in the gospel" it seems probable that in Mark it stands as an added invitation that Christians extended to all men to commit themselves confidently to the good news that the age of fulfillment of God's purposes, proclaimed by the prophets, was at hand in Jesus as Christ whose life, resurrection and coming again in future glory should lead all men to repent and to enter a new life under God's rule.

After a mention of successful teaching in Galilean synagogues, Luke reports an early visit of Jesus to Nazareth which Matthew and Mark place later in his ministry. Luke not only prefers this special placement but he also introduces by this dramatic story some of the important themes which run through his Gospel. There is the program of anointment by the Spirit, good news to the poor, aid to the needy, fulfillment of prophecy, rejection of Jesus by his own people with the consequent aid to Gentiles and finally victory over his foes.

The scene in the home synagogue highlights only certain actions and utterances. There is no mention of the Shema, nor of the bene-

[3] C. T. Craig, *The Interpreter's Bible* (New York, 1951), VII, 145.

diction, nor of the reading of the Law which with the reading from
the prophets and the instruction made up the service of the time. It
is clear that Jesus was a regular attendant, that he was selected to
read the scripture, an honor open to any qualified male member of
the synagogue, that he stood to read and sat to teach according to
custom. He received and returned the roll of scripture from the
attendant. This "hazzan" held an honored position to which he was
appointed by the elders. He cared for the rolls which were stored in
the ark, directed services and selected the participants. The passage
which Jesus read from Isaiah is a fourfold program of good news, of
help for the poor, of relief of distress and of the year of the Lord, but
it differs from the fourfold summary of Mark. This quotation based
on the Septuagint shows freedom in the use of scripture since it omits
a phrase (Isa. 61:1) and adds another (Isa. 58:6) and fails to mention the day of vengeance. The claim of fulfillment of this scripture
is important because God's purposes are thus realized in the graceful
words of Jesus who won witness and recognition as the son of a
known neighbor, Joseph. The proverb, "Physician, heal yourself," was
well known but its application is not so clear since it is Nazareth
people who expected some deed done not upon Jesus but for them.
It seems to show that his fellow townsmen wanted immediate evidence at home of what Jesus had done abroad. But a hindrance
arose because a spokesman for God is rejected in his native place.
The evidence for this attitude is plain from the great prophets and
Elisha (I Kgs. 17:8-9; II Kgs. 5:14) who helped foreigners like a
starving Phoenician widow or Naaman, a Syrian leper, instead of
Israelite widows and lepers. This pointed comparison of Jewish and
Gentile relationships with prophets resulted in mob action sufficient
to threaten Jesus' life. Nazareth lies saucerlike on the slope of a hill
where rocky places can be found from which to pitch a man down
but the traditional spot called the Mount of Precipitation can scarcely
be accepted. How Jesus escaped is not explained but Luke sees him
move to safety by a marvelous passage through the crowd. Imaginative speculations that the neighbors cooled while traveling to the hill-
top or that his friends intervened or that memory of good days in the
past defeated a hastily hurt pride are interesting but historically useless. Luke knew the brevity and the selectivity essential for a powerful preamble to the unmatchable life he had to unfold. He may have
expanded Mark's story or have found the incident in one of his
sources.

In Matthew and in Mark the announcement of the Kingdom in

the preaching of Jesus is followed by the call of four Galilean fisher-men as disciples. Though the story does not state it, they are taken to be the first ones. They stand at the head of later lists and are the most frequently named disciples. Jesus summons them to follow him with the promise that he will make them into something new and greater as fishers of men. Their response was immediate. The broth-ers, Simon and Andrew, were quickly joined by two other brothers, James and John. There is no report of previous acquaintance with Jesus but his call is sufficient to secure disciples who embark with Jesus who himself is the "Big Fisherman." The tradition that Peter's reminiscences stand back of Mark is well supported by the lifelike details at the lakeside: Jesus walking, the use of proper names, the actual throw of the net by fishermen near enough so Jesus could speak while others mended a net far enough away so he had to call to them, and the father left in the boat with hired servants. Matthew omits the hired servants, stresses the brotherhood of the men and adds the name of Peter to Simon. These actualities are far better seen as historical rather than as decorative details of an idealized scene. Reduced to essential facts they could be used as an example to win new followers of Jesus who must leave all to obey him and share his mission. Still the air of a real, remembered call lingers as strong as sea smell. It was common for Jews to see rabbis whose work was to raise up disciples and to teach them the commandments of God so they could practice them but Jesus struck out in his own way. He taught and he gained disciples but their mission was first to follow him and then to find men who would also accept God's rule. Jesus' words, "Follow me," reflect the custom in which disciples walked be-hind their teacher in travel after they had left their homes to live with and serve him while they learned. Probably these fishermen knew Jesus and had heard him preach around Galilee before they accepted his invitation (John 1:35-42) but this background was not indicated as the story was told in the Synoptics.

20

First Exorcism and Healings

Mt. 4:23–25, 8:1–17; Mk. 1:21–45; Lk. 4:31–5:26, 7:1–10
(12–17, 45, 46)

THE SHORTEST shelf space in the study of the Gospels is occupied by the books on miracles. This is in marked contrast to the Synoptics and to Mark especially, though not to the letters of the New Testament. In Mark 30 per cent of the verses are related to miracles. Matthew and Luke repeat most of Mark's miracles and add a few of their own. "The miracle stories form an essential and inseparable part of the gospel tradition and their aim, like that of every other part of the tradition, is to deepen the understanding of the mystery of who Jesus is and to set forth the implications of this recognition for the whole life and conduct of those who seek to follow him." [1] These miracles can be classified as exorcisms, healings, resuscitations and nature-wonders. In the first three groups unusual changes are reported in people, in the last group the objects affected are nonhuman, like bread or water. Critics like Dibelius [2] and Bultmann undertook new classifications of miracles according to literary form. They discovered definite patterns in the circumstances, the cures and the impressions. They attempted distinctions between earlier and later stories and explanations of their origins. They reported many affinities and analogies with Rabbinic and Hellenic wonder tales. The rabbinical stories can be read in the Mishnah, translated by Danby and in the Soncino Talmud. The Greek stories are well represented in the *Life of Apollonius of Tyana* in the Loeb Classical Library. It was written in the third century by Philostratos about a famous Greek philosopher, traveler and miracle worker of the first century. A thorough criticism of the Form Critics has been made by McGinley who holds that the stories of healing in the Gospels have some traits in common with Rabbinic and Hellenic tales but are completely different in historical and spiritual tone.[3]

[1] A. Richardson, *The Miracle Stories of the Gospels* (London, 1941), 1.
[2] *From Tradition to Gospel*, 70–119.
[3] L. J. McGinley, *Form Criticism of the Synoptic Healing Narratives* (Woodstock, 1944), 48–154.

The first question, as Richardson indicates, is not "Did these events happen?" but "Why are these stories an integral part of the Gospel?" [4] It is important to know something of the history of miracle and of the effect of faith on mind and something of theories of reality in order to understand a subject as old and complex as miracles. There is no easy answer about them except for the skeptic who denies them completely and for the dogmatist who accepts them entirely. Both solutions short-circuit the events and the discussions about them. Historical study of them is the first step. Each story needs to be traced to its earliest form and accounted for, as far as possible, by known laws. Some elements defy explanation and at times one must suspend judgment about historicity. A miracle is also a symbolic statement about the way God entered experience, especially through the personality of Jesus.[5]

Mark and Luke agree that the first miracle occurred in a synagogue where the people were astonished at the authority of Jesus in teaching and in casting out a demon. Luke mentions power as well as authority. Matthew gives a complete editorial summary which shows that Jesus taught in all Galilee, that he preached the gospel of God and healed every disease. His fame spread northward throughout the Roman province of Syria. Great crowds flocked from Galilee and from the Greek Ten-City region eastward and from the Jewish areas of Jerusalem and Judea southward. Luke alone mentions preaching in Judea but he uses the term for the whole country of Palestine. All kinds of disease, demon-possession, epilepsy and paralysis yielded to the power of Jesus. Mark's story seems to be a sample Sabbath in which the authority of Jesus is manifested. Authority is closely related to power and in Luke the words appear to be synonymous.

4 *The Miracle Stories of the Gospels*, 34–37.

5 J. Wendland, *Miracles and Christianity* (London, 1911), 1–122; A. C. Headlam, *The Miracles of the New Testament* (London, 1914), 1–69, 182–220; W. A. Brown, "Permanent Significance of Miracle for Religion," *Harv. Theol. Rev.* VIII (1915), 298–322; E. R. Micklem, *Miracles and the New Psychology* (London, 1922), 31–42, 130–36; F. R. Tennant, *Miracle and its Philosophical Presuppositions* (Cambridge, 1925), 1–95; C. J. Wright, *Miracle in History and Modern Thought* (New York, 1930), 3–41; 273–323; B. W. Bacon, *Studies in Matthew* (New York, 1930), 369–74; C. H. Dodd, "Miracles in the Gospels," *Exp. Times* XLIV (1933), 504–9; H. S. Box, *Miracles and the Critics* (London, Milwaukee, 1935); C. F. Rogers, *The Case for Miracles* (London, 1936), 1–138; A. Richardson, *The Miracle Stories of the Gospels* (London, 1941); C. S. Lewis, *Miracles* (New York, 1947), 15–22, 67–75, 121–70; G. T. Manley, *New Bible Handbook* (London, 1948), 57–68; F. C. Grant, *Introduction to New Testament Thought* (New York, 1950), 144–59; W. K. L. Clarke, *Concise Bible Commentary* (London, 1952), 284–300; R. M. Grant, *Miracle and Natural Law* (Amsterdam, 1952), 153–208; *Catholic Commentary on Holy Scriptures* (London, 1953), 117–20, 778–79; H. E. W. Turner, *Jesus, Master and Lord* (London, 1953), 156–84.

These words must be read not only in their ordinary sense but in their religious meanings.[6] "Power" is another name for God (Mk. 14:62) or the strength of the Holy Spirit. It defines Christ (Rom. 1:16) or it may describe an outpouring of God's might at the end of time (Mk. 9:1) or it may mean a miracle or the ability to work one. Used in the plural it may refer to heavenly beings (Mk. 13:25). Essentially the gospel writers see a mighty activity of God, beyond words to explain, in the power of Jesus to preach or heal. In his life, God is at work.

Authority is the potential energy or capacity to exercise power. Authority stands behind power as an office affords position to use power. Hence Jesus acted with divine authority, not only to cast out demons and to heal the sick but to forgive sins (Mk. 2:10). But there is another meaning for authority especially as related to the teaching of Jesus. Rabbinic powers indicate that authority was conferred in Palestine by a solemn rite in which a rabbi laid his hands on the head of a candidate and conferred on him the responsibility to lay down doctrines and decisions with binding force. Thus he shared the wisdom that was believed to have descended from Moses. Early Christians followed a similar practice when they set men apart for missionary work or prayed for a descent of the Holy Spirit (Acts 6:6; 8:17; 13:3). In the synagogue Jesus taught with authority and not as the scribes who had levels of authority from the topmost learned theologian to the copier of records and the elementary teacher. Matthew sees the authority of Jesus in teaching since he places his reference to it at the end of the Sermon on the Mount. In theory the divine Law was unchanged but new situations and cases required changing interpretations to meet human needs. The new teaching of Jesus was not as one authorized as a scribe to teach. He did not spend much time citing past interpreters of the Law. "Underived power rather than novelty in content was probably the impression which Jesus gave in his teaching. His self-assurance and heroic radicalism were well-matched by his powerful influence over those distressed in mind, body or estate."[7] The content of his teaching was mostly similar to the faith of his fathers in Judaism. Newness was related to his manner, to his personality, to his radical emphasis on certain aspects of Jewish teaching and to his intense emotional demands.

[6] Barrett, op. cit., 71–82; J. Starr, "Meaning of Authority in Mark 1:22," Harv. Theol. Rev. XXIII (1930), 302–5; D. Daube, "Authority in Mark 1:22, 27," Jour. Theol. Stud. XXXIX (1938), 45–59; Richardson, op. cit., 1–19.

[7] H. J. Cadbury. Jesus: What Manner of Man (New York, 1948), 72.

"Jesus' teaching gained prestige from his miracles. There can be little doubt that these are the two features of his career that loom largest in all the gospels. . . . Miracles suggest Messiahship, miracles authenticate teaching." [8] These are the aspects put together by Mark in his first report of the career of Jesus whose exercise of authority results in teaching and in control of demons.

In the miracle stories exorcism of demons cannot always be sharply separated from healings but Mark has four stories in which demons are the focus for defeat by Jesus (1:23; 5:2; 7:25; 9:17). This power was also delegated to his disciples. The idea of demons dwelling in people rather than in things finds little expression in the Old Testament and the Apocrypha. Demoniac possession and expulsion were well known to the Rabbis but "there is a remarkable infrequency of reference to the subject in the Mishnah and Tannaite literature" while the great influence in Jewish circles of belief in demons dates A.D. 150–450. [9] Exorcism was practiced in New Testament times (Mt. 12:27; Acts 16:16–18) and parallel stories appear in Greek literature. In the Gospels the stories of exorcism contain these features: (1) the condition of the demoniac; (2) the demons recognize Jesus as supernatural; (3) he speaks to them and expels them by command; (4) the onlookers are astonished. [10] The Messiah was expected to defeat Satan and his hosts and these exorcisms in the Gospels are special signs of God's power and kingdom. Exorcisms are not magic nor are they peculiar to Jesus. They are visible events which show that divine might resides in Jesus, that this power subdues the evil adversary, that the rule of God is thus come among men and that Jesus is the Messiah. However, these actions both reveal and conceal these facts according to the response of those who accept or reject the exorcism as "the finger of God."

These exorcisms today receive varied interpretations. There are those who believe the stories as told. For such people there is no question about the events, the dialogues and the actual existence of demons who still influence mankind. Others believe the stories literally but think the world has changed so that demons no longer possess people. There are skeptics who regard the stories as pious folklore fabrications expressive of popular religious beliefs by people who needed helpful explanations of their faith. [11] But since these stories are an

[8] *Ibid.*, 110, 111.

[9] Abrahams, *Studies in Pharisaism and the Gospels*, I, 110.

[10] Barrett, *op. cit.*, 55, 56.

[11] S. V. McCasland, *By the Finger of God* (New York, 1951), 1–11.

essential part of the gospel record, there are those who regard them as reports of real experiences which have rational, historical and psychological explanations which entitle them to be regarded as facts.[12] They think demon possession is a first-century condition known today as mental illness. Insanity covers a tremendous range of troubles which affect both mind and body. Demon possession and exorcism are ancient ways to explain and cure these troubles. But there remain those who believe there is no easy nor entirely satisfactory explanation of the demons in the Gospels. "Demonic possession in the New Testament is still an unsolved problem," as a Scottish doctor insisted,[13] but much help has come from psychiatry and from present-day reports where demons are still believed to flourish. Some insight and understanding come from numerous similar stories current outside the Gospels but the most aid is found in a careful study of each account in the Synoptics, plus some confidence in the experience of 2,000 years in meeting queer human ailments.

The first exorcism in the synagogue at Capernaum was successful when a man questioned Jesus in the midst of his teaching. The man's question alternates curiously between singular and plural and reflects the belief in many demons who question or assert their possible destruction. They make a double identification of Jesus. The second title, Holy One of God, added to his known name and home is unusual since it appears in the Synoptics only in this incident. This title had been applied to Aaron the first high priest who mediated the things of God to Israel (Ps. 106:16). Since the title is bestowed by demons, they thus publicly recognize Jesus in a way the people of the synagogue did not see. This recognition is not an involuntary tribute but a defiance of their destroyer. "It is an identification of the Messiah who is going around among people without letting his real nature be known."[14] It was a common belief that control over a person or a spirit was gained when the true name was known and used for defense. To reveal the name of Jesus as the Holy One of God would lessen his power. Jesus' answer to this challenge was a command to silence and to leave the victim. With a convulsion and a shout the demon departed. Luke adds that no harm was done and places the shout at the beginning. Amazement followed the exorcism and Mark emphasizes the speed of the fame of Jesus' authority. It is notable that Jesus used no conjury and no sorcery. One command

---

[12] *Ibid.*, 63; E. Langton, *Essentials of Demonology* (London, 1949), 148–74.

[13] W. M. Alexander, *Demonic Possession* (Edinburgh, 1902), vii.

[14] McCasland, *op. cit.*, 85.

was sufficient. This is a distinctive aspect of the exorcisms in the Gospels.

The healing of Peter's mother-in-law is an example of the cure of the sick which appears in the Gospels as a parallel power to casting out demons. Here again the starting point for study is not modern medicine but the views of Jesus and his contemporaries. The idea that disease was due to sin was well known in the Old Testament. The anger of the Lord brought leprosy on Miriam, the sister of Moses (Num. 12:10). The Lord promised Israel, "I will smite you . . . seven times for your sins" (Lev. 26:24). Suffering and sin constitute the problem of Job, the masterpiece of the Bible. Healing was evidence that the power of sin was broken. The idea that God created and directed all things, both usual and unusual, made it natural to think the unusual events were the most striking evidence of divine action. Holy men were believed to work miracles. Clusters of marvelous deeds hung around names of Moses and the prophets, Elijah and Elisha and the pagan world teemed with stories haloed in wonder. Some miracles could be worked by evil powers.

The gospel writers are not interested in theories of miracles nor in complete descriptions nor in analyses and explanations. They report a variety of miracles, about thirty-five in number most of which are about healings which occurred in the early Galilean ministry. Their miracles are written as a natural and an essential part of the story of Jesus. They believe not only in the miracles which he worked but also in miracles about him, especially the resurrection. They see the miracles as proof of God's power in Jesus and as signs of the Kingdom of God, useful for Christian instruction and defense. For the term "miracles" they used words like "powers," "mighty works" and "signs" or "wonders." It is evident that the latter two pointed to something beyond them. Miracle as a mere wonder or as something incredible has no place in the Gospels and this word often misleads the modern reader who should note that "miracle" appears seldom in the American Standard Version New Testament and not at all in the Revised Standard Version. Miracles are signs that by divine aid Jesus could forgive sins, show compassion for the sick, respond to faith, overcome illness of both body and mind, defeat the devil, answer John the Baptist's question about the Coming One and establish the rule of God. This Kingdom is already present in these deeds of Jesus.

The stories of healing vary in their patterns but an order can often be discerned in them: (1) the sufferer appears with some named ail-

ment; (2) the healing comes by some physical act by Jesus as in
Mark or by a word; (3) the cure is complete as proved by an act or
a word; (4) there is astonishment or fear or glory to God or acknowledgment of Jesus as a prophet or Son of God. Matthew and
Luke report the same stories as Mark, with a few added, but they
feel free to heighten some details or omit others through reverence
for Jesus or from special motives like the exaltation of Peter, but in
general the Synoptics are alike in their view of miracles. They see the
miracles as important actual events which always bore meanings
about God, his Kingdom and Jesus in which men shared in repentance, faith, belief or righteous action. But there are negative aspects
which show that the disciples did not understand the miracles, that
enemies maligned Jesus because of these wonders, that he was unable
to do mighty works in his native region, that he denounced Capernaum and Bethsaida because these works did not lead them to repent
and that he refused to perform wonders when challenged by Pharisaic opponents or a sensation seeker like Herod. As a whole, the
Synoptists view the healing as part of the power of God, often mediated by the Spirit and wrought by the hand or the word of Jesus
whose amazing might moved them with awe. They see these works
of Jesus as immensely significant as they met men's dire needs, overcame the powers of evil and proved the Expected One and the Kingdom had come. If men failed to perceive these signs, it was because
they had eyes and ears but did not see and hear.

From these pages of the past to the present is a long journey but
the entire way is dotted by strange stories of cures of disease through
the aid of religion. Men are still excited by healings in Protestant
faith groups, in Christian Science mid-week meetings and at Roman
Catholic shrines. The fact that people recover from both trivial and
desperate, apparently hopeless, illnesses is indisputable. The explanations of recovery are disputed. These explanations start from basic
assumptions which ought always to be recognized and set forth. For
modern man these assumptions are religious or scientific or a mixture
of both. Man assumes in religion that it is rational to believe that God
exists, that he is living, creative, righteous and knowable. The world
and man have their being under his active direction. The health of
man, physical and mental, lies within the purpose of God and depends on conformity to that purpose. Conformity follows moral and
physical laws. These laws are formulated by man as far as he knows
them. He follows them to health but also faces ill health at times.
When ill, he may reach the limit of his co-operation with God ac-

cording to known laws of health. Then he takes a leap of faith that God's will may be done in a situation exceeding human aid. He does not trust his ignorance but rather believes that God knows best, that he wills good for him and that he is greater than any laws man discovers. Sometimes this leap is followed by a return to health, not explainable by present knowledge. The man asserts God cured him and testifies to a miracle. "A miracle is God's use of his own law-abiding powers to work out in ways surprising to us his will for our lives and for the world." [15] "A miracle may be defined as a sensible phenomenon contrary to the ordinary course of nature and effected by God." [16]

Since God is not a subject for scientific demonstration, modern man as a scientist assumes it is rational not to believe in miracles. He believes in a certain structure of the universe, based on observations collected by the methods of science and verified in the light of further observations according to the rules of science.[17] Health and ill health can be observed, described and aided by known causes and laws. The unknown for the scientist must be explored and verified by scientific means. The relationship of body and mind still presents unsolved problems. In this relationship health has roots which are not completely known. It is possible to look to science alone for the cure of all of man's illnesses. It is possible to find help through religious faith. Science and religion in spite of past battles are not enemies but essential pathways to reality. In each avenue there are resources for man's health. Modern man differs mostly from ancient man, both in science and religion, in the thought that God and the universe must be understood in orderly not capricious processes.

Mark's story of Peter's mother-in-law is simple, lifelike and historical. The place, the person, the illness, the action of Jesus and the result follow rapidly. The account is reduced to essentials. There are no words, no explanations, no discussion of the length of the illness or of the fever though Luke calls it great. The Evangelists agree on the fact of the cure but differ on the way Jesus was informed of the illness and in the manner of the cure. In Mark Jesus was told of the fever, in Matthew he saw the woman and in Luke he is requested to aid her. Mark pictures the vivid action as Jesus took her by the hand and raised her up, in Matthew a touch is sufficient and in Luke he stood and corrected the fever by word. Luke emphasizes the immediacy of the cure and agrees with Mark that it was complete since the woman got up and served her household. Matthew shifts to the more devotional idea that her service was to Jesus. This story cites a human need and the power of Jesus to meet that need.

The mention of sundown that day makes clear that Sabbath observance ended at that hour and it was then legal to labor to bring the demoniacs and the diseased to Jesus. Rumor ran like wildfire and hope for help for affliction moved crowds to the door. Mark reports many sick healed and demons cast out and controlled into silence lest they identify Jesus publicly through their supernatural knowledge. Matthew and Luke report that Jesus healed all by word or by laying on hands. Matthew follows his familiar theme that the cures of Jesus fulfilled the prophet Isaiah who wrote of a great Servant who took away weakness and disease (53:4). Luke plainly gives the words of the demons who recognize Jesus as the Son of God and he explains the command to silence as due to demonic recognition of Jesus as Messiah. This recognition did not extend to the people around Jesus. In this early period Jesus had work to do but his mission was not according to some current Messianic hopes; hence silence about identification with the Messiah was imperative lest popular hopes misinterpret his true mission. It is necessary to distinguish between the time of writing of the Gospels when the Messiahship of Jesus was believed and proclaimed and the unsuspected situation during the activities of Jesus when he was unrecognized as the Messiah except by people inhabited by supernatural spirits. Shortly before Jesus went to Jerusalem, Peter declared him the Messiah but was held to silence by Jesus. The Synoptists show such reserve about Jesus' own words about his Messiahship that disputes still linger about whether Jesus ever accepted Messiahship. Certainly his disciples eventually saw and preached him as the Messiah and certainly Jesus did not follow the conventional Jewish expectations about the Messiah. Most of his fellow Jews never thought of him as Messiah.

Matthew and Luke tell of a decision by Jesus to leave Capernaum for a time. Mark's brief passage is remarkable for its light on the prayer, the purpose and the work of Jesus. Peter probably supplied the actual story but beyond the history are religious overtones to lead the reader to face the example of Jesus. After the teaching, the cures and the crowds Jesus went out in the dark, long before dawn, to a lonely spot to pray. Three times Mark reports Jesus at prayer alone: (1) at the beginning of his work after a busy day in Capernaum (1:35); (2) in the middle of his mission after feeding 5,000 (6:46); (3) at the end in Gethsemane, shortly before he died (14:32). To these may be added his last cry from the cross which is not named a prayer but which is directed to God (15:34). These are windows which permit glimpses into the devotion of Jesus to God but their panes also reflect some celestial light in the dark of human tension.

When Peter and his companions tracked Jesus and reported everyone was searching for him, Jesus declared his decision, reinforced by prayer, to proclaim the gospel to the next towns since that was his mission. According to Luke the searching crowd, probably more interested in wonders than in the words of Jesus, came to him to keep him with them. Luke states that Jesus' preaching was the good news of the rule of God and that he was sent to other cities also for preaching. Jesus had a wider work than in Capernaum. Crowds gathered because of healings and exorcisms but the main purpose was expressed in words about God which he spoke in synagogues in all Galilee.

Luke has his own story about the call of Peter to follow Jesus. He uses little of Mark's report of the first four disciples. Luke's story has some parallels and perhaps some relationship to a post-resurrection account about Peter in John (21:11) when Jesus also directed a great catch of fish, conversed with Peter and forecast his future. There are symbolic meanings in Luke's story though Luke did not mean it as an allegory. It is a story which contains important interpretations rather than exact history. Only Luke calls the preaching of Jesus "the word of God" which points to the divine origin of his words. Luke alone rightly refers to the "lake of Gennesaret." This name comes from the plain at the northwest end of the lake. Since his readers were Gentiles, Luke uses "Master" and "Lord" not "Rabbi" when followers of Jesus address him. Luke pictures the pressure of the people upon Jesus as he taught them from Simon's boat, seated as was customary in teaching. Next he directed Peter to let down nets for a catch. He obeyed and enclosed a great haul of fish. Astonished, he fell down before Jesus and acknowledged his sin and separation from Jesus who relieved his fear and assured him he would have a new occupation to take men alive. Then Peter left all and followed him. This story puts Peter into prominence in that he aided Jesus with his boat, in his obedience in the face of apparent failure, in his confession of sin, in his recognition of the supernatural in Jesus and in his new promising task of catching men in which James and John join. A big catch of fish is not necessarily a miracle, nor do the words of Jesus indicate one, but Luke makes plain the awe of Peter and his partners and illustrates the popular motif of wonder-working which Jesus himself rejected in the temptation to leap from the pinnacle of the Temple.

The cleansing of the leper is vividly told by Mark. The plague of leprosy had detailed supervision by the priests who were health officials. They identified the disease, decided about the condition of the victim who offered the sacrifices required on recovery and restoration to normal society (Lev. 13–14). Pending recovery the leper was unclean in a religious sense and had to dwell alone with garments rent and hair loose. With covered lip he must cry his warning, "Unclean, unclean." His leprosy differed from the modern disease. It seems to have been some skin affliction, perhaps elephantiasis, that changed appearance in a few days and from which a person could recover. The cause and the cure are not given. Later rabbis regarded leprosy as punishment for grave sin. In the second-century Egerton papyrus this leper states he caught his disease from journeying with lepers.

This leper broke the law in his approach to Jesus and he did not obey Jesus' command for silence and for cleansing with the priest at Jerusalem. He came with confidence that Jesus could cleanse him. Mark reveals striking emotional aspects as Jesus was stirred with compassion while the man besought him and as he disregarded ceremonial defilement when he touched the leper. When the leprosy left, Jesus strictly commanded silence and obedience to the Mosaic Law but the man went out and talked so freely that great crowds compelled Jesus to stay in the country and people came to him from everywhere. For Mark, the pity of Jesus, his sudden sternness, his limitation of movement appear naturally as part of his narrative but Matthew and Luke abbreviate these points. They join in the immediacy of the cleansing for which the modern reader finds no satisfactory explanation except superhuman power. Luke accents the bad condition of the man as he came and the news of the cleansing to the great multitude who came to hear and to be healed. Then Jesus withdrew to the wilderness for prayer. Matthew and Luke report that the leper addressed Jesus as "Lord." This is a name for Jesus almost unknown in Mark (7:28). It came into wide use in the early church to show the exalted relationship of Jesus to his followers but during Jesus' ministry his disciples called him "teacher." "Lord" has many meanings.[18] It could be used for polite address as "Sir" is now used. It was applied to an owner of a slave or of property or to a father, a governor

[18] E. D. Burton, *Galatians* (New York, 1920), 399–404; Jackson and Lake, *The Beginnings of Christianity*, I, 409–18; J. A. Smith, "Meaning of Kurios," *Jour. Theol. Stud.* XXXI (1930), 155–60; Taylor, *The Names of Jesus*, 38–51.

or a king. In a religious sense it was a title for the gods and in Hebrew scriptures it meant God. "Lord" on the lips of the leper was an acknowledgment that Jesus had power to cleanse him.

Q is known to lack miracles. It contains one cure and one exorcism (Lk. 7:1–10; 11:14) but its nature as teaching explains their absence, except for this healing of the centurion's servant which Matthew and Luke place at Capernaum after the great sermon by Jesus. The climax of this story is not the cure but an important saying about the faith of a Gentile which Matthew emphasizes by the use of "truly" and Luke by the climactic position of the saying. The healing, however, had its significance especially since it illustrated that Jesus by a word could cure a sufferer at a distance. How the servant was paralyzed is also not explained. But this story is one of the few where Jesus deals with a Gentile. This fact had special meaning for Gentile Christians. Luke tells of aid to a Roman officer who had built a synagogue because he loved the Jews and who in turn had help first from a delegation of their elders and then from friends. These men became the media by which Jesus sent help. So also later the Jews had aided Gentiles to their faith as Christians. The centurion's faith exceeded the faith of Israel. Thus many from outside Judaism would share the fellowship of Israel's faithful people while unbelieving Jews would be cast into darkness. These points could be used to show the importance of faith in the divine authority of Jesus.

Since Matthew and Luke largely agree on the dialogue but differ on the setting of the story, it appears that each writer supplied the narrative framework and that Matthew's simpler report is nearer the actual situation. The centurion deals directly with Jesus, beseeching him for his "boy" who may be either son or servant, and who lay in distressing paralysis. In humility and unusual confidence the centurion suggests, on the analogy of his own soldiers, that Jesus had power to command the healing with a spoken word. His utter assurance makes Jesus marvel and he receives as his reward the cure of the boy at that hour and a commendation that exalts his faith which is the apex of his virtues which include humanity, generosity, humility and wise courteous co-operation. Luke does not name the deadly disease of the slave but he contrasts effectively the tribute of the elders, "He is worthy," with the soldier's disclaimer, "I am not worthy." He omits any word or action of Jesus about the healing as he directs attention of the multitude to faith. The forecast about foreigners who would come first in the Kingdom he places as part of a rebuke which Jesus gave to unreceptive Jewish villagers while on his way to Jerusalem. This is a setting for the saying entirely different from Matthew.

This section has set forth the power of Jesus to cast out demons, to dispel fever, to win Peter as a disciple, to cleanse the leper and to cure paralysis. The summaries indicate a great range of control over demons and disease. Surging crowds came and were amazed. Each story contains actions and words of Jesus which show authority over evils which beset mankind. Each story teaches by living example the astounding benefits people receive through him. Each story had helpful lessons which rise from events in the past but which convey like benefits to the reader. Each story requires separate study to determine its history and its religious truth. The gospel writers regard the events as actual and real but they do not stop there. They see in the events a relationship between God, Jesus and man which they intend to share with the reader. Competent historians must judge, as far as possible, about the actuality of the events and they do not always agree, owing to differing presuppositions. They have no yardsticks for complete measurement of Jesus. "Of the reality and phenomena of faith healings in their general character no historical critic today will entertain any serious doubt." [19] Any reader can discern in these stories a religious life, mysterious yet accessible, which is as open to him as to the first believers. For the health of body and mind of the present reader there are the marvelous unfolding resources of science and also the age-old but inexhaustible power of the Good News.

[19] B. W. Bacon, *The Gospel of Matthew* (New York, 1930), 392.

21

First Conflicts

Mt. 9:1–17, 27–34, 10:1–4, 12:1–50; Mk. 2:1–28, 3:1–12, 20–35; Lk. 5:27–39, 6:1–11, 11:14–32, 8:19–21 (52–54, 56, 57, 69–71, 85–89)

THE POPULARITY of Jesus as a teacher and a healer soon aroused opposition from scribes and Pharisees. Mark presents a cycle of five conflict stories in which Jesus faces adverse criticism about forgiveness, eating with sinners, fasting and Sabbath observance. These controversies display the opponents, their grounds for opposition and the victories of Jesus which result in a decision to destroy him. Matthew and Luke arrange these stories according to their plans which scatter them differently from Mark. These stories show that Jesus did not teach in generalized statements but in living situations where he made decisions about actual cases.

The cure of paralysis is a double miracle since forgiveness of sins is added to a physical change. It is possible to see the story as originally two separate accounts of healing but it is rather a single conflict about Jesus which has been modified to meet conflicts when Christians faced Jews. Mark describes the event in Capernaum where Jesus was preaching "at home" evidently with Peter. The crowds filled the house and the doorway. The "word" which Jesus preached soon acquired the technical meaning of the gospel. Luke mentions not only the teaching but the presence of Pharisees and scribes from all over Palestine and that Jesus had power from God to heal. It is characteristic of Luke to stress healing. Matthew reduces the narrative but keeps the dialogue in which all three writers agree remarkably. Four men carrying a paralytic upon a small mattress interrupted the preaching. They went up an outside staircase which led to the flat roof which in Palestine serves as another room during the half-year drought. They unroofed a place to lower their friend before Jesus. Luke thinks of tiles rather than of the common clay-and-branches roof.

When Jesus surprised everyone by his declaration of forgiveness for the paralytic, he faced an immediate charge of blasphemy and met it by the claim that the Son of Man had authority to forgive sins and to cure the paralysis of the man who obeyed his command to rise, pick up his pallet and go home. Amazement seized the people who glorified God at this strange sight. Luke writes that the man also glorified God while Matthew reports the people were afraid. He credits God with the gift of such authority to men as shown in Jesus.

This is one of the stories about Jesus which occasions most discussion because of: (1) the unusual aspects of the miracle; (2) the relationship of illness and sin; (3) the meaning of "Son of Man." In view of the faith of the paralytic Jesus declared the man's sins forgiven without a confession or sign of repentance or a requirement of any kind to make good for evil-doing. He did not say, "I forgive your sins," though he declared the Son of Man had such authority. To the scribes and the Pharisees this forgiveness appeared as blasphemy since it usurped God's authority and contained no stipulations about repentance. It made forgiveness appear too free from moral requirements. The cure came without sanctions. Jesus acted for the welfare of the mind before he dealt with his body. How far Jesus shared the belief that sin caused calamities can scarcely be known from the evidence. His words to the paralytic lifted the bar of sin and set him free to receive healing. He said the Son of Man had authority on earth to forgive sin though in Jewish thought even the Messiah was not expected to forgive sins. The proof of this inner change was established by an outward change as the paralytic walked. A deed exceeded a declaration. He did not clarify the meaning of the term, Son of Man, but the early church used this saying to verify the important belief that forgiveness of sins and healing were mediated through Jesus who was believed to be the Son of Man.

The relationship of illness and sin arouses endless discussions. Disease was caused by sin as the friends of Job argued or it was attributed to Satan or to demons. "Healing and forgiveness of sin are inseparable in the teaching both of the synagogue and the early church." [1] "The prayer of faith shall save him who is sick and the Lord shall raise him up and if he have committed sins, it shall be forgiven him" (Jas. 5:15). "A sick man does not recover from his sickness until all his sins are forgiven him as it is written [Ps. 103:3] 'who forgiveth all thy iniquities who healeth all thy diseases'" (Nedarim 41a).

Unusual aspects of this story appear at several points. The breaking up of the roof shows the perseverance of the friends but ignores any

---

[1] Bacon, *The Gospel of Matthew*, 391.

damage to property. Jesus saw their faith and also into the thoughts of foes. He called the paralytic "Son," a term to express intimate concern but one he does not use elsewhere. Matthew adds a word of encouragement to the "son" but Luke uses the ordinary term "man." The scribes question in their hearts but Jesus could perceive their ideas. Luke puts these thoughts into audible speech and shifts to a question of the identity of Jesus whereas in Mark the scribes ask why Jesus had spoken. Jesus declined to work miracles when challenged by the devil and the Pharisees (Mt. 4:7; Mk. 8:12). Yet here is a story with no parallel except one in Luke (7:47) in which a miracle proves authority to forgive sins. It is possible that the dialogue (Mk. 2:5-10) originated in the early church which believed that Jesus had been authenticated by miracles. The alternative to this theory is that the dialogue is an essential part of the conflict which Jesus faced when he related forgiveness to healing. This is the view of the gospel writers.

"The use of the phrase 'the Son of Man' in the Gospels is of extraordinary difficulty." [2] The literature on this term is interminable.[3] Several meanings will be distinguished and then the use of the term by Jesus and by the Gospels considered. (1) "Son of Man" is a literal translation, a Hebrew expression which may simply mean the man or an individual man or humanity as marked off from angels or animals. The parallelism of Hebrew poetry in which the second line repeats the meaning of the first makes clear this usage. "What is man, that thou art mindful of him? And the son of man, that thou visitest him?" (Ps. 8:4). Ezekiel is often addressed by the Lord as Son of Man (2:1). (2) In Daniel "a son of man" is applied collectively and descriptively to the "saints of the Most High" or Israel. Their glorious future is contrasted with the heathen empires symbolized by beasts (7:13). (3) In Enoch the Son of Man is a supernatural

[2] G. F. Moore, *Judaism* (Cambridge, 1927), II, 335.

[3] R. H. Charles, *Book of Enoch* (Oxford, 1912), 306–9; E. F. Scott, *The Kingdom and the Messiah* (Edinburgh, 1921), 175–208; B. W. Bacon, "The Son of Man in the Usage of Jesus," *Jour. Bib. Lit.* XLI (1922), 143–82; C. G. Montefiore, *Synoptic Gospels* (London, 1927), I, 64–80; Jackson and Lake, *The Beginnings of Christianity,* I, 368–84; T. W. Manson, *The Teaching of Jesus* (Cambridge, 1931), 211–36; R. Otto, *The Kingdom of God and the Son of Man* (London, 1938), 159–261; A. T. Cadoux, *Theology of Jesus* (London, 1940), 179–213; P. Parker, "The Meaning of Son of Man," *Jour. Bib. Lit.* LX (1941), 151–57; Bowman, *The Intention of Jesus,* 119–53; W. H. Curtis, *Jesus Christ, the Teacher* (London, 1943), 127–57; J. Y. Campbell, "Origin and Meaning of the Term Son of Man," *Jour. Theol. Stud.* XLVIII (1947), 145–53; G. S. Duncan, *Jesus, Son of Man* (London, 1947), 135–53; C. C. McCown, "Jesus, Son of Man," *Jour. of Religion* XXVIII (1948), 1–12; M. Dibelius, *Jesus* (Philadelphia, 1949), 88–102; Taylor, *The Names of Jesus,* 25–35.

being, a Messiah probably, chosen before creation, whose power will uphold the righteous, bring light to the Gentiles and judge the wicked from his throne of glory (48:2-10; 62:5-14). (4) In the Synoptics Son of Man appears sixty-nine times, always on the lips of Jesus. It is a synonym for "I"; it is equivalent to man; it is used almost exclusively in the last days of Jesus in reference to the sufferings and the death of Jesus and to the idea that he or some mysterious celestial being will come again. The mists hang low over its exact meaning in many places. (5) It was soon dropped out of Christian use since it appears not at all in the epistles of the New Testament which greatly popularized the use of "Christ," a term Jesus avoided. It seems probable that Jesus used Son of Man because its multiple meanings best suited his purposes. The term revealed and concealed; it was many sided and elastic; it carried the thought of a common humanity which might deeply love and suffer and it shared either a Messianic or a non-Messianic significance; it was associated with the people of God; and it looked to an exalted future when God's goals would be gained. It is too simple to say that the title exhibited the humanity of Jesus or veiled the mysterious Man coming on the clouds of heaven. This self-designation of Jesus is a mold into which he poured his manifold relationships to man and God. It was the phrase most favored by Jesus himself but it was only one in the long list of names his followers used as they taxed their vocabulary to label one who exceeded all labels. The term aroused no concern among its hearers at its first appearance and it may be understood in the story of the paralytic to claim that man could forgive sins on earth but more probably that Jesus could forgive sins.

The call of Levi introduces the next conflict which concerns Jesus' dinner with sinners. Mark alone provides the setting by the sea with crowds gathered to hear Jesus teach. The tax collector, known to Mark and Luke as Levi, is called Matthew, one of the later twelve disciples (Mt. 10:3), whose Gospel bears his name. Mark names his father, Alphaeus, and gives no indication that he knew that Levi was also Matthew. Levi worked at a tollhouse near the sea border of Herod's domain. His business involved contacts with Gentiles which a pious Jew avoided. Since the collection of taxes was farmed out for certain times and amounts, the publican made as much as he could. His profits lay in the difference between his tax exactions and the amount he paid to Herod. While he gained money, he also reaped ill will for his possible frequent graft. He was known as a sinner or robber. Moreover, he was in an irreligious business because taxes in the Holy Land were regarded as the Lord's peculiar property. That Jesus called a tax collector as a disciple shows a remarkable interest beyond any ordinary Pharisee who would not seek sinners. Jesus invited a follower from a despised group and by his initiative opened a new field of religious interest in people who would not or could not keep all the separatist requirements of the Pharisee. Sinners were those ignorant masses who did not know the Law. They used unclean clothes or food or dishes and failed to consecrate their meals with prayer. They violated moral standards. They were sometimes known as "people of the land" and were accursed (John 7:49). Such people could only contaminate others yet Jesus mingled freely with them.

Levi responded at once to the call of Jesus. Luke emphasizes his complete response as he left all and prepared a great reception for Jesus which resulted in a complaint against his disciples who ate and drank with publicans and sinners. Matthew and Mark show that the protest is against Jesus as the latter mentions the sinners four times in a brief story. The reply came not from disciples but from Jesus that his mission was not to those who are righteous but to the neediest. His answer may contain a touch of irony. Luke makes clear that his call was not simply to a meal but to repentance while in Matthew he urged the Pharisees to study Hosea (6:6) who had set forth God's call for kindness above offerings. This pivots on Jesus' call to sinners but it contains the picture of Jesus in free association with a low-grade class from which he even called a follower in the face of objection by top-grade religious leaders.

The third conflict concerns fasting for which three word pictures of a wedding, a garment and wine illustrate the answers. The questioners in Mark are indefinite people; in Matthew they are disciples of John and in Luke scribes and Pharisees. They ask why Jesus' disciples do not fast when disciples of John and of the Pharisees do fast. Fasting was not stressed in the Law, apart from the Day of Atonement. It was used to avert national calamity like war or drought and in individual mourning or repentance. The Pharisee fasted twice a week, traditionally Thursday and Monday, the days when Moses went up and came down from Mount Sinai at receipt of the Ten Commandments. But these fasts were not written laws. They were voluntary and regarded as acceptable to God. Judaism was not an ascetic religion. God created the good world not for man's denial but for his enjoyment.

A time will come for fasting but the present was no fit time for disciples to fast. Jesus depicted the present time as a wedding when fasting was out of the question. It is time for the new since no one successfully patches an old shrunken garment with a new unshrunken cloth nor puts new wine into old inelastic wineskins which could not stand the pressure of fermentation. Luke widens the teaching with a parable of newness. He pictures an absurd situation where a man tears a piece from a new garment which cannot match an old one. He adds a saying about those who prefer old to new wine which recognizes that some people take no stock in new opportunities. This rejection of fasting for the present and the mixture of new and old illustrates some of the radical thought of Jesus. In the Sermon on the Mount he said that his disciples would fast and that his mission was to fulfill the old Law but these sayings look in another direction. There is a time for joy and feasting even though sorrows lie in the future. There is a new life which must have its own importance. Jesus made a fresh beginning that led men to see his coming as a new creation. The old was soon seen as Judaism and the new was the preaching and the presence of Jesus which could not continue united within the older forms of faith. His words about the taking of the bridegroom were remembered with an added significance when they were read as a forecast of later tragic events. His figurative language aroused no question at the time he spoke. When Mark wrote, the crucifixion was history and he notes a fast for "that day" while Luke writes "those days." Jesus may have felt his doom early in his work but the first plain mention of it privately to his disciples was incredible to them (Mk. 8:32). Fasting was soon established in the church. "You must fast on Wednesday and Friday" (Didache 8:1). Yet Jesus set up no rule though his reference to future fasting provided evidence for the practice.

In accordance with his topical arrangement Matthew presents a cycle of ten mighty works in chapters eight and nine which illustrate the power of Jesus to heal, his authority and the importance of faith. Among these are two brief miracles, found only in Matthew. Since there are similar accounts later in Matthew (20:30; 12:22), it is possible that these are double reports of the same events. Matthew has a favorite interest in prophecy. These stories fulfill the glowing hopes of the prophet who foretold the glorious age when the eyes of the blind would open and the ears of the deaf would be unstopped (Isa. 35:5; 32:3; 29:18). The two blind men hail Jesus with the Messianic title, "Son of David." [4] This title is not a popular one in the Gospels.

[4] G. Dalman, *Words of Jesus* (Edinburgh, 1902), 316–24.

Neither Jesus nor his disciples used it. Matthew uses it nine times which is more than the combined total, eight, in the other Gospels. But it was a title for the Messiah which was based on the idea of a son descended from the family of David (Isa. 11:1; 9:6) though its first use as a title is late in the second century B.C. (Pss. of Sol. 17:28). The blind men may have repeated a rumor which was not taken seriously by those who heard it but more probably this early mention reflects Matthew's confident belief in Jesus as a Messiah of Davidic descent as his genealogy shows. There was a national, political and royal coloring to the name, Son of David, which was far from the ideal of Jesus. The question of Jesus, the answer of the men, the assurance "according to your faith" and the coming of sight show that faith is the pivot on which sight returns and that this is Matthew's main point. The disregard of the stern charge for silence is a typical result since faith that brought open eyes was news too good to be quieted.

Two conflicts concern Sabbath observance. There was the written commandment to keep the Sabbath holy and there were oral commandments, "the tradition of the elders," which gave strict and detailed directions about the kinds of labor forbidden on the Sabbath. These oral laws were held by the Pharisees to be binding. Food was prepared the day before the Sabbath which was holy because God rested on the seventh day after the creation of the world (Ex. 20:11) and because working Hebrews needed rest and to remember that God freed them from their slave labor in Egypt (Dt. 5:14-15). The old law required that anyone who worked on the Sabbath should be put to death (Exod. 31:14) but how much it was enforced in the days of Jesus is uncertain.

As they passed through a field on the Sabbath, the disciples of Jesus plucked heads of grain for food. This was permitted by hand but not by sickle (Dt. 23:25). But to reap grain on the Sabbath was considered forbidden labor unless life were at stake. In Mark and Matthew the Pharisees question Jesus about his disciples' violation of the Sabbath but in Luke the disciples not only reap the grain but thresh it in their hands and the Pharisees attack them. Jesus defends them first with a question from the scripture about the Hebrew hero, David, who with his men ate holy bread, the twelve loaves placed each Sabbath on a table before the Lord (Lev. 24:5-9) which only the priests could eat. David was hungry and his need justified breaking the law of the showbread. Since Ahimelech is named as priest in the story (I Sam. 21:1-7) and Mark by mistake or by another tradition wrote "Abiathar," son of Ahimelech, as the priest, Matthew and Luke omit Abiathar. The second defense by Jesus is in Mark only and is also known in early Talmudic teaching. "Both he and the Rabbis use and cite the maxim 'The Sabbath was made for you, you were not made for the Sabbath' but only Jesus drives the maxim home." [5] This saying appears in the Rabbis later than Jesus and it seems not to have relieved the irksome Sabbath rules. "Jesus differed fundamentally from the Pharisees in that he asserted the general right to abrogate the Sabbath law for man's ordinary convenience while the Rabbis limited the license to cases of danger of life." [6] Man or the Son of Man in Mark is master even of the Sabbath. Matthew adds another illustration which states that the priests work in the Temple on the Sabbath without guilt and he quotes Hosea's words (6:6) which show that the Lord desires mercy more than ritual requirements. This is not a good parallel to the action of the disciples but it proves that as the Temple is not subject to rules of Sabbath work so "something" greater (the Son of Man) is also free to serve man and God. Matthew and Luke both understand the Son of Man to be Jesus as lord of the Sabbath and they omit Mark's saying which puts man in that position as lord. Jesus worked not to do away with the Sabbath but for an observance which aided men to use the day to do good. He gained enemies when he established freedom to help the needy as a true remembrance of the holy day.

The fifth conflict came in a synagogue when scribes and Pharisees watched Jesus to see if he would heal on the Sabbath. They questioned him in order to file a charge against him. Jewish persecutions were not based on ideas held contrary to authority but on actions which breached the law. Jesus did not face heresy hunters but men like the Herodians whom the Pharisees invited in counsel. The Herodians are unknown but are probably influential, political followers of Herod Antipas who had killed John the Baptist and who was rumored later to wish to kill Jesus (Lk. 13:31).[7] In Mark Jesus requested the man who had a withered hand to stand forth while he asked the Pharisees a question which they could but did not answer. "Is it lawful on the Sabbath to do good or harm, to save life or to kill?" Angered and grieved at their hard hearts, Jesus told the man to stretch out his hand. He obeyed and found it normal. Any diag-

---

[5] C. G. Montefiore, *Rabbinic Literature and Gospel Teachings* (London, 1930), 244.

[6] Abrahams, *Studies in Pharisaism and the Gospels*, I, 128–35.

[7] H. H. Rowley, "The Herodians in the Gospels," *Jour. Theol. Stud.* XLI (1940), 14–27.

nosis of the condition of the arm is impossible for lack of evidence. Luke states that it was the right hand and Jerome quotes the Gospel to the Hebrews in which the man informs Jesus that he was a mason and entreated aid so that he might not beg for food in shame.[8] Matthew introduces another question by Jesus as he cites to the Pharisees the humane custom which allowed merciful work to be done on the Sabbath such as lifting a sheep out of a pit. Luke uses this question in the cure of the man who had dropsy (14:5). Such actions for similar human aid were subjects of debate. In Matthew Jesus exclaims about the relative value of a man and a sheep. Matthew and Luke omit Mark's reference to the anger of Jesus lest it be misinterpreted. Jesus kept the Sabbath but he held that human need preceded oral laws and eventually his resurrection changed the holy day from the seventh to the first day of the week.

Mark has a comprehensive summary which unites the general situation with important details. Jesus and his disciples withdrew from the synagogue to the seaside where great crowds from every direction came to him and he healed many. This popular success stands in contrast to the deadly opposition of the religious leaders. Two details stand out. A little boat, probably Peter's (Lk. 5:3), had to be kept ready if necessary to escape the pressure of crowds. The people with unclean spirits recognized him, fell down and declared him to be the Son of God. But Jesus strictly silenced this Messianic recognition. This follows Mark's familiar thought that Jesus was truly the Messiah but this was a secret which Jesus kept till near the end of his life. Matthew mentions the withdrawal and the crowds and their general healing but these are the people charged not to make him known. Matthew sees these events as a fulfillment of the prophecy of Isaiah (42:1-4) whose wonderful Servant originally was Israel but whose ideals were accepted by Jesus and later proclaimed by his followers as a forecast of Jesus. The Lord had a chosen beloved Servant or Son who in quietness and gentleness brought justice to the people of the earth. When Matthew wrote his Gospel, Jesus had long since been accepted as the one sent from God who combined the influential ideals of the Servant of the Lord, the Davidic Messiah and the coming Son of Man.

It was to be expected that the foes of Jesus would oppose him but Mark tells of friends who heard of crowds so great that eating was impossible. Hence they went to seize him since it was said (or they said) he was beside himself. They thought that he was out of his

---

[8] James, *Apocryphal New Testament*, 4, 5.

mind as the situation showed. It was aberration rather than insanity. Those who went to get him can never be identified beyond dispute. Since the Greek lacks a noun, the reference may be taken to be his people, friends, relatives or family. It is generally accepted that these are the same as his family whose arrival is described a few verses later. The crowds were so great his folks could not reach him and when they asked for him, his reply might have encouraged their concern. "Who are my mother and my brothers?" His answer, as he looked on those seated around, affirms kinship with those who do God's will. Luke enlarges the answer with the thought about anyone who hears the word of God and does it while Matthew exalts Jesus' relationship to his disciples to whom he gestures with a hand as he claims them in kinship. This unusual saying which places action for God above any physical ties to a family is one of those piercing insights which relate Jesus to all who do God's will first, no matter the cost. The brevity of these reports starts innumerable guesses about Jesus and his family. Their plans for him on this visit, their attitude toward him and his new disturbing work, their absence from discipleship during his public ministry occasion speculation. Zealous attempts to eliminate his mother from concern for his conduct show reverence for her but give no real information. In the Synoptic account of Jesus' public life the failure of his family to share his work for the Kingdom or his last days in Jerusalem only makes more poignant the revealing words of Jesus that a prophet has no honor among kinsfolk and in his own home (Mk. 6:4).

The two parts of the story of the visit of Jesus' relatives are divided by the darkest charge made against Jesus in his Galilean days. Who made the charge is variously stated. In Mark, which appears most historical, the scribes from Jerusalem, following the rumor about the mind of Jesus, are responsible. In Matthew the Pharisees by their charge upset a hope among the people that Jesus might be the Messianic Son of David after he healed a dumb and blind demoniac. In Luke some of the multitude make the charge after Jesus cast out a demon so a dumb man could speak. Jesus has power over demons hence he is possessed by Beelzebub who is prince of demons. He controls demons by league with their head. Guesses, now made about Beelzebub, indicate that he might be a Fly-lord or a Filth-lord, or a False-lord. The answer of Jesus is clear-cut as he called the scribes to him and gave two illustrations to show that the charge was ridiculous. Division in a kingdom or a house or in Satan's household means their end. A strong man's house cannot be robbed until the man is bound. Matthew and Luke add a further defensive question by Jesus. By whom did the exorcists among his accusers cast out demons? They did work similar to the exorcisms of Jesus and their work can constitute judgment. The final point in rebuttal by Jesus is that the rule of God has come since he cast out demons, not by Beelzebub, but by the finger of God. In such actions which Jesus credits to the Spirit of God the Kingdom established its presence.

Then Jesus changed from defense to offense. In this battle against evil there could be no neutrality. One must take sides. One had to be for him or against him. In one of his warnings which begins with truly (Amen), indicating emphasis on a new thought, he gave his most serious answer to the most serious charge. Forgiveness will be granted to all sins and blasphemies except one, speaking against the Holy Spirit. Matthew doubles this warning about the Spirit and Luke puts it in a charge to the disciples (12:10) and agrees with Matthew that anyone who speaks against the Son of Man can find forgiveness. In Mark it is the sons of men who will be forgiven. The unforgivable sin as Mark explains it was to charge Jesus with an unclean spirit. This sin is to slander him by the claim that his goodness from God is evil. Blasphemy "against the Holy Spirit" has grown centuries-old thickets of explanation in which lost sin-stricken people have wandered. The idea of no forgiveness was known in scripture when the sin of Eli's descendants was not to be expiated forever (I Sam. 3:14) or the one who despised the word of the Lord should be utterly cut off (Num. 15:31). Amid the endless debates Jewish teachers felt a man was beyond the pale of pardon if he profaned God's name or caused many to sin or denied the truth of the Law or of Judaism.[9] But with God all things are possible (Mk. 10:27) and he will abundantly pardon the wicked who forsakes his ways (Isa. 55:7). The Rabbis retained the hypothetically unforgivable sin but found excuses and extenuations for the unforgiven sinner so he was in fact forgiven.[10] When Jesus found his work against demons was credited to them, he declared it a terrible sin. As long as men made evil their good, they could not be forgiven. Forgiveness comes to those who seek it. He emphasized the sin but omitted the punishment. This sin is a perversion of man's highest capacity to distinguish good from evil. Luke does not stress the eternal aspects of unforgiven sin like Matthew and Mark. Jesus elsewhere taught an unlimited forgiveness (Mt. 18:22). Man can deny God's presence and never know his for-

[9] Abrahams, op. cit., I, 142–49.
[10] Montefiore, op. cit., 248.

giveness. From the standpoint of God it is important for man not to assume that he knows the limits of God's wisdom, power, justice or mercy.

It is possible to relieve Jesus of this stern saying because: (1) it does not accord with his other teachings about forgiveness; (2) he taught little about the Holy Spirit in the Synoptics though there is much about the Spirit after his death and historically the Pharisees could not be expected to distinguish between him and the Holy Spirit; (3) unforgiven sin was the answer the apostolic church made when they defended themselves and their work against severe Jewish attacks. This change of source for the saying still does not unlock its difficult meanings.

In Matthew Jesus gave a condemnation of the Pharisees like John the Baptist's as he named them a brood of vipers who as evil men could not speak good. A good or a bad man speaks according to his inner life of good or evil. When the day of judgment comes, men must give an account for every purposeless word. There was a popular idea that the words of a man would be the standard by which he was judged by God. This warning about idle talk as an index of destiny can be balanced by the parable of the last judgment where deeds of mercy determine a man's future (Mt. 25:46).

22

The Sermon on the Mount

Mt. 5–7; Lk. 6:20–49, 11:1–4, 9–13, 33–36, 12:22–34, 13:22–30, 16:16–18 (18–44, 73–78, 146, 165, 176)

THE MOST famous collection of Jesus' teachings is the Sermon on the Mount which appears in Matthew with parallels in Luke's Sermon on the Plain and in other different settings.[1] The origin, the sources, the setting, the people addressed and especially the meaning require consideration. It is traditional to see the Sermon as literally delivered at one time by Jesus. This is not impossible since it is shorter than most sermons. But the parallels and the differences between Matthew and Luke and Matthew's well-known method of topical grouping and the custom of Jesus to teach briefly rather than in longer discourses lead to the conclusion that both Matthew and Luke have collected teachings originally separate. This does not mean that they created the content of the sermons which are the essential teachings of Jesus. Most of their material comes from Q but which one stands nearer the original Q is debatable though Luke is usually favored. The Sermon on the Mount draws on the rich store of teachings in the scriptures and in late Judaism. The teaching is not novel but original in its intensity, selectivity and purity. The ore of Judaism is stamped with the seal of the creative heart and mind of Jesus. There are parallels to Jesus' teachings in Jewish writings but there is no parallel to the Sermon as a whole.

Matthew places the Sermon early in his Gospel after a general summary of the activities of Jesus because he regards Jesus as a second Moses who had divine teaching for his disciples. Luke places his Sermon after a considerable ministry of Jesus in Galilee following a

[1] C. Gore, *The Sermon on the Mount* (London, 1899); J. Moffatt, "The Sermon on the Mount," *Enc. Bib.* (London, 1907), IV, cols. 4375–91; C. W. Votaw, "The Sermon on the Mount," *Hast. Bib Dict.* (New York, 1912), V, 1–45; H. Marriott, *The Sermon on the Mount* (London, 1925); T. W. Manson in *Mission and Message of Jesus* (New York, 1938), 338–54, 442–71; republished, *The Sayings of Jesus* (London, 1949), 46–62, 150–79; M. Dibelius, *The Sermon on the Mount* (New York, 1940), E. T. Thompson, *The Sermon on the Mount* (Richmond, 1946); H. Windisch, *The Meaning of the Sermon on the Mount* (Philadelphia, 1951); A. M. Hunter, *Design for Life* (London, 1953), 9–116.

night of prayer on a mountain when he chose his twelve disciples. For the setting of the Sermon Matthew states that Jesus went up into a mountain while in Luke he spoke at a level place. There is no geographical identification of the site but traditions arose which put it on the west side of the lake. Both writers state that the words were addressed to disciples though crowds fill the background. Matthew's Sermon is four times as long as Luke's though they have similar beginnings with Beatitudes and they end with a parable of two builders. Luke scatters elsewhere in his Gospel a number of teachings found in Matthew's Sermon. He has four woes to balance four Beatitudes. Matthew omits the woes because he collects them later. Matthew has eight Beatitudes for his opening section though he uses the "blessed" nine times. Luke omits most of the discussions about Jesus and the Mosaic Law which interested Matthew's Jewish Christian readers but not Luke's Gentiles. The order of the topics is generally the same in each writer. Luke is briefer but Matthew's arrangement is a superb form for teaching.

Jesus as a teacher was following an important line of predecessors in Judaism. Moses taught the Torah to Israel, the prophets proclaimed that men must learn and apply the purposes of God, the wisemen perfected their thought as in the Proverbs, the scribes transmitted and interpreted the scriptures with great learning. All this teaching was based on the belief that the knowledge and the will of God were revealed to men and that men could know and use God's words in their lives. The words of the Lord required trust in him, obedience to his commands and righteous conduct toward men. There was no line drawn between religion and ethics. Jesus taught in stories or parables, vivid and lifelike and in brief illustrative sentences, maxims and precepts which are poetic in form and practical in purpose. Therefore they stand out at times as commands and prohibitions. Some teachings are reported in brief narratives and often in dialogue. The Sermon contains but one parable at its close. For all its fame it is not a complete summary of Jesus' teachings but it contains many of his outstanding truths about God and his requirements for man.

While the Sermon appears as a somewhat formal address in a particular place, it illustrates also the informal, popular, outdoors aspect of Jesus' teachings. He spoke in synagogues but also in homes, or by the sea or along the road. He used all the usual experiences of life as an area for discovery of God. He looked at life as it was lived and at the world as he faced it and saw some wonderful meanings that he could share with other men. His hearers might be many, few or one. His main aim was not teaching though "Teacher" is one of his more popular titles in spite of the fact that he had no professional training as a rabbi or priest. He proclaimed the rule of God and used teaching to make clear the kind of living which was required of the children of God. "Not as a teacher expounding a thesis is he to be understood but as the prophet of the kingdom and the shepherd of lost sheep." [2] Yet men treasure his sayings beyond pearls and rightly regard him as one of the world's greatest teachers since his words vitalize powerfully the mind and the action of those who know and heed them. But while the interest of his followers was aroused by his words, they were even more concerned about who he was and what he did for people because God had anointed him and was with him to enable men to be rid of their sins (Acts 10:38).

The Sermon has generated an endless interest in its meanings. Can its startling requirements be met? What is its essential character? Matthew as the editor meant it "to be a code of law for individual and social control of Christian behavior" and the question arises as to the extent that Jesus thought of himself as a legislator like Moses.[3] The Sermon may be taken as an outline of the ideal Christian life to be studied with the Church in its indispensable role as guide.[4] It may be regarded as a platform of principles for individual ethical conduct or for social reform but not as literal legislation. It is a "Life of a Disciple of Jesus." [5] It may be declared emergency ethics, as Schweitzer famously claimed, which can be followed by a few only in the brief span before the end of the age. In that case it is not intended for long-range application though it remains as invaluable inspiration. It may be held to be a paradoxical symbol intended not as possible commands to be kept but as sharp-thorned examples of God's demands for a new "being" as Dibelius thought. It may be considered theologically as a counsel of despair, too high for men and therefore they must find in the cross of Christ a saving correlation to the Sermon as Kittel argued and Windisch has criticized.[6] It may be rejected as impossible in practice as compared with Rabbinic ethics as Klausner judged the Sermon.[7]

[2] B. H. Branscomb, *The Teachings of Jesus* (Nashville, 1931), 97.
[3] S. M. Gilmour, "Interpreting the Sermon on the Mount," *Croz. Quart.*, 24 (1947), 47–56.
[4] J. Lebreton, *Life and Teaching of Jesus Our Lord* (London, 1835), I, 125–99.
[5] Ropes, *The Synoptic Gospels*, 48.
[6] Windisch, *op. cit.*, 44–61.
[7] J. Klausner, *Jesus of Nazareth* (New York, 1925), 381–97.

Three questions face the one who would know the Sermon: (1) What did Jesus mean? (2) What did Matthew and Luke mean? (3) What does the Sermon mean to the reader and his time? Windisch has wisely shown that historian and theologian must work separately and with mutual criticism for there is danger that either alone will be lopsided. Men criticize the Sermon but even more the Sermon criticizes men. It must be read in the light of the rest of Jesus' teachings and of the rest of the New Testament and with the aid of the Old Testament and of later church experience and thought and with the most responsive moral and religious insight that men can summon. It must be read with the recognition that the Sermon presents manifold claims of Jesus which are radical, final and decisive for anyone who would follow him. Windisch rightly holds that the Sermon is not a theological unity but contains four interests each of which is conceived as absolute. (1) There is a rule of God which is also fellowship with him. When a man recognizes this Kingdom, he must decide about his response to it which determines God's decision or judgment about his present and future existence. (2) There is a true Law which man must obey wholeheartedly and which rightly relates him to God and man. (3) There is the radical goodness of God manifested in nature and to his followers who in prayer and service must be perfect as God is. (4) There is Jesus who stands as teacher, legislator, prophet, witness and judge of the community of those who hear and do his words.

The Sermon can be divided into three main parts: (1) the happiness and the influence of Jesus' disciples in the Kingdom (5:1–16); (2) examples of the Law of Moses as fulfilled in the true law of Jesus (5:17–6:18); (3) various warnings and commandments about right and wrong conduct (6:19–7:29). The first two sections are clearly defined topics, the third is a miscellany in which Matthew has gathered a fund of valuable teachings. Each main section has numerous well-marked subdivisions.

Jesus as a true son of Israel taught that God's will was to be done on earth. In the Beatitudes he begins with promises of happiness for disciples who possess certain qualities here and in the future. A logical line can be drawn between being and doing though in life the two are interwoven. The Beatitudes portray a certain kind of character. What the prophets preached and the Psalmist sang is now received and will be realized. The Beatitudes are bounded by the Kingdom. They begin with the poor in spirit and end with the persecuted and both already share the Kingdom, the greatest good and goal which God gives man. The other six kinds of people are sure of future blessings though these distinctions about present and future possession of the Kingdom may not have been indicated in the Aramaic which Jesus spoke.

The gifts of God come to those who possess attitudes which are avenues for happiness. Jesus names those who are blessed or happy and indicates what they receive. The "poor" had a double meaning in Jewish literature. They were the literal poor who lacked worldly goods but they were also pious ones who faithfully believed in God and obeyed his commandments. Often their only help was in God (Ps. 72:2, 4; Isa. 61:1; Pss. of Sol. 10:7). By contrast "the rich" was often a synonym for the wicked. The poor in spirit are those who know their need. They who seek will find. Their happiness is not due to poverty but because they now possess a place in the realm of God. Luke's Beatitudes reflect physical hardships as his use of "the poor" indicates but Matthew widens the meanings to include moral qualities. Luke's Beatitudes are thought to be an earlier form because they are simpler and because they are addressed directly to disciples in the second person. In Matthew Jesus speaks in the third person about the blessed ones except for the latter part of his blessing upon the persecuted.

Those who mourn may lament their sins or share the sorrows of their people (Isa. 61:2-3) or weep over the woes which precede the Messiah's coming but they are blessed because their consolation is assured. Their encouragement will come. No one escapes the way of sorrow whether from sin, suffering or death and the gracious words of Jesus relieve a deep human need. Paul, in this world, knew the comfort of God through Christ whose comfort could be shared with anyone afflicted (II Cor. 1:3-6). John saw in the world to come that God would wipe away all tears when sorrow and pain are passed away (Rev. 21:4). In Luke there is a sharp contrast between loud weeping and merry laughter to replace weeping when the Lord brought his people back from captivity. "They that sow in tears shall reap in joy" (Ps. 126:5). The future will reverse the present.

The third Beatitude is a quotation from a Psalm (37:11). These humble-minded disciples are similar to those in the first Beatitude who were the poor who were often oppressed. The meek submit to God, as the Old Testament indicates, rather than to man and by his promise shall receive the earth which God will purge of its evil. Pride has pitfalls and humility its rich rewards. In the past the promise of inheritance of the earth was associated with the covenant which gave

the promised land of Canaan to the Lord's people. Its literal fulfillment is not the point nor is the promise only about a new earth in
a future age. But the meek shall receive from God the rewards which
their gentleness creates in this world. Their way leads to life.

It was a common hope that when God's rule was established it
would be like a great feast. In Matthew the desire for righteousness
like the driving needs of hunger and thirst will be amply met by the
Lord who filled the hungry soul with good (Ps. 107:9). Righteousness was the goal of life because it meant character and conduct like
God's. As food and drink satisfy necessities so will those who seek
God and righteousness find a full response to their needs. In Luke
the hungry shall be filled. The lack of food was too well-known to
many people who heard Jesus and his promise renewed hope that
their famine would turn into a feast. Matthew and Luke together
illustrate the truth that food for mind and body are essential for man
to live as God intended. "If there is no meal there is no Torah, if
there is no Torah there is no meal." [8]

To the merciful the Lord had shown himself merciful (Ps. 18:25).
Happy are those whose kindness reaches out to all without limit for
as they give they will receive whether from God or man. Like calls
forth like. God's mercy was especially associated with his forgiveness
and there will be plenteous forgiveness for those who are forgiving.
Micah (6:8) had taught that one of God's great requirements was to
love mercy. The Psalmist delighted in the mercy of the Lord. This
regard for mercy springs from God who grants it to man who gives
it to his neighbor. Jesus assures his followers that loving-kindness, as
mercy might be translated, is a prominent part of one's relationship
to others. He does not use the word "love" in the Beatitudes but
mercy is the attitude nearest to it.

To see God is figurative language for the highest good that man
could seek. Man might see him here or in the world to come. God's
presence dwelt in the Holy of Holies in the Temple but also in the
humble and contrite heart. To appear before God was to see him.
There were defilements of body and sins of the soul which barred
men from the sight of God. Jesus said nothing of ritual outer washings. Like the Psalmist he knew that the man who could stand in
the holy place before God had clean hands and a pure heart (Ps.
24:4) but he promised happiness to anyone anywhere who had an
inner unalloyed devotion whose reward would be the vision of God.
The presence of God satisfied the Psalmist when he awoke with his

[8] R. T. Herford, *Pirke Aboth* 3:21 (New York, 1945), 91.

likeness (Ps. 17:15). The "heart" meant the whole inner life whose sincerity and purity enabled God to be known. The sight of God has always defied words but this inner vision whether seen by Isaiah, Paul, Aquinas or Pascal brings the seer more than he can say.

The blessing on peacemakers has often been selected as the one Beatitude which required something to be done though the others imply righteous activity. The ideal of peace which should have no end was part of the prophetic program (Isa. 9:7). Under the heel of Rome this ideal was not popular in seething Galilee but Jesus proclaimed the kinship of peacemakers to God. But peacemaking was not only resistance to war, however important, it was overcoming enmity with good will wherever needed. All kinds of peace depend upon peacemakers. The best thought of God called him a God of peace. When Hebrews met, their greeting was "Peace." Hillel said, "Be of the disciples of Aaron, one that loves peace, that loves mankind and brings them nigh to Torah." [9] "Sons of God" was a familiar phrase to describe a favored position of the Hebrew people with God. He had chosen and aided them in endless ways (Hos. 1:10). Jesus called peacemakers "sons of God" as an honor for their efforts. Sons of God were to inherit his Kingdom.

Joy in persecution appears impossible. It is one of the paradoxes that portray the originality of Jesus. This Beatitude appears in two forms in Matthew, one of which from Q is shared with Luke. The longer form of this Beatitude reflects both the anticipation of Jesus and the actual opposition his disciples faced when the Gospels were written. Persecution would come falsely on account of Jesus or the Son of Man as Luke shows. There is a threefold statement of persecution in Matthew and a fourfold form in Luke who adds that disciples would endure hatred, ostracism and slander. A name and its object were one in reality. When Christians rejoicingly suffered dishonor for the name (Acts 5:41), they meant Jesus. "Your name" in the Beatitude is a reference to the fact that disciples of Jesus were identified in a sense with him. Their joy is justified because they would receive compensation already prepared in the future and because they stood in the line of great prophets who had also suffered. Rewards for unjust persecution are to be expected from a God of justice. There is no expectation that men should be good without reward.

Against these four Beatitudes Luke sets in exact order four woes upon the rich, the full, the laughing and the unduly popular. These

[9] Herford, *op. cit.,* 31.

are warnings of pity, not cursing, for those whose rewards do not include the Kingdom. These woes do not describe disciples but such men as may have been in the multitude or Luke may have gathered the sayings from other circumstances. These woes do not describe all such men absolutely. They say "also" for those mistakenly content in wealth, satisfaction and reputation so that they seek no part in the reign of God. The "rich" was often a synonym for the wicked as the poor stood for the pious. Such rich had been paid in full but only by money. "They lack nothing but the things that really matter." [10] Stuffed and laughing in an abundant present they will lose and weep in the future. Flattery is no blessing for the false prophets had accepted it to their destruction.

After the impressive introduction of the Beatitudes which show the character and the results for disciples who enter the Kingdom of Heaven the influence of these disciples stands forth like salt and light. Salt with water, fire and iron was listed among the necessities for the life of man (Ecclus. 39:26). It was known for seasoning and for preservative effect. Salt evaporated from Dead Sea water was not pure salt and because of tax it was sometimes adulterated; hence it could lose its savor and become useless. Luke makes clear that such salt had no value even for the customary use of manure. Then he adds the warning to use one's ears. Light for illumination, for guidance and for life is a favorite figure in religion. The Lord was an everlasting light. His servant was sent as a light to the Gentiles to the ends of the earth (Isa. 49:6). Jesus is the light of the world (John 8:12). With the Law a Jew was a light to those in darkness (Rom. 2:19) and the Philippian Christians were lights in the world (Phil. 2:15). Rabbinical writers described Adam, Israel, the Temple or Jerusalem each as a light to the world.[11] Jesus saw his disciples, not as hidden but shining like a light to all in the house, that is, within their own group and before men outside. In a different context in Luke the light is for all who enter which may mean converts. The good deeds expected of disciples will lead men not to praise them but their Father in heaven, a term characteristic of Matthew, who presents God in this Jewish phrase both in relation to his fellow believers and to Jesus.

For the Evangelists the scriptures constituted an authoritative word of God yet they found a further authority of God in Jesus. There was an old and a new revelation, both authentic. The relationship of the scriptures and Jesus was a constant problem.[12] It was part of the

---

[10] Manson, *The Sayings of Jesus,* 49.

[11] Abrahams, *Studies in Pharisaism and the Gospels* II, 15–16.

[12] B. H. Branscomb, *Jesus and the Law of Moses* (New York, 1930), 72–122.

larger issue as to whether Judaism and Christianity would remain one or separate. Eventually the church kept the Jewish scriptures but accepted Jesus as the primary word of God. Mark and Luke wrote for Gentile readers who felt free from the ceremonial requirements of the Mosaic Law. While Matthew, writing for Jewish Christians, believed that the whole Law hung upon the love of God and of neighbor and that Jesus was a second Moses, yet he had received traditions which affirmed the entire validity of the scriptures. Hence his Gospel looks back as well as forward with Jesus. In the Sermon Matthew devotes a large section to the words of Jesus concerning the Law and its practices.

As an introduction Jesus states that his mission is to fulfill the scriptures. They must be kept to the last dot yet in order to enter the Kingdom his disciples must exceed the scribes and the Pharisees in righteousness. "To fulfill" means: (1) to complete in detail; (2) to cause to stand and confirm the true meaning. Matthew took the first meaning and set forth Jesus with a blanket endorsement of every detail in the Law until the end of time. Yet the Pharisees attempted to keep every written detail in addition to many oral regulations. Jesus stands nearer the second meaning. In view of the illustrations which follow in the Sermon as well as other uses of the scriptures by Jesus and in view of the new requirements for disciples to exceed the scribal minutiae it may be held that Jesus believed the scriptures to be the word of God but that he confirmed their true meanings and fully expressed them with some of his own independent insights. "All that Jesus taught about the will of God is only a commentary on the legislation revealed in the Old Testament." "Christianity means to reverence Jesus as Lord and to render active obedience to the will of God which he proclaimed." [13]

The first illustration of fulfillment of the law deals with murder and it sets an antithetic pattern for the five which follow. The older Law of Moses was heard when read in home and synagogue. "But I say to you" repeated for each illustration shows that Jesus required some added or new understanding and action for his disciples. His commands are positive rather than negative. "Thou shalt not kill" faced the penalty of a life for a life (Ex. 21:12; Dt. 17:8-9). But the antecedents of the action must be prevented. Anger, insult, scorn of a fellow man, who is a brother, lead to punishment. The climactic action comes when Jesus says one cannot rightly approach God in the Temple until all is right with a brother. But the step to recon-

[13] Windisch, *op. cit.,* 68, 71.

ciliation must be taken not by the offender only but by the one offended against. Likewise in facing someone with a court claim a move must be made to settle the trouble in friendliness lest the worse result of prison should come. Both the brother and the accuser appear as aggressors but their enmity can be cleared by the right attitude. Luke also has this court case in words spoken by Jesus to the multitudes in a more suitable context than Matthew. Jesus asks a significant question that assumes that his listeners within themselves possess the capacity to judge the right. This moral sovereignty in the common man has immense importance.

In the second illustration concerning adultery Jesus discusses not the penalty which was death (Lev. 20:10) but the prevention of the adultery of the eyes which are aids to action. The lustful imagination is morally guilty as it plans the actual offense. An ounce of moral prevention is better than a pound of regretful cure. Thoughts are deeper than deeds. The eye and the right hand are normal and natural members of the body but even sight and contact can lead to hell. Evil sexual impulses must be controlled lest the entire body be lost. God can punish when man cannot. Hell or Gehenna was the name for the final place of punishment of the wicked. It took its name from the valley of Hinnom which ran steeply south of Jerusalem where both the fires of the city rubbish and of the long past terrible child sacrifices in the worship of the god Moloch had made the place abhorrent. Both Matthew (18:8-9) and Mark (9:43-49) later repeat these sayings about the hand and the eye which can cause one to stumble.

The third antithesis between Moses and Jesus concerning divorce is more amply discussed in all three Synoptics later when in Judea Jesus responds to a Pharisaic inquiry. In this brief statement in the Sermon Jesus shows his independence of the religion of his day especially in its attitude toward women. In three ways he was their champion: he is strict about divorce; he associated freely with women, contrary to custom; he was merciful toward them. "He makes a new departure of enormous significance and importance. If he had done no more than this he might justly be regarded as one of the great teachers of the world." [14] Divorce in Jesus' day was in the hands of the husband alone (Dt. 24:1-4). A wife was sent away with the document of divorce. The sufficient cause of divorce was debated by the strict school of Shammai which restricted it to unchastity and by the liberal school of Hillel which allowed divorce for "any unseemly thing" which

[14] Montefiore, *Rabbinic Literature and Gospel Teachings*, 47.

might be a burned breakfast. The Sermon sides with Shammai since there is an exceptive clause which allows divorce for fornication. Since Mark and Luke elsewhere report the words of Jesus with no exception for divorce it is often believed that the clause is an addition by Matthew or a step down from the ideal in the practice of the early church. The alternative on the one hand is to hold that Jesus gave two differing commands on this vital subject or on the other hand to ignore or explain away the plain permission of divorce for unchastity. The Sermon sets forth the results of divorce which lead to adultery in fact though a couple may legally be married. Adultery was more serious than divorce and a man who divorced his wife and married another was responsible for adultery.

The fourth illustration which is a quotation about swearing combines two elements which are given exactly as found in the scriptures (Lev. 19:12; Num. 30:2). The two points are that the truth must be told and that a vow to the Lord must be kept. Jesus departs from rabbinical teachings which never forbade swearing though they condemned useless swearing. It was customary to avoid the use of God's sacred name in oaths as Jesus indicated when he named four kinds of oaths as forbidden. Such oaths infer a reference to God and men must not swear because they revere God. This is the ultimate reason for no oaths. There is the further point that simple honesty stands in its own right when backed by a truthteller whose "yes" or "no" needs no swearing.

The fifth and sixth examples are found also in Luke's sermon. Eye for eye, tooth for tooth were famous statements of even-handed justice of the law which advanced beyond the earlier uneven demands of revenge exceeding injury (Ex. 21:24; Dt. 19:21; Lev. 24:19). Jesus required his disciples to live above tit for tat. They must forbear more than insist on their rights. In the admonition not to resist evil it is not possible to determine whether an evil person or thing is meant. To resist meant active hostility. The turned cheek, the given cloak, the second mile, gifts to the beggar and the borrower are examples of overcoming evil with good at the individual level. They are not literal rules, nor a platform for all public justice, nor are they to be read as an indifference to evildoers or approval of evil actions. They are religious commands. Back of each response is the good will of the disciple of Jesus which is to be greater than the evil. This radical teaching of Jesus stuns or startles or inspires the hearer. It involves a willingness to endure injury rather than inflict it. It roots out retaliation and revenge. Jesus did not discard the law of justice but commands a response that replaces hostility with helpfulness. Luke's examples are briefer and placed significantly in the section on love of enemies. They describe a theft of the outer cloak, used both for clothing and bedding, instead of a lawsuit over a coat and the offender is a robber rather than a borrower. He does not mention the military custom which allowed Roman soldiers to requisition a Jew as baggage carrier for a mile or more but he does place the Golden Rule in the midst of these commands about retaliation.

The final contrast concerns love of enemies. The command to love one's neighbor was well known (Lev. 19:18) but a command for hatred of one's enemies was not in the Law. It was an inference from the experiences in Israel's history when oppressed by its conquerors and especially when they hated Israel's God. The cursing Psalms illustrate plenty of prayers for vengeance on adversaries. Jesus widened the circle of love so that it included not only the neighbor who was customarily identified as a fellow Jew, not only the resident alien who was accepted as a proselyte but one's enemies without reserve. For the enemy there was not to be hate nor negative restraint from injury nor silent embittered endurance but a powerful good will, which Luke who omits the contrast with the Law portrays in fourfold form as love, doing good, blessing and prayer. This is not love as an emotion so much as ethical action. It is a regard for foes which is ready to help them to do good. It is eager aid without limit, not fondness for one's enemy. Luke also has longer questions with a poetic refrain about what credit can be given for love or service or a loan if an equal response is required. The purpose of love is the good done, not an expected return. Love exceeds expectation, since it is no fifty-fifty affair. Even tax collectors and Gentiles, the despised classes, do as much on the basis of an equal exchange. The one sufficient reason for love of enemies is that it is the way to be sons of God, the most high Father. It is God's way to send sun and rain on both the evil and the good. Luke has no mention of the good and the just but he shows God's kindness reaches to the ingrate and the selfish. The goal according to Luke is to be like God in mercy since his loving-kindness endures forever. The goal according to Matthew in one of the greatest sayings in a great Sermon is for disciples to be perfect as God is perfect. This seemingly impossible ideal shows how strongly Jesus expected men to act according to religious principles. God's children must be like him. Thus Jesus fulfilled some Old Testament commands. "Thou shalt be perfect with the Lord thy God" (Dt. 18:13). "Be ye holy; for I am holy" (Lev. 11:44). Noah and Job were called perfect which meant without moral blemishes or wholehearted toward God. "In the Old Testament the epithet 'merciful' is given to God, hardly ever to man; and the epithet 'perfect' to man never to God." [15] The perfection of love in Matthew in contrast to Luke's perfection in mercy remains unparalleled in Jewish literature.[16] It is the glowing, commanding confidence of Jesus that God's abounding love falls like sun and rain on all and that men as they meet one another must live this godlike life.

Matthew next sets forth in Jesus' teachings three of the best-known acts of Jewish piety. He assumes his disciples will give alms, pray and fast. For each of these acts he first warns about what is not to be done and then sets forth directions about what must be done and finally promises God's reward. These duties are not for ostentation which has no reward from God. Many obligations for public and private charity appear often in Jewish writings.[17] God's law required care for the poor. Men like Job and Tobit exemplified the importance of almsgiving. It was recognized that charity should not be for praise to the giver nor debasement of the receiver. The hypocrites were not identified by name with the Pharisees but such givers were known. They are those who pervert God's commands about charity. Trumpets were blown for certain devotions but Jesus used them as metaphors for publicity in synagogue and street when gifts were made. The true almsgiver provides privately for the needy. His motive is to help unselfishly. He acts not to win God's reward but God who sees all will reward him because he knows his inner attitude. There is no explanation in the Sermon about when or how or where God's recognition will be given but its coming is assured.

No section of the Sermon is so well known as Jesus' teaching about prayer.[18] It lays open his life with God. He warns first of the public prayer of the hypocrites in synagogue and street who want men to see them at their devotions. He adds the faulty example of the Gentiles whose prayers are needlessly long. Then he positively directs prayer to be made in private and God's rewards will come. God knows men's needs prior to prayer. This teaching found in Matthew alone is expanded into the Lord's Prayer which Luke gives in

---

[15] Manson, in *Mission and Message of Jesus*, 347.
[16] Abrahams, *op. cit.*, II, 151.
[17] G. F. Moore, *Judaism*, II, 162–79.
[18] C. Gore, *Prayer and the Lord's Prayer* (London, 1898, 1945); J. W. Thirtle, *The Lord's Prayer* (London, 1915); E. F. Morison, *The Lord's Prayer* (London, 1917); Abrahams, *op. cit.*, II, 94–108; Moore, *op. cit.*, II, 212–38; E. Underhill, *Abba* (London, 1940); E. F. Tittle, *The Lord's Prayer* (New York, 1942); E. F. Scott, *The Lord's Prayer* (New York, 1951).

briefer form but places after a prayer of Jesus had led his disciples to ask him to teach them to pray as John had taught his disciples. Rabbis also gave set prayers to their disciples. But the fact that Matthew and Luke have different forms of prayer suggests that Jesus gave no ritual pattern for exact repetition. Luke uses "Father" only and omits petitions about the will of God and about deliverance from evil. Judaism had its incomparable book of prayers, the Psalms, as well as its stories of heroes of prayer which nourished Jesus. It had fixed public and private prayers. In the synagogues men constantly used the Shema (Hear), the Kaddish (Holy) and the Shemoneh Esreh (Eighteen Benedictions) which are now easily found in the Authorized Jewish Prayerbook. Jesus was a man of prayer, like Jeremiah, as his actions and parables prove. He taught his disciples to come to God in secret, in brief, insistent, simple, sincere and reverent words of faith. His prayer breathes the faith of his people since it echoes familiar Jewish thoughts except the condition about forgiveness. But his prayer is profoundly original in its full embodiment of older prayers, in its unity, in its universality, in its choice of fundamental points for prayer and in its perfect confidence in God's dealings with man. As the poet puts common words into uncommon beauty so Jesus united the faith of his fathers with his own for a perfect prayer.

The perfection of the Paternoster, the title known from long centuries of Latin usage, is dulled by familiarity. To understand and appreciate this prayer is of highest importance. Its brevity is baffling and its living mystery clothed in ancient scriptural words but by its magical phrases men mount to God. There is an invocation to God followed by two main parts in impressive parallelism. In the invocation God is trusted as Father but the plural pronoun relates him to all men though his dwelling place is above men and earth. The first part of the prayer contains three petitions all of which converge in God: "thy name," "thy Kingdom," "thy will." The second part turns upon three of man's needs: "give us," "forgive us," "lead us." Here is ascending recognition of God and descending aid from God. To hallow the name of God is to hold God himself as holy in reverent obedience, worship and service. "The hallowing name as the supreme principle and motive of moral conduct in Judaism" meant to live so that men would see and say that the God of Israel was the true God.[19] His name is also sanctified by the Lord himself as for example when he took Israel from captivity and other nations saw the Lord made holy in Israel (Ezek. 36:23). So the disciples of Jesus are to

---

[19] Moore, *op. cit.*, II, 103.

pray that God be acknowledged and reverenced both by his own mighty deeds to help men and by their own good works and lives. The coming of God's rule is the great theme of Jesus' preaching. All his purposes find focus in the phrase "the Kingdom of Heaven." This part of the prayer looks to the future for its complete fulfillment but God is a living ruler who has purposes which affect men in their obedience and trust on earth. The Kingdom is in God's hands, its hour and power he disposes and Jesus' prayer is a hope for its full coming as he makes man's first obligation in life to seek it (Mt. 6:33). God's will alone is perfect and all-inclusive. His will stands over lesser wills of believers whose use of this prayer acknowledges God's will above their own. It is a will not to be put into words alone but into action. Its area is on earth lest men regard it as remote from them but its goal is perfection on earth as in heaven. Its content defies definition for man is not God but man must trust and obey its eternal design which he can discern as far as he does it.

The prayer is both to God and for man. Like the angels on Jacob's ladder, the prayer first moves up and then down. For man to do God's will there are needs to be met in their lives. Jesus recognized these needs for food, forgiveness and freedom from evil. Bread is not a luxury but a necessity. The word translated "daily" is rare and its meaning uncertain. The sages had prayed for needful bread (Prov. 30:8). The word may mean continual or for the morrow. The disciples lived as the common people who possessed no economic reserves. Since the earth was the Lord's, Jesus taught them to pray for everyday food. But they also had needs for minds freed from the weight of wrongs done or unmet obligations. Probably "sins" or "debts" both translate the same Aramaic word, used by Jesus, which meant either one or the punishment due to them. In Matthew God's forgiveness is conditioned to the fact that man has forgiven. Luke maintains the present tense that as a man is willing to forgive so he prays for divine forgiveness. Jesus moved beyond the usual teaching of his time (Ecclus. 28:2). He placed responsibility for restoration on the one who was hurt by the sin according to Matthew but in Mark (11:25) the responsibility lies with the offender. This was the usual Jewish requirement. In Jesus' thought God's mercy must be shared. Forgiveness is inevitably linked both to God and to one's fellow sinners.

Temptation has two meanings: a test or an incitement to evil. Temptation was a word used for persecution when loyalty to God was at stake. The disciples must pray for guidance not into trials

which life often presents but for God to set them free from the power
of evil. This is the one petition which has a negative which required
further positive explanation. The form of this request is troublesome
because it appears that God may lead into temptation. But God
tempts no man to evil (Jas. 1:13) though as Creator and Ruler the
world is under his final direction. The petition may be understood
as a request that disciples not be led into trials beyond endurance.
Deliverance from evil may refer to an evil one like the devil or to
man who defies God or possibly to deliverance from evil impulse.
The closing doxology, well known in Protestant though not in Roman Catholic usage, is not in Matthew or Luke and is not a part of
the original prayer but it appears as early as the second century in
the Didache and in many manuscripts though not in the earliest
ones. It is a liturgical addition which smooths an abrupt ending. It
is adapted from the book of Chronicles (I, 29:11).

Fasting is expected of disciples but not with gloomy faces nor with
disfigurement caused by no washing or by ashes used on the head
instead of the usual perfumed oil. Such outward signs marked the
hypocrite. Jewish fasting was both public and private. In public fasts
like the Day of Atonement or for some national calamity like a
drought trumpets summoned all to fast.[20] The extent of private fasts
cannot be accurately fixed in the time of Jesus. Fasting was part of
penitence or might accompany sacrifice or as preparation for beginning some new religious venture or to gain a message from God. The
prophetic ideal stressed repentance and charity as a fast acceptable to
God (Isa. 58:3-9). This ideal set the need to help the needy above
any fasting. The hypocrite missed the mark by a public display. Jesus
commanded his disciples to fast for God's sight alone from whom
reward would come.

The third main section of the Sermon has no central theme but
consists of a variety of counsels. (1) There is entire trust in God,
man's true treasure, who dispels anxiety. This completes the sixth
chapter of Matthew. Then follow smaller sections: (2) on judging;
(3) on care for the holy; (4) on God's gifts; (5) on the Golden
Rule; (6) on the two ways; (7) on the test of good deeds illustrated
by the two builders. Only about one half of Luke's parallels are placed
in his sermon, the rest are scattered in various settings.

Jesus taught a boundless trust in God by an effective parallelism
which showed negatively the folly of trust in earthly treasure like a
blind man in the service of mammon. Positively true trust is a heav-

---

[20] Moore, *op. cit.*, II, 55-69; Abrahams, *op. cit.*, I, 121-28.

enly treasure like seeing men who serve only God. The heart feels secure in its treasures but earthly ones suffer damage or theft. Treasures in heaven are related to God but Jesus did not ruin his figures of speech with prosaic definitions. In Luke the purses that are permanent are obtained by almsgiving in view of the coming Son of Man and the end of this age. Generosity provided heavenly wealth in Jewish thought. The bountiful eye shall be blessed (Prov. 22:9). A donor gained treasure for the day of necessity (Tob. 4:8). Jesus promised treasure in heaven to a would-be follower if he gave his goods to the poor and followed him (Mk. 10:21). One needs to see this truth as the normal eye provides sight or perhaps as a generous eye shares wealth. But one can be blind to it and in Matthew there is an exclamation over such darkness while in Luke there is the warning lest such light become darkness. In Luke there is a repetition about the body full of light (11:35) which leads Creed to think this is an "intolerably platitudinous meaning." [21] There can be no divided loyalty in trust of God. Mammon is an Aramaic word for wealth of any material kind. Man cannot be a slave of riches and of God. A choice must be made. Luke sets this teaching for disciples as one of the lessons from the parable of the shrewd steward.

Anxiety about things must never eclipse God and his rule which remains the all-inclusive search. In lines of poetic beauty Jesus summons his followers to a life free from corroding care. Food, drink, clothing have their place but that place is to aid life not to worry it. God has an infinite care even for the birds which he feeds and for wild flowers which breathe out beauty. The birds are not cited for idleness but for freedom from anxiety. "They are not always worrying that the supply of worms may run out yet they do not expect the worms to crawl down their beaks." [22] The flowers flourish because God decks them but for a day before they go for fuel in the small ovens of Galilean cooks. If these little things exist under God's helping hand how much more does his care reach to man. God knows men need the things of everyday life but the disciples must seek God first. Then he provides the lesser things within the larger circle of entire trust in him. Moreover, anxiety is useless since it adds nothing to the length of life or stature. Anxiety about things imitates Gentiles, or nations of the world as Luke calls them, who do not put their trust in God. Matthew adds that one day at a time is enough. Let the morrow worry over its own situation. The trouble

---

[21] *Gospel according to St. Luke*, 164.
[22] H. K. Luce, *Gospel according to St. Luke* (Cambridge, 1933), 231.

of today is sufficient. This is a proverbial phrase. "The attempt to square it with Jesus' faith in the fatherly providence of God may be regarded as wasted labor." [23]

Jesus sees men as brothers who deserve brotherly treatment. Like produces like. One gets what one gives. A pitiless man is no help. To accept his judgments is to "fall into his faults." [24] Luke's fuller and more poetic passage abounds in illustrations. Judgment belongs to God. Not only must there be restraint in judgment and in condemnation of others but there must be forgiveness and giving of full measure in dealing with others. Yet this command about judgment does not mean lack of moral choice or inability to decide about good and evil. Jesus holds his followers responsible for their conduct. Correction begins with oneself lest one fall into the ludicrous position which sees a splinter in a brother's eye and ignores a big plank in one's own eye. The attitude in judging others and in improving oneself determines the way God deals out judgment.

The command to safeguard holy things from dogs and pearls from pigs sounds foreign to much of the teaching and the action of Jesus. Dogs were scavengers and pigs unclean for Jews. The passage stands apart in Matthew only. It has been read as symbolic caution by Jesus to save his disciples from needless exposure of their faith to evil men. Warnings about the liability of attacks on disciples are well known. It has been regarded as a primitive church direction about "holy things for holy people" as in the Didache (9:5) when the Eucharist was limited to baptized people.

Jesus urged his disciples to expect good gifts from God. They came in response to asking, seeking and knocking in the presence of God. In three rhetorical questions he affirms the certainty of God's gifts which rest on his goodness as a heavenly Father. Even an earthly father will meet his son's requests for food. The description of parents as evil is to be understood to mean they are less good than God but they do right for children. How much more God will meet requests. The lack of a comparative in Semitic speech results in statements which sound like direct contradictions when a comparison is meant. Luke places this famous promise of Jesus after a story of persistent prayer. A father will not give his son a serpent which bites or a scorpion which stings when he wants a fish or an egg. God will not fail to give the Holy Spirit. References to the Holy Spirit are notably scanty in the Synoptics, therefore the promise in Matthew of

[23] Manson, in *Mission and Message of Jesus*, 465.
[24] B. S. Easton, *Gospel according to St. Luke* (New York, 1926), 90–91.

"good things from God" is taken as nearer the original teaching of
Jesus. Also in Matthew the son asks for bread not an egg and his
father does not hand him a stone. Fish and bread were the common
Galilean food.

The Golden Rule is a new name for an old principle which had
received a negative statement in Judaism before the days of Jesus.
The thought appears in Tobit (4:15) and Hillel taught, "What thou
hatest do to no man," and added that this is the whole law (Shabb.
31a). The Rule stands in Matthew as Jesus gave it in positive form
as a general summary of activities for disciples. When Jesus says it
is the law and the prophets, he meant that it sums up God's commands in the scriptures. Its universal scope covers all things done. In
Luke the Rule is in the midst of Jesus' teaching about love of enemies. The greatness of this Rule is matched only by its difficulty. It
is a principle rather than a rule, in spite of its popular name. Its simplicity pierces the dark complexities of human relations with a clear
guiding light. Its meaning for followers of Jesus must be correlated
with the rest of his teachings. Its truth, creatively and imaginatively
applied in all situations, can move men to a mutual good beyond all
calculation.

The Sermon points out two ways, the one easy, the other hard.
The first leads to death, the second to life. That life is like a way or
a road was so widely taught in Jewish and Christian writings that it
became a commonplace. But its importance remains in the fact that
the rule for right living in Judaism (Halachah) was named from the
verb meaning "to walk" and in Christianity the Didache and the
Epistle of Barnabas both undertook to give complete warnings and
directions about the two ways. In earlier days Moses was reported to
have set forth the same choice for Israel (Dt. 30:15, 19). Jeremiah
repeated the fateful word of the Lord, "I set before you the way of
life and the way of death" (Jer. 21:8). Jesus said the wide gate is entered easily, without effort by many, but its destination is destruction
or "death with no hope of life as opposed to life with no fear of
death." [25] The narrow gate for the few who find it by decisive effort
admits to life here and in the world to come. Life is attained by determined effort not from thought or emotion. The contrast lies between struggling and strolling. The proverbial difficulty of all things
excellent still provides an outcome that is utterly important. Luke
differs considerably as he tells of a questioner who asked Jesus if few
would share in the coming Kingdom. This question was often de-

[25] Manson, *op. cit.*, 467.

bated in Judaism with varying answers. The answer of Jesus is that
entrance is not by two gates opening into two roads but by one door
opening into a house where many would seek entrance. Men must
strive to enter. God's purpose is not to exclude them but their own
shortcomings can debar them.

The final sections of the Sermon cluster around tests of deeds done.
The importance of Jesus' teachings is found in their results in the
lives of his disciples. Fruits, fit or unfit to eat, are the reliable evidence about a tree. Good fruits come from their own stock. Matthew
uses this test as a means to distinguish false spokesmen for God who
look like sheep but devour like wolves. In Luke Jesus points out that
good and evil within man produce their corresponding results and
adds that speech pours out of the abundance of the inner life. It is
proof in action of a person's character.

The next test looks to the future. The Kingdom had its day of
coming. The day of the Lord meant a decisive future action when
the power of God would be shown. He would judge men and establish his Kingdom in righteousness. In Matthew this expectation is to
be realized in the near future. The fate of some disciples who
preached, expelled demons and did wonders in the name of Jesus will
be complete rejection as lawless men. This is the future judgment on
false prophets who do not follow the new law of the Sermon. This
stress on doing God's will rather than making false claims on the
authority of Jesus combines what Jesus taught with the later experience of the church which had to ban impostors who hid words and
actions with a Christian cloak. Luke has a piercing question of Jesus.
To call him "Lord" is a respectful acceptance but to put his words
into practice is the essential point. Why did his hearers not do it?
There is a rejection of those who had eaten with Jesus and heard his
teaching which Luke places in another setting as he pictures a narrow door closed by a houseowner as he sends away the workers of
unrighteousness. These severe words of rejection, quoted from a
Psalm (6:8), are applied to those who associated with Jesus yet acted
lawlessly.

The last test is told in a rhythmical story of two house builders. In
Matthew the setting is especially natural to Palestine where flash
floods of winter rains and storms test the two houses, one built on
rock, the other on sand. The man who builds on the rock of hearing
and doing the words of Jesus has a house of life which endures in
crisis. The house on sand built on hearing without doing falls. Luke
closes his sermon with a similar parable but begins with those who

come to Jesus and also hear and do his words. The builders are not described as wise and foolish but as one who built on a rock foundation and one who laid no foundation for his house which then fell not in a tempest but in a flood. Matthew ends the Sermon with the first use of his formula by which he closes each of his five great discourses. Jesus had "finished" his teachings. The crowds wondered at the words of Jesus for his teaching had the authority of his own unique insight into God's will rather than the repetition of a past message from God.

The commandments of the Lord were not too hard for Israel for they were in their hearts (Dt. 30:11-14) nor does Jesus think his commands to do God's will are impossible for his disciples who were to be like God. "The idea of impracticality appears absolutely senseless within the framework of a correct understanding of the Sermon on the Mount. Jesus gives new commandments, principles and examples for the true expression of piety, not only to convince men of the correctness of his prescriptions but also to bring about full obedience among men to God." [26] His Sermon contains laws to be observed, wise sayings to be put into conduct, prophetic declarations of divine words and some warnings and promises about the Kingdom and the future which God would determine. The Sermon is not the complete teaching of Jesus, it is not a rejection of Judaism, it is not a blueprint for Utopia, it is not a code of ethics, it is not a charter for a church and it is not a theological creed. It is a wonderful collection of the words of Jesus, who believed that he knew God's will and could do it and that men could hear and do the same. This confidence in God and man the followers of Jesus will live to maintain. "Every generation, every Christian thinker has to weigh the words of Jesus, to ponder their substance and to translate them into language current at the time. No undertaking is more serious or more delicate, none is more necessary or more profitable." [27]

[26] Windisch, op. cit., 96.
[27] W. A. Curtis, Jesus Christ the Teacher (Oxford, 1943), 215.

23

Teaching by Parables

Mt. 13:1–52; Mk. 4:1–34; Lk. 8:1–18, 10:23–24, 13:18–21
(84, 90–103)

THERE IS NO place where Jesus and his teachings can be better known than in the stories he told. "His parables were miracles in words and his miracles were parables in deeds." [1] By their variety, beauty and significance his parables place Jesus in a unique position. By their realism, irony and range of characters they portray both the life of Galilee and the mind of Jesus and sometimes the skill of the Gospel writer. "As long as literature shall have any meaning the parables of Jesus will stand as models of sincerity, stories with not a word too much nor a word too little." [2] Their popularity has produced a host of commentators on these entrancing tales. [3]

Three questions need discussion: What are parables? Why did Jesus use them? How are they to be understood? In biblical use a parable is a picture in words which by the use of comparison illustrates some moral or religious lesson. A parable is a "like saying." The usual form for a parable is a story which is true to life which distinguishes it from the fancies of a fable or an allegory. But in the Gospels there are shorter forms like a simile or a metaphor, for example, "Physician, heal thyself" (Lk. 4:23) or "How can Satan cast out Satan?" (Mk. 3:23). There are allegorical explanations of parables like the one about the Sower (Mk. 4:10–20). An allegory is like a parable but it has many lessons, often fantastic, which are based on metaphors whereas a parable is a realistic, simple comparison, based

---

[1] W. A. Scroggie, *A Guide to the Gospels* (London, 1948), 553.

[2] C. Barry, "The Literary and Artistic Beauty of Christ's Parables" *Cath. Bib. Quart.* X (1948), 379.

[3] G. A. Buttrick, *The Parables of Jesus* (New York, 1928); W. H. Robinson, *The Parables of Jesus* (Chicago, 1928); C. J. Cadoux, *The Parables of Jesus* (London, 1931); Manson, *The Teaching of Jesus*, 57–81; C. H. Dodd, *The Parables of the Kingdom* (New York, 1936); W. O. E. Oesterley, *The Gospel Parables* (New York, 1936); H. Martin, *The Parables of the Gospels* (New York, 1937); B. T. D. Smith, *The Parables of the Synoptic Gospels* (New York, 1937); A. E. Barnett, *Understanding the Parables of Our Lord* (New York, 1940); C. W. F. Smith, *The Jesus of the Parables* (Philadelphia, 1948); J. A. Findlay, *Jesus and His Parables* (London, 1950).

on similes. There are no sharp lines of distinction but it is possible to distinguish: (1) a simple simile or metaphor; (2) an extension of them which is sometimes called a similitude; (3) a story which is the parable proper; (4) the allegory. The variety of use results in no agreement on the number of parables in the Gospels. Manson lists sixty-five parables and Robinson fifty-seven.[4] The Old Testament is the source for this wide range of meanings for a parable because the Hebrew word for parable (mashal) with a root meaning of likeness may refer to a riddle, a popular saying, a proverb, a prophetic utterance, an allegory or even to a poetic discourse. The scriptures are too lifelike to fit into any neat literary classification.

Jesus used parables because he inherited a language and a literature which were concrete, pictorial and figurative, a language of senses and a literature of a living people who felt a divine significance in their doings and who expressed these truths not in abstractions but in natural poetic imagery and in human history. Jesus told parables because he was a poetic storyteller who saw everywhere illustrations of the ideals he wished to teach. "He found them ready-made by the Maker of man and nature." [5] He created parables because they portrayed the experiences of himself and his hearers rather than the law of the scribes and he quickened his listeners to realize what God is like and how he expected men to deal with one another. Parables stimulated both thought and action.

To understand the parables it is necessary to think of them as Jesus told them. They mirror the everyday life of Galileans and also the unexpected play of Jesus' mind as he pictured these people. The stories stuck in the memories of his auditors. They repeated and spread these storied teachings of Jesus to new followers and guided them in their faith. Sometimes explanations and general sayings amplified the stories and collections of separate parables were gathered. When the gospel spread beyond Palestine, the parables took on added meanings and applications in the new churches but these changes were comparatively slight and under the guidance of the Spirit. The genius of Jesus sparkles in his parables and few can equal it. When Mark composed his Gospel, he included few parables but Matthew and Luke found and arranged them in large numbers. The disciples did not understand some of the parables. When they asked Jesus about them, they remembered his answers "in a glass darkly." They are the first in an endless line of interpreters. The Church Fathers

4 Manson, *Teaching of Jesus*, 66–68; Robinson, *op. cit.*, 10–12.
5 C. H. Dodd, *op. cit.*, 22.

allegorized the parables so that every point like a crossword puzzle had to be read with imported biblical and theological meanings. Figurative language always has to be figured out. Eventually it was claimed by Jülicher (1888) that Jesus never used allegories and that his parables had to be read historically for one main teaching point. The interpreter of a parable looks at the story as it was told and undertakes to read and enjoy it for its own sake and its own setting in the Gospels. Then the meaning of the story appropriate to its own time and hearers as it was intended by Jesus or by his immediate followers including the Evangelists must be considered. Finally, since parabolic stories can be read in any language or age, these glowing word pictures still creatively excite the imagination to discover their timeless truths and to wonder if the teller of these tales is not himself the great Parable. No interpreter faces a more common error than to make a parable mean what he thinks it ought to mean rather than what it actually teaches. But he must discover its permanent significance for himself as well as for the past.

Matthew arranges seven parables in a single chapter midway through his Gospel. Mark gives a lakeside setting to his three parables about sowing and seeds. Jesus, facing a great crowd, climbed into a boat, seated himself and taught the people many things. In the first parable the seed of the sower fell in four different places and produced four kinds of results. Only the final one was a good harvest. The seeds on a hard road, shallow ground, a thorny place and very fertile soil, for which Galilee was famous, show that the words taught by Jesus and his followers met some unusual responses. The threefold failure is balanced by the threefold success. This point appears plain but the following explanations in Mark present only perplexity. The warning to use one's ears points to the need of understanding. Mark shows Jesus alone with his disciples who ask about parables. In Luke they ask about this particular parable and in Matthew they question why he speaks to the people in parables. The answer in Mark is that the secret of the Kingdom is given to the disciples while in Matthew and Luke they are given to know the secrets of the Kingdom. Everything for outsiders is put in parables so that they may not understand and be forgiven. This answer is shortened and softened in Luke who limits it to this one parable and omits the reference to forgiveness. Matthew changes and enlarges the explanation. Parables are spoken *because* the people do not understand. More will be added to the disciples' understanding by explanation but those who lack their faith will lose what the parable contains.

Thus they are like the people described by the Lord to Isaiah at his call whose hearts and ears and eyes are so unresponsive that their condition forbids their answer to the Lord.

That Jesus told parables to conceal rather than to reveal the truth seems incredible but it was not incredible to Mark. Jesus gave parables for illustration so that the common people could hear him gladly but Mark also thought that parables served to condemn evil people. Explanations divide into two camps: (1) those who hold the words of Jesus (Mk. 4:10–12) to be historical; (2) those who think the words are an early church interpretation. (1) Since the words are historical, so also are Matthew's which prove that Jesus told parables to help people because they did not see and understand. Matthew must be given precedence because the whole mission of Jesus was merciful. In any single passage which is uncertain the context and the whole teaching of the Bible must be used for verification. Mark should be read in the light of Semitic forms of thought which may sound strange to modern ears. His Semitic statement, like Isaiah's prophecy, does not distinguish between cause and result. Since people failed to understand, Jesus was expressing the consequence, not the motive of parables.[6] Moreover it is possible that Jesus had need to guard his message against enemies and stories made attacks more difficult. (2) Those who think Mark gives an explanation later than the life of Jesus, point out that Mark's thought cannot be forced into modern concepts. The Christians of Mark's day felt sharply the differences between themselves and non-Christians, especially when the latter were persecutors, whether Jew or Roman. There were those who were outside and had to be addressed in figurative language for the sake of those inside who had access to all things but had to be protected in their faith. The Kingdom of God was a secret known but to Jesus and his disciples. Mark's language is so unusual as to indicate a development of later thought. Since the Jews as a whole did not accept Jesus, a theological explanation for this hard fact was advanced. God had chosen his followers of Jesus just as he had destined the Israelites to be his people. God's purposes are beyond men. Another possibility is that the translation from Aramaic into Greek has caused the difficulty. Parables must be for those *who* do not understand, not *in order that* they may not understand.[7]

Matthew and Luke give a blessing upon the disciples who have an opportunity that the best and greatest men of the past had hoped

---

[6] G. A. Denzer, *Parables of the Kingdom* (Washington, 1945), 119–72.

[7] Manson, *op. cit.*, 78.

for but had not realized. In Matthew happiness comes to disciples because they see Jesus and hear his parables. This beatitude in Luke follows a prayer of rejoicing by Jesus when seventy disciples reported to Jesus the success of a mission. They are happy because of what they see. Instead of giving his disciples a blessing Jesus asks them if they understand. The number of questions, about fifty, which Jesus asks in Mark reveal him, like Socrates, as a great interrogator. Matthew and Luke turn the reproving questions into positive introductions to the detailed allegorical explanation of the parable of the Sower. This combination of parable and explanation has made the Sower one of the most popular parables. This explanation with the one about the weeds (Mt. 13:36–41) is remarkable because such detailed applications do not appear for other parables. This interpretation of the Sower may be "an illustration of the history of Christian mission-preaching." [8] Its present form shows adaptation to situations faced by Christian teachers though the substance of the ideas came from Jesus. The interpretation by its impressive repetition of the parable and its unraveling of meanings is an effective statement of the possibilities of teaching not only among the first hearers of Jesus but among his followers as they spread his words with varying results. The "word" is most emphasized in Mark who in his sevenfold reference to it illustrates the way the teaching of Jesus is snatched by Satan, dies in rootless lives when persecuted and is smothered by cares, rich delights or desires for other things. But there are good results in those who accept, or, as Matthew puts it, understand the teaching and produce abundant harvests. What Matthew calls the Word of the Kingdom Luke identifies as the Word of God which the devil or trials can cause men not to believe. Luke adds pleasures to the other things which choke the word. But those who hear and retain the teaching in an honest, good heart produce not the varying results noted in Mark but a harvest in patience.

These explanations are followed in Mark with a question and an answer about a lamp. Then follows a warning that nothing can be hid. Therefore, one must hear and heed because one gains more as he gets more. This purpose of parables is opposite to the earlier one which made them open to disciples but blinders to those outside. In Luke the light is for those who enter. This refers to the Kingdom or the church. How one hears (Luke) is different from what one hears (Mark) though both Greek words may come from the same Aramaic word. The promise of more is repeated but the threat of loss is di-

[8] B. T. D. Smith, *op. cit.,* 128.

rected to the one who can be mistaken in what he thinks about care-
lessly.

The parable of the seed growing of itself is in Mark alone. It reflects the farmer in Palestine whose day was reckoned to begin at
sunset. So short a story should make its point without a quibble but
four meanings are argued: (1) the kingdom is like a seed with its
own mysterious vitality from God not man; (2) the kingdom is like
a seed which grows steadily from grain planted to grain grown; (3)
the kingdom is like man's co-operation as he plants seed though he
cannot explain its life; his work is done and then he waits in quiet
patience until the harvest time; (4) the kingdom is like a ripe crop;
the time of reaping is the end of the age. The idea of growth is so
congenial to an age fat and fatuous with the idea of progress that it
is not easy to realize that the kingdom might mean something different to Jesus. "The kingdom he preached did not grow—it comes and
its coming does not depend upon its acceptance by the world but
upon the will of God." [9] The kingdom has a future aspect like the
day of the Lord (Joel 3:13) when the prophet commanded the sickle
to cut down the wicked. This harvest of judgment which haggles
over the identity of the harvester and the time of his coming requires
too much importation into this short story. Jesus did not teach a
kingdom of man and the point of the parable probably lies in the
first suggestion. Perhaps Matthew and Luke omitted it because its
point was not clear to them.

The parable of the weeds is found only in Matthew and its explanation is delayed until two more parables are related. The kingdom
is like a man who sowed wheat but found weeds sowed by an enemy.
These tares are taken to be darnel which resembles wheat. The un-
kind sowing of weeds was known among farmers. To sort out the
growing weeds would be difficult before the harvest time. The owner
let them grow until the harvest showed the taller wheat and the
darker darnel, then the wheat was gathered and the weeds burned.
Jesus may well have thought that God is the final judge of men at the
harvest of their lives and that the separatism of the Pharisees was an
undue effort to judge good and evil men before the issue of their
lives had ripened. When he said the kingdom is like an action with
several aspects he means that the kingdom cannot be pinned down
to one thing. It appears that in this parable the kingdom in this
world has various possibilities which can be properly determined by
the outcome of their growth. Meanwhile an enemy is also in evidence.

[9] *Ibid.*, 120.

The explanation of the weeds is detailed enough to reflect later conditions though given by Matthew in the words of Jesus. The style is stilted and stereotyped. The use of "Son of Man" in two different senses is a reflection of thought about Jesus and the ideas are conventional apocalyptic ones. The allegorical interpretation is an unusual addition found but twice in the parables. The interpretation reflects the difficulties of the first days of the church when the presence of true and false followers of Jesus required some explanation of evil and its relation to the kingdom and the final fate for good and bad men. Strong influences have flowed from this interpretation. Certain phrases recur like refrains which beat into the thought of the hearer. The end of the age signified the belief that there was a transforming change coming when the present age with its dominance of evil would pass away. Existing in both ages the kingdom included sons who had to live with sons of Satan now but eventually the kingdom was to be cleared of all scandals and lawlessness and the righteous would shine like the sun in God's Kingdom. The Son of Man or Christ appears in both ages. At present he sows the sons of the kingdom but in the coming time he will act as a judge whose reaping angels will throw the evildoers into hell. This furnace of fire causes weeping and teeth gnashing which is compared with the bright bliss of the righteous with God. These apocalyptic pictures are among the most difficult for a modern man to estimate justly. Their imagery comes from some Jewish writings which dealt with an unknown future with no clear line between literal and symbolic meanings. Apocalyptic writings constitute a first-century fantastic framework for some important religious ideas about the separation of good and evil and about God's purposes for the future of man. To what extent Jesus shared these pictures and how much his disciples mixed his ideas with theirs as well as how they must be viewed today remain questions under dispute.

Mark's parable of the mustard seed is preceded by one of Jesus' many questions which Luke also repeats: What is the Kingdom like? It is like a tiny mustard seed proverbial for its small size, which grew quickly in fertile Galilean soil to a plant, ten to twelve feet tall, large enough for birds to share its shade and nest in its branches. In Palestine it was a plant of the field rather than of the garden. This herb cannot literally be called a tree though it is like a small one. Matthew and Luke use tree as a metaphor. This parable suggests ideas about the Kingdom: (1) that it grows like the mustard from seed to a great plant; (2) that it is certain to fulfill its destiny; (3)

that its great size contrasts with its small beginnings; (4) that it attracts outsiders. Gradual growth is not the point because the mustard seed grows quickly and this idea is not in accord with Jesus' teachings about the Kingdom. The disciples must maintain hope for the greatness of the Kingdom no matter if they share its tiny origins. Moreover they can expect others to share the Kingdom for the scriptures had similar ideas. Ezekiel had foreseen an ideal restoration when the Lord would plant a goodly cedar in Israel where birds would dwell in its branches and shade (17:22). So the Kingdom would also attract men's attention.

Matthew and Luke have a parable about leaven, or yeast, which is almost a twin to the mustard seed. This story is drawn from women's work of making bread. They had to grind the grain by hand and set the dough with yeast. Three pecks of meal took real labor to prepare for baking. The leaven has been taken to symbolize: (1) that the Kingdom grows; (2) that its coming is sure; (3) that it works unseen; (4) that it affects everyone it touches. Leaven in Jewish thought stood for evil influence since its working was thought to be a bad ferment. No leavened bread was used at Passover (Ex. 12:8). Paul warned his Corinthian Christians concerning fornication among their members, "A little leaven leavens the whole lump" (I Cor. 5:6). Some interpreters think the leaven cannot represent the Kingdom. But Jesus cannot be kept in a strait jacket of tradition. The infectious power of evil was accepted. "Jesus claimed the same power for good." [10] The point of this parable is that the realm of God affects everyone it touches.

Mark ends his list of three parables with the double observation that Jesus spoke the word (gospel) with many such parables, as the people could understand, but he also explained everything privately to the disciples. The first statement shows that he adapted his pictorial method to the needs of his hearers and the second reinforces the earlier difficult idea (4:10–12) that the disciples had an inside track for understanding his teachings. This part may reflect the hard situation in which disciples were sharply set off from other people or it may emphasize the great opportunity which came from the direct teaching of Jesus. Matthew sees that Jesus' use of parables fulfilled the prophet's words. Strictly speaking, his quotation is not from a prophet but from one of the Psalms (78:2) in which the poet reviewed the history of his nation and promised to speak in parables when telling of revelations which reach into the ancient past.

[10] *Ibid.*, 123.

Matthew has twin parables about a hidden treasure and a costly pearl which illustrate the same point that the Kingdom is of great value. A man gives all that he possesses in order to obtain it. In the story of the hidden treasure a man chances upon it while the merchant is seeking for the pearl but both give all they have to get something more valuable. Jesus did not foster dishonesty by telling about the buyer of the field. He illustrated what a man would do to gain a treasure. The main purpose of the parable is to be kept in mind and not every detail of conduct which might include good and bad behavior. Nothing is said about who buried the treasure nor how it was found since the purpose is not to chronicle every fact but to select highlights for teaching that the Kingdom is most valuable to men. Jesus used the familiar facts that hoards of coins were banked in the ground in Palestine and that merchants traveled to the Persian Gulf for pearls.

The final parable in Matthew's chapter is a twin to the one about the weeds. A fisherman's large seine, often worked from two boats, enclosed all kinds of fish, which the men sorted, keeping the good and throwing away the inedible ones or those forbidden by law such as those that had no fins or scales (Lev. 11:10). So the Kingdom was intended to include all men. But an apocalyptic interpretation is added like the one which followed the parable of the weeds. It centers about the end of the world and teaches the final separation of good and bad. The point of the parable which deals with the present purpose of Jesus and Kingdom is preferable to the point of the allegory which looks to an unknown end of the age. When Jesus asked his disciples if they understood all these things, they gave a confident "Yes." Their assurance exceeded their wisdom so Jesus added a wise counsel, found only in Matthew, who himself exemplified this ideal. The Kingdom had its scribes as did the Law and they had to be trained for it and be able to draw out its treasures both new and old. This saying provided a place for the learned man and stressed his competence as he used the new truths of the Gospel and the old truths of Judaism.

24

Concerning Discipleship

Mt. 9:35–11:1; Mk. 3:13–19, 6:6–13, 8:34–39; Lk. 6:1–12, 10:1–22, 12:2–12, 49–56, 14:25–35 (58–63, 72, 109, 123, 139, 140, 160, 171)

JESUS SELECTED a group of men known as the Twelve. He purposed to form a group to live with him as members of God's Kingdom. This is one of his most significant acts since this small number is like a little lake whence a mighty river (the church) takes its beginnings. "This intention of our Lord was as unique as its fruitage has been in the religious history of mankind."[1] This new move by Jesus has three aspects: (1) the appointment of the Twelve; (2) their names; (3) the field, the methods and the results of their work. Mark gives both a setting and a purpose for their selection which is separate from a later commission to begin work (6:7–12). Jesus went to a hillside and summoned his followers who obeyed at once. He then appointed the Twelve. The number indicated the founding of a new Israel of the Righteous Remnant of prophets. This scene parallels the Old Testament situation when the Lord called Moses and his people from Mount Sinai as a new nation with twelve tribes formed of those who escaped the wrath of Pharaoh. So Jesus formed a new group after his foes took counsel to destroy him (Mk. 3:6). The Twelve were chosen for fellowship with Jesus and then for departure to preach and control demons. This meant discipleship when the Twelve learned from Jesus and apostleship when he sent them forth on a mission. There was no ceremony of ordination for the informal group. Luke states that Jesus after a night of prayer chose the Twelve and named them apostles or messengers. Matthew formally lists them by the same title which soon came into use in the early church for the Twelve and for those who had authority from Christ to do missionary work. Mark only once names the disciples as apostles (6:30). They had both power and authority over all demons and to cure diseases. With this commission Matthew agrees but he gives it a different setting. The call and the work are directly connected. The reason for the call is that Jesus saw the people troubled and prostrate like helpless sheep

[1] Bowman, *Intention of Jesus*, 224.

with no helping shepherd (I Kgs. 22:17). Then he told his disciples that few laborers were at hand for the full harvest.

The Twelve are listed by name once each in Mark and Matthew and twice in Luke including Acts 1:13 but John omits this roll. These men, later called saints and glorified by interesting and unreliable legends, are surprisingly unknown in the Gospels. Peter heads all lists and Judas, the traitor, stands always at the bottom. The first four appear enough to give some clues about them but the rest are little more than names and on one of the names the lists do not even agree. Perhaps Judas or Thaddeus had two names which might account for the variation. Simon, Peter, Cephas, the rockman, was like a firm foundation but his stability came after the resurrection. The sons of Zebedee, James and John, were sons of thunder and stories show their driving quick-tempered dispositions (Mk. 9:38; Lk. 9:54). Andrew and Philip are Greek names. Thomas is the Aramaic word for twin. Simon was a Cananaean which is not a reference to the land of Canaan but probably to an Aramaic word for Zealot as Luke translated it. A party of Zealots or violent revolutionaries was known in the great revolt against Rome A.D. 66.[2] But zeal for the Law was well known and Luke's term may mean Simon the Zealous. Simon may thus have been a man of religious zeal or of fiery patriotism. Judas had a second name which gives no light on the traitor. Iscariot is often taken to mean "man of Kerioth." This may be a reference to a Judean village known only in the distant past (Josh. 15:25). But it is only a guess that Judas was a Judean. Kerioth might mean "the false" one. This list of the Twelve, as far as known, shows that the disciples of Jesus came from the common walks of life but he gave them most uncommon opportunities with him and obligations to him.

The directions for work which the Twelve were assigned had importance for the advancement of Jesus' mission and for the later intense missionary program of the early church. This work supplemented the mission of Jesus and trained the disciples for their future work after Jesus' death. In Mark this work stands later than the call of the disciples but in Matthew the work follows directly upon the call while in Luke there are two reports about it. There is a mission of the Twelve and of the Seventy. The second contains directions similar to those to the Twelve so that they can be studied together. The work of the Seventy included preparation for the coming of

[2] Josephus, *Wars*, IV.3.9; cf. *Ant.* XVIII.1.6; Jackson and Lake, *Beginnings of Christianity*, I, 425.

Jesus. It is possible that the number seventy is symbolic in Luke's thought for the nations of the world since they were thought to total seventy. The "marching orders" for the Twelve required them to repeat the words and the works of Jesus, to travel light, to be good guests, to expect persecution, to fear none but God, to lose life and gain it for Christ's sake and to expect to be received and rewarded as his disciples.

According to Mark Jesus sent his disciples with authority over demons. They went out by twos as did the Seventy later in Luke. This accorded with Jewish custom and also worked successfully in the early church (Acts 8:14). According to Luke the disciples were to preach the Kingdom of God and to heal while in Matthew there was a full program which covered the field of service as well as their words and actions. Their field was limited to their own fellow Jews in this particular enterprise. This beginning among their own lost people answered to an immediate need and provided the best chance for a good start. Gentiles scorned the Jewish religion and Samaritans believed only part of it as they had their own temple, priests and Pentateuch for scripture. The disciples were to preach that the Kingdom was near and they were to aid the sick, raise the dead, cleanse lepers and release those possessed by demons. They were to give as they had received without charge. This free service could be rendered because they lived by the hospitality of their hosts and they traveled only short distances. They had an urgent mission for time was short. They took no baggage nor money. In Mark the equipment included a staff and sandals which reflect a real journey. Matthew and Luke forbid even these aids. Perhaps they thought the mission was sacred like the journey into the Temple which prohibited these articles. These variations reflect different traditions about preparations for missions where exact rules for equipment meant less than the general purpose that this important work had to be done at once with the expectation that the disciples' needs would be met as they went along. The workers deserved to be supported. Paul claimed that the Lord commanded that those who proclaimed the gospel should get their living by it (I Cor. 9:14). Luke's directions to the Seventy include prohibition of salutations on the highway which probably refers to dallying greetings which hindered the journey. Many of Jesus' commands are stated in extreme terms which made men think even though they could not literally obey them. Brief overstatements were more effective than long carefully hedged qualifications.

In Mark the guest disciples were bidden to stay in one house dur-

ing their visit and if refused hospitality and hearing, they were to
lose no time but were to shake off the dust from their feet. This act
was evidence probably that the people of the place were like the Gentiles whose dusty land defiled the good Jew. By this common gesture
the disciples gave witness about the responsibility of the people who
did not accept them or their message. This mission with its repentance, exorcisms and healings is like the work of Jesus except for the
use of oil in healing. There is no report that Jesus used oil for healing
though it was much used in medicine and later it was prescribed
with prayer for the Christian sick but it was the Lord and not the
oil that was to raise up the ill (James 5:14-15).

In Matthew and to the Lukan Seventy directions for arrival at a
town were more specific. The disciples had to discover a peaceful,
worthy man. An actual greeting to the host is given in Luke. "Peace"
was a customary greeting. It was to carry a real blessing to the hearer
but if not accepted it would return to the speaker to bless him. This
special power of the spoken word was a belief of the time. Luke with
his usual interest in eating and drinking twice states the requirement
to eat what was provided. The food was to be eaten, as it was given,
with hospitality. The Seventy were to heal the sick and to say that
the Kingdom of God had come near. The rejection of disciples by
a town would lead to a most serious fate on the judgment day which
would be worse than the fate of Sodom which for its serious sins
was destroyed by "fire from the Lord out of heaven" (Gen. 19:24).
The warning to repent had not reached Sodom and Gomorrah as it
had the towns visited by the disciples. This same warning which
Luke relates to the work of the Seventy is repeated by Matthew in
the following chapter when he names Chorazin, Bethsaida and Capernaum as cities of Galilee which Jesus reproached because they did
not repent at his mighty works. The Gentile cities of Tyre and Sidon
would have repented in sackcloth and ashes if they had known such
an opportunity. Sackcloth, a coarse material woven from black goat
hair, was worn in mourning and ashes were sprinkled on the head
as signs of humiliation. The coming fate of Capernaum in Hades
can be pictured from prophetic poetry where the mighty king of
Babylon was tumbled from his high throne down into shadowy
weakness in Sheol (Isa. 14:10). These ominous words about a judgment and a fate in Sheol have been traditionally accepted as the dark
side of Jesus' teaching not only about the fate of unrepentant Jewish
towns but as a forecast of the doom of all who hear his words and
refuse to turn to God. The serious consequences of such conduct are

inevitable though the figurative biblical language should not be read literally. Repentance is dateless and determinative. It fits all ages and influences the fate of everyone. But there are those who think these forecasts have been partly formulated by Christian teachers in the generation following Jesus. This is due to the floating repetitious character of the forecasts and to the fact that Jesus did not fail in Capernaum and to the idea that it was unlike him to make mighty works the basis of repentance.

Jesus said his disciples must go like sheep among wolves. This advice in Matthew is addressed to the Twelve who had to be wise as the proverbial serpent which wrought such momentous changes in the Garden of Eden and as undamaging as the doves which were birds of the air under God's care. The life among wolves is foretold by Matthew who describes a persecution (10:17–23) that does not fit the first tour of Galilean towns by disciples. Mark and Luke put the same forecast by Jesus in his last week in Jerusalem where it should be studied more fully. The passage on persecution closes with directions to move to another town and gives the promise that the Son of Man will come before the disciples reach all the towns of Palestine. This extraordinary expectation, not given elsewhere, reads as if the Son of Man would appear before the mission of the Twelve was completed. It differs from other predictions which stated that only God knew the time. "It seems to be impossible to interpret this verse of a coming of Christ to his missionaries during his lifetime." [3] This forecast reflects one of the early Christian beliefs that the second coming of Christ would occur before persecution became inescapable.

The disciples must expect persecution but they are to be fortified for it. They are to be like their teacher. This is a saying which Luke puts in his sermon on the plain (6:40). A servant is like his master since the master of the household (Jesus) was called Beelzebub. This term of abuse has no certain meaning. It was the name of the Philistine god of the city of Ekron (II Kgs. 1:2). With the spelling of Beelzebul found in Greek manuscripts it might mean the Lord of Dung or the Lord of the House. It appears to be an equivalent name for Satan but there is no other such use in Jewish literature. The disciples are to have no fear of men because the gospel which they heard privately from Jesus must be made known publicly. The dark and the light, the whisper and the housetop symbolize the difference between secrecy and open knowledge. They are to fear God alone, not men who can injure only the body. This fear of God is not cowardice

[3] W. C. Allen, *Gospel according to St. Matthew* (New York, 1907), 107.

but voluntary, reverent submission. Only God has power over both
soul and body, even to destruction in hell. Gehenna, the name for
hell, came from the valley of Hinnom near Jerusalem where refuse
was thrown and burned. This name was first given in the second
century B.C. to the place of punishment for impious Jews after the
last judgment and then it became the fate of all evil men. The name
was also applied to the place where men were punished while await-
ing the Judgment. Man was thought to be a single product of dust
and spirit. "In the Rabbinic conception body and soul were to be
judged together and when cast into Gehinnom were cast there together." [4] The thought of the Rabbis about man's destiny included
both punishment and annihilation. "On the whole the Rabbis seem
to have thought that every Israelite who did not deliberately turn his
back upon the Law would undoubtedly be saved. He might be pur-
gatorially punished after death but it would be for purification and
not eternally." [5] In Matthew the possible fate of man is called destruction of body and soul together. This is but one point in the
teaching of Jesus who knew that to love God was better than to fear
him. The third appeal to disciples not to fear was based on God's
constant and universal providence which let no sparrow fall without
notice though they were sold as the cheapest birds in the market at
two for a penny. God's infinite knowledge can number every hair on
a man's head. Disciples count for more than many sparrows. Moreover as the disciples remained loyal to Jesus before men so Jesus
would acknowledge them before God while a failure before men
meant repudiation before God.

Luke has a passage parallel to Matthew about fear. He and Matthew had a common source in Q but Luke has some instructive differences. Matthew sets the passage in the mission charge but Luke
pictures Jesus in the presence of a crowd of thousands as he warned
them about the hypocrisy of the Pharisees. The disciples are to make
public what they had previously spoken privately. Jesus calls his disciples "my friends" which is the only use of this affectionate title in
the Synoptics. In addition to the refrain about fear Luke shows the
emphasis of Jesus by a threefold use of the words "I tell you" or "I
will warn you." Luke gives a slightly different price for sparrows and
declares that God does not forget them. Luke agrees with Mark that
the Son of Man will acknowledge everyone before God who ac-

[4] Abrahams, *Studies in Pharisaism and the Gospels*, II, 45; cf. Manson, in *Mission
and Message of Jesus*, 398–400.
[5] Montefiore, *Rabbinic Literature and Gospel Teaching*, 229.

knowledges Jesus before men. This raises the possibility that the Son of Man is different from Jesus and also the inquiry whether Matthew or Luke more clearly reflects the original saying of Jesus. More important than these undecided questions is the fact that each writer assures the disciples that faithful service will be recognized before God.

One of the most difficult results of discipleship is division within families. Tender relationships are split because a household fails to agree on religious loyalties. In Luke this is the tragic tension which Jesus felt between his duty to God and its consequence to families. Jesus said his work was like fire or a baptism. Mutual hostility between parents and children is destructive as a fire. A flood of troubles comes like deep water in baptism. Jesus wished that the fire were kindled and that the baptism were accomplished because he realized that his demands for God's rule would result in sharp cutting of the closest ties of life. He was under intense pressure until his work was done. The weariness and the sadness of these verses guarantee their authenticity.[6] He did not lull his followers with an opiate future. His call took first place if a choice came between discipleship and relatives. He was a realist whose ideals blazed in some shocking statements. Luke gives one demand which Jesus set before the multitudes but Matthew puts it before his disciples. Not only the command to honor parents or to cleave to one's wife or to care for children and brothers and sisters must be secondary but whoever comes to Jesus must hate them. This hyperbole drives home the all-encompassing truth that loyalty to Jesus is greater than other claims. It is not literal hate but it means that one cannot love Jesus less than one's folks. All family loyalties, even life itself, stand within the greater circle of discipleship with Jesus. They are second always to the rule of God which Jesus preached. His disciples must be willing to face the cross and to carry it to its dire outcome. This dreadful death was a common sight under Roman rule. It is used as an illustration by Jesus not as a forecast of his own particular fate. Jesus knew the hostility of evil forces which could inflict suffering and death and his disciples had to accept these risks with him. Jesus said he brought a sword which sharply symbolizes lack of peace when children rise against their parents. In Luke the hostility is mutual. This division is quoted from Micah (7:6) whose words warn of foes in a man's household. There is no conscious exaggeration about hate but one must not love parents or children more than Jesus. There is no mention of the wife.

---

[6] H. K. Luce, *Gospel according to St. Luke,* 135.

Jesus gives his powerful paradox about finding and losing life for his sake. This is one of those sayings which ceaselessly sound in the mind of any hearer. Some claim it as the greatest of Jesus' words. It was well known among his first followers who knew its meanings both literal and spiritual. Martyrdom was not a word but a possibility for them. Matthew sets the saying in this special mission charge to disciples and again to disciples after Peter's recognition of him as Christ (16:24-25). Mark has it after the forecast of Jesus concerning his coming suffering shortly before he started to Jerusalem (8:35). Luke gives it twice, first like Mark, as Jesus started toward the cross (9:23), and again in Jerusalem as Jesus taught about the astounding day when the Son of Man was to be revealed (17:33). Since the Synoptists agree in placing the paradox just after Jesus predicted his suffering, it is probably in its historical setting. A paradox points to a truth from apparently contradictory positions. It is one of Jesus' best-known forms of speech which pricked the minds of his hearers as well as provided a way to a many-sided truth too great for a one-angled statement. In the paradox of life lost and saved Jesus used life in a double sense. It is the present natural physical existence and yet it is also the future eternal blessedness of spiritual existence. One can find or save himself by an escape from physical death and lose true life. One may be put to death for Christ's sake and thus find or save life eternal with God.

Luke's setting for the cost of discipleship is before Jesus started forward into the dangers of Jerusalem. Jesus gave two illustrations which invited the multitude to think of future discipleship with most careful planning. A builder of a tower must count the cost lest he be ridiculed for his inability to finish his project. Stone towers were often built and lived in temporarily as an owner watched his ripening vineyards or harvests. Palaces also had expensive corner towers. A king with 10,000 men takes counsel about meeting 20,000 enemies and undertakes to make peace. In these warnings about the outcome of discipleship Jesus urged his listeners to determine by serious thought how much it costs to be a disciple and to be willing to renounce everything for this priceless privilege. With danger ahead Jesus desired no faint hearts, no fickle enthusiasts and no divided interests. This is one of the places where Jesus expected much more than is found in his Jewish heritage. Greatness engenders greatness. To renounce all that one has, to give up family and fortune, to risk life itself in order to follow Jesus and to share his cause is the highest possible ideal. There is no other point at which Jesus both by his words and example sets forth such utter commitment, scorn of danger and entire loyalty. His disciples had to count life well lost to gain life with him in the Kingdom of God.

Matthew closes his account of Jesus' instructions to the Twelve by directions which pass from the disciples to those who receive them. These sayings begin with a promise, later repeated by Matthew (18:5) and by Mark (9:37) and Luke (9:48) as they report Jesus' teaching about children. The disciples were to go, braced by the assurance that they represented Jesus and God. Thus their reception was not for themselves alone but for the ones in whose cause they traveled. Some of these directions appear adapted to Christian travelers. They reflect the work of prophets and righteous men. Hosts for these men would receive the same rewards as their good guests. Even a small service like a cup of cold water to a disciple new in the faith, a "little one," would be recompensed. These promises of hospitality to messengers of the faith were important because inns were few and unfit for Christian fellowship. Such aid put Jesus' teachings into actions and kindness to his disciples was done to Christ and God.

25

Concerning John the Baptist and the Father

Mt. 11:2–30; Lk. 7:18–35, 10:13–22 (64–68)

MATTHEW AND Luke share reports, based on Q, about Jesus as he answers a question from John the Baptist and as he prays. Both of these topics had importance for the early church. John was held in prison by Herod. In Luke his disciples told him of "these things" which refer to the preceding mighty works and perhaps to the Sermon. In Matthew John heard about the deeds of the Christ. This shows Matthew believed in Jesus as Christ though historically there had been no such recognition at this time except by some demoniacs. John asked, through his disciples, if Jesus were the coming one. This coming one is not identified by John but he had preached of a mightier one coming to baptize by the Spirit and to judge. John's question has been taken in two ways: (1) he had thought Jesus to be the Messiah but now doubted; (2) he had not known Jesus as the Messiah but asks hoping that he is. In any case he desired a direct answer from Jesus who gave no mere verbal assent. In Matthew his answer to the messengers is for them to tell John what they saw and heard. The scene is described by quotations from the Messianic promises of Isaiah which combine marvels of mercy with good news preached to the poor. Then Jesus adds a blessing upon the one who found no offense in him. This may mean a rebuke of John if he doubts or an assurance in view of the things done by Jesus. Luke has the view that Jesus is verified by miracles and he reports many of them as the answer for John as well as the prophetic passages. That Jesus tried to convince John by miracles is not in accord with his commands for secrecy about them nor with his rejection of them at the temptation nor with his belief that he came to teach and preach the good news as the climax of the quotation from Isaiah helps to prove (Isa. 35:5–6). However, Jesus also saw the rule of God coming because demons were cast out. His answer, given partly in prophetic passages, best assured John because it showed people aided to a new life by what was done and heard. There is no evidence that John received this message from Jesus before Herod beheaded him.

When John's disciples had gone, Jesus turned to the crowds with rhetorical questions about what they saw and why they traveled to the wilderness after John. It was not the scenery nor a man in gorgeous garments but one who was a prophet and much more who had attracted the crowds. Then Jesus quoted Malachi (3:1) to identify John as the messenger of the Lord to herald the Messiah and added that there never was born a greater man than John yet paradoxically the least in the Kingdom was greater than John. This triple praise of John puts John on a pedestal above many later estimates. It also provided some puzzles. The quotation in Malachi is spoken by the Lord for his own messenger who prepared the way not for the Messiah but for the Lord. In the Gospels Malachi's words read as if spoken by the Lord of a messenger to prepare the way for the Messiah. This change points to the prophecy as an early proof text about Jesus and John which was in use among Christians. Mark used the same passage at the opening of his Gospel. How the least in the Kingdom could be greater than John is not easily explained. (1) The Gordian knot is cut by those who see the saying as not from Jesus who valued John greatly and who would not exclude him from the Kingdom. The saying is from those Christians who contrasted the old order of Judaism with the new order of Christianity and who saw John as less important than Jesus. This short statement about the least and John was added to emphasize the opportunities in the Kingdom and to lessen the importance of John. But a difficult saying is not cleared by attributing it to the first generation who preached the gospel. (2) Jesus saw John as a hero of righteousness whose work and hopes had ended in prison. He paid his tribute to him. Before him there was none greater yet he preceded the Kingdom which Jesus preached and which the prisoner John could not actively share. The least disciples had an opportunity in the Kingdom that made them, not greater in deeds, but greater in immediate possibilities and privileges than anything known before Jesus preached. (3) Finally there are those who think the saying is one paradox that remains a surd.

Luke has a comment on the different ways in which John had been regarded. The common people, including even tax collectors, had acknowledged John by their acceptance of baptism but the Pharisees and the lawyers had frustrated God's purposes as they refused baptism. Matthew and Luke each have an obscure saying about the Kingdom and violence in which the meaning varies widely. The saying occurs in Luke in a later chapter (16:16) when Jesus rebuked the Pharisees and made a distinction between the Law and the prophets, God's past revelation, which had prevailed until John and the good news of the rule of God which had been preached since John. This is a view of Jesus' message as something which succeeds the law and the prophets rather than fulfills them. Men everywhere force their way into the Kingdom or are pressed into it. In Matthew the meanings are difficult to determine. For those who are willing to hear and accept the truth, John is Elijah. This identification was not made by John himself. Elijah had been so great a prophet that later ages looked for him to return to share in the last days of this present age, to prepare God's ways, to precede and announce the Messiah and to restore the tribes of Israel (Ecclus. 48:10). This expectation of a miraculous return of Elijah is still symbolized in each Passover celebration by an opened door. The prophets and the Law spoke until John came. Since the days of John the Kingdom has endured harsh treatments and men of violence made it their spoil. This means persecution. A different idea is that the Kingdom has been coming violently with its own force and that men undertake to establish it by force. This means compulsion was used to achieve a good goal or to enter a new age.

Jesus knew the games of children and he used one of them for a comparison of the way the Pharisees treated John and himself. Children played first a glad wedding game for dancing and then a sad funeral game for weeping but in neither case could they persuade their peevish playmates to share the games. So it was with John whose severe life of self-denial reflected his preaching about judgment. He was called crazy. Jesus enjoyed food and drink and did not keep all the fasts (Mk. 2:19). Of him it was said he ate too much, drank too much and gave his friendship to publicans and sinners. The common people had accepted John's baptism and had heard Jesus gladly but the religious leaders had refused both John and Jesus. The work of John and the gospel of Jesus both came from God. Wisdom is justified by her deeds or by her children. Wisdom was often regarded as the representative of God's action in creation and history. In Matthew the works done by John and Jesus establish divine wisdom. In Luke the children or sons of wisdom may mean that Jesus and John justify the divine wisdom.

In Matthew after a rebuke of the Galilean cities for unrepentance Jesus gave a prayer of thanks to God. In Luke the prayer follows the return of the Seventy. There are few recorded prayers of Jesus but the essence of religion is in them.[1] This one is significant because of

[1] W. E. Bundy, *The Religion of Jesus* (Indianapolis, 1928), 170–209.

its revelation of God's will and because of its statement of the relationship of Father and Son. It is an easy mistake to look at the Gospels by modern standards of thought only but they have their own outlook which needs to be known first. In Luke the attitude of Jesus in prayer is a combination of thrilling joy in the Holy Spirit. This is one of Luke's special contributions. The invocation unites the most important thoughts about God, his Fatherhood and his Lordship. God is sovereign over all that exists but his motives are fatherly.[2] God is ruler with power and eternal purposes surpassingly great, yet they are founded on mercy or kindness. When God is addressed as Father, it is usually with some pronoun or qualifying word which, out of reverence, paves the way to the Father. But Jesus' brief prayer has a remarkable immediate approach to God. His references to God as Father are reserved in the Synoptics mostly for his disciples. "It is the Johannine writings primarily which have made 'Father' the natural name for God for Christian people." [3] "These things," which were willingly accepted by the "babes" or humble unlearned followers, refer to the teaching the disciples accepted and the work they had reported to Jesus. The "wise" who were learned in the law and the "understanding" who had high natural ability to comprehend it had rejected these things. Jesus did not thank God that the learned are blind but that some simple folks believed and acted though the wise lacked faith. The form of his prayer states not a purpose but a result.

The "Father-Son" part of the prayer is remarkable since it has but one parallel in the Synoptics when Jesus disclaimed knowledge for the Son of the time of the end of the age (Mk. 13:32). This famous relationship is everywhere developed in John's Gospel. This prayer is not an extract from John but it shows that Jesus spoke occasionally of a special knowledge given to him from God and shared by Jesus with others. The things delivered to Jesus refer to his teachings and his ability to do mighty works which Jesus divided with his disciples. The knowledge of God in biblical thought is widely used for what in modern times would be called religion. Knowledge meant both moral insight and action. Knowledge of God was not merely intellectual information but recognition and acceptance of all that God means to men plus the ensuing activity which made the knowledge effective in human life. To know who God or the Son is, as in Luke, does not differ from knowledge of them, as in Matthew. Jesus spoke of a unique knowledge between Father and Son and of the mission

---

[2] Manson, *The Teachings of Jesus*, 89–115, 144–70.
[3] *Ibid.*, 99.

of the Son to share the revelation of God with others. This has been read as if there is no knowledge of God except through Jesus but God is not without his own witness among all peoples before and since the coming of Christ. This prayer is a window into the fathomless depths of the will of Jesus to share his knowledge of God with all who will accept it. When the prayer changes from second person to third person, its form may have been set by the needs of the early church to make clear and strong its confidence in a sacred Father-Son knowledge which was the living source of their faith.

Matthew alone gives the lyric words of Jesus as he opens the way for those who toil and endure burdens to come to him, to take his yoke and to learn from him. He would give rest to their souls as Jeremiah had promised to those who sought the old paths of the Lord (Jer. 6:16). These weary ones may be those who knew the work and the heat of the day or the burden of evil doing or more probably those who found the many heavy requirements of the Law too much for them. The yoke was a symbol for discipline and shared labor but it was a term used especially for those who undertook the many duties of the Law. By contrast the yoke of the Kingdom which Jesus asked men to take of their own choice was good, valuable and easy to bear. They were to find release especially from the load of the unwritten Law which bore heavily upon them. They were to find relief from the weights of sin or worry or fear or ills which dragged them down. These entrancing promises point to amazing claims stated with confidence and candor. Jesus expected the weary to come, to find his promises answered and most of all to discover these pledges are based on himself. This treasured invitation provides insights concerning the one who made the promises. He invited the heavy laden to himself, to share his easy yoke and light burden and to find in fellowship with him that he was gentle and humble. He had depths and heights within himself and in his mission not measurable by any ordinary standards. It has been held that he was paraphrasing a quotation from Jesus, the son of Sirach (Ecclus. 51:23-27) who had portrayed wisdom with an invitation to put the neck under its yoke and to find peace. This is possible but the main purport of Jesus is different since he invited men to follow him, share his promises of God's rule and find soul rest. He does not mention wisdom as the answer for wearied men. As Matthew arranged this remarkable section (11: 25-30) there is first the prayer of thanks by Jesus, then a statement of his relationship to the Father and finally a gracious invitation, "Come unto me."

26

Famous Mighty Works

Mt. 8:23–34, 9:18–26, 13:53–58, 14:13–36; Mk. 4:35–6:6, 14–16,
30–56; Lk. 8:22–9:17, 7:11–17 (105–108, 110, 112–114, 80)

IN SOME parts of his Gospel Mark uses a topical plan. After some parables he puts a cycle of mighty works which are related to the mission
of the Twelve and to Herod's superstition about a return of John the
Baptist after his death. These miracles cover almost all the kinds
which Jesus worked and especially some nature miracles which are
the hardest for a modern man to grasp.

Whether we can "explain" them or not—and I doubt if we can "explain" them to the satisfaction of the mind of our generation—they had
better be left as they stand, as an indispensable element in the gospel
story and as the evidence (for the first century) of the stupendous power
and true value of the oncoming kingdom of God, the proof of "the powers
of the age to come" (Heb. 6:5) and the assurance that the ministry of
Jesus, and continuous with it, the spread of the church was not human in
origin or devising, but was the mighty act of God for the salvation of
men.[1]

In all the centuries since Jesus men have looked for repetition of his
miracles physically and discovered that it is their spiritual significance
which is enduring.

The story of the stilling of the storm, in Mark especially, contains
concrete details and also religious overtones. The evening scene, the
start across the lake, the other boats, the storm, wind, waves, the
sleeper on the cushion, the frantic question of disciples, the assured
answer of Jesus and the sudden calm make a realistic account. But
over these human scenes there falls a feeling of mysterious might and
overpowering awe where faith conquers fear and the awakened
Sleeper subdues the storm with the same words with which he expelled an unclean spirit (Mk. 1:25). Storms rise and fall with equal
suddenness on the Galilean lake which lies 650 feet below sea level

[1] Grant, *An Introduction to New Testament Thought,* 158.

with hills high above. An interpretation of a coincidence suits a reader today but it is not Mark's meaning. The rebuke of the disciples for their fear and lack of faith is understandable but the rebuke of a storm, except in fancy, is passing strange. Instead of the attempt to explain the first century by the twentieth it is more profitable to look at the story for the teachings that had continuing significance for those who first heard the Gospel. His disciples saw in Jesus a power superior to wind and waves. Moses had controlled the sea and so could Jesus. The effects of the miracles on the disciples are more important than on the sea. As Mark wrote, "They feared with a great fear." Their question at the end, "Who is this?" could be asked not simply to one another but wherever they told the story. Their rescue from danger because Jesus was with them and their lesson of faith that overcomes fear could be retold to all hearers. These religious teachings could be used in daily life again and again and meant more than an escape in the storm, an event which remained in the past. An incident in the past supported a present faith but the faith counted most. The nature miracles baffle a modern reader but they are natural to the Gospels and to the gospel writers who felt no differences in a mighty power whether known in man or in nature.

In the disciples' appeals for aid Jesus is called Master, Teacher and Lord but Matthew and Luke omit the part of the question from which it might be inferred that Jesus did not care if his disciples drowned. They also save the face of the disciples somewhat as they moderate his direct question, "Have you no faith?" Mark writes that the disciples took Jesus into the boat but Matthew stresses the initiative of Jesus as the disciples follow him into it. Matthew shows that Jesus dealt with the disciples before he calmed the storm whereas in Mark and Luke he first spoke to the storm.

Mark usually gives the most details in miracles. Matthew especially abbreviates the story of the Gerasene demoniac though he increases the demoniacs cured from one to two. Perhaps this increase is due to his omission of an earlier demoniac story (Mk. 1:24). The name of the region varies. Matthew gives it as Gadara, a place about ten miles from the lake. The large well-known city of Gerasa was thirty miles southeast and inland. Origen named a place near the lake as Gergasa but it has not been clearly identified. These puzzles about the place, plus secular motives in the story, plus the transfer of demons, plus the destruction of pigs, plus the possible misinterpretation of events by the swineherds and the disciples about Jesus' belief in demons, plus the command of Jesus to proclaim, not silence the miracle, plus his failure to teach among the Gerasenes have led to a divorce of the original story from Jesus. "If this story were originally related of a Jewish exorcist in a Gentile country and only afterwards ascribed to Jesus, it would contain nothing surprising." [2] But this still leaves the story as the responsibility of the Evangelists. It is maintained that a modern spot, Kursa, on the east shore is the best identification for the site of the miracle [3] and that the story is not secular but reflects first-century views not "inconsistent with the character of Jesus or devoid of profound spiritual teaching." [4] The demons recognize the superior power of Jesus and since they had to live somewhere, Jesus was humane in his permission for them to inhabit swine rather than hell and he did not intend any destruction of property. There was nothing offensive to Jewish minds about unclean spirits in unclean animals. Pigs were forbidden for Jews to eat (Lev. 11:7). "A man freed from the power of an evil spirit was worth infinitely more than a whole herd of swine." [5]

The transfer of demons from the victim to the swine was not a visible transaction. It could be an inference by the disciples from the conversation between Jesus and the demoniac and from the swine frightened by the crazy behavior of the demoniac. The acceptance of the demons by Jesus was part of a first-century outlook as common as the belief that the sun rose, though long later scientific man rejected both. When Jesus told the cured man to go home and tell his friends what God had done for him, it was in a Gentile area where Jesus was not living and where silence was not necessary to protect him from overwhelming crowds of miracle mongers. Jesus did not stay to teach since the people of the region begged him through fear to leave. As a whole the story is lively and popular, true to its time and a vehicle of the truth that Jesus could bring God's mercy to an untamed madman though the cause of the madness would be diagnosed differently today.

The story of Jairus' daughter is notable because a second narrative is interwoven and because it is one of the two stories of resuscitation in the Synoptics. On a westward return from the east shore of the lake a great crowd gathered as Jairus, a president of the synagogue, fell at Jesus' feet and earnestly asked him to come to aid his little daughter who was near death. Luke states that she was his only

[2] M. Dibelius, *From Tradition to Gospel* (New York, 1935), 89.

[3] Dalman, *Sacred Sites and Ways*, 179.

[4] Richardson, *Miracle Stories of the Gospels*, 73.

[5] Lebreton, *Life and Teaching of Jesus Christ* I, 271.

daughter. In the crowd that pressed Jesus as he went toward the home he was touched by a woman who had endured a hemorrhage for twelve years with no medical relief. Luke shortens the mention of her failures with doctors and Matthew omits it. Her complaint made her ceremonially unclean (Lev. 15:19), a condition which could be transferred by touch to other people or things (Lev. 15:25). She believed a touch, even of Jesus' robe, could cure her. Matthew and Luke mention her touch on the blue tassel which Jewish men wore in the corners of their garments as a reminder of the commandments of the Lord (Num. 15:38–39). When Jesus questioned who had touched him, his disciples reminded him of the pressing crowd. When Jesus looked around, the woman confessed her condition and cure and received from Jesus the assurance that her faith had made her well. The frequent "look" of Jesus is the one reference in the Gospels to his physical appearance though it is not intended to be descriptive of him. Mark's explanation of power within Jesus to effect the cure as an inward perception is reported in Luke as a declaration of Jesus to the crowd. One early influence of this story is found in Eusebius,[6] who wrote that in Caesarea Philippi, the home of this unnamed woman, he had seen on a stone platform two bronze figures of the suppliant and of Jesus.

News came that the girl was dead, therefore the Teacher was not to be troubled further. But the response of Jesus was to tell the father not to fear but to believe. Luke's addition that the girl would be well is a promise which indicates illness rather than death. When Jesus came to the wailing people at the home, though he had not seen her, he said that the girl was not dead but asleep and they laughed at him. He permitted only the parents and three disciples in the room with the girl. Then with a grasp of the hand and in Aramaic words he told the girl to arise. When she obeyed and walked, he commanded silence about it and food for the child. This food met her need and also proved her alive.

Matthew reports that it was the father who told Jesus his daughter was dead. Matthew and Luke omit the unusual Aramaic in Mark. Jesus' words about sleep and the statement that the girl rose up bear a double meaning. Sleep is a synonym for death and to arise may mean to get up or to return from death. Luke says her spirit returned. The Evangelists write because they believed Jesus was Lord over death as well as over the other aspects of man's life. This story was the best proof of this power. This confidence in someone greater than

[6] *Eccles. Hist.* VII.18.

death had incalculable influence on Jesus' followers which his later
resurrection more surely established. The facts of life and death are
ineluctable but Jesus defeated death with life. But as long as Mark's
story of the little girl is read there will be the question, not of Mark's
purpose in the story but of the meaning of Jesus' words about the
girl before he saw her. The crowd laughed as if they thought he
meant ordinary sleep. His action and words to her and the request
for food support that view. It is congenial to many readers to think
of a deathlike coma from which Jesus aroused the girl by prompt
action. Death sometimes is a lengthened process with no sharp line
drawn upon life. Others join Matthew and Luke who know the dam-
sel was dead. Mark's marching scenes lead toward one climax. The
response that Jesus made to the father's first pitiful plea, his fear-
banishing words as he overruled the death message of the messengers,
his strong questions to the mourners and his climactic life-giving
words to the girl all point in fourfold fashion to One mighty in word
and in power to overcome death and to restore life.

Matthew has a formula to mark the close of each of the five great
discourses of Jesus. This formula states that Jesus finished his parables
or teachings. Matthew places a visit to Nazareth after a section on
parables but Mark puts it after the collection of miracles. This is the
visit which Luke located at the beginning of Jesus' work (4:16–30).
Jesus went home followed by disciples and remained for teaching on
the Sabbath when many heard him with astonishment. But the wonder of his neighbors turned into questioning his wisdom and mighty
works. The sad outcome was offense at him. Jesus recognized that no
prophet was honored in his own country, among relatives or in his
own home. Matthew states that he could do few mighty works there.
Mark bluntly reports that he could do no mighty work except healing a few ailing folks. Jesus could only marvel at their continued
unbelief. Matthew omits mention of astonishment at their lack of
faith. This unbelief in spite of Jesus' teaching and touching the sick
is the point in Mark's account because the rule of God could come
only to those who accept it. This authentic story is verified by its own
hard nature. That Jesus shared the usual prophet's rejection and that
his own family are not named among his followers discloses a bitter
experience. The quaint fact in the rejection is that his occupation and
family were too well known. At home Jesus had worked as an arti-
san. This means he was not simply a carpenter but also a worker in
stone or metal. Justin Martyr, born at Neapolis, south of Nazareth,
wrote about a century after Jesus that he made plows and yokes and

taught both by signs of righteousness and by a life of energy.[7] His neighbors called Jesus Son of Mary, which is unusual since a man was named as a son of his father whether dead or alive. The mention of four brothers by name and of sisters indicates that Jesus grew up in a family of at least seven children. Since the father is not named, he is usually thought to be dead though in Luke Jesus is called "Joseph's son" (4:22). When Matthew refers to Jesus as the son of a carpenter, he avoids mention of him as a humble workman as in Mark and identifies both parents of Jesus. The brothers of Jesus are the subjects of an old, lengthy controversy. As a defense of the later theory of the perpetual virginity of Mary the brothers were declared to be half brothers by the eastern Greek church and cousins by the western Latin church. No basis exists in the Gospels for either of these theories though "brother" could be applied to relatives beyond the closest blood ties. These brothers of Jesus are known or named in Acts and by Paul and by Josephus. One of them, James, became a strong leader in the early church in Jerusalem.

The fame of Jesus reached the ruler of his region. The tetrarch, Herod Antipas, shared the speculations about Jesus and his powers. These rumors asserted that Jesus was John the Baptist resurrected or that he was Elijah who had gone to heaven in a strange chariot and would appear again before the Messiah or that he was like one of the old prophets. Herod accepted the first rumor. These ideas show the influence of Jesus and the kind of men he resembled. They also show the fantastic ideas that were current about some unusual righteous men who might come back to earth soon or late after their death. Matthew gives no theory but Herod's who thought Jesus was John but Luke has a more probable report that Herod was perplexed about the rumor but curious enough to try to see Jesus.

The only miracle reported by all four Evangelists is the feeding of the 5,000. In addition Matthew and Mark each relate the feeding of 4,000. This total of six stories of feeding bears some relationship to the Lord's Supper which became the outstanding rite of the church. Mark, as usual, is more complete with lifelike details blended with an act beyond human comprehension. The tide of people, coming and going, gave no time even to eat. Jesus suggested a rest and led his disciples by boat to a deserted place. Recognized by the crowds who followed on shore, Jesus looked with pity on their shepherdless state and began to teach them, as he had the disciples, many things.

[7] *Trypho* LXXXVIII.8.

Luke explains that he spoke of the Kingdom of God and he and Matthew add that he healed their sick.

The time came for the customary main meal of the day at evening but there was no food. The dialogue between Jesus and his disciples is notable in Mark. To the disciples' suggestion to send the crowd away Jesus countered with a word to the disciples to feed them. Matthew and Luke omit the astonished question of the disciples about buying two hundred denarii ($40) worth of food. In reply Jesus asked them to go and see what they had on hand. Five loaves, usually the size, the shape and the thickness of a small dining plate, and two fish, usually dried and salted, made the total. It was the common food of the poor. He commanded the crowds to sit on the green grass in orderly fashion as for a meal, took the food, looked to heaven, gave the blessing, broke the loaves and gave them to the disciples to set before the people and he divided the fish among them. These actions accord with the dining customs of the day when the father or the host presided at a meal. The blessing probably followed the words, "Blessed art Thou, O Lord our God, King of the world, who causest bread to grow out of the earth." This devout custom blessed not the food but God, the giver of bread.

To this point this outdoor scene in springtime at sunset with Jesus as host is an interesting believable sight. But all ate and were satisfied and twelve baskets of broken pieces were gathered. These twelve baskets probably refer to the wallets of the Twelve in which most Jews carried their food on journeys to insure "clean" food. The pieces prove that food was plentiful. A total of 5,000 ate. Matthew magnifies this twice over by adding "besides women and children." These astounding results caused no reported comments though Mark states (6:52) that the disciples with hardened hearts did not understand about the loaves and later Jesus rehearsed the situation and ended with a question still unanswered, "Do you not yet understand?" (8:21).

This lack of understanding has continued 2,000 years, yet Jesus evidently expected some understanding. But there are varied responses: (1) an open skepticism which declares the whole story unbelievable; (2) an equally open credulity that accepts it as entirely believable but too sacred and divine for understanding; (3) traditional allegorical explanations of which the earliest is the Gospel of John which has no record of words and actions of Jesus with bread and wine at the Last Supper. Hence it interprets this story as the Eucharist where Jesus is the bread of life to feed men's faith. Augustine thought that as God makes all the harvests of the world from a few seeds so Jesus by the same power multiplied five small loaves. Men wonder not at food great enough for the whole world but at the rarity of this food to feed 5,000. (4) The influence of Hebrew history molded the story. God fed the Hebrews forty years with manna under Moses' leadership. Elisha could cause twenty loaves to feed one hundred men. Hence the disciples of Jesus said that he could provide food for the hungry. (5) The expectation of the Messiah created the account. In the future the coming Messiah would provide a banquet with food in abundance or the Lord had promised a shepherd to feed his people. Hence Jesus gave a foretaste of the coming days of the Messiah. (6) Rational explanations hold that Jesus set an example as host even with a little food or he gave small bits to many and the crowds inspired by his words and actions brought out their hidden stores to help their hungry neighbors. The miracle was in the changed attitudes. (7) The story reports an actual meal but with added interpretations. The outcome, as given by the Synoptists, is highly supernatural. That Jesus performed this miracle they had no doubt. They knew that Jesus requested understanding about this meal. They also knew that food came by natural means. The followers of Jesus did not expect to feed people actual food by a repetition of the story but they did expect them to find much food for living as Christians. They were to see Jesus, not only as powerful enough to feed the hungry but as one who taught, who had pity for crowds far from home and who trained disciples to satisfy hunger under his direction and help. Fulfilling his commands both disciples and needy people had abundance. These interwoven events and meanings of the Gospels will continue to defy both mere historical analysis and unexplainable theological assumptions.

Luke omits the story of walking on water as he does several other miracles in this section of Mark. It has been conjectured that he did so to avoid misinterpretations of Jesus or else his copy of Mark did not contain the miracles. This story contains some of the same motives as the one about the stilling of the storm. There is the complete confidence that Jesus had power over wind and waves and that he could rid disciples of their fear and rescue them in time of danger. Jesus required his disciples to go by boat to Bethsaida while he took leave of the crowd and went into the hills to pray. This is the second of three times of prayer by Jesus as reported in Mark. The disciples alone in the boat had trouble with the high wind in the morning watch (3:00–6:00 A.M.). But their deep trouble was cleared by Jesus.

He saw them, came to them, spoke to them and got into the boat with them. All these actions had much religious significance to the first disciples but they also could be shared spiritually when dangers faced them in later days. When the disciples were in peril in the earlier story of the storm, Jesus was asleep in the boat with apparent indifference. In this story there seems to be a parallel in the puzzling mention that Jesus meant as if to pass them as he came to them. Matthew omits this perplexity as he does the statement about the hardened hearts of disciples which made them so they could not understand these miracles. Walking on the sea has been given the easy rationalization that Jesus was walking in the water at the edge of the sea and that the storm and the fright of the disciples left them unable to report clearly the actual situation. One difficulty with this explanation is that Matthew and Mark have no such idea. Matthew had a tradition which looks like a pious legend about Peter. He exalts Peter by showing that he alone tried to walk to Jesus on the water. Then he uses Peter to teach that fear reduced him to a man of little faith who was saved only because he appealed to Jesus who caught him but rebuked his doubt. In Matthew the worship of Jesus as the disciples acclaimed him Son of God appears as a historical anachronism which shows well the transforming faith of the early church at the time the Gospel was written.

Jesus and the disciples landed not at Bethsaida in the northeast but at the Gennesaret plain in the northwest. Mark notes the little details at the landing. They moored, stepped out of the boat and the crowds came on the run. They thronged Jesus at once wherever he went in country, village or city. They brought him their sick who sought to touch even the tassel of his robe. These many healings reflect the power of faith even though tinged with magic that a garment of Jesus contained curative power. This summary closes the section in Mark in which he showed Jesus in his mission around the Sea of Galilee. Henceforth the story moves in wider circles northwestward and eastward before the final fatal southward journey.

Following the story of the illness of the centurion's servant, who was saved from the point of death, Luke alone relates the restoration of life to the dead son of the widow of Nain. This graphic narrative first depicts the story and then states its impressive results. Nain, a village known only from this story, is located a few miles southeast of Nazareth. When Jesus went there with his disciples followed by a great crowd, he met a sad procession as a widow wept over her only son who was being carried out for burial. In biblical days a woman

bereft of husband and an only son faced her worst disaster. Aroused
to compassion, the Lord spoke first to her, "Do not weep," and to
the son, "Arise." When the dead man sat up and began to speak,
Jesus gave him to his mother. In Jewish law if a person touched the
dead, he became "unclean" for a week but Jesus did not hesitate to
touch the bier. Awe seized both the crowd with the widow and the
crowd with Jesus. That a prophet had come and that God had visited
his people occasioned praise to God while the news about Jesus spread
everywhere.

Luke thought of Jesus as the Lord whose pity for the widow and
whose power over death were equally natural. Some modern readers
who linger over physical details more than spiritual significance in
the story suggest that the son was in a coma and find some support
in the fact that burial in Palestine was often promptly arranged on
the day of death. In that case they do not dissolve the wonder nor
understand Luke. Others, noting the idea that a great prophet had
arisen and that Nain is two miles from Shunem where Elisha had
raised a dead son (II Kgs. 4:32–37), think the narrative about Jesus
is a symbolic story, patterned upon Elisha, to illustrate life-giving
spiritual power. This idea may have been in Luke's thought but he
also believed that he reported an actual event.

27

Defilement · Wonders · Leaven

Mt. 15:1–16:12, 12:38–45; Mk. 7:1–8:26; Lk. 12:54–56, 11:24–25, 29–32 (115–121, 87, 88)

EXTRAORDINARY NEWS about Jesus reached Jerusalem. Scribes and Pharisees came to him and precipitated a long dispute about defilement and the "tradition of the elders." This ceremonial uncleanness was of great importance to Judaism and early Christianity. The issue was not hygienic since sanitation had not developed but ritual cleanness which arose in early times in Israel when things were believed to contain a power to contaminate or to make holy. Certain foods like pork or things like a corpse were unclean or dangerous. Certain people like priests or things like an altar were clean or holy. The Law supported these regulations on the clean and the unclean but the prophets put moral cleanness before ritual purity. They saw that religious defilement and purity were in people rather than in things. How much and in what manner the power and the life of God is in things is still debated. When the Gospels were written, there had been great controversy over the question of the observance of Jewish laws for Christians. Some held that the Jewish laws were obsolete, others that they were not to be followed literally but allegorically and others that the only Christians who needed to keep the laws were converted Jews.

In Mark the question of defilement from unclean or unwashed hands required an explanation for his Gentile readers which Matthew could omit. There had grown up in Judaism the "tradition of the elders." These oral requirements were intended to aid men to observe the written law which specified how God's will was to be done. The traditions of the elders were sponsored by the scribes and the Pharisees who believed that four centuries earlier Ezra had especially developed them though there was a legend that Moses started oral commands in addition to his written ones. The immense development of these oral teachings is reflected later in the Mishnah and eventually in the Talmud. They lay heavily on all who kept them. The disciples of Jesus who ate without the ceremonial washings neglected the tradition. This offended the Pharisees who had recently developed a traditional practice of hand washing before and after meals. It was an act of consecration since food was God-given but it was made a rigorous rule with many others which tended to become burdensome formalities. Mark has a generalization that all Jews washed hands and had ritual washings for household dishes. This was not literally correct for all Jews since there were many common people like the disciples and the Sadducees who did not agree with the Pharisees on washings.[1]

Jesus is credited with three answers about defilement. One is a quotation from Isaiah, the next is an illustration about "Corban" and the last concerns clean and unclean food. This answer was addressed to a crowd and later explained to disciples. These answers bear the marks of editorial adaptations to issues among early Christians. The quotation from Isaiah (29:13) makes the point that Pharisaic hypocrisy professed honor to the Lord but in reality dropped God's commandments and taught the precepts of men. This idea is based not on the Hebrew text but on the Septuagint form of quotation. Therefore, it is thought to be an early proof text used in controversies between Jews and Christians rather than an exact quotation of Jesus who probably did not use the Greek of the Septuagint. But its ideas are those which Jesus shared. He charged that the Pharisees put their oral commands above God's since they allowed a man to evade his responsibility to honor his parents by the use of Corban or a vow formula. This vow to God took precedence over the needs of parents; hence there was a current shift of responsibility when a man claimed Corban released him from duty to parents. Thus Jesus condemned the tradition which voided a commandment of God. Jesus incurred an increased hostility from Pharisees who condemned him in good conscience. Nothing is more deadly than the risk which comes from opposition to religious ideas which are held by men who think they are the only custodians of God's law. In this situation there was the whole issue as to what duties stand first in religion. Jesus upheld the position that human duties to parents preceded the validity of vows. Eventually the descendants of the Pharisees took the same position. Finally Jesus called the people and gave one of his greatest principles. Moral and spiritual defilement comes only from within a man. It is personal, not in things outside a man. He did away with distinctions between clean and unclean things. "Jesus speaks here like a new

[1] E. Schürer, *Jewish People in the Time of Jesus Christ*, Div. II, II, 90–105; Montefiore, *Synoptic Gospels*, I, 129–144.

Amos or Isaiah. It is one of two or three most original sayings in the Gospels." [2] Matthew reinforces the argument by a report of disciples that the Pharisees took offense at this saying but that Jesus answered figuratively that God alone provides a proper planting, otherwise a plant will be rooted out. Avoid the Pharisee for he is a blind leader of the blind. Privately the disciples with Peter as spokesman, according to Matthew, asked Jesus about his answer. His reply was a sharp question about their lack of understanding. He repeated his point that nothing outside a man defiles him. In a parenthesis, which Matthew omits, Mark explains that he made all foods proper for man. This represents the view of the Gentile Christian who believed that the Jewish regulations on clean and unclean goods were wiped out. By contrast there come from within man's heart the things which defile him. Then follows a list of thirteen evils in thoughts and actions which reveal what constitutes real defilement. Among these vices the evil eye means jealousy or envy. In this catalogue of evils, which is reduced to seven by Matthew, who models the actions upon transgressions of the Ten Commandments, there is more of the Greek method which made lists of virtues and vices rather than the short, living illustrations of them characteristic of Jesus and Jewish writers. Though the present listing is probably editorial in Mark the point is that these things within man degrade him rather than his food.

Jesus went into the region of Tyre, a seacoast, Gentile area, beyond the territory controlled by Herod Antipas. No reasons are given by Jesus for this trip. It is guessed that he wished to avoid the curiosity or the animosity of Herod, or that he felt the need for rest and privacy, or that he wanted an opportunity to train the Twelve, or to plan his future moves in the face of rising Pharisaic opposition. This journey is usually thought to mark a decisive change in the public work of Jesus and it covers one of the few contacts of Jesus with a Gentile. The woman who begged help for her demon-possessed daughter was a Greek, which here means Gentile, and a native of the Phoenician region. Matthew called her a Canaanite. Speculations about the language of the dialogue are idle. Jesus or the woman may have talked both Greek and Aramaic. The answer of Jesus sounds harsh though a kind tone and manner can modify words. Children's bread goes first to children and not to little dogs. Unlike some commentators the woman showed no distaste for these words of Jesus. With quick wit she caught up his answer and turned it to her advan-

---

[2] Montefiore, *Rabbinic Literature and Gospel Teachings*, 254.

tage. The dogs do eat the children's crumbs under the table. For this ready reply Jesus assured the woman that she could go and find her daughter free of the demon.

This story contains the only record in Mark where Jesus is called "Lord." The woman used it like the respectful "Sir." It is also the only cure wrought at a distance. Nothing is known about the child's trouble. It is not unlike a modern saying that indefinitely reports an illness as due to a microbe or "bug." The woman was rewarded for her perceptive words which insist on the sharing of household food with both children and household pets. The contrast between children and dogs implies that Jews and Gentiles do not first share the help of Jesus but eventually both receive aid. This is a natural situation which shows that Jesus felt the need to work among his own people. His first words to the woman reflect his need for privacy after he had faced the deadly opposition of Herod and the Pharisees. Mighty works would upset any chance for quiet. His attitude to the Roman centurion whose servant he healed in Capernaum and to other foreigners shows that he did not share the contempt of some fellow Jews for Gentiles. Dogs are disdained in biblical records though in Tobit (6:16; 11:5) a dog appears as a friendly companion on a journey. Jesus' reference to a dog appears to be friendly. This story had significance for Mark's Gentile readers because it showed that Jesus did help a foreign woman who sought his aid.

Matthew tells the story with interest especially in teaching Jewish Christians. He mentions no entrance of Jesus into a home in Gentile territory and reports that the woman came out to Jesus. He adds the Messianic title, Son of David, to the woman's appeal to Jesus. The disciples intervene to send her away. Jesus in his answer limits his mission to his own people with the further claim that it is not fair to feed children's bread to dogs. Yet the woman answered that dogs do share crumbs from the master's table and Jesus grants her request because of her great faith so that her daughter was healed instantly.

In Mark the journey that Jesus made from Tyre northward through Sidon and eastward through the Decapolis to the east side of the Sea of Galilee is circuitous and uncertain. He remained outside Herod's domain. Matthew shortens the travel by omission of Sidon and Decapolis but enlarges an editorial statement about the wonder of the crowds who praised the God of Israel for many people healed. In Mark there is one miracle in which a deaf man with a speech impediment is restored. This act of Jesus caused great astonishment among the people who acclaimed him as one who did all things well.

Since he caused the deaf to hear and the dumb to speak, he fulfilled the prophecy of Isaiah (35:5). The methods of cure are vividly described. These include the separation of the man from the crowd, the touch of hand upon his ears, the use of saliva for his tongue, the look upward to heaven, the sigh, the Aramaic formula, "Be opened," and the repeated charge for silence about the cure. By these actions Jesus communicated help to the deaf mute. Two particulars need comment. The curative power of saliva was believed both by Jew and Gentile to be effective for healing or even for magic. The use of a native word for a cure is not simply a historical remembrance because the use of a formula in cures, especially in another language, was thought to convey unseen powers.

The feeding of the 4,000 may be a doublet that is a second account of the feeding of the 5,000 or it may be the story of a second feeding. Because of similarities it is often held to be a doublet. If so the interest lies in comparative reports of the same event. The crowd, their hunger, the compassion of Jesus, his questions to disciples, the bread and the fish, the blessing, the breaking and the distribution by disciples, the left-over fragments and the immediate departure in a boat indicate an essential likeness. Would the disciples have asked a second time how to feed 4,000 if they knew about the 5,000? Two accounts of the same situation grew up with some differences and when Mark found both, he understood them as separate events. Luke refused to do likewise. But Mark, followed by Matthew, had two separate feedings in mind. He states that a great crowd gathered again and stayed for three days with Jesus who took the initiative to aid them. The loaves number seven, there are a few fish, the crowd sits on the ground, there are seven baskets left over. Mark uses a different word for basket. This container was one especially used for fruit or fish. There are 4,000 in the crowd. When they were fed, Jesus got into a boat with his disciples and they started for Dalmanutha, a place unknown today. In all these details Mark provides differences from his story of the 5,000. Possibly he thought one feeding was for Jews and the other for Gentiles since Jesus was in a Gentile region though Gentiles might not have praised the God of Israel. Both feedings illustrate the same truths about Jesus. The question as to whether the accounts are separate or duplicate is settled: (1) by those who follow Matthew and Mark as sufficient evidence for two feedings; or (2) by those who, like Luke, think there was only one, even though there are two narratives about it.

A teacher or leader or even the Messiah was sometimes expected to convince people by a sign or a wonderful work which would authenticate a prophet's word or a teacher's authority. In Mark some Pharisees argued with Jesus to produce some supernatural evidence to satisfy them or perhaps if the demand were not met, Jesus would be discredited. The answer which Jesus gave as he sighed deeply was surprising but in keeping with his decision at the Temptation. He asked why a sign was sought and declared none would be given. Then he left them. Jesus did not refuse mighty works if needs arose but he refused to do them for proof about himself, his teaching or work. He would not appeal to a miracle to verify religion at the demand of enemies. This refusal stands in sharp contrast to his reply to the messengers of John the Baptist when he appealed to things seen and done and to the gospel preached.

The importance of this topic is shown by Matthew and Luke, who following Q give it twice in different settings. In the first instance, seeking for signs is credited to scribes and Pharisees by Matthew and to crowds by Luke. The answer of Jesus is not flat refusal and departure but a declaration that an evil people seek signs and no signs would be given except the kind evident in Jonah and Solomon. Jonah preached to Nineveh, the great evil capital of the Assyrian enemy who had devastated Israel, but Nineveh repented. The queen of the south, Sheba, came far distances to Jerusalem to listen to the wisdom of Solomon. Both Nineveh and Sheba would fare better at the judgment than the people who asked for a sign. There is something here greater than Jonah or Solomon, namely, the Son of Man, whose preaching was sufficient without signs. But Matthew has introduced another idea about the sign. He explains how Jonah was a sign not only by preaching but by his three-day stay in the whale which was an action in forecast of the Son of Man who would be three days and nights in the grave. This interpretation belongs to Matthew rather than to Jesus who had named his preaching as evidence for his questioners and who had rejected the request for heavenly pyrotechnics. There is no evidence that the Ninevites knew about the whale nor did Jesus later stay three nights in the tomb.

The second instance of a sign desired from heaven occurs when both Pharisees and Sadducees make the request, according to Matthew. In Luke Jesus addresses the multitude, who do not question him, about the signs of weather which they can read correctly. West wind from the sea meant showers and south wind meant dry heat.

These weather signs are exactly Palestinian. Why could the crowds not read the meaning of their time as they faced Jesus? In Matthew the leaders could read a red sky at evening or dawn as meaning fair and foul weather respectively but they could not read the appearance of their own spiritual climate.

The disciples forgot to take food on a boat trip. They found one small loaf but it was insufficient. Jesus gave some warnings and asked some questions on this trip which remained unanswered. He warned about the leaven of Pharisees and of Herod. Leaven had different meanings besides yeast. It could refer to ordinary bread or to an evil disposition in men. The disciples thought he meant bread while he apparently was speaking of dire influences from religious Pharisees and the political Herod. When the disciples misunderstood, Jesus released a hail of seven questions concerning their mistaken discussion about bread, their dull eyes and ears and their failure to understand about the fragments left from feeding the 5,000 and the 4,000. Mark does not give the results of this Socratic method of Jesus. Matthew lightens and lessens the questions but states that Jesus rebuked the disciples for their little faith.

Mark alone tells of a second miracle in Bethsaida which is almost a twin to the one about the deaf, stammering man. The people bring the needy one to Jesus and beg his aid. There is the same privacy, use of saliva, touch by hand and command to avoid publicity. The miracle is notable for the references to the actions of Jesus who led the blind man by the hand out of the village and twice put his hands on his eyes. His gradual restoration to sight came in two stages as he saw men first blurred and then distinctly. The confidence that the saliva of a great man could effect cures is vividly described by Tacitus [3] when a blind man in Alexandria begged aid from Vespasian. The emperor demurred at first but finally granted the request and the blind man received sight.

Matthew and Luke tell of Jesus' teaching about an unclean or evil spirit which leaves a man and finds no rest in the desert where demons were thought to dwell. Upon its return to its former residence it finds its home swept and orderly. Matthew adds that it was empty. The unclean spirit found seven others more evil to dwell with him. Therefore the man, inhabited by evil powers, is worse than before. Matthew gives this illustration following Jesus' condemnation of an evil sign-seeking generation. He compares the condition of this gen-

[3] *Hist.* IV.81.

eration to the worse state of the demon-haunted man whose empti-
ness invited the return of evil spirits. Luke does not report this comparison with the evil generation. He places the teaching in a different
sequence and holds to its significance for an individual man who,
freed from evil, must carefully guard against its reinforced return.

28

The Declaration of Peter · Coming Suffering · Transfiguration

Mt. 16:13–17:21; Mk. 8:27–9:29; Lk. 9:18–43a, 17:5–6
(122–126, 180)

CAESAREA PHILIPPI, formerly Paneas, was the capital which Herod Philip had rebuilt and named to honor his emperor Tiberius. It stood near the foot of lofty Mount Hermon about twenty-five miles north of the Sea of Galilee. Jesus journeyed with his disciples in villages and on a mountainside near the city where a cycle of significant events show him recognized as Christ, transfigured, and as a mighty healer. In Mark this is a momentous situation. Though Jesus was declared the Christ, he required silence about it and began to teach about the coming sufferings of the Son of Man. These awesome predictions recur three times (Mk. 8:31; 9:31; 10:33–34) on the journey through Galilee toward Jerusalem and each time the disciples object or fail to understand in fear and amazement. In retrospect Mark saw Jesus as Christ and also as the suffering Son of Man who forecast his fate but his secret as Messiah was known only to disciples and not acknowledged publicly until the night before his death at his trial before the high priest. Sometime on his northward travel Jesus decided he must go to Jerusalem. From Caesarea Philippi to Jerusalem was a long way of sorrow but the outcome was not defeat but the triumph of resurrection. The historical difficulty is to determine what the situation was in prospect because the known outcome has somewhat colored the steep dramatic ascent to the last days. Three questions require answers: (1) Did Jesus consider himself the Messiah? (2) Who is the suffering Son of Man? (3) What part did the disciples have in the suffering?

On the way toward Caesarea Philippi Jesus reversed the usual role of a rabbi who answered questions from his students. He asked directly about the common opinion about himself. Matthew changes the first personal pronoun used by Jesus to the "Son of Man." The answers about John the Baptist, Elijah or one of the prophets showed that the people thought Jesus to be some kind of powerful leader and spokesman for God. Both John and Elijah were thought to be related to a coming one. Matthew names Jeremiah whose sufferings were outstanding among the prophets. When Jesus pushed the inquiry for the opinion of his own disciples, Peter, as spokesman, gave the highest identification possible, "You are the Christ." Then Jesus charged them to tell no one about him. Peter's answer in Luke and in Matthew is enlarged to show that the Christ is of God or is the Son of the living God. Since Jesus never made a direct claim to be the Messiah except before the high priest when friendly witnesses were absent and since the evidence is therefore debatable, it is asserted that Jesus himself never claimed Messiahship. "I am personally of the opinion that Jesus did not believe himself to be the Messiah." [1] Jesus was a prophet who prepared his people to do God's will and to accept his rule. Messiahship had been no part of the personal religion of Jesus. "Messianic self-interpretation has not concerned him." [2] It was a designation of his followers.

Opposite to this view is the belief that Jesus was plainly conscious of his Messianic vocation as proved by his baptism, temptation, acceptance of Peter's declaration, claim at his trial, condemnation and crucifixion.[3] Jesus was primarily conscious of his sonship with God and his work as a bringer of the Kingdom yet his Messiahship, though secondary, is historically valid throughout his public life. Since the Messiahship meant many differing ideals to many people and since it might arouse political suspicions, Jesus did not declare his Messiahship until the end of his life. "Jesus was certainly convinced that he was the predicted and awaited Messianic King of Israel." [4]

Between these two views it is possible to see that the later developed belief in Jesus as Christ, as Son of David, as Son of Man and as Suffering Servant has influenced the Gospel records. But at the time that Peter declared Jesus to be Christ this term was not a proper name. "Messiah is essentially an adjective meaning consecrated or appointed by God and was not the prerogative title of any single person until later than the time of Christ." [5] It was applied to Israel, to patriarchs,

[1] R. Bultmann, *Jesus and the Word* (New York, 1934), 9.

[2] S. J. Case, *Jesus* (Chicago, 1927), 377.

[3] H. G. Hatch, *The Messianic Consciousness of Jesus* (London, 1939), 127–28.

[4] C. J. Cadoux, *The Historic Mission of Jesus* (London, 1941), 51; cf. C. T. Craig, "The Problem of the Messiahship of Jesus," in *New Testament Studies,* ed. E. P. Booth (New York 1942), 95–114.

[5] Jackson and Lake, *The Beginnings of Christianity,* I, 362.

to kings, to prophets and even to the Persian, Cyrus the Great. Hence Peter's declaration meant that Jesus had a mission to fulfill to which God had appointed him. Christ is not a popular term in the Synoptics and they reflect accurately the fact that Jesus guarded its use.

The "Son of Man" is especially used by Jesus in his forecasts of suffering. The idea of a suffering Messiah is not Jewish. It was first accepted by Jesus and then applied to him in the light of his teaching and death. He knew the famous Suffering Servant of Isaiah who was not the Messiah in Jewish thought. That Jesus faced his dangerous future with open eyes is clear. That he had difficulty in teaching his disciples about suffering is evident. Peter rebuked him for speaking plainly of his unhappy future. In Mark there is a graphic roadside scene as Jesus turned and saw the other disciples who might have heard Peter's words. He severely called Peter a Satan who stood with men but not with God. Matthew gives Peter's shocked words but adds in Jesus' answer that he was also a hindrance. That Jesus thought of himself as the heavenly Son of Man who would inaugurate a new day as he came in the clouds to judge the world may be doubtful but his death and resurrection established this view for his followers.[6] In the Gospels the term "Son of Man" appears with several meanings but mostly in relation to the suffering, the dying, the rising and the coming of Christ. The ambiguities in the term will always cause difficulty but it is possible that Jesus used the title for himself with new and unique meanings which he merged into a creative, inspiring idea. This ideal linked him with his own people for whom he was willing to suffer and die and it also carried some hope for exaltation in the future. He felt that his leadership fulfilled the Messianic hopes of the past as he understood them and as he prepared his people for God's rule. Yet his mission required the humility of suffering and death. Still there was the power of God entrusted to him which would lead to an eventual, living triumph in a short time (three days). The exactness of details about the future as written in Mark (8:31) shows the knowledge of actual events after Jesus' death as well as the insight and the hopes which Jesus, in the limits of humanity, would know in general rather than in specific form before he reached Jerusalem. His disciples knew he had foretold an incredible future which had amazingly come true.

Matthew alone has a Petrine passage (16:17-19) which has led to widely divergent ideas and actions. When Peter declared Jesus was Christ, he received a blessing from Jesus who said the heavenly

---

[6] B. H. Branscomb, *Gospel of Mark*, 143-52.

Father, not man, revealed this truth to him. Then in a change of his name from Simon, Son of Jona, to Peter, the rock, Jesus made two promises: (1) that upon this rock he would build his church and the gates or the power of death would never succeed against it; (2) that he would give Peter the keys of the Kingdom of Heaven with an authority to control the lawful and the unlawful on earth with the sanction also of heaven.

Two claims based on this passage have had immense historical influence. The first claim is the primacy of Peter who is the rock on which the church is built and whose power had final authority over prohibitions and permissions in the church. These claims could be true for Peter without any certainty that they could be handed on to those who believed that they were his successors. The second claim is that the church and the kingdom are the same since the two are named near together in the promises. This identification is an inference which receives support from the fact that Jesus preached the Kingdom of God in the Gospels while the rest of the New Testament is written about the church. The validity of this inference varies as the words and the deeds of Jesus for the Kingdom are compared with those of men for the church. For Jesus the Kingdom is God's will active among men. The Kingdom is a gift of God's grace and power. It had come in Jesus and in his activities and yet it had a future fulfillment. That Jesus looked for the kind of institution which the church later became is much disputed. However, there are pointers in Matthew's Gospel that an institution was on its way (16:19; 18:18).

These Petrine verses have been viewed in three ways: (1) as a historical saying of Jesus; (2) as a composition by Matthew; (3) as some of each of the foregoing. First, the text of these verses is authentic. All Greek manuscripts and ancient translations contain the verses. Even if the verses were written by Matthew, they could come from a genuine tradition of Jesus. The passage is Jewish in language and thought and similar in style to other sayings of Jesus. It accords with the prominence of Peter throughout the Gospels. The church can be understood as the gathering of disciples who were called together by Jesus and who were to gather others to join in a community which Jesus intended to perpetuate against any powers of the underworld.[7] The rock means Jesus himself according to several early Church Fathers or it means "this" revelation of Messiahship which Peter declared in faith or it means Peter himself. This last under-

[7] K. L. Schmidt, *The Church* (London, 1950), 35–50; R. N. Flew, *Jesus and His Church* (New York, 1938), 123–36.

standing is enforced by a play upon the word "Peter" (rock) both in Aramaic and Greek. The keys to the Kingdom are symbols of authority rather than literal power to control entrance to the church or to the world hereafter as later claimed for Peter. The power to bind and loose was like that exercised by men learned in the Law who gave verdicts on things forbidden and lawful. Such power is illustrated by Josephus who wrote that the Pharisees arose to authority in the native Jewish state under Alexandra, the queen (76–69 B.C.), so that they were at liberty "to banish and recall, to loose and to bind whom they would." [8]

Second, this passage is a composition by Matthew who especially favors Peter as shown in his call, his leadership, this declaration and a special experience at the resurrection. The other Evangelists do not know of this passage about Peter. The word "church" never appears in their writings. Its appearance twice in Matthew indicates a development later than Jesus. The equation of the Kingdom of Heaven to the church is entirely different from Jesus' teachings elsewhere. "The identification of kingdom and church is impossible for Jesus." [9] The church is a new and distinctive fellowship that is the result of the resurrection. Jesus promised the Kingdom to his followers. If Peter had received special authority, he would never have asked what he would receive for following Jesus (Mt. 19:27) nor would the disciples have disputed about the greatest (Mt. 18:1) if Peter had been made the rock. To give Peter an exalted position does not accord with his designation as Satan nor with his conduct which was far from rocklike. The power to bind and loose was also committed by Jesus to all the disciples (Mt. 18:18). Perhaps these verses about the primacy of Peter belong to a post-resurrection tradition about him which arose when he deserved the favor. They are then thought to be placed by Matthew in the earlier setting at Caesarea Philippi.

Third, it is possible that Jesus commended Peter for his insight as shown in verses 17–18 but that verse 19 has been conformed under the direction of the Spirit to the views of those who saw Peter at Antioch as the chief leader whose interpretation of the new law for a new Israel was superior to that of any other Jewish Christian like James or Paul. "Whatever the words meant as originally spoken, it is hard not to suspect that they have been modified by some controversy between followers of different leaders in the early church." [10]

[8] *Wars*, I.5.2.

[9] G. Johnston, *The Doctrine of the Church in the New Testament* (Cambridge, 1943), 51; cf. 46–58.

[10] Streeter, *The Four Gospels*, 258; cf. 504.

Following the forecast by Jesus of his suffering, the warnings were for disciples to be ready to carry their own crosses in following him. This saying has already been discussed in another setting. However, there is a sequel concerning the consequences of disloyalty. In Mark the influence of evil, apostate people may induce shame of Jesus and his words. In that case the Son of Man will disown the disloyal follower when he will come in the glory of the Father with his angels. This glory is one of the ways in which the Son of Man was to be known. Glory is a many-sided word which showed that God made himself known in radiance or in historical events or in some aspect of nature. Matthew states that the Son of Man will act as a judge to give every man what he has earned. It is difficult to know whether Jesus distinguished himself from this coming Son of Man. Opinion is much divided on this point. The Gospel writers identified Jesus with the coming Son of Man after the resurrection and looked for his coming as they adapted the imaginative pictures of Jewish writers about the future to a second appearance of Christ. Matthew makes a notable change in which he states that the Son of Man will be seen coming in his Kingdom. Luke gives the prediction that some will see the Kingdom of God come and Mark that they will see it come with power. They distinguish the coming of the Kingdom from the coming of the Son of Man though the two comings may be equivalent. These predictions were to be fulfilled before the death of some of the hearers of Jesus. The thought that the Kingdom would come quickly and powerfully showed the confidence of Jesus in God. In the lifetime of some of his disciples the Kingdom did make great advances. The prediction in Matthew about the Son of Man coming in his Kingdom had no literal visible fulfillment and eventually the church changed to a more spiritual hope for the future. These hopes about the days to come were repeated and amplified in Jesus' last days in Jerusalem but they were expressed in thought forms of time and space of the first century which differ greatly from present ideas.

The mystery in Jesus rises to splendor in the Transfiguration.[11] Endless wonder circles about the story. In Mark it is the second exalted part of a mysterious cycle of which the forecast of the suffering Christ is first and the wonder-worker who healed an epileptic is third. About a week after Peter's declaration Jesus took Peter, James and John to a high mountain. There three wonders occurred. Jesus

[11] J. B. Bernadin, "The Transfiguration," *Jour. Bib. Lit.* LXX (1933), 181–89; G. Boobyer, *St. Mark and the Transfiguration Story* (Edinburgh, 1942), 1–26, 48–87; A. M. Ramsey, *The Glory of God and the Transfiguration of Christ* (London, 1949), 101–27.

was transfigured, Elijah and Moses appeared and a divine voice spoke from a cloud. This secrecy and the strange nature of the story have caused numerous suggestions about it. These suggestions can be centered about two questions. What is the nature of the experiences and what is their meaning? Matthew quotes Jesus who describes the experience as a vision which is the best term for it. The narrative has been read as a crisis in the inner life of Jesus when he was strengthened to go as Messiah to Jerusalem. The story has been called a myth or perhaps a post-resurrection appearance which has been placed in an earlier period of Jesus' life. It has been thought a part of the theology of the early church in which the vision is a forecast of the glory of Christ in his second coming. But the present position of the story is preferable. It is an event which has been saturated with religious significance, and included a special assurance from God to Jesus and the disciples about his Sonship.

The place is not named and there is no certain identification of the mountain. Since the fourth century Mount Tabor, near Nazareth, has been the traditional site and it still has its churches and annual ceremonies. But it is improbable because Tabor is not a high mountain, nor near Caesarea Philippi. It is in Galilee which Jesus had avoided in his northland travels. He did not pass through Galilee until on his way to Jerusalem (Mk. 9:30). A probable historic spot would be somewhere on the slopes of mighty Mount Hermon. The mountain may be a historical remembrance or an idealization patterned after the famous Sinai-Horeb where Moses and Elijah had known appearances of God. The mountain visit was a time for prayer according to Luke whose longer account may be based on more complete sources or upon his own inferences drawn from Mark.

The meaning of the Transfiguration for Jesus and for his disciples has been the subject of wide discussion. Many people have reported visions which cannot be dismissed as fancies because of their effect upon the ones who see them. People like Isaiah, Paul, Augustine and Joan of Arc were changed by the power and the purity of their visions. Some visions are worthless. They are best judged by their ethical and religious content and by their practical outcome. Luke is the first to see the story with more emphasis on Jesus while Mark and Matthew are more concerned to stress the experiences of the disciples. Jesus had recently announced his way of suffering and the Transfiguration can be seen as a time of prayer when he gained added strength for the hard road ahead and when he felt supported by the great leaders of his people and especially by God. But in Mark this narrative is an interpretation of the experiences of the disciples which Jesus shared with them. He was transfigured "before them." Elijah and Moses appeared "to them" and a voice spoke for their information and direction. When the vision ended, they saw Jesus only. That they were afraid and did not know what to say, were heavy with sleep, puzzled and silent about the experience are indications of a mystery beyond their measurement.

Religion lives in men's lives because there is some real otherness, partly fathomed, partly unfathomable. The whole story is intended to verify for the disciples some most important points of faith about Jesus so that they would be prepared for a dangerous future yet they did not understand until later. Jesus appeared to them for a time in a blazing light. This is reminiscent of Moses who faced God on Mount Sinai to receive his laws and who came down not knowing that the skin of his face shone (Exod. 34:29). For a moment the disciples saw Jesus changed from an earthly to a heavenly appearance. Elijah and Moses, the most notable men in the history of Israel, appeared to converse with Jesus. Luke reports that they talked of his coming departure (death) in Jerusalem. Jesus and Moses and Elijah appear in glory. This reference to glory reflects the thought of an exalted, celestial life with God which Christ attained after his death and resurrection. The vision of glory granted to the disciples was a forecast of the life Jesus would enter after death. Peter's suggestion to build three booths indicates a desire to prolong their experience or it expressed the hope that the Lord would dwell with his people in a tabernacle as he had done in Israelite history. The final part of the vision repeats the baptismal experience for the benefit of the disciples. The cloud and the voice were familiar ways to localize the presence or Shekinah of God. The voice declared the status of Jesus as the beloved Son and commanded the disciples to listen to him. Moses had been promised a prophet like to himself to whom the people must hearken (Dt. 18:15). Mark reports fear in the disciples at the sight of Jesus with Moses and Elijah but in Matthew and Luke they were awed by the cloud and the divine voice. Matthew says that Jesus comforted the disciples as he touched and reassured them after the vision faded.

The effects of this vision are centered in three points: (1) the resurrection; (2) the coming of Elijah; (3) the suffering Son of Man. Jesus charged the disciples to keep quiet until the Son of Man should rise. They could only question among themselves about it since they had no idea of a Son of Man in resurrection. When they asked Jesus about the meaning of the current expectation of Elijah who was to come before the great and terrible day of the Lord (Mal. 4:5), Jesus met their question with another. Elijah was expected to come before the Messiah to restore all things to an ideal situation but he had already come and met an unhappy fate. Why must the Son of Man suffer contempt? This, as Matthew explained, showed the disciples that the current hope about the coming of Elijah had been fulfilled by John the Baptist who had endured the same fate that the Son of Man would soon face. The suffering Son of Man seemed incredible to the disciples and it is no wonder that Jesus' question was left unanswered. The disciples thought the Son of Man was to come in power and glory but Jesus foretold his suffering. The Transfiguration was a real experience of the disciples. They saw in a vision some strange meanings in an unusual appearance of Jesus which they could only understand after Jesus' death.

The ascent of the mountain, the vision on the mountain and the mighty work at the foot of the mountain belong together. In Matthew and Mark the descent follows immediately after the vision but in Luke it comes the next day. Jesus and the three found the rest of the disciples in an argument with scribes in the midst of a large crowd who greeted Jesus in amazement. When Jesus asked about the subject of discussion, a man reported that he had brought his epileptic son whose demon the disciples could not cast out. Jesus wondered how long he could stand these faithless people. Mark gives details about the violent convulsions of the son and the diagnosing dialogue between Jesus and the anguished father who alternated between belief and unbelief. The power of faith flows in Jesus' words, "All things are possible to him that believes." When Jesus commanded the spirit to leave permanently, the boy had a convulsion but Jesus took him by the hand and he got up. The former condition of the boy is described in Mark as due to a dumb spirit and in Matthew as moonstruck. In treatment of the boy's fits Jesus followed the methods of exorcism of his day. The unusually complete symptoms indicate epilepsy. Luke alone reports the astonishment of everyone at the majesty of God. Matthew reports the cure as instantaneous. Both of these comments exalt the ability of Jesus to meet a need that the disciples could not meet. When they asked him privately about their inability, Jesus answered that prayer alone could drive out such a demon. Some later manuscripts add the necessity of fasting. Prayer was one of the best attacks on demons according to Jewish beliefs. The answer of Jesus points to an important truth but it is not the expected answer in view of the stress on faith in the narrative. It may have been spoken by Jesus at another time and used here by Mark for teaching or it may be one of the several occasions when Jesus surprised his disciples by an unexpected teaching. Matthew gives the expected answer of Jesus as he points to the little faith of the disciples and adds that tiny faith could move a mountain. "Nothing will be impossible to you." To move mountains was a picturesque Jewish manner of speech for doing what seemed impossible. Jesus proved the power of faith by the cure and he wanted his disciples to share this faith. Luke puts this same teaching for the disciples much later in his Gospel and changes the figure of the mountain to a mulberry tree uprooted and planted in the sea by faith. These conscious exaggerations aroused his disciples, as no prosaic statement ever did, to believe that faith could achieve insuperable goals.

29

The Fate of the Son of Man · Greatness · Temptation · The Sinning Brother

Mt. 17:22–27, 18:1–35; Mk. 9:30–50; Lk. 9:43b–50, 17:1–4, 11:23
(127–131, 134–136)

ACCORDING TO Mark Jesus and his disciples came through Galilee secretly. As he taught them about the Son of Man whose betrayal, death and resurrection lay ahead, they did not understand this incredible idea and feared to ask him. Matthew favors the disciples as he omits their ignorance and states they were greatly grieved. In Luke Jesus warns the disciples to let his words sink into their ears but he gives only the forecast of betrayal. He explains the ignorance of the disciples as part of a prearranged divine plan which concealed the meaning for a time. This second prediction about the fate of the Son of Man should have been clear to the disciples if it was as detailed as given in Matthew and Mark. But in fact the disciples came soon to Jerusalem and when the deadly crisis arrived, they fled as if unprepared. It appears more probable that the less definite forecast in Luke constitutes the early warning rather than the detailed account of betrayal, death and resurrection which were made clear after their accomplishment in Jerusalem but not on the way there. The ominous words of Jesus about the future were fulfilled and the actual events rounded out the memories of the disciples as they told of teachings before Jerusalem which were clarified after Jerusalem.

Matthew with his special interest in Peter tells of his part in the payment of the temple tax at Capernaum. This tax was required of every Jewish man from the age of twenty as "a ransom for his soul unto the Lord" (Exod. 30:11–13). This poll tax was paid annually for the support of public worship in the Temple. The amount required, in modern value, was about seventy-five cents. Peter assured the tax collector that Jesus paid the tax. When Peter came home, Jesus asked him whether kings took customs and head taxes from their own people or from aliens. When Peter answered that the latter

paid, Jesus said sons were free but nevertheless Peter was to pay the
tax for himself and Jesus. When Jesus said Peter would find a shekel
in the mouth of a fish, he was speaking illustratively of the way in
which fishing would provide money. The story showed that Jesus
paid his religious tax even though not required. It is possible also
that the story was used by Matthew for a later situation when Jewish
Christians had to decide about the continued support of the Temple.
In that case they had an example from Jesus for voluntary support.

Also at Capernaum Jesus asked his disciples about their discussion
on the road. Their silence indicted them. Mark explains that they
had discussed who was greatest. Perhaps this grew out of selection of
the three who had been up the mountain or, as Matthew suggests,
their interest was in the future Kingdom. Jesus both spoke and acted
to teach them. He sat down, called the Twelve and in paradoxical
words declared the first was last of all and servant of all. Then he
took a child in his arms and said that anyone who received or dealt
kindly with such a little one received himself and also God who sent
him. Matthew relieves the disciples of the dispute among themselves
and it is they who ask Jesus about the greatest rather than Jesus who
questioned them. Matthew also writes that Jesus put the child among
the Twelve rather than in his own arms and that Jesus told the disciples they must become like little children. He omits the reference
to the reception of the one who had sent Jesus. These changes give a
different meaning to Jesus' acted illustration with the child.

In Luke Jesus reads the thoughts of the disciples in the argument,
teaches that the reception of the child is the reception of himself and
of God and concludes with the saying that the least among the disciples is greatest. The thought of greatness in humility and service
in this story is highly significant because it appears two more times
in Matthew (20:26–27; 23:11–12), also in Luke (18:14, 17; 22:26)
and once in Mark (10:43–44). Jesus recognized the drive of ambition
in his disciples but he turned it to greatness in helpfulness, even to a
little child. His care for children is beautifully pictured by Mark who
shows him with a child in his arms as he teaches grown men the
importance of a little one. Anyone who is kind for the sake of Jesus,
even to a child, serves both him and God. This profound relationship
makes all greatness truly humble and helpful. It bears the remembrance that whatever is done to another is to be done as to Jesus and
to God. To be great is to be kind, to be first is to be ready to be last,
to aid the least child is to know God.

John, the son of Zebedee, is the sole speaker in one place only in the Gospels. He stands third in the inner circle of Peter, James and John who are the favored ones of the Twelve. As a "Son of Thunder" he forbade an exorcist to use the name of Jesus as a formula to cast out demons because the exorcist was not with Jesus and the disciples. Jesus commanded tolerance. Anyone who used his name to defeat evil demons could not soon speak evil of him. Such a worker is not an enemy but a friend. An opposite form of this saying which states that anyone not with Jesus is against him appears later in Luke (11:23) and Matthew (12:30). The contradiction can be understood as due to different circumstances. In the latter sayings Jesus was speaking of a battle against Satan where no neutrality was possible. Jesus felt that the exorcist, forbidden by John, was an ally whose work should not be stopped. Even a small gift of a cup of water to disciples would receive a reward. The phrase "because you belong to Christ" sounds like an addition from the later time when the followers of Christ were thus designated. Jesus had just forbidden any mention of Christ to the disciples at Peter's declaration. They did not bear the name of Christ while they were with Jesus. Luke has a briefer account and changes the command for tolerance so that it refers to the disciples exclusively rather than to include Jesus with them. Exorcism in the name of Jesus is not reported elsewhere in the Gospels though his name was used for exorcism soon after his death. Names of gods and of great men were part of the formulae for healings or exorcisms. Or a person could be afflicted or bound by some demon's name. Since the early church used the name of Jesus, it faced the problem of its use by those outside the church as some strolling Jews once tried to use it, only to have the man with an evil spirit attack them (Acts 19:13-16). The story about John reflects the need for some answer from Jesus about exorcists with no official connection with the church. It taught toleration of others doing good in the name of Jesus though outside the church.

The sternness of Jesus' warning to those who put stumbling blocks in the way of believing little ones shows how strongly Jesus felt about offenses against innocency or helplessness. He said temptations to sin would come but it would be better to drown with a millstone in the sea than to lead little ones into sin. This millstone was not the small one used by women to grind grain but the larger one turned by a donkey which would be ample to sink a man in the sea. The statement about little ones in Matthew refers to children whose ill treatment arouses strong feelings. But in Mark and Luke the little ones are the humble beginners who believe in Jesus but who are not strong enough for defense against evildoers. Jesus sometimes called his disciples "children"; hence it is not always clear whether little ones refer to children or to those new in the faith. In Matthew the little ones must not be despised because the messengers of God who watch over them have direct access always to God's presence.

The next warning turns with equal sternness from others to oneself. The hand, the foot, the eye can lead into sin and Jesus in vigorous language insists that it is better to lose part of the body than the whole of it. To enter the Kingdom is worth any sacrifice. In Matthew entrance into life replaces entrance into the Kingdom while Mark uses life and Kingdom interchangeably. Opposite to life is Gehenna, named for the steep ravine where the garbage of Jerusalem was dumped and burned. Gehenna is a metaphor for the place of punishment for the wicked. It is unfortunate that in English hell has been used to translate both Gehenna and Hades because the latter is not properly hell but the world of the dead. The pictorial aspects of Gehenna arouse horror but do not give information about its location and ultimate outcome. In Mark the worm and the fire are quoted from a prophecy of Isaiah (66:24) who described the fate of sinners against God. Jesus taught that self-discipline could lead to life while the lack of it led to hell. The importance of the future was decisive as one chose the Kingdom or Gehenna. Discipline was essential for those facing possible martyrdom.

Three short sayings about salt illustrate the way some of Jesus' declarations were linked together because they shared a common word. Salt appears with three different meanings. The only connection is verbal. "Everyone will be salted with fire" is a baffling expression but may mean that one will be purified by the fire of persecution. Matthew and Luke omit the saying. Torrey, who has set forth the problems of translation from Aramaic into Greek, holds that "it obviously is as impractical to salt a person with fire as it would be to fire him with salt." Since Aramaic and Hebrew were written only in consonants, some of which are much alike, ambiguity could easily arise. He translates the saying, "Anything spoiling is salted." [1] The next saying about the salt which loses saltness signifies those who become useless through lost devotion. The final meaning of salt is that it is a symbol of friendship and peace among the disciples.

Matthew has a passage in which he refers to a brother in the church. "In Jewish usage 'brother' stands for a co-religionist, fellow-member of the Jewish religious group. It is distinguished from 'neigh-

[1] Torrey, *Our Translated Gospels*, 13.

bor' which means fellow-member of the Jewish people or nation." [2] The specific directions for dealing with a sinning brother are different, both in form and in thought, from the usual ideals of Jesus. There is a shorter saying in Luke that a sinning brother is to be rebuked, then forgiven if he repents. An unfailing forgiveness must be willing to accept the repentant sinner even seven times in a day. Seven was the number which stood for completion or perfection. From this kind of general saying the exact rules in Matthew were developed to deal in four steps with an erring brother. The rules are followed by assurances about the authority of the disciples and about the power of prayer when two or three agree. The first step with the offender is a private appeal, as the Law required. If it fails, the next step is to take others to testify about the sinner. The Law required two or three witnesses (Dt. 19:15). If the offender refused any settlement, then the matter is to be put before the church. A final failure there will require avoidance of the offender as if he were a Gentile and a tax collector. This last step of separation is opposite to the association of Jesus with tax collectors in Galilee. Since Jesus did not teach religion by the use of rules and since the word "church" appears in this passage, these four steps are regarded as a development of church regulations for which the authority of Jesus was cited. All the disciples were given the power to bind and loose which earlier had been conferred on Peter. The great significance of prayers, united and harmonious, is assured by the promise that the Father will answer them. The absolute form of this promise about God's response and about the presence of Jesus among two or three united in his name points toward an independent saying of Jesus which has no connection elsewhere but Matthew has placed it to support decisions to bind and to loose. The belief that God hears and answers prayer even of two people in agreement and that those who gather for Christ's sake can know his spiritual fellowship "in the midst of them" has had immeasurable effects upon the devotional life of Christians. The great promises of Jesus had rooting in Malachi (3:16) who had written that the Lord hearkened and heard those who reverenced him and spoke one to another. A century after Jesus a rabbi promised "if two sit together and the words of the Law are spoken between them the Divine Presence rests between them." [3]

In Matthew Peter asked about forgiveness for a sinning brother and generously suggested seven times as the limit because it was com-

---

[2] Manson, in *Mission and Message of Jesus* (New York, 1938), 502.
[3] *Pirke Aboth* 3:3; Danby, *The Mishnah*, 450.

mon belief that there was no obligation to forgive more than three times. But he received from Jesus the astounding reply "seventy times seven" or possibly "seventy-seven times." This is in contrast to the seventy-sevenfold revenge exacted by the patriarch Lamech (Gen. 4:24). As there had once been revenge without limit so Peter had to learn that forgiveness was unlimited. To enforce this ideal Jesus gave the parable of the unmerciful servant which accords with the thought of his day on forgiveness. The best Jewish teaching urged forgiveness of an injury so that in one's own prayers his sins would be forgiven (Ecclus. 28:2). One must speak peaceably to a sinner with no guile against him and forgive him when he repents (Test. Gad. 6:3). Jesus did not tell the parable to illustrate repeated forgiveness, as in Peter's question, but to teach readiness to forgive. As one deals with another so must one expect God to deal with him. There was a trusted servant of a king who had to give an accounting for a loan. The sum of 10,000 talents which he owed appears incredibly large. A talent equals about $1,000. The sale of himself and family to meet his debt was stopped when he pleaded for patience and a chance to pay. The king did better than the debtor dreamed. He canceled the whole debt. This generous forgiveness was lost upon the servant who then threw a fellow servant into jail because he owed him twenty dollars. Compared with the ten-million-dollar debt of the first servant, this debt was a trifle yet the hardhearted creditor had no mercy. When the king heard of this situation, it is no wonder that he turned over his unforgiving servant to the torturers who would find any hidden assets and hold him until he paid. As the king had set the example of forgiveness, so God's mercy sets the standard for his children to forgive one another.

30

Events and Parables Mainly in Luke

Lk. 9:51–62, 10:1, 17–20 (137–140), 29–42; Mt. 8:18–22 (114, 145, 49); Lk. 11:5–8, 27–28 (147, 151), 12:13–21 (156), 13:1–17, 31–33 (162, 163, 166), 14:1–14 (168, 169), 15:1–16:15, 19–31, 17:7–10 (173–175, 177, 181–183), 18:1–14 (185, 186)

LUKE HAS a central section (9:51–18:14) which constitutes almost one third of his book. It is the "center and core of the Third Gospel." It makes no use of Mark and shares about one half of Q.[1] Luke has special events and parables complete enough to lead to the suggestion that he had a special source and that he used part of it for this section before he found Mark. There are four brief mentions of the way which led to Jerusalem (9:51; 13:22–23; 17:11; 18:31) but basically the section is composed of teachings of Jesus. There are four notices of Samaritans which illustrate Luke's interest in non-Jewish people.[2] Its parables, such as the Prodigal Son and the Good Samaritan, are the best known of Jesus' stories.

The section opens with an exalted earnest look ahead to the time when Jesus would be received up. This is a reference to the Ascension which followed his death and resurrection. Jesus faced the upward way to Jerusalem with utmost determination. As he headed south, his messengers were refused hospitality at a Samaritan village. There had been bitter feelings between Samaritans and Jews since the days of Ezra and Nehemiah, four hundred years earlier, when a religious feud developed after Jews refused Samaritans any share in rebuilding the Temple (Ez. 4:3–5). The Samaritans accepted only the Pentateuch and developed their own priesthood and temple. The Jews looked on them as half-breeds in race and religion, "a foolish nation" (Ecclus. 50:26). Jews usually avoided travel in Samaria. From Galilee they took the longer road down the east side of the Jordan to Jerusalem. Jesus had headed straight south where he met inhospitality. The stormy sons of Zebedee believed that Jesus like Elijah, the mighty

---

[1] Streeter, *The Four Gospels*, 203.
[2] M. S. Enslin, "Luke and the Samaritans," *Harv. Theol. Rev.* XXXVI (1943), 277–97.

prophet, could permit destruction of enemies by fire from heaven (II Kgs. 1:10–12). But Jesus turned and rebuked them for their vengeful suggestion and went on to another village.

Three would-be disciples received stern replies from Jesus. Matthew identifies two of them as a scribe and another disciple. Luke does not name them. To the first man who volunteered to follow anywhere Jesus replied that he would have to endure homelessness. Even foxes and birds had their dwellings but the Son of Man had no place to lay his head. The next candidate asked leave to bury his father before he came. Burial of the dead was a duty important enough to demand risk of life and property (Tob. 1:19–20). Yet Jesus said to let the dead bury the dead and to go and herald the rule of God. In Matthew the requirement is to follow Jesus. This hard demand can scarcely be literal because the dead cannot act, hence it is thought to mean that a man could not wait for his father to die before he became a disciple, or spiritually dead must look after the physically dead while the disciple entered into the more urgent work for the Kingdom. The next man wanted to go home to make farewells which might be elaborate and delayed. Jesus required disciples to be like a man with his Palestinian one-handled plow who had to look ahead if he did his work. No man who divided his attention was fit for the work. These renunciations seem harsh but they must be read in the light of Jesus' own example and of the danger ahead in Jerusalem. Jesus wanted no faint hearts, no sudden enthusiasts, no doubtful disciples but rather those who could endure a homeless life, who could give first place to the Kingdom and who could go forward ungrieved over the past.

The appointment and the work of the Seventy may be a doublet of the sending forth of the Twelve or it may be meant to include the fact that Jesus had a wide circle of disciples to whom he gave the same instructions as to the Twelve. Or it may be Luke's device to suggest a ministry to Gentiles since there were thought to be seventy nations in the world. Only Luke records the appointment and the report of the Seventy. Their return, with joy at their control of demons by the name of Jesus, led him in one of his vivid phrases to see Satan, chief of demons, fallen like lightning. It was a common hope that Satan would be overthrown as part of his final defeat. Jesus encouraged his followers by assurance of their power over the enemy. Treading on serpents and scorpions, which were often regarded as half demonic, is a metaphor of success. That nothing could hurt the disciples was a triumphant claim for faith over physical facts. Yet this success over evil spirits was not the most important reason for joy. The idea of a heavenly book where God had written a record is known in both Old and New Testaments. It was a book of life which named those who were destined to live with God (Exod. 32:32; Dan. 12:1; Phil. 4:3; Rev. 21:27). There was also the idea that the book was a record of men's deeds for judgment (Isa. 65:6; Rev. 20:12). The Seventy were to rejoice in their enrollment in the book as citizens in the coming Kingdom. This privilege took precedence over control of demons. The prayer of rejoicing by Jesus has been discussed earlier.

With its moral penetration, its memorable simplicity and beauty, the parable of the Good Samaritan takes first rank among popular stories. In Luke the parable has an introduction which is a dialogue between a lawyer and Jesus about eternal life. In Matthew and Mark the question is about the greatest commandment and it comes in the last week in Jerusalem. Since the lawyer quoted the command to love one's neighbor as oneself, he asked Jesus, "Who is my neighbor?" In answer Jesus gave the story of the Good Samaritan. The scene of the brutal attack on the unnamed traveler is the steep road which winds down seventeen miles from the heights of Jerusalem to Jericho. Deep deserted ravines, barren cliffs and caves made the region a favorite one for robbers. The priest and the Levite were important officials at the worship in the Temple. Perhaps they were on their way home to Jericho where many priests lived at the completion of their period of service in Jerusalem. There is no explanation of their actions as they passed by the victim of attack and robbery. To relieve their callousness it has been guessed that they shared the belief that misfortune was God's judgment on sin and they hesitated to interfere in an act of God or that they could not risk ceremonial defilement from a possible corpse.[3] But it was evident that the man was left half dead by the act of man and human need took precedence over ritual. A parable, like a popular story, does not stop for all possible explanations. Even the helpless traveler is unidentified. The Samaritan was a layman, perhaps a trader, despised by Jews for his race and religion but he had pity. His aid to the victim, with the use of oil and wine, a common remedy for cleansing and healing wounds, and his provision of a place and money for future care constitute the point of the story. "The moral is not that a Samaritan is better than a priest but that a loving Samaritan is better than a loveless priest."[4] When Jesus asked the lawyer who proved a neighbor to the man, his question was a

---

[3] Oesterley, The Gospel Parables, 164.
[4] Easton, The Gospel according to St. Luke (New York, 1926), 171.

radical shift from the starting question of the lawyer, "Who is my neighbor?" When Jesus commanded the lawyer to do as the Samaritan had done, he transposed a question into moral conduct.

In the Synoptics Jesus appears once as the guest of Mary and Martha. Luke does not name their village though John's Gospel (11:1) gives it as Bethany, which is near Jerusalem. This scene of home hospitality is the kind of story Luke enjoyed. The hospitality of the sisters took differing forms. Mary sat at the feet of Jesus, the position of a pupil. Martha worked diligently at preparation of an elaborate meal. Her heated question frankly asked Jesus if he had no care that Mary gave her no help. "Tell her then to help me." Since the manuscripts have variant readings, Jesus' whimsical reproach has been taken with two different meanings. Martha had been worried about many things to eat when few or one would be enough. Mary has chosen the "best dish" as Moffatt translates and she is not to be dragged away from it. She had listened to the teaching of Jesus. The other meaning becomes allegorical as Martha is thought to represent the practical person or the many things of the Jewish law or Jewish Christianity while Mary represents the devout person or spiritual concerns or Gentile Christianity or the Gospel as "one thing." When the allegory comes in, its fancies easily exceed control. This household scene portrays Jesus as the Lord throughout the story. He came as a guest who commended the higher duty and opportunity to hear his teaching in which the lesser duty to things in the kitchen must not interfere.

After the Lord's Prayer Luke relates a parable of prayer about a friend at midnight. Perhaps the midnight guest had traveled to avoid the excessive day heat. The home in Palestine had small food stocks and hospitality required bread for a guest. The host had none so he awoke a neighbor for a loan of three loaves. The neighbor was gruffy and reluctant to get up. He did not answer with friendliness. He did not want to disturb his children who were literally with him on mattresses on the floor. The shut door kept out any unclean spirits who dwelt in the dark. He could not get up because he had no will to do it. But the persistent neighbor allowed him no sleep until his request was granted. If friendliness did not work, then his importunity would bring results. The man in bed is not like God but in contrast to him. If a neighbor will give all that is needed, how much more God will answer prayer especially when it is for another's need. Importunity in prayer depends upon the importance of the request.

One brief mention in Luke corresponds in part to an earlier visit of Jesus' relatives when he had emphasized the importance of spiritual kinship (Lk. 8:19-21). A woman exclaimed in complimentary fashion at the teaching of Jesus that the mother who bore him must be happy. The answer of Jesus may be understood as a rebuke of flattery or as a counsel of wisdom. "Jesus was not deluded by people who made pious noises and he brought them back to realities by the shortest possible route." [5] But the woman's admiration for Jesus, expressed indirectly by a reference to his mother, may better be taken as conceded by Jesus but also corrected to show that true happiness for all lay in hearing and doing God's word.

Jesus told the parable of the rich fool when an unknown man asked him to settle a dispute over inheritance. Since the Mosaic law covered all obligations, religious, civil and criminal, rabbis were consulted for decisions in disputes. Jesus refused to be a judge in a case where two brothers of the same faith quarreled over property. Since he warned next about covetousness, it appears that the man was not in need of justice but had sought to use Jesus in his schemes for more wealth. Though a man has abundance, his life is not essentially in his possessions. He owns his wealth, it does not own him. A rich farmer in the midst of his plenty said to himself that his future consisted in building bigger barns and in a life of ease when he would eat, drink and be merry. He thought there was nothing better under the sun for a man to do (Eccles. 8:15). "Man proposes but God disposes." The man's monologue to himself has a postscript as God said to him, "Fool, this night your soul is required from you." As a final barbed question God asked him who would get his things (Ecclus. 11:19). The man was a fool not because he did wrong but because he saw life only in "my crops," "my barns," "my grain" and "my goods." He lost these riches with his life. He lacked riches with God who is man's true treasure.

Disasters must be endured by those who suffer them but their meanings are many. When Jesus commented on the two recent disasters, he turned the thought about them into a new direction. Luke does not state why Jesus was told about the Galileans Pilate had killed during their sacrifices in Jerusalem nor why they were slain. Probably their quick tempers met Pilate's cruelty since he always had trouble in his rule of Judea. These unfortunate victims were like the eighteen who died in an accident when a tower in Siloam fell on them. Siloam was a pool into which emptied an aqueduct which brought water to Jerusalem from the south. Jesus denied that these dead were sinners above all others. A current belief asserted suffering was due to sin. But not all sinners meet misfortune measured to their sins. Jesus directed attention not to the sin of the dead men but to the sin of his hearers who had to repent or perish. It is far easier to comment on the hard luck of others than to correct one's own evil ways. When Jesus said men must repent or all would perish, it is uncertain whether he had individuals or his nation in mind though the latter is favored. To reinforce repentance he told the parable of the barren fig tree which only used up space in the vineyard. It was customary to plant fig trees in vineyards. The owner wanted the useless tree cut down and the area filled by a fruitful tree. The caretaker pleaded for one more chance for the tree which had had no fruit for three years. He would cultivate and fertilize it and try one more year. The parable points out that repentance was open but the time was short.

The healing of the bent woman is told only by Luke. Her condition looks like some curvature of the spine which she had endured for eighteen years. It is described as a spirit of weakness and a binding by Satan. When Jesus saw her in the synagogue, he called her, laid his hands upon her and declared her free from her infirmity. Then she praised God and all the people rejoiced at the glorious things done by Jesus. There is a secondary aspect in the story since the synagogue ruler scolded the people and told them there were six days in a week to work and not to come to be healed on the Sabbath. Jesus questioned this command as he cited the law which allowed mercy to animals who needed water on the Sabbath and thus an Israelite woman should be freed from the power of evil on the holy day. This story combines the power of Jesus to heal, which he regarded as warfare against Satan, with the assertion that to do good on the Sabbath did not break the law of God.

As Jesus journeyed toward Jerusalem, some Pharisees told him that Herod wanted to kill him. The Pharisees may have been friendly in their warning and wished to save him from a fate like John the Baptist or they may have been hostile in order to frighten him out of Herod's territory or perhaps they were spokesmen for Herod. The strong reply of Jesus gives Herod the uncomplimentary but deserved name of fox, an animal known in the Bible for its destructiveness. It was also cunning and worthless. Jesus showed no fear as he sent his defiant message to Herod. He would continue his work but in a short time he would say, "I am finished." This meant his life and work. He would go his way shortly but not from fear or threats. Then in strange words of sorrowful irony, he gave as his reason for departure that a prophet could not appropriately die away from Jerusalem. This so-called holy city had killed and rejected its messengers from God. This incident, like the warning Jesus gave after Peter's declaration, proves that Jesus felt danger in his coming visit to Jerusalem.

Only Luke describes a cure of dropsy which occasioned another dispute over the Sabbath. The setting is in the home of a Pharisaic ruler where Jesus dined. The healing of the man is related briefly. Whether he came as a guest or on his own initiative is not explained. Jesus took hold of him, healed him and sent him out. The Pharisee refused to answer Jesus' question about the lawfulness of Sabbath healing and Jesus used his familiar comparison. If one would pull an animal out of a well on the Sabbath, how much more should a man be helped. This issue of the Sabbath is set in the framework of general Pharisaic opposition to Jesus. They watched him but he was not stopped by suspicion. They had no reply to his questions nor to his action as he healed the man.

This dinner with the ruler also showed Jesus the selfish seekers for favored places. Then Jesus told a parable to the guests and added some words to his host. These comments bear two interpretations. The parable may mean that Jesus had in mind the common thought that the Kingdom of God is like a great banquet and that there is a certain behavior expected of those who desire to enter and to enjoy the feast of the Kingdom. Position in the Kingdom is in God's hands and it is not awarded by one's own estimate of his own importance. Thus Jesus used etiquette to teach the great lesson of humility. "Pride goeth before destruction. And a haughty spirit before a fall" (Prov. 16:18). The poor in spirit possess the Kingdom.

But it is possible that Jesus spoke of the actual courtesies in receiving and giving hospitality which was a superior virtue in Palestinian life. Jesus had an eye for all mundane affairs but he saw in them the power of right purposes. To guests he indicated perhaps that "it is not the purpose of humility to get promotion but only the humble can be promoted." [6] To be invited up is better than to be told to step down (Prov. 25:7). To hosts he said, perhaps partly in humor, that a good time at banquets is less important than meals for the poor, the cripples and the blind. To invite your friends, relatives or the rich might mean they would return the invitation. This is hospitality traded, not given. True happiness comes and an eternal reward will be gained by food shared with the needy. Those who give such aid

[6] H. Balmforth, *Gospel according to St. Luke* (Oxford, 1930), 232.

will share "the resurrection of the just." This is a Pharisaic phrase for the life that God bestows upon his good people in the future. Jesus gave some suggestions about etiquette for hosts and guests at actual dinners but such behavior was also related to the final eternal purposes of God.

No parables of Jesus are greater favorites than those which tell of the lost sheep, the lost coin and the lost sons. However, in each case the real point centers in the shepherd, the woman and the father who rejoice that the lost is found. "What was certainly new in Christ's teaching was his belief that it was God's will that the sinner should be sought and not merely mourned for." [7] In Luke Jesus relates the parables when tax collectors and sinners came to hear him. They recognized his sympathy and interest in them and listened to his requirements. But the Pharisees and the scribes, the religious elite, complained at the contacts of Jesus with sinners. Matthew gives the story of the lost sheep in another setting as Jesus was talking to disciples. In Matthew the sheep strayed and the owner went on the possibility that he might find it. When he found it, he rejoiced over it more than over his ninety-nine safe sheep. In Luke the shepherd searches until he finds the sheep he had lost. Then he invites neighbors and friends to rejoice with him. At the end there is more joy in heaven over one sinner than over ninety-nine righteous persons. "In heaven" is used to avoid the sacred name of God but it means that God is glad.

The lost coin led the woman to search diligently until she located it. The dark house with few windows required a light for the hunt. The floor of rock or hard earth had to be swept. When the coin was found, there was the same joy with friends as there is in heaven over one repentant sinner.

The father who shared his property at his younger son's request was generous and trusting. The laws of inheritance gave double to the first born (Dt. 21:17; Num. 27:8–11). Division of property could be made before death though it was not good practice (Ecclus. 33:19–23). The younger son was reckless with money and careless about companions. He sank to the worst degradation for a Jew. He had to feed swine and even share their food which was the pod of the locust tree. In desperation from hunger, he thought of home, prepared a speech of repentance and returned home. His father's pity and love welcomed him. According to some manuscripts the father did not wait to hear his son's entire speech of repentance. His quick com-

---

[7] Smith, *The Parables of the Synoptic Gospels*, 190.

mands for the first-grade robe, the ring, the shoes, the finest food and merriment show the father's joy in his returned son who was again within the family home and bounty. The elder son, like the Pharisees, was hard on his sinning brother. His father with patience went out to him, as he had gone out also to the prodigal, to explain the situation. But in anger and jealousy he accused his father of neglect and his brother of wasting wealth in harlotry. He said he never had a small kid from his father but a large calf was given to this wastrel "son of yours." Still the father called him "son" as he did the prodigal and reminded him that everything was his but it was right to rejoice that "your brother" who has been lost was found. God is like the father who stands before each son with love and forgiveness and with joy over repentance and recovery.

The elder son has had his defenders in the name of justice. But a parable does not illustrate a whole system of morals or theology. The parable is about God's mercy and joy and love. The first need of the returning, repentant son was for forgiveness and restoration. The father could act only as he did, in affection as a father, at the time of the return of his son to his heart and home. The father is not God but God is like the father. Many questions could be asked about the past and the future of each member of the family but like a great painting this story is selective of a certain beautiful, essential truth which Jesus set forth to perfection. Spare simplicity of scene, vigorous action, warm affection, living dialogue, realistic morals, religious depth and a consummate sureness of style combine into unsurpassed excellence in this parable. Something of Luke's artistic writing genius appears in this story but he has creatively and perfectly blended his art with the still greater originality of Jesus.

No parable has elicited more comments about its point than the one about the unjust steward. One reason for the variations is that Luke has added a list of sayings which contain many suggestions. No parable has aroused more questions about its morals. But a parable is not an allegory. Not every detail can be pressed for a religious meaning. This shrewd steward is drawn from life and as in the parable of the hidden treasure not all actions are ideals because they appear in a story. The wealthy man who demanded an accounting from his dishonest manager before he dismissed him found that the manager was able to feather his own nest for the future. He had a time of panic as he faced the loss of his job and felt too soft to labor and too proud to beg but he concocted a clever plan. He had various debtors rewrite their own contracts at a reduced figure so that the debtors owed him rather than the owner. The debts were payable in kind. A measure of oil was about nine gallons and a measure of wheat about ten bushels. The debtors had a substantial saving from the steward's reduction of their obligations.

The difficulties begin with the statement that the lord commended the steward for his prudence. The "lord" has been understood to be either the wealthy master or Jesus. It is hard to see why either should commend him but there is no adequate reason to take the lord as a reference to Jesus since throughout the story all other references to the lord mean the owner. It is possible that the master praised the steward not for his cheating but for his clever plan to insure his own future. The second difficulty is to decide whether the statement about the wisdom of worldly people is the comment of the owner or of Jesus. This comment is better understood as the point of the parable in which Jesus said men like the shrewd steward deal more wisely in this life with people of their own kind than do the "sons of light." These men cannot be identified except that they are those who share the light of God. The main idea is that men should take forethought for their spiritual and eternal welfare with as much ingenuity as keen-witted men plan their future with material things. The third difficulty is to understand the saying about making friends by use of unrighteous mammon and to decide whether it is also a point of the parable. Luke took this saying as an application of the parable. There is probably no better understanding of it. Jesus may not have been so limited to one idea for each of his stories as are some modern commentators. In this saying Jesus advised his disciples to use money which often is tainted by misuse or by a false trust in it more than in God so that when money fails or death comes, friendship will endure and in the eternal dwellings even God will accept the one who makes this kind of investment. As the shrewd steward used his wealth to make his future secure in the houses of his creditors so might the followers of Jesus use their money, not unrighteously, but wisely to gain treasure in heaven. The final difficulty concerns sayings which Luke has piled up at the end of this parable. These sayings deal with the relation of the riches of the earth to the true riches of life under God's rule but they have only a topical likeness to the parable and did not originally belong in it. They are important sayings of Jesus by which Luke wished to safeguard the understanding of a difficult parable. Fidelity in the use of wealth is essential. No dishonesty can be allowed even in a small matter. If one cannot be trusted in handling worldly goods, how can one be trusted with the genuine wealth of spiritual blessings? If one is untrustworthy in the use of another's belongings, how can one expect possessions of his own? A man must be honest about money which God has loaned him in order that God may give him eternal possessions which stay with him as no transient earthly goods can ever remain. The saying about God and mammon appears also in the Sermon on the Mount where it has been discussed.

Luke commented that the Pharisees were money lovers. This characterization has often been accepted but it has also been denied. "This designation produces a situation that is historically false." [8] The Sadducees deserved the title more than the Pharisees and the saying may have originally been directed against them.[9] But the issue of the incident is not in money but in the answer of Jesus to the Pharisees who heard his teaching and turned up their noses at him. Some of them may have regarded wealth as evidence of God's favor but their self-justification before men was not the same as God's estimate. He knew their hearts. A good standing with men can be loathsome in God's sight. Some Pharisees were more interested in high positions among men than in inward standing with God.

The parable of the rich man and Lazarus further illustrates Luke's interest in the use of riches. This parable has some distinctive aspects. It is the only one in which a proper name, Lazarus, is used. This is an abbreviation of Eliezar which means Helped of God. The unknown rich man has been named Dives from the Latin adjective in the Vulgate. In this parable Abraham, father of the Hebrew people, plays a prominent part. This story pictures in considerable detail the popular concepts of life after death. Jesus may have adapted one of the current tales of the time.

A brief setting on earth shows the rich man in the luxury of the finest clothing and food. By contrast Lazarus, prostrate and ulcerated, in his poverty depended on food dropped from the rich man's table. He was so weak that he was defenseless against the dogs, unclean animals, that nosed him. But at death these conditions were reversed. Lazarus had an angelic escort to a special honored place. Abraham was believed to dwell in Paradise in the presence of God. Lazarus shared Abraham's care. The rich man at death received the last honorable act of burial which had great importance in Judaism but he passed to torment in Hades. This region appears with some of the features of Gehenna or hell with flame and anguish. In earlier thought Hades or Sheol had been simply the dark underground world of the

[8] Easton, op. cit., 247.
[9] Manson, op. cit., 588.

dead and later it became a waiting place for both sinners and right-eous before final judgment. In the vivid dialogue the rich man made two requests of Abraham who denied them with two important an-swers. Dives could see Lazarus afar off; when on earth, he could not see him at his gate. Dives called Abraham "Father," a claim which he could make as one of the covenanted people of Israel. In later thought Abraham was believed able to help the wicked in hell. Abra-ham addressed the man as "Son" but refused his request for Lazarus to return to earth to warn his five brothers. Abraham replied that they had ample teaching for their future welfare in Moses and the prophets and not even one from the dead would make repentance more possible when they ignored the revelation of God in the Scrip-tures.

This parable requires some negatives. Jesus need not be denied as its author because of the equivocal morality which seems to teach that the rich are tormented and the poor blessed after death. It need not be held that certain verses (26–31) are a later addition to teach about the resurrection of Jesus though Luke may have been influ-enced by that thought. It should not be read as a final, complete, eternal picture of life after death because it embodies many popular ideas about the future in dramatic form. Jesus told a picturesque story about a rich man, a beggar and Abraham. Dives never looked at the diseased beggar in this world but in the next world, when he finally saw him, he wanted to use him to aid himself and his brothers. Abraham, father of all faithful Hebrews, taught that he must expect some essential equality of good for evil things and that the scriptures contain all things necessary to salvation. Not miraculous appearances from the dead but recognition of human obligations and of the pres-ent teachings of Moses and the prophets would insure repentance and a life to come.

A brief parable on a slave's duty has been given many titles of which "Unprofitable Servant" is best known. Jesus described the slave who worked all day in the field and came into the house for more work still to be done. The owner evidently had but one slave. Oesterley states that there were four kinds of workers.[10] There was the bondman who did not have a hard condition among Jews because the Law regulated the master's obligations. Above the bondman was the higher household servant who had a confidential position in the houses of the wealthy. Below the bondman was a lower slave who was subordinate to the bondman. Finally there were hired servants

[10] Oesterley, *op. cit.*, 185–86.

who were free men but had no assurance, beyond casual labor, of work or support. In this parable Jesus spoke of the bondman who would not expect to be served at table when he came in from the field but who had to go to the kitchen to serve his master before he had his own meal. He did not expect to dine before his master nor to receive thanks for doing his duty. Thus men who face God's endless claims have an obligation, which they must acknowledge, not to claim reward nor thanks from God, but to feel that they have done what is due as servants of little worth. In view of obligations to God man must keep his commandments and realize that he never can put God in debt to him. Even the most learned man was obligated. "If thou hast wrought much in the Law claim not merit for thyself, for to this end wast thou created." [11]

The story of the healing of ten lepers exalts a Samaritan whose gratitude was great and whose faith made him well. It stands in contrast to the other nine who probably were Jews. The locality of the incident between Samaria and Galilee accounts for the mixture of companions in misery since Jews and Samaritans normally had no dealings. The lepers observed the isolation required and called from a distance for mercy from Jesus. He likewise followed the Law as he directed them to the priests in Jerusalem who supervised the required sacrifice and official cleansing. The cure of their disease which is not identified with modern leprosy caused the Samaritan to praise God and to return to Jesus whose words arouse questions for a reader of the story. If he sent the ten to the priests, why should he question about the nine who did not return to him? Praise to God could be rendered anywhere. Was it required in the presence of Jesus? Was the Samaritan released from priestly health requirements? Why should the mention of the leper's faith come after the cure? Consequently there have been two explanations of the story: (1) that it is a historical incident as reported; (2) that it is a composition by Luke, an expansion of an earlier cleansing (5:12–16) which was adapted by Luke to teach the important truth that even a foreigner received aid and commendation by Jesus.

The brief answer of Jesus to the Pharisee who asked when the reign of God was coming has negative and positive aspects which have been endlessly interpreted.[12] The Kingdom is not to come by

---

[11] *Pirke Aboth* 2:8; Danby, *op. cit.,* 448.

[12] C. H. Roberts, "The Kingdom of Heaven," *Harv. Theol. Rev.* XXI (1948), 1–8; G. Cope, "The Kingdom of Heaven—When and Where," *Croz. Quart.* XXVIII (1951), 232–39.

signs nor can it be seen. The Pharisees favored signs for evidence about the Kingdom but such outward miraculous proof could not forecast it nor could it be spotted so men could point to it in visible form. There are riddles in the Gospels for which men attempt answers which exhibit fertility rather than certainty. To the Pharisees Jesus said, "The Kingdom of God is *within* [or among] you." Perhaps his Aramaic word for Kingdom had more than one meaning as does the Greek in which the Kingdom is God's rule and also those whom he rules. (1) Those who prefer to view the Kingdom as unseen and spiritual within men's hearts think that Jesus' answer countered a misplaced Pharisaic concern for an observable physical Kingdom. An objection to this long-favored view is that Jesus addressed the Pharisees and the Kingdom was not in them, else they could have asked why Jesus opposed them. To avoid the idea that Jesus declared that the Kingdom was within the Pharisees it is possible to understand that "within you" is an impersonal reference to man or within man. Still Jesus taught elsewhere that men enter the Kingdom, not vice versa. (2) Those who point out that Jesus nowhere else has the thought of the Kingdom as inward prefer to think that he meant that the Kingdom was in the midst of his hearers. It was already realized in the presence, the miracles and the teaching of Jesus. There was no use to ask the time of arrival because it is present. It has a divine existence with its own potential world order which men share but do not produce. The Pharisees still looked to the future when they should have discerned the Kingdom in the situation they faced. (3) It is suggested from papyri usage that the meaning is neither that the Kingdom is within you nor among you but within your grasp. It is at hand and ready for your possession if you want it. (4) Finally it is possible that Jesus made the statement that the Kingdom did not come by observation and that some Christian writer under the guidance of the Spirit felt the need to make the Kingdom realizable in the hearts of men because of the delay in the coming of the Kingdom in any outward observable manner. In that case the concluding statement that the Kingdom is within men is a doctrinal extension to the preceding statement by Jesus. In the next teaching to disciples about the day of the Son of Man they were warned not to be misled "there" and "here" because there would be delay in the day to come.

The parable of the unjust judge encourages prayer with perseverance. Luke placed the parable at the end of a discussion of the future revelation of the Son of Man which shows that prayer must continue in the face of difficult conditions. It is similar to the parable of the importunate friend who asked bread at midnight. The widow is known in the Bible as a helpless victim whose clothing could not be taken in default (Dt. 24:17). Pure religion is to visit the orphan and the widow in their affliction (Jas. 1:27). Luke has a special interest in widows whereas Matthew has no story about them. A judge faced standards in the Law, "Thou shalt not wrest justice" (Dt. 16:19) but the judge in this story was indifferent. He put off any settlement for the widow but he finally acted for the widow who demanded continually that vengeance or justice be done but he met her need merely to save himself from her ceaseless pestering. She made no polite request but demanded her due. The point of the parable is that the unrighteous judge granted the request and in contrast a righteous God will answer prayer for those who pray perseveringly. Persistence in prayer is not to weary God into an answer. It is the natural expression of great need, earnestness and sincerity. Perseverance lifts the one who prays into accord with God's will and it becomes the avenue by which his will is achieved.

In the explanation which follows the parable two questions are asked and answered, and a comment follows. The questions deal with the delay of God's vengeance for his elect who appeal unceasingly to him. The elect are the people or the individuals whom God has chosen for his service. Israel was a chosen people and a David was a selected servant (Isa. 65:9, 15; Ps. 89:3, 19). "It is noteworthy that the idea of Israel as God's elect should appear not in the days of national importance and prosperity but in the period of humiliation and impotence." [13] The answer is that God will quickly vindicate his wronged people. But a question, still unanswered, shows the troubled wonderment that clouded the thought of Jesus as he peered into an unknown future. Will faith stand steadfast on earth in the heart of the individual believer or in his whole fellowship. "Better God's delay than the unreadiness of man." [14]

Luke states that Jesus spoke the parable of the Pharisee and the publican to some people who trusted in themselves and despised others. Hillel, like Jesus, had to rebuke undue pride. "Trust not in thyself until the day of thy death and judge not thy fellow until thou art come to his place." [15] The prayer attitude which made a man right in the sight of God was illustrated by the two men, the highest and

[13] Manson, *op. cit.*, 599.
[14] Cadbury, *The Making of Luke-Acts*, 296.
[15] *Pirke Aboth* 2:5; Danby, *op. cit.*, 448.

the lowest in Hebrew piety, who went up to pray at the Temple, probably at one of the appointed hours such as three o'clock (Acts 3:1) though private prayer was also offered between the services. According to custom the Pharisee stood for prayer and whispered by himself, as Hannah did (I Sam. 1:13), a prayer to God. He thanked God for what he was not and for what he did. He was not like evil men, especially not like the publican, who was also there for prayer. The Pharisee did more than the Law required. Fasting twice a week was not obligatory for him or any Jew but he may have done it in penitence for the sins of Israel. Tithes were limited to payment for the increase of land, oil, wine and animals (Dt. 14:23) but he tithed all that he acquired, perhaps his garden herbs (Mt. 23:23) or all that he bought, sold or ate if gotten from "people of the land" who were careless about the Law. Such careful living was practiced by some Pharisees though this man's prayer does not picture all his practices. But Jesus shows him as the man with the wrong attitude.

The tax collector also prayed but not with pride nor with thanks for his goodness nor with contempt for a fellow worshiper nor to inform God of his good works. He stood humbly afar off and dared not look up but beat his breast as he begged God's mercy upon his sinful self. He knew his need and trusted God to forgive. God's mercy had no limits. He did not deal with man according to his sins, nor desire the death of a sinner. He removed transgressions as far as the east is from the west. The one condition to receive forgiveness was repentance before God. The publican's penitence in prayer made him acceptable to God while the Pharisee, whose prayer showed trust in himself rather than need for forgiveness, missed his meeting with God. Justification with God "does not mean that a tax collector is a better man in God's eyes than a Pharisee but that a penitent tax collector ranks in his sight above a self-satisfied Pharisee." [16] Luke adds a saying about humility which does not deal with the main point of the parable but which he regards as widely suitable since he (14:11) and Matthew repeat it twice (18:4; 23:12). With this parable Luke completes his special section and returns to the Marcan narrative which describes the events on the road to Jerusalem.

[16] Smith, *op. cit.*, 178.

31

Teachings about Family · Riches · Kingdom · Greatness

Mt. 19:1–20:34; Mk. 10:1–52; Lk. 18:15–19:10 (187–194)

ACCORDING TO Mark, whose geography is hard to follow, Jesus started for Judea and went into the region east of the Jordan where crowds came to him and he taught them. Matthew begins his section with the fourth use of his formula that Jesus had "finished these sayings." He adds that the crowds were large and that Jesus healed them. Matthew and Mark report a test of Jesus by Pharisees on the subject of divorce which is followed by a story of children brought to Jesus. Luke omits the discussion on divorce since he had given one statement about it (16:18) but he gives the account about infants. This section on marriage, divorce and children makes up important teaching about the family.

Marriage was the only vocation open to women. They were given in marriage by the father to the husband who made proper gifts in payment. Marriage was a private affair for those concerned. No religious or civil official had charge and no license or public record was required. Divorce was a burning question of the day when it was brought to Jesus for discussion.[1] John the Baptist was killed because he rebuked Herod Antipas for marriage to his brother's wife. She had divorced her husband contrary to Jewish law which placed the right to divorce only with the husband. The Pharisees came to test Jesus with the thorny question of divorce. Marriage was safeguarded by the Jewish law which required death for adulterers (Dt. 22:22; Lev. 20:10) though the infliction of this penalty is disputed. The law allowed a man to divorce his wife for "some unseemly thing" provided he gave her a written statement which allowed her to remarry (Dt. 24:1–2). This paper safeguarded her against a charge of adultery. The meaning of an unseemly thing is not clear. Childlessness

---

[1] R. H. Charles, *The Teaching of the New Testament on Divorce* (London, 1921), 1–38; Abrahams, *Studies in Pharisaism and the Gospels* I, 66–81; B. S. Easton, "Divorce and the New Testament," *Angl. Theol. Rev.* 22 (1940), 78–87.

especially led to divorce. Women had no legal power in the decision about divorce which was private and easy. The husband was the owner of the wife and could dispose of her at his will. A thousand years passed before divorce required the assent of Jewish women. Divorce was different with Romans since either husband or wife had the power to divorce. Among the Greeks both the husband and the wife could divorce but the wife needed the consent of a magistrate.

In Mark the Pharisees asked Jesus if divorce was legitimate. In Matthew the issue is different. Since they knew divorce was legal, they asked Jesus about the grounds for divorce. In Mark the reply of Jesus was a question about the command of Moses whose authority backed all Jewish law. When the Pharisees cited his permission for divorce, Jesus answered that divorce was allowed because men had hard hearts. Jesus did not discard this permission but pointed beyond Moses to the origin of marriage by quoting twice from Genesis (1:27: 2:24) to prove God's purposes when he created man and woman for a united life which man should not separate. God's plan called for purified not hard hearts. In Matthew the answer of Jesus is an immediate appeal to the beginnings in Genesis and the Pharisees then asked why Moses allowed divorce. Jesus gave the answer about hard hearts and added that any man who divorced and remarried was an adulterer, except in the case of unchastity, which meant that the marriage bond was broken by sexual irregularity. In Mark the disciples, perhaps disturbed by the rigor of Jesus' ideal, asked him again about divorce and Jesus said that any man or woman who divorced and remarried committed adultery. It is remarkable that the woman is cited as able to divorce. This absolute statement is also given by Luke (16:18) except that he limits the adulterous action to the man in the divorce of his wife and marriage to another or to a divorced woman. Paul repeated a similar command of the Lord that Christian married couples must not leave one another (I Cor. 7:10, 15) yet he gave his advice that a Christian was no longer in a marriage bond to an unbeliever if deserted by the pagan.

Marriage and divorce present complex situations for which the Gospels show not one solution but various ones. Scholars try to establish the original words of Jesus but the evidence points to plural traditions. The issues can be put into three statements, oversimplified for brevity: (1) Jesus granted divorce for unchastity alone; (2) Jesus granted no divorce; (3) Jesus gave no rule about divorce but stated an ideal. Each of these statements must be examined. (1) It is claimed that Mark had been edited from a Gentile viewpoint since no woman could divorce her husband in Judaism, that Matthew (19:1–9; 5:32) is not based on Mark and that Paul's advice permitting divorce from a pagan is an interpolation (I Cor. 7:11a). "The teaching of our Lord is truly and explicitly set forth in Matthew." [2] (2) Since Mark and Luke agree that Jesus gave no exception for divorce, marriage is indissoluble. He prohibited remarriage as long as both parties to the first marriage were alive. Matthew's report meant that Jesus granted a man the right to send away his wife for infidelity lest he condone her sin. But this repudiation is man's doings. God's law cannot be changed hence no remarriage is possible.[3] (3) The clause "except for unchastity" was added by Matthew in an "attempt to adjust the absolute teaching of Jesus on the indissolubility of marriage to existing practices in the Jewish church." [4] Jesus' teachings are often given in strikingly radical form and this teaching on marriage and divorce is an absolute ideal. It is not a rule to be enforced contrary to human necessity since Jesus spent much time in opposition to the rule-making religion of his day. Marriage was made for man and not man for marriage. God created man and woman for lifelong devotion to each other but with a responsibility to God to maintain their lives together. This ideal grants no man the right to separate husband and wife but it does not maintain that every marriage undertakes to fulfill God's plans. To turn an ideal into a rigid rule may even deny the intention of Jesus to make marriage a co-operation with God's purposes. The church has never taken Jesus' saying about divorce in an absolute sense. It has always developed rules about marriage. From the third century onward married couples came for church blessing upon them but the wedding itself remained a secular affair for over a thousand years. No canon law required a priest to officiate until the thirteenth century.

Matthew has an obscure passage about celibacy. The disciples appear to think that it is best not to marry if the strict standards of Jesus take from man the power to divorce. Or else the disciples raise the question about the expediency of marriage which originally had no connection with the preceding discussion of divorce. In any case Jesus required no asceticism for his disciples. This saying indicates that celibacy is not for all men. Some men stay unmarried because they are sexually defective from birth or castrated or devoted to the Kingdom. It is improbable that men literally made themselves

---

[2] Charles, *op. cit.*, 33.

[3] M. J. Lagrange, *Gospel of Jesus Christ* (London, 1938), II, 85–92.

[4] Major, in *Mission and Message of Jesus*, 128.

eunuchs for the Kingdom because the Law barred a man from the assembly of the Lord if he were a eunuch (Dt. 23:1). Judaism accepted marriage and children as the creation of God and while celibacy had made some headway among an extreme group like the Essenes, Judaism never sponsored sex mutilation. Voluntary renunciation of family, according to Jesus, was possible in order to enter the Kingdom but he did not require men literally to pluck out an eye or to cut off a hand or sexual organs. Neither did he make any law or time limit about those who put the rule of God ahead of physical desires. He left the decision with the individual. The physical conditions are not possible for all men. Some can also make a choice not to marry if marriage appears inexpedient with a call into the Kingdom. Peter had a wife, while Paul was unmarried, but both served the Lord.

There is a singular beauty in the story of Jesus as he blessed children. Those who brought the children are unnamed but they are probably the parents who desired a blessing in accordance with the Jewish custom when fathers or rabbis placed their hands on the heads of children or disciples as a special favor. This blessing was believed to convey actual aid, not merely good wishes. Such blessings are well known in the Old Testament. Matthew states that Jesus was expected also to pray for the youngsters. Luke thinks of the children as infants. Why the disciples objected is not stated. It is assumed that they did not want the Master's blessing freely given without preliminary sifting or that they did not think that Jesus should be bothered by small folks or that he was too burdened by petitioners of all kinds or that the Kingdom was too important for little ones.[5] Both Matthew and Luke omit Jesus' anger with his disciples and his embrace of the children in the bend of his arm as he laid his hand upon them. His memorable words open wide the way for children. They are to come to him for the Kingdom belongs to children and to those who receive it like them. Jesus loved children who possessed the Kingdom and were examples for others to enter it. It is no wonder that this scene was soon used to justify infant baptism which may reach back into the first century. The child is an example of receptivity. In his trust and in his need he is willing to receive from those on whom he depends. Anyone who desired the Kingdom had to be like a child. "The Kingdom of God is for babes but the gospel is hard to understand. When we call it simple, we mean that we are resolved to find nothing paradoxical or mysterious about it, only a few platitudes like being good and loving one another. In reality there never was a teacher who gave his disciples so many surprises as Jesus did." [6]

The designation "rich young ruler" is a combination from Matthew who called him young and from Luke who states that he was a very rich ruler. His rule is not political but probably over his estate. Mark pictures him as one who, on the wayside, ran and knelt to Jesus. The story has three parts in which Jesus converses with the rich man, teaches disciples about the entrance to the Kingdom and replies to Peter about rewards. The title of "Good Teacher," given to Jesus by the rich man, was spoken in sincerity, not flattery. He desired to do something to be secure in the coming life or Kingdom. The humble humanity of Jesus led him to point to God alone as good. Jesus believed in God's incomparable goodness even when he faced Jerusalem. He said that the man knew the commandments. Then he listed five of the Ten though not in their present order and added another one which forbade fraud. The man affirmed that he had kept them from his youth, which probably meant from age twelve when Jewish youth undertook to obey the whole Law. He must have been an attractive man since Jesus looking at him loved him. This is a rare statement of affection and both Matthew and Luke omit it, perhaps because the man refused to follow Jesus when Jesus told him that he lacked one thing. The love of Jesus summoned him with an alarming demand. He had to go, sell his goods, give to the poor, gain treasure in heaven and come and follow Jesus. But his face fell as he preferred his great possessions to the new opportunity with Jesus. He went away sorrowful. Jesus did not usually make this requirement about wealth nor should it be made a law in his name for his followers.

Matthew has a different report of this story. With an exalted idea of the goodness of Jesus he would not repeat the question of Jesus, "Why do you call me good?" lest it be used against Jesus. He avoids the sacred name of God and also the affirmation of Jesus that God alone is good as he gives the question, "Why do you ask me about the good?" He adds the love of neighbor to the list of commandments, omits "Do not defraud" and states that the young man acknowledged his lack even after he had kept these laws which Jesus declared essential for life. Then Matthew reports that Jesus with a counsel for perfection invited him to renounce his riches and to become a disciple. "If you would enter life" and "If you would be perfect" may be taken as references to the same ideal condition though

[6] W. Lowrie, *Jesus according to St. Mark* (London, 1929), 382.

the mention of "perfect" has been often understood as intended by Matthew for a special class of people in the church. This incident has led to much discussion about the sinlessness of Jesus which his goodness soon led his followers to affirm. But the negative idea of sinlessness is not the issue with Matthew who defends the goodness of Jesus against any possible attack.

When the rich man left, Jesus looked at his disciples and to their great astonishment made two comments about the extreme difficulty for the rich to enter the Kingdom. The second comment is dropped by Matthew and Luke and there is serious manuscript divergence about the use of the word "for those who trust in riches." Luke changes Mark's report as he states that Jesus spoke to the rich man and that the astonishment was in the crowd rather than in the disciples. The wonder at Jesus' declaration about the rich may be due to the proverbial belief that God's blessings helped to make men rich. But the Psalmist often held that the rich were wicked. Jesus exceeded contemporary views in his warnings about the dangers of wealth and in his blessings on the poor.[7] The rich were expected to give alms but not to give all as Jesus required of his questioner. In this requirement Jesus was concerned not primarily with distribution of wealth to the poor but with the condition of the giver. Jesus emphasized the danger of wealth by a humorously exaggerated metaphor. A camel cannot go through the eye of a needle yet that is easier than for the rich to enter the Kingdom. There is no historical probability in the suggestion that Jesus meant a small rope or a small gate. His disciples were shocked at this impossible saying as they questioned who could be saved if a rich man with all his advantages failed. But Jesus had limitless faith in God, as earlier in the story he showed belief in God's incomparable goodness. Compared with man's inability God was able to save even a rich man. It may be that though the rich man refused to follow, Jesus still had hopes for him for all things are possible with God. He has power to do all possible things, not all things since no man is saved against his will.

Peter reminded Jesus that the disciples had left all and had followed him. They had done much that he had demanded of the rich man. In his reply Jesus looked to the present and the future. It was customary to think of two ages, one here and one to come, which God or his Messiah would inaugurate. Jesus promised that anyone who left home, relatives and property would receive one hundredfold

---

[7] Abrahams, *op. cit.*, I, 113–17; Montefiore, *Rabbinic Literature and Gospel Teachings*, 274–85.

with persecutions in this present time and eternal life in the coming time. One hundredfold is a manner of speech to assure disciples that their life would be rich with more than they gave up. They found their riches in fellowship and service if not in actual material wealth. The reference to persecution was a grim note quite different from the other hopes. It is only in Mark and may be an addition from the actual suffering of early Christians or it may be irony by which Jesus tempered the great expectations of his disciples. In the list of relatives surrendered for the sake of the Kingdom Luke adds a wife but omits the sisters. Discussions of the manifold promises for the future must be based on figurative not literal fulfillment of this matrimonial possibility. In Matthew Peter bluntly asked what the disciples were to receive. Jesus' answer of manifold rewards is not for the present time but in the new supernatural world. Views varied about the coming of the new world. The "regeneration" meant the end of this present world and a new creation from God to replace it or a divine transformation of this world into an ideal one like the beginning of creation. When the Son of Man would come to reign, he would sit on a glorious throne. This was an idea known in Judaism from the book of Enoch (55:4). The promise to the disciples was that they were to have twelve thrones and to judge the twelve tribes of Israel. This is an adaptation of the popular idea that in the future thrones would be set for the judgment by God and that his saints would share the judgment and receive a kingdom (Dan. 7:9, 22; Ps. 122:5).

This Jewish hope was transferred to Jewish Christians who expected to share Christ's glory and to judge the world. Paul promised this kind of future to the saints in Corinth (I Cor. 6:2). "The twelve tribes of Israel" was a name for the Hebrew people but it may mean the new Israel or church. These hopes for future rewards were varied as shown by Luke who reports that Jesus gave a similar promise about thrones and judgment to the Twelve at the Last Supper because they had faithfully stayed with him during his trials. As God appointed Jesus to the Kingdom, so he gave a promise to the disciples that they were to eat and drink in his Kingdom. This was a traditional expression for sharing the abundant blessings of the coming of the Messiah. Luke blends the idea of a banquet with sitting on thrones to judge. With this picturesque language about rewards it is difficult to know how much Jesus used the thought forms of his day and how much the disciples understood about the future. Matthew and Mark agree that in the future many would find their present positions reversed. Luke puts this saying about the first and the last at a time when Jesus answered a public question about who might be saved (13:30).

Matthew illustrated the idea of rewards and reversed positions in the future with a parable told by Jesus about the Kingdom which is like a householder who hired laborers to work in his vineyard at different hours of the day and yet paid each one the same sum. When one who had borne the brunt and the heat of the day kicked because payment for one hour of work equaled pay for a whole day from sunrise to star shine, the owner cleared his policy. He had paid the agreed fair wages for the day and he had also chosen to pay as much to the later laborers. His generosity should not be envied. He could do as he pleased with his own possessions. The payment was made according to his will and not according to the work done.

Matthew has stressed the idea of the last who will be first which appears both before and after the parable. The Kingdom is open to all, even late-comers. The equal reward for all workers stands in contrast to the reward, especially to the Twelve, which had been promised in response to Peter's question about what the disciples would be given. It also reinforces the next promise of rewards to everyone who sacrificed for Christ's sake. But the parable may have been told originally without the setting given by Matthew. In that case the speech of the owner is the point rather than the comment about the last and the first. The parable teaches that the Kingdom comes to a man not because he earned it but because God gives it. Jesus opposed some of the current Jewish conceptions about the way men earned rewards as they obeyed the Law and accumulated credit for actions which exceeded its requirements. A fast, a prayer, an act of charity, an observance of Sabbath, a restraint of temptation could gain extra merit for a man and bring rewards in the future life. In opposite fashion every evil brought calculated retribution and punishment. A good man was thought to claim his credits with the Lord just as the all-day workers expected more pay in the parable. Not all Jewish teachers stressed the value of works but this teaching was dominant.[8] Jesus showed that God deals with men not according to their deserts but according to his abounding generosity. Man has no claim on God who is sovereign in goodness, shared alike with those who labor much or little. The parable does not teach that God is indifferent to the good deeds but that all rewards are due to God's grace which is infinitely greater than a man can claim.

The third prediction of the suffering, the death and the resurrec-

---

[8] Oesterley, *The Gospel Parables*, 100–111.

tion is more detailed than the earlier ones. This repetition was to prepare the disciples but they failed when the crisis came. It also shows that Jesus was aware of danger. For the first time Jesus named Jerusalem as the goal. Mark pictures a scene on the open road where Jesus strides ahead and the disciples follow amazed and afraid. Luke explains that the disciples understood nothing about these things because the saying was hidden from them as if some divine purpose could open or close their minds. These forecasts have been tempered somewhat by the actual later events in Jerusalem. Matthew specifies death by crucifixion and Luke omits the condemnation of Jesus to death by Jewish leaders. It is remarkable if Jesus mentioned six details about his fate before he went to Jerusalem that the disciples were entirely unprepared for the tragedy.

In Mark, James and John moved up level with Jesus on the road and asked a special favor. In an approach, naïvely cunning as a child's, they wanted Jesus to do whatever they asked. They desired chief places, either at a banquet or in authority as disciples, in his glory. The coming glory was part of the hopes for the Messiah when his power and radiance would be established. Jesus first asked if the brothers knew what they requested and if they could share his cup and baptism. His coming fate is symbolized by a cup to drink and a baptism to be undergone. Since they were confident, Jesus promised they would enter into his experiences. (James was later beheaded by Herod Agrippa, Acts 12:2. The fate of John is uncertain.) But he could not allot the chief places. Such honors are assigned but Jesus did not explain the basis of choice though Matthew adds that it is made by the Father.

The ten other disciples were indignant that James and John had stolen a march on them. But Jesus dealt wisely and kindly with the ten as he had with the misdirected ambition of the two. His high ideals fall into the rhythmic parallelism found in Hebrew poetry. The great men of the Gentiles lorded it over their subjects but among the Twelve greatness depended on service, even readiness to be slave of all. As final evidence the Son of Man is cited as one who came to serve and to give his life as a ransom for many. This famous utterance is usually understood as a reiteration by Jesus of his Servant theme and as the first clear statement of the purpose of his death. A ransom had several meanings. It was a price paid to free a slave or to compensate for a crime. In a religious sense it was the price a Hebrew gave for his life to the Lord to avert plague at a census (Num. 3:51), or it was the amount required in place of the sacrifice of the

first born (Num. 18:15), or it was the offering of the suffering Servant whose death made many righteous as he vicariously bore their
sins (Isa. 53:10–13). Since Luke has a different statement (22:27) and
since the thought of ransom is rare in the Gospels, it has been held
that his interpretation of Jesus' death comes from the church rather
than from Jesus. But the thought of blood poured out for many is
spoken by Jesus at the Last Supper (Mt. 26:28). It is good sense to
hold that Jesus, rather than some unknown Christian, knew Isaiah's
prophecy and adopted his ideal of service in life and sacrifice for
others in death. "The great saying, despite its omission by Luke, is
in probability genuine." [9] Luke sets his version of the saying at the
Last Supper where a dispute among the disciples about the greatest
had arisen. Jesus counseled that the greatest must become like the
youngest and that he himself lived among his disciples as one who
served.

Mark's incident about the ambitious scheme of James and John
caused some difficulty for the later Synoptists. Luke has no place for
it and Matthew gives the mother of the brothers the responsibility
for the request. She knelt and asked Jesus to command the places for
her sons. The answer of Jesus goes to the sons, not to the mother. It
is probable that Matthew felt a need in view of the later fame of the
disciples to credit the mother with their apparently selfish hopes for
the future.

The journey to Jerusalem is marked by two stories at Jericho. All
the Synoptists report a miracle of sight for the blind but Luke alone
tells of the salvation of Zaccheus, the rich tax collector. Jericho of the
New Testament was located about a mile west of modern Jericho on
the edge of the Jordan valley at the mouth of a valley (Wadi Qelt)
which leads toward Jerusalem. Herod the Great had built a magnificent winter palace and the city had a hippodrome, a theater and
swimming pools. Villas of the rich were surrounded by fertile irri-
gated lands with famous balsam and palm groves. At the Passover
season when Jesus was traveling, the country was covered with spring
flowers. Southward the Dead Sea sparkled in sunlight, eastward rose
the blue flat mountains of Moab, northward lay the jungle of the
Jordan valley and westward towered the steep high slopes of the
wilderness of Judea.[10]

Mark's story of the blind beggar reads like an eyewitness report.

[9] Rawlinson, *St. Mark,* 147.

[10] J. T. Kelso, "New Testament Jericho," *Bib. Arch.* XIV (1951), 34–43; Josephus,
Wars, I.21.4; G. Dalman, *Sacred Sites and Ways,* 244–48.

Jesus leaves Jericho with his disciples and a great crowd. The beggar, Bartimaeus, sits by the roadside, he hears rumors, and shouts his appeal for help to Jesus, Son of David. The crowd tries to silence him, then encourages him as Jesus calls him. The beggar throws off his cloak, springs up to go to Jesus who asks what he wants. With respectful address he replies, "Rabboni . . . my sight." Jesus assures him he can go since his faith made him well. But he follows Jesus on the way toward Jerusalem. There are no explanations about the length or the condition of the blindness and the cure is accomplished by a word. The physical results are but part of the purpose of the story. The title, Son of David, is Messianic. Until this point in Mark only the demoniacs had recognized Jesus by this name and they had been silenced. But here the title received no rebuke for soon in Jerusalem it would be publicly proclaimed. This Messianic title could easily arouse revolutionary hopes in Jews and repressive action by the Roman authorities. The beggar pinned the label on Jesus in hope of help. Sight restored to Bartimaeus led him to join the followers of Jesus. Luke adds that he glorified God as did all the spectators. Luke places the miracle at the entrance of Jesus into Jericho since he followed it with a story about Zaccheus. Matthew reports that two beggars were cured as Jesus touched their eyes. Matthew's variant report may be due to another tradition or to a wish to enhance the miracle or to attempt to combine two healings into one account since he omitted an earlier healing of a blind man (Mk. 8:22–26).

Personal names are infrequent in Luke but he knew of Zaccheus, the wealthy tax collector in Jericho, one of the richest districts of Palestine. His name is an abbreviation of Zachariah. Though a Jew his business gained him a reputation as a sinner. His short stature and his curiosity led him to hustle up a tree to see Jesus. When Jesus saw him and invited himself to his home, he hastened down with joy. But the point of the story is in his resolve, publicly stated to Jesus who had honored him when others would not cross his threshold. He promised to give one half of his property to the poor and to repay fourfold to anyone wronged. The Law required a stolen ox to be paid for with five and a stolen sheep had to be replaced by four. Stolen property if recovered had to be doubled (Exod. 22:1, 4, 7). Jesus did not call Zaccheus to be a disciple as he did Levi nor require him to give all his goods to the poor but the charity of Zaccheus is amazing. His actions verify his appreciation of Jesus who declared salvation had come to him and to his family. He was not to be estranged as a sinner but regarded as a true Jew. A "son of Abraham" was expected to share all the blessings that their founder knew as the friend of God. Salvation is a term, not found elsewhere in the teaching of Jesus. Its meaning is shown in the mission of the Son of Man to seek and save the lost such as Zaccheus. The emphasis of Jesus on "today," twice repeated, shows that salvation is a present experience. The visit of Jesus and the righteous resolve of Zaccheus combine to effect salvation.

32

The Triumphal Entry · The Cleansed
Temple · The Fig Tree

Mt. 21:1–22; Mk. 11:1–25; Lk. 19:28–48, 13:34–35 (196–201, 167)

THE LAST days of Jesus in Jerusalem fall within a short span in the
Synoptics. All the events and the teachings are crowded into a few
days. The traditional calculation of this time is covered by Holy
Week as celebrated later in the church. There has always been an
open question whether Jesus had only a few days of ministry in Jerusalem as found in the Synoptics or whether he made repeated visits
to the south as John's Gospel indicates. Luke is least interested in any
chronology. These days in Jerusalem form the climax of Jesus' career.
They are packed with teachings and events but not with miracles.
They deal with the most difficult question of the crucified Messiah.

The entry into Jerusalem has been called triumphal though there
is not much to justify the description. Jesus made some plans as he
came near Jerusalem. Eastward about one half mile, the Mount of
Olives arises above the city. The deep Kidron valley lies between the
Mount and the city. Beyond the Mount lay the villages of Bethphage
and Bethany though the former has not been located except in some
Talmudic references as somewhere near Jerusalem. The road from
Jericho passed through Bethany about two miles east of Jerusalem
and thence along the southern slope of the Mount whence the ancient
walled city can be seen across the Kidron valley. In this region Jesus
sent two disciples to a village to find a colt. They carried the message
that the Lord had need of it and would return it soon. Mark describes
the colt as tied at a door in the street where the message of Jesus was
required to release it. Whether Jesus had arranged for the colt ahead
of time or whether the owner was a friend or whether the message
was superhumanly effective is not stated. Matthew omits the questioning of the disciples by the owners but adds that there were two
animals, an ass and her colt. He quotes the prophet Zechariah (9:9)
who had written of a king coming to Jerusalem to speak peace to
the nations. In poetic parallelism in which one line repeats the pre-

ceding one, Zechariah depicted the king as lowly and riding on an ass, on a colt, the foal of an ass, though he meant but one animal. Matthew understood the poetry literally as if it described two animals. He thus illustrates an interest in prophecy so great that he does not pause to explain how Jesus could ride "upon them" instead of one. A colt unridden suggested newness and sacredness. Carpeting the way with clothing was a gesture usually accorded a royal leader. Mark tells that the road was also spread with a litter of leaves from the fields and Matthew adds that branches were cut from trees. There is no mention of palms. In Mark some of the cries of the people are quoted from a Psalm (118:25-26) which was the welcome called to pilgrims coming to Jerusalem. This was followed by a blessing upon the coming kingdom of David. This was an expression of hope for ideal days ahead. "Hosanna" meant "save now" and was usually addressed to a king or to God especially at the feasts of Tabernacles and of Lights. Originally a prayer, it had become a greeting. There is no identification of Jesus in Mark but Matthew calls him the Son of David, which meant the Messiah. Luke inserts "king" into the quotation from the Psalm but he drops the foreign word "Hosanna" and the reference to the kingdom of David. He emphasizes the multitudes of disciples who praised God for all the mighty works they had seen which recalled Galilean days. The exact meaning of peace and glory in the highest is not clear but the words reflect the feelings of the disciples while they praise God.

Jesus' purpose in the entry has been much debated. Matthew and Luke see Jesus hailed as a Messianic king who presented himself in public, peaceful humility to Jerusalem. Mark also shows that Jesus received Messianic greetings but the disciples and others did not name him as Messiah. The crowds thought him a prophet. It is improbable that they saw him as Messiah in the popular sense else this rumor would have been used against Jesus at his trial when the charge of Messiahship was raised against him. Consequently, there is one view that the idea of Messiahship was constructed on the basis of prophecy to explain the incident which originally was an enthusiastic greeting of pilgrims rejoicing over their leader in the Holy City, the goal of their journey. Another view points out that the details describe an actual event. The Evangelists understood the entry as a Messianic demonstration but the intent of Jesus did not coincide with the customary expectations of the Messiah. He knew that in the history of his people prophets had appeared in Jerusalem who had taught by actions as well as words. Since he came to fulfill the Law and the prophets, he acted symbolically to present himself in a peaceful humble manner to his disciples and to the city. His mission was not in might and earthly greatness but in service and sacrifice.

Luke puts a protest of the Pharisees to Jesus in a dramatic sequence to the acclamation of the disciples. Jesus answered that the stones would cry out if the disciples did not. Then the sight of the city led him to weep. This view from the shoulder of the Mount of Olives over the valley westward across the city had incomparable beauty. The walled city enclosed the gleaming gold-encrusted stones of the Temple with its clouds of smoke from the great altar. Near it rose the towers of the Antonia castle and farther beyond at the edge of the city stood the Herodian citadel. The slanting sunrays clothed the stone homes of rich and poor in celestial radiance. Jerusalem in her beauty, seen from Olivet, entrances all who behold it. Proud priests, Roman soldiers, common people, their fates intertwined, stirred Jesus. He shared a patriotic love for the Holy City which remains one of the marvels of Judaism. "If I forget thee, O Jerusalem, let my right hand forget her cunning" (Ps. 137:5). Jesus lamented that his beloved city did not know the things that make for peace. Like Jeremiah he felt the alarms of war resounding in his ears long before the day of actual conflict. He felt the fate of his own people as their enemies would gather to besiege and destroy them and their fair city. The Romans grimly fulfilled his words within a generation (A.D. 66–70) as Josephus, an eyewitness, has recorded in his *Wars*. But the Jerusalemites neither saw nor knew their opportunity as their Man of Peace visited them and sorrowed over them.

According to Mark Jesus entered Jerusalem late in the day, visited the Temple, surveyed the situation and went to Bethany for the night. Matthew and Luke report that he cleansed the Temple on the same day as the entry. Matthew writes that the whole city was stirred by the coming of Jesus and that the crowds answered a query about him when they identified him as the prophet from Nazareth in Galilee. Since prophecy was thought to have ceased in Israel, this reply could arouse great concern as the preaching of John the Baptist proved. Excitement over the entry of Jesus is much greater in Matthew than in Mark.

The fruitless fig tree illustrates the fact that the first writers about Jesus found no difficulties where later ones spilled ink profusely to explain a difficult situation. Mark spaces the story over two days. On the morning of the first day Jesus and his disciples were going to Jerusalem and Jesus was hungry. He saw a fig tree which had leafed out but he found no figs on it. He remarked that no one would eat fruit from that tree in the future. On the next morning his disciples noticed the tree and Peter remarked that the tree which Jesus had cursed had withered away. Then Jesus gave the disciples some teachings on the power of faith and prayer. The story is difficult: (1) because the teachings at the end do not fit the story; (2) because it records an apparently petulant act of Jesus, who cursed the tree; (3) because Matthew states that the tree withered away at once after Jesus said it would never have any more fruit. Commentators recognize that Matthew and Luke tell the story to illustrate the marvelous power of Jesus but a mere show of power does not comport with the character of Jesus. Explanations are varied. (1) The actual incident is lost and there is no use to try to regain knowledge of original circumstances. There is no moral or religious value for readers today. (2) The story was originally a parable of a barren fig tree such as Luke told (13:6–9). He omits the incident perhaps because he found it difficult or had already told of a barren fig tree. (3) The story is historical. The loss of one fig tree was incidental to the great teaching for the disciples but any petulance or anger of Jesus is incredible. He gave a parable in action as the prophets did to show the disciples that barren lives bring condemnation. (4) The actual event had perplexities and was not correctly understood by the disciples. The Passover season was too early for figs and it is puzzling to know why Jesus expected fruit. The leaves gave promise of fruit but the early crop of figs did not begin before late May or the first of June. The comment of Jesus was not a curse according to Mark but a poetic observation addressed to the tree, as prophets sometimes spoke, and possibly based on a scrutiny of the condition of the tree. The next day Peter made a deduction and an interpretation. The withered tree led him to claim that Jesus cursed it. The fruitless fate of the tree is the point of the story. The following teachings on faith and prayer had great significance because they appear elsewhere in Matthew (17:20) and in Luke (17:6). They declare that the apparently impossible is possible. Mark has placed them as a part of this incident but their immediate connection is not obvious though their truth is most important. The power of prayer backed by believing faith and a forgiving mind works tremendous changes in those who pray and in the causes for which they pray.

The cleansing of the Temple is the only incident when Jesus made a physical attack upon an evil situation. He had laid his hands on sufferers to heal but in the Temple he put his strength to drive rob-

bing merchants and money-changers out of the Temple as he over-
turned their tables and seats and stopped the desecration of the holy
area by those who made it a traffic course. This was a surprising
drastic action which sealed his fate in Jerusalem because the chief
priests and the scribes then planned to destroy him but feared open
action because he was popular with the people on account of his
teaching. Luke adds that he taught daily in the Temple. Both Luke
and Matthew abbreviate the actions and the words of Jesus. Matthew
omits the plan of the Jewish leaders but adds that Jesus healed the
lame and the blind in the Temple and met the protests of priests and
scribes who were indignant at both his wonderful doings and the
children who sang Messianic praises to Jesus in the Temple as they
repeated the acclamations of the entry. Jesus replied with a quotation
from one of the Psalms (8:2) which stated that perfect praise comes
from babes. Matthew gives the quotation in the Septuagint version
and he sees Jesus as accepting the Messianic acclaim.

The attack by Jesus is backed by his charge that the Temple was
a house of prayer for all people yet the merchants made it a den of
thieves. In this accusation Jesus combined quotations from Isaiah
(56:7) and Jeremiah (7:11). Jesus cleared the Temple primarily because its main purpose of worship was perverted by merchants' trade
and by robbery in their methods. The Temple proper, built of white
marble and adorned with gold, had a courtyard for the Gentiles with
open spaces where the necessary business of the Temple was trans-
acted. Shortly before the Passover the half shekel poll tax (Mt. 17:24-
27) had to be paid in the silver Tyrian coinage. Not the bronze coins
of Judea nor the Roman coins but the excellent Phoenician silver was
required in payment of the temple tax.[1] Money-changers were essential and they may have overcharged on their fees. The buying and
the selling of sacrifices for use at the great altar, like the money
changing, were in the hands of the priests. Pilgrims met a financial
monopoly when they offered sacrifices which priests not only sold
but had to approve for perfect condition, fit for offering to the Lord.
The power and the greed of some merchant priests aroused rebuke
and opposition which Jesus spearheaded. To cheat or to overcharge
under the guise of temple regulations was especially odious. The
worship of God was adversely affected so that Jesus felt he had to
stop the evil. He reinforced the sacredness of the place of prayer as
he forbade the use of the Temple for a way of traffic. To anyone who

[1] Abrahams, *Studies in Pharisaism and the Gospels*, I, 82–89.

has seen the abuse of religious shrines by money making and the exploitation of the poor to support wealthy religious institutions with powerful leaders so that prayer is ruined by outrages carried on in the name of God it will not seem strange that Jesus risked his life to cleanse the Temple. From this incident arise many of the ceaseless arguments about the relative amount of force which followers of Jesus should use in the fight against evil.[2] The answer cannot be found in one single story or rule of thumb but rather in the whole teaching and example of Jesus, together with the co-operation of individuals and peoples who seek God's continued guidance.

[2] E. F. Scott, *The Crisis in the Life of Jesus* (New York, 1952).

33

Questions · Parables · Woes to Pharisees

Mt. 21:23–23:39; Mk. 11:27–12:44; Lk. 20:1–21:4, 14:15–24, 10:25–28, 11:37–12:1 (202–212, 154)

THE ATTACK by Jesus was countered by his opponents who sought to discredit him by difficult and dangerous questions which were sprung on him without warning by the shrewdest of his enemies. These four questions are about his authority, taxes to Caesar, the resurrection and the first commandment. Their order is interrupted by parables pointed at the foes of Jesus. He answered the questions and in return asked a final one about David's son which his antagonists left unanswered.

In Mark's plan these questions start on the third day in Jerusalem while Jesus was walking in the Temple probably in its much-used courts and porches. The main authority, civil and religious, in Jerusalem rested in the Council of Seventy or Sanhedrin which was composed of the three groups, high priests, scribes and elders who encountered Jesus. The double form of their question about the authority of Jesus to do "these things" needed only one answer. The "things" may refer both to the cleansing of the Temple and to his teachings but Matthew inserts the fact that he was questioned as he was teaching. The answer of Jesus in which he asked about John's authority was not simply the use of the current rabbinical method which met one question with another, nor was it an attempt to evade a direct reply. It dealt with a basic issue. Jesus began his work when John baptized him. If John's authority was from God, Jesus was completing John's work. If John's authority was only human, that fact affected the things Jesus did. The questioners of Jesus found the tables turned as they faced a dilemma which they escaped by a claim of ignorance about John. They refused to risk an answer because they had not believed in John and they feared the people who revered John. They proved their incompetence to decide about either the source or the use of authority by Jesus. Therefore, Jesus would not tell them about his authority.

Matthew strengthens the authority of John by a parable of two sons in which Jesus challenges priests, scribes and elders with the question, "What do you think?" Then he ends with another query for their decision between two sons, one of whom stubbornly refused to work for his father but later repented and worked and one who politely promised and later did not work. There could be but one answer as to which did the father's will. Thus the tax collectors and the harlots entered the Kingdom of God ahead of the leaders in Jerusalem because they believed John while the leaders disbelieved. The final comment about this parable stresses the attitude of the leaders toward John whereas the main point is their attitude toward God in doing his will. It may have been a statement from Jesus, originally independent of the parable, which Matthew used to connect the parable with the context.

The parable of the wicked husbandmen or farmer-tenants is the second of three which Matthew collects about the leaders in Jerusalem. Though named a parable it is nearer to an allegory. For Jesus and the Evangelists the word "parable" covered a wide range of meanings. A man prepared a vineyard, rented it to tenants and left the country. When he sent different servants to collect the rent, they were beaten and killed. Finally he sent his beloved son who also was slain by the tenants who hoped to hold his inheritance. The owner would come eventually and destroy the tenants and lease the vineyards to other good tenants. One of the Psalms (118:22–23) tells of a rejected stone which later was put into position as a cornerstone. This scripture is given as a kind of proof for the changed position of the tenants. In Luke the stone becomes the means of destruction to anyone who falls on it or on whom it falls. In Matthew there is a plain statement that the Kingdom of God would be taken from the Jewish leaders and given to a nation which acted justly. The owner is God, the vineyard is Israel, the tenants are the Jewish leaders, the servants are prophets, the son is Jesus, the nation means Christians and the outcome is a forecast of what would happen to the leaders.

The authenticity of this parable as told by Jesus is both denied and supported. It is denied because (1) the conduct of the owner and the tenants is not as realistic as in Jesus' parables. The owner was too long-suffering and the tenants too foolish in their hope to inherit the vineyard. (2) It is more allegorical than customary with Jesus. (3) Jesus did not foretell his death to enemies or make Messianic claims as the Psalm suggests to them. The authenticity is supported because (1) the story is adapted to its purpose which did not require realism at all points though many details of the vineyard are true to the Palestinian scene. The leniency of the owner is intended to show God's mercy and the tenants may have thought the owner would not return. (2) Jesus could easily use allegory since he had a similar example about the Lord and his vineyard in Isaiah (5:1-7). There is a reference to the death of the Son but none to the resurrection which would have been cited if the early church composed the allegory. (3) Jesus did foresee his death and he desired to try to win his enemies from their fate by his warning about God's possible judgment. In this division of opinion it is probable both sides have some merit. The ideas of the parable could well be spoken by Jesus though the section about the beloved son and his treatment appears to have been adapted by the followers of Jesus as they preached about him and his effect upon the leaders of his people.

The third of Matthew's parables about the chief men of Jerusalem compares the Kingdom of Heaven to a marriage feast given by a king for his son. When servants twice brought news that everything was ready for those who had been invited, the guests would not come but went on with their business. Some abused and even killed the servants. Then the king destroyed the murderers and their city. Servants again invited everyone they could find, both good and bad, and these guests filled the feast hall but one was thrown out because he had no wedding garment. By this parable Jesus made plain to the leaders that though they did not choose to enter the Kingdom the invitation would reach all kinds of people who would accept it. But there are elements in the parable which point to a perspective in which Matthew has made some allegorical references to situations which developed in the interval between the death of Jesus and the writing of the Gospel. The abrupt unreasonable killing of servants who only brought a wedding invitation and the consequent punishment for the killers is probably a veiled reference to the Jewish persecution of Christians and the destruction of Jerusalem. The guests, good and bad, gathered into the Kingdom reflect the problem of the church with unworthy members. The man without a wedding garment could hardly be expected to have one under the hurried conditions of his sudden invitation. This part of the story may have been another parable by Jesus which Matthew adapted to show that a man could not stay in the Kingdom unless he were properly prepared. The wedding garment may be seen as a symbol of righteousness. His fate is an outer darkness which probably meant Gehenna. The concluding comment about the many called and few chosen, though true, does not well fit the story since all but one had been called and stayed at the feast though other bad guests might have been discovered. This parable shows considerable editing by Matthew.

The ideal future was often set forth in Jewish thought as a feast which God or his Messiah would make for all people. Luke reports a parable by Jesus when he was at dinner at a Pharisee's home somewhere on the way to Jerusalem. Someone remarked how happy would be the one who should eat bread in the Kingdom of God. In reply Jesus told the parable of a great banquet to which guests declined to come by giving flimsy excuses about business or home concerns. The host sent servants twice everywhere to urge all to come, even the poor, the maimed, the blind and the lame. Those first bidden had no banquet. Hospitality had great importance in Palestine and it helped to illustrate the truth that the Kingdom is filled when God issues invitations which men decide to accept. Jesus "sees the deepest tragedy of human life, not in the many wrong and foolish things that men do or in the many good and wise things they fail to accomplish but in their rejection of God's greatest gift." [1] This parable may be independent of the one in Matthew because it has a different setting and small differences in details. Jesus could use the same theme more than once in his stories. But it is more probable that Luke gave the more original version of the same story than Matthew since the main outline and the teaching are the same. These two stories had a common origin but they were remembered and retold in different areas by different writers.

The second trapping question put to Jesus concerned the Roman poll tax. If Jesus supported it, he would alienate his fellow Jews who believed that the Holy Land belonged to God (Lev. 25:23) and that any taxes should go to him. The Jews detested the tax as a subjection to a foreign power. If Jesus refused the tax, he could be charged with sedition before Pilate. In A.D. 6 Judas, a Galilean, had led a revolt against the Roman tax (Acts 5:37). The dilemma that Jesus faced was cunningly arranged and the outcome was serious. Pharisees and Herodians who usually kept separate ways combined to try to catch Jesus. Luke, who never mentions Herodians, states that priests and scribes sent spies so as to be able to turn Jesus over to the governor. The Evangelists mention their malice, hypocrisy and craftiness though they opened their talk with Jesus with smooth flattery about his truth, independence, impartiality and loyalty to God. The answer of Jesus was first a question, "Why put me to the test?" then an action and finally a declaration. The action was to look at a Roman

---

[1] Manson, *Mission and Message of Jesus*, 422.

denarius which he had brought to him since he evidently had none. The tax had to be paid in silver and this coin, if it represented the current emperor Tiberius (A.D. 14–37), showed his head and official titles on the obverse and an image of his mother in a seated pose on the reverse.[2] As a concession to the Jews the local bronze coins had no human images. Render to Caesar and to God the things that belong to each one respectively. Amazement followed his answer and his opponents were silent according to Luke and left him according to Matthew.

This declaration of Jesus has had enormous influence on theories of church and state. Its meanings have multiplied in the minds of men. It has been understood in various ways: (1) as an adroit evasion so as to escape the trap; (2) as advice which caught his trappers with the obligation to return to Caesar his own property since they had in hand his idolatrous coin; (3) as an endorsement of the Roman poll tax similar to the advice Jesus gave to Peter to pay the temple tax (Mt. 17:24–26); (4) as a reiteration of the Jewish position of loyalty to God and to the existing government except when it demanded apostasy which is not the issue in the story since sacrifices were offered for the Emperor twice a day in the Temple; (5) as a recognition of obligations which were intended for all men to follow though the declaration left to them the decision between the things of Caesar and of God. In view of Jesus' primary interest in the Kingdom and in his efforts to get men to acknowledge God and to give him his due in all things, he granted it was lawful to pay taxes due the government but he stressed the duties which men owed to God as the climax of his statement.

New and strong opponents, the Sadducees, brought the third difficult question to Jesus. From these aristocratic people came most of the priestly leaders in Jerusalem. Their conservatism led them to reject the more recently developed beliefs in the resurrection of the body which the Pharisees advocated but they probably did not deny an after life. They followed the written Law but not the oral traditions and the Law had little to support a resurrection. Sheol was the dark pit where the dead were not remembered by the Lord nor could they praise him (Ps. 88:3–12). But this traditional view had been enlarged by the Pharisees into a bodily resurrection which was a distinctly different view from the Greek idea of immortality of the soul. Since the Sadducees appear in Mark and Luke only in this incident, they

---

[2] H. Loewe, *Render unto Caesar* (Cambridge, 1940), 65–116; J. S. Kennard, *Render to God* (New York, 1950), 51–102.

had few contacts with Jesus but probably they had heard enough about his teachings concerning the future life to think that he believed in a resurrection. Current Jewish views fluctuated between popular thought which pictured an after world much like the present one and a more refined, shining, starlike existence (Dan. 12:2–3).

The Sadducees set up a ridiculous supposition based on an ancient law of Moses (Dt. 25:5–6) which required the brother of a dead man who had left no child to marry the widow. The first-born son would then bear the name of the dead brother. Thus the family name was saved from extinction and property holdings maintained within the family. This requirement was later known as the Levirate law from the Latin *levir* or husband's brother. The law probably was not enforced in the first century but the issue was debated long after the time of Jesus. The Sadducees assumed that Jesus believed life in the next world would duplicate this one, hence the embarrassment to decide which of seven brothers should have the one wife. In Mark Jesus asked them a question but in Matthew and Luke he made a statement. The Sadducees quoted Moses but they were wrong on two points. They did not really know the scriptures nor the power of God. God had created an order of existence where marriage was not essential for continuance of life. The Sadducees are thought not to believe in angels but Jesus said that the dead were like angels who were believed to be spiritual and immortal (Enoch 15:6). In Luke Jesus emphasizes the equality of the dead with angels and calls them sons of God who are accounted worthy to reach resurrection. In the story about the burning bush (Exod. 3:6) God had revealed his name and nature to Moses. He had spoken to Moses as the living God of Abraham, Isaac and Jacob. These men had died centuries earlier but God did not outlive his friendships and these men, long dead, were yet alive with God. Jesus used the well-known method which quoted one scripture in rebuttal to another or to establish an argument. It has a limited value because mere quotation can prove too little or too much but the thought of Jesus did not depend solely on this method. His answer, as a whole, has scope and faith because it is based on the nature of God. He stressed not the nature of the resurrection but life continued from God. He rejected the notion that the next world duplicates this one physically while his confidence for the future depended upon God's character. He believed that God maintained a relationship with man which was independent of the event of death and that man should trust not his own potential, but the power of God for a future life.

The last question came from a scribe according to Mark and from a lawyer according to Matthew and Luke. In Luke this incident stands early as an introduction to the parable of the Good Samaritan. This variation in position shows that the story was known in Q as well as in Mark. Luke used Q and omitted the narrative from his report of the last week while Matthew followed Mark's order and combined the Marcan and the Q stories. The lawyer asked a stock question about the first or the great commandment but in Luke he asked about eternal life. There were so many commandments in the Law of Moses that scholars made attempts to determine some few basic principles. One rabbi of the third century stated that Moses imparted 613 precepts, 365 negative, 248 positive. All were binding upon a Jew but in the list of precepts the question of priority or of "light" and "heavy" commands was often debated. The lawyer may have been both wise and sincere because he answered his own question and in Mark Jesus commended him as not far from the Kingdom. This favorable comment about him is not repeated by Matthew nor by Luke who reported that he had wanted to test Jesus.

The famous answer, whether by Jesus or by the lawyer, united the love of God and of neighbor. The command to love God came from Deuteronomy (6:5) and the one to love one's neighbor was written in Leviticus (19:18). This combination had been made, probably in the preceding century, in the Testaments of the Twelve Patriarchs (Iss. 5:2, 7:5; Dan. 5:3) though it is uncertain how widely it was known. Other parts of scripture were also chosen in answer to the question about which commandments were first. Hillel gave the negative Golden Rule as the basic principle of the Law.[3] In Mark the answer of Jesus began with the Shema which every Jew repeated daily and which was written on a miniature roll in his phylactery. The Shema declared that God is one and that one must love him with one's whole being. It is remarkable that Matthew, the Jewish Christian Gospel, omits this monotheistic affirmation. Duties to God and to man constitute the essence of the Ten Commandments. The prophets proclaimed the Lord required justice and mercy among men and humility before God (Mic. 6:8). When Jesus declared that God is one and then united love of God and love of man into the first and great commandment, he set forth principles of most influential worth. He gave not one answer but three in one. To believe in God alone and to give to him first the highest and entire devotion of

[3] Abrahams, *Studies in Pharisaism and the Gospels*, I, 18–29; Montefiore, *Rabbinic Literature and Gospel Teachings*, 312–22.

life and then to link one's love of others to God stands as an ultimate ideal for followers of Jesus.[4] "This commandment have we from him, that he who loveth God love his brother also" (I John 4:21).

When Jesus turned the tables and asked a question about the Son of David, he not only received no answer but he took the risk that it would remain unanswered. Later readers find as much trouble with a reply as his first listeners. In Mark he taught in the Temple but his hearers are not named. In Matthew they are Pharisees in dialogue with Jesus. In Luke they are indefinite though they appear to be scribes. They taught that Christ was the Son of David yet David inspired by the Spirit wrote, "The Lord [God] said to my Lord [Messiah], sit at my right hand" (Ps. 110:1). Since David thus called the Messiah Lord, how is he his son? This is the usual quotation of holy scripture to prove a point. Luke is unique among New Testament writers as he used the title of the book of Psalms in place of Mark's statement about their inspiration. David was regarded as the author of the entire book rather than the author of part of it as in modern study. Matthew comments that no one could answer Jesus nor dared ask him any more questions.

The intent of Jesus' question is hard to discern but two possibilities are present. (1) The question leads to a denial of Jesus as Son of David and therefore it is not authentic but due to some Christian group who wanted no Jewish Son of David. But it is improbable that the Evangelists, who strongly believe in the Davidic descent of Jesus, had any idea that the question could be understood as against this descent. (2) The question considers the nature of the Messiah as related to David. It suggests that though he is descended from David, he is much more the Lord of David because God would put him at his right hand on a throne far above David. This suggests that Jesus felt his mission was greater than anything conferred by a great ancestor. This Psalm was highly favored in the early church as a Messianic forecast. It is frequently quoted in the New Testament to support the final exaltation of Jesus after his death.

The intense feeling between Jesus and the leaders in Jerusalem moved rapidly toward a crisis as he cleansed the Temple, taught the people and attacked the leaders. They resented him as a religious rival, tried to trap him and plotted his destruction. The chief men of Jerusalem had position, wealth and power, undergirded everywhere by long-established religious authority. They would not tolerate any other possible rival or leadership nor any criticism of their conduct.

[4] E. Stauffer, "Love," in G. Kittel, *Bible Key Words* (New York, 1951), 45–53.

They were not all evil but they had serious flaws. Jesus named their evils and they resented it. In Mark the common people heard him gladly as he finished the siege of questions. Then he warned about the learned men, the scribes, who explained and administered the Law. Jesus condemned the scribes for their undue desire for special privileges, for exploitation and for hypocrisy. They liked flowing robes, deferential greetings, the best seats at synagogues which were probably reserved for them while the common people stood. They also desired the chief places at banquets. They covered their grab of widows' property with long prayers. Their pretense would lead to greater condemnation. Luke follows Mark in his brief indictment of the scribes in Jerusalem but in an earlier chapter (11:37–52) he presented a heavy condemnation of the Pharisees and the lawyers (scribes) in which Jesus pronounced six woes upon them, three upon each class. This discourse has a setting of Jesus dining with a Pharisee. Matthew has the sharpest and longest denunciation of scribes and Pharisees in which there are three parts; first a description of Jesus' foes with instructions for disciples, then seven woes upon them and finally a lament over Jerusalem. These indictments by Jesus have their origin in real conflicts. His enemies would not have killed him for light words or ineffective actions. But the edges of the indictment have been sharpened by the dire persecutions inflicted on the first Christians by the Jews. There are no sufferings more bitter than those inflicted through conscientious scruples when men undertake to destroy heretics. When the Evangelists wrote, the serious strife between synagogue and church had colored their report of the words of Jesus. Jewish scholars regard the attack on the Pharisees as overdrawn and as an indictment of a whole party for the sins of some of them. It is notable that Matthew is responsible for this wholesale condemnation. All Pharisees were not evil but some of them were ready to destroy Jesus and later tried to crush his followers. The condemnation of the Pharisees and the scribes was not for their teaching of the Law but for specific actions which exceeded or abused the Law. An uncritical use of the Gospels has resulted in a derogatory view of the Pharisees whose name has been treated with contempt. The Gospels give more space to the unfavorable than to the favorable aspects of the Pharisees but modern study has resulted in a better-balanced estimate of the Pharisees.

In his opening description Matthew reported that Jesus noted their position on the seat of Moses. This refers to the stone chair where sat the most distinguished learned man in the synagogue. The Law of

Moses was the supreme authority. It was expounded by scribes who taught that its commandments must be obeyed but their learning did not always result in their own practice. Not all theologians are saints and the ones in Jerusalem liked to display their piety by outward show. Their broad phylacteries were small leather boxes, containing scripture. They had leather straps so that they could be worn on the head and on the left arm at prayers morning and evening or the pious could wear them all day. The wide fringes on their garments reminded the wearers of God's commandments. The Pharisee liked to be called rabbi, a new, much-honored title. Jesus forbade his disciples to use rabbi or father or master which fed the egoism of oneself. They were brothers under one teacher and God's title had to be kept for him alone, with Christ the only master. With them the greatest among them was to be the humble servant.

The woes in Matthew and Luke can be best seen in a comparative arrangement. The italic indicates that the passage appears in one Gospel only.

Mt. 23:	13 Kingdom closed	Lk. 11:	42 tithes
woes	15 *proselytes*	woes upon	43 best seats
upon	16 *swearing*	Pharisees	44 unseen tombs
scribes	23 tithes		
and	25 deception	upon	46 burdens
Pharisees	27 whitewashed	lawyers	47 prophets' tombs
	tombs		52 key of
	29 prophets' tombs		knowledge

The word "woe" is best understood not as a curse but as pity such as is expressed by the word "alas." The first complaint in Matthew is placed last in Luke. The Law was God's will for men yet the learned men who were its custodians had a monopoly in their myriad interpretations which excluded rather than helped themselves and others to a knowledge of God. Judaism sought converts in the first century and they came because Judaism taught one righteous God and high standards of conduct yet they became more zealous than the leaders who were headed for Gehenna. The wars with Rome and then the eventual struggle against conversion to Christianity led the Jews to abandon missionary efforts. Distinctions in swearing misled men to believe some pledges did not hold. The Pharisees were blind guides who could not see that all swearing, even if it avoided the name of God, implied the use of his name in reality. The Law required a tenth of the increase of seed (Dt. 14:22) and it was mistaken zeal to exceed the Law and to tithe small garden herbs, some of which like mint did not require the tithe, and then to neglect the most important elements like mercy, justice and faith. Such leaders who took great pride and care for endless details should not miss the love of God. They strain out gnats and swallow camels. It was customary to strain wine through cloth so that no insects would be swallowed. Ritual cleanness for dishes or for oneself had great importance in Judaism and the rules were long and complicated. The Pharisee kept a clean exterior to cover an interior full of robbery, greed and incontinence. Luke has a similar condemnation but he does not include it among his woes. He adds the thought that God created both the outer world as well as the souls of men. To give alms from within is a curious statement which may mean from a pure heart or from generosity or Luke has mistranslated an Aramaic word, "give alms," which is very similar to "cleanse" which is Matthew's translation. A tomb, if touched, defiled a man for a week (Num. 19:16) and the sepulchers were whitewashed to warn pilgrims especially at Passover season. In Luke the Pharisees were likened to graves which polluted people. In Matthew the contrast is between an outer good appearance and an inner rottenness in the tomb. In the past prophets were murdered when they tried to reform Israel. To build tombs to these honored dead men was easier than to obey their truths or a living prophet. Monuments to the dead displaced righteous conduct as a response to the preaching of the prophets. Easy talk about the past ignored the present messengers which God in his wisdom had sent. The willingness of these leaders in Jerusalem to kill and persecute could only lead to hell. Such attitudes and actions made them responsible for the continuance of the murders recorded in scripture from Abel, the first victim, to Zachariah, the last one.

The lament of Jesus over Jerusalem reads much the same in Matthew and Luke but the latter places it when Jesus started on the road to the Holy City after he had a warning that Herod wished to kill him. There is no way to decide where Jesus spoke the words but it is natural to suppose that he was moved at sight of the city as Matthew states. The scriptures do not report many prophets killed in Jerusalem but the capital stood for the whole nation. This poetic dirge disclosed the deep sorrow Jesus felt for his national city. He had often longed, as a mother hen protects its chickens, to save its people but he met a hostile rejection. This passage is sometimes understood to indicate that Jesus visited Jerusalem often, as John's Gospel states, but it expresses longings rather than actions though it is possible that

Jesus made repeated attempts to prepare Jerusalem for the Kingdom. He felt the danger of the future when the "house," which may mean the Temple or the nation, would be desolate. Jerusalem would not see him until it spoke the welcoming words for pilgrims. "Blessed be he who enters in the name of the Lord" (Ps. 118:26). In Luke it is possible to see these words as a forecast of the triumphal entry but Matthew inserts the word "again" which looks to the future glorious return after death.

The Temple had a treasury which appears to have been a room in the Court of the Women where according to later tradition there were thirteen trumpet-shaped receptacles marked to receive various kinds of gifts. Priests supervised the amount of the gifts. Jesus sat and watched the givers. The rich gave much and a widow put in two coins, the smallest in circulation. Jesus called his disciples and with the words, "truly I say to you," used twelve times in Mark, when an impression was intended, he exalted the widow as one who gave the most of all because she gave all her living. Her gift was greatest because it cost her most as it came from a heart wholly generous. Jesus saw in her action the ideal expression of a gift to God. Yet for Mark it is not the widow but Jesus who is the central figure in the story as he observes the gift and teaches his disciples with marvelous discernment.

34

What is to Come in the Future?

Mt. 24–25; Mk. 13; Lk. 21:5–38, 17:22–37, 19:11–27, 12:35–48
(213–230, 184, 158, 159)

A MODERN reader feels a strangeness of thought in the Gospels when he opens the chapters which discuss the future. Eschatology or the teaching about last things is a technical word to describe ideas about the future of the world and of men and of their possible life beyond the present existence. It deals with the final purposes of God as men face their ultimate destinies. Apocalyptic or an unveiling or revelation is a certain kind of eschatology which pictured the future in visions in which God was believed to disclose coming events. The literature of apocalyptic of which Daniel and Revelation are outstanding examples in the Bible flourished from the second century B.C. to the second century of the Christian era. The Jewish people had national hopes in which they thought God would act for their good and for the destruction of their enemies. He would establish a sovereignty over the Jewish people and over the whole world. The prophets had preached about a day of the Lord which would also be punishment for evil-doing as well as a good time for the nation. Since the nation suffered long centuries of foreign domination, apocalypticism arose after prophecy as a compensation which pictured a supernatural world to answer all the deferred hopes of the present one. The end of this age would come and a new heaven and earth would replace the present situation. This new age, sometimes the work of God himself or of his Messiah, was pictured in symbolic scenes with glowing imagination. It would suddenly come after certain trials or woes with a climax of supernatural signs and of great conflicts with evil powers, superhuman and human. Then a final judgment would condemn the wicked and establish the righteous in an ideal life in a world to come. A mysterious heavenly Son of Man who would come in power and glory was added to an earlier hope of an earthly Son of David who had been expected to reign in a glorious restoration of the Jewish nation. These hopes had many aspects but they were all grounded in a belief that God would soon end the present age and inaugurate a new one since the Jews were not able to establish an ideal world. Otherworldly apocalyptic pictures are full of imagery, often too bizarre for literal meaning. They cannot be reduced to a system of logical thought but they can be examined for essential ideas which they contain. There was confidence that God is active in history and that there is a goal which it is God's will to establish. Sufferings must come in the face of evil but courage and hope would aid endurance. There is an urgent need for action because an end is coming and there is hope for the hereafter in which God judges the good and the evil.[1]

There are unresolvable difficulties in the unending attempts to distinguish: (1) between the Jewish hopes about the future for the nation or for individuals and the extent to which Jesus and his disciples shared them and (2) between Jesus and the added hopes of the early church which developed until the Gospels were written. During the nineteenth century much study emphasized Jesus as one who taught primarily for this present world. Schweitzer in 1901 startled his readers with his *thoroughgoing* eschatology in which he taught that Jesus expected an immediate end of the age and the coming of the Son of Man.[2] This one-sided emphasis on the future has been balanced by Dodd with his *realized* eschatology which stresses the present aspects of God's purposes in the field of human affairs. The hidden Kingdom of God was already revealed in the actual experience of the followers of Jesus.[3] In the present study of Jesus' teachings about the future there is recognition of a *balanced* eschatology. It is held that Jesus had definite ideas about the future for himself, his disciples, the Temple, his nation, the end of the age and the part God would take in everything. He accepted some of the apocalyptic figures of speech but he was not bewitched by them. He did not proclaim his teachings by visions. He was a prophet, not an apocalyptist. He believed that there were both present and future aspects to God's activity. He admitted limits to his knowledge. He had the practical purpose to prepare his disciples for the future and to equip them with an attitude of watchfulness and faith and readiness for the future.

Jesus predicted that the Temple would be destroyed when his dis-

[1] H. H. Rowley, *The Relevance of Apocalyptic* (London, 1944), 140–68; J. Bloch, *On the Apocalyptic in Judaism* (Philadelphia, 1952), 28–70.

[2] A. Schweitzer, *The Mystery of the Kingdom of God* (New York, 1950).

[3] C. H. Dodd, *Apostolic Preaching* (Chicago, 1937), 135–67.

ciples admired its wonderful building with its gold-encrusted stones, marble pillars and gleaming appearance. Other prophets like Micah and Jeremiah had foretold with sorrow a destruction of Jerusalem. Jesus did not live to see his prediction fulfilled about the destruction of the Temple but the Romans burned the Temple and laid low the city in dreadful ruin in A.D. 70. In Mark four of the disciples asked Jesus about his prediction as they sat on the Mount of Olives overlooking the Temple. They questioned when it would happen and what would be the sign. The form of the question in Luke, Mark and Matthew corresponds to the ascending order of interest these writers took in apocalyptic. Luke has the simplest question while Matthew introduces two ideas which show his special concern for the future. The disciples asked Jesus about his coming (Parousia or appearance) and about the end of the age. His coming refers to the expectation that Jesus would come again in power and glory because his first coming, which ended in an early violent death, had been far different from their dreams of a Messiah. This was one of the strongest hopes of the early church and had taken two forms. The first was a visible, audible, powerful, physical coming in the near future; the second was a spiritual, invisible sense of Christ's presence as an inner spirit. The end of the age expressed the common belief that God worked in two periods, a present one which had started at creation and was soon to end and a future one which would realize in ideal form the purposes of God.

The answer which Jesus gave is unusual in Mark which contains no other long discourse. It refers to a reader (13:14) when Jesus is supposed to be speaking. It has much more apocalyptic imagery than is usual in the teachings of Jesus. There has been wide acceptance of the theory that a written Jewish document has been adapted by a Christian editor together with sayings of Jesus or possibly the adaptation was made by Jesus himself. The topics of discussion can be summarized as follows: (1) the beginning of suffering for disciples; (2) terrible tribulations; (3) false leaders; (4) the coming Son of Man; (5) the time; (6) watch.

Jesus warned his disciples not to be misled by those who would use his name to beguile them. Matthew states they would claim to be Christ and Luke that they would proclaim that the end is near. But the end would not come though wars, famine and earthquakes came. In apocalyptic thought a period of suffering was expected to precede the new age. Persecution would come for Christ's sake but the disciples had to bear their testimony. The gospel had to be preached first to all nations, according to Mark. Any defense that the disciples make would be given them by the Holy Spirit. Matthew mentions that it is the Spirit of the Father who would speak through them. In Luke Jesus would give them speech and an overcoming wisdom. But the disciples were to face family divisions, death and hatred. Matthew probably reflects his own age as he adds that many would fall away and be misled by false prophets and as wickedness waxed so most men's love would wane. Endurance to the end would bring salvation. Luke omits the mention of the end and writes that the disciples would gain their lives by endurance. Matthew promises that the gospel of the Kingdom will be preached throughout the whole world and then the end would come.

There was to be a special sign for the disciples to flee in haste when they saw the "abomination of desolation" set up "where he should not be" as stated in Mark. Matthew identifies this strange phrase about desolation as from Daniel (9:27) and says that "the abomination" is to stand in the holy place in the Temple. This "profanation that appalls" in Daniel was the altar to Zeus set up by the Syrian ruler, Antiochus IV, in 168 B.C. for the sacrifice of unclean swine in the temple (I Macc. 1:54). Because of this sacrilege this curious phrase came to stand for the Man of Sin or Antichrist who would force a horrible conflict between good and evil powers. It was part of the current interpretation of the future that there would be a final, terrific, unprecedented conflict of supernatural powers. This great tribulation would affect everyone so none would survive unless God shortened it for the sake of his chosen people. He was believed to be able to hasten or to delay the end. Luke omits any reference to the desolating sacrilege and puts the siege of Jerusalem as the sign for the flight from the city because its people would die by the sword and be sold into captivity until the Gentiles fulfilled their time as forecast in scripture. Apocalyptic schemes usually set forth a temporary domination by the heathen before the end came. Mark, written before the city was destroyed, makes no mention of its fall. In the effort to find some historical setting for the sacrilege at the Temple it has been suggested that the written forecast of profanation was influenced by the order of the emperor Caligula in A.D. 40 to set up his statue in the Temple. Such sacrilege would never have been tolerated by the Jews and it was fortunate Caligula's order was delayed and that his death saved a probable revolt.

The warning about false leaders, claiming to be Christ or prophets, repeats the opening statement (Mk. 13:5-6). Their success in deceit would be due to signs and wonders. Luke places this passage as a warning to all the disciples at an earlier date after a Pharisee asked when the Kingdom would come. In his answer Jesus cautioned that many would want to see the day of the Son of Man but it would be sudden, unexpected and destructive like the flood in the days of Noah (Gen. 7:23) or it would be like the fire from heaven in the days of Lot (Gen. 19:24). On both occasions people had lived in entire disregard of warnings. There would be no time for any care for earthly goods. The fate of Lot's wife should be remembered because she became a pillar of salt when she looked back to her possessions in the evil city of Sodom. As people slept or worked, some would be taken for salvation and others left for destruction. The disciples asked Jesus, "Where?" and he replied in proverbial words about the vultures which appear above any dead body. This answer may refer to the sudden swift speed of these birds as symbolic of the coming of the Son of Man or it may mean simply that any cause produces consequences.

The climax of the future would come with cosmic convulsions which would darken and shake the sun, the moon and the stars. Luke adds an earthly distress as nations and men are filled with bewildered despair, fear and foreboding. Then would come the Son of Man in the clouds and his angels would gather his chosen ones from the ends of earth and heaven. Luke changes the situation as he drops out the work of the angels and concludes that these things are to be signs of hope to disciples who could anticipate a new order as the old one broke up. This passage sets forth the strong hope of the first Christians about the return of the risen Christ in great glory. It is similar to the Jewish hopes in one of Daniel's visions (7:13–14) of the Son of Man coming on the clouds. Jesus had hopes for his own future even beyond death but it is extremely difficult to know his hopes clearly when they appear in imagery and are later interpreted by his disciples.

The time of these things can be judged because they indicate the Son of Man is near as the leaves of a fig tree foretell summer. Luke makes the significant change that the Kingdom of God, not the Son of Man, is near and thus shows less interest in apocalyptic imagery. Matthew and Mark show an immediate expectation of these events since they were to come within a generation. The astounding claim is made by Jesus that his words would remain although all else passes. But the exact day or hour is known not by anyone, angels or the Son, but only by the Father. Luke has no mention of this ignorance of

Jesus about the time. There is difficulty in the fact that the end of the age did not come in a generation. "All these things" did not come to pass as predicted in a short time. This difficulty about time has been resolved in different ways. Some Christians have thought that the Lord's time and man's time do not coincide and they have revived at intervals the idea that the world would end soon, especially as great disasters threatened. This view crystallizes the ideas of the time scheme of Jewish Christian apocalyptic into permanent acceptance. Concepts of time have never remained static and apocalyptists had no final view of time. Others have argued that Jesus used the thought forms of his day about time as readily as he did those about space. The world was thought to be flat and the earth to have begun in time about 4000 B.C. and to end within a generation. But some first-century ideas about time and space, though shared by Jesus, have no validity for modern man since religious issues are not involved in many space-time concepts. Still others have held that the imagery and the metaphors of apocalyptic cannot be taken literally and that it is to be expected that varying ideas about the time of the end would appear among Christians as they mistook "these things" to mean the end of the world whereas Jesus meant the end of Jerusalem.

It is important to remember that in Jesus' teaching the coming of the Kingdom of God is not identical with the coming of the Son of Man. "The Son of Man has no kingdom and the Kingdom of God has no Son of Man" except in a few passages where the connection in one Gospel fails to find support in the parallel passage.[4] It is also important to note that the concluding section of this discourse about the future stresses not the time but the attitude required. In Mark Jesus repeats the requirement to watch three times. Watch because the time is unknown; watch because it might come any hour of the night; all must watch. In Luke prayer is added with safeguards against drunkenness with its nausea and against the common cares of life which prevent readiness for the day of the Son of Man. Both Matthew and Luke liken the hour of coming to the unexpectedness of a thief. A wise and faithful servant will be happy and rewarded for doing his daily work but a wicked one who abuses his position will suffer punishment at the unanticipated return of the master. Thus the disciples as they face the future had to take care, watch, pray and be faithful to their entrusted work.

Matthew concludes his section on the future with three famous

[4] H. B. Sharman, *Son of Man and Kingdom of God* (New York, 1943), 89.

parables, each of which includes the idea of a crisis and a fateful separation of people into good and bad. The story of the ten maidens may be adapted from actual conditions or it may be more allegory than parable with an interest in various ideas rather than fidelity to the facts of a wedding. Comparing the Kingdom with a wedding seems to combine elements of both parable and allegory. The Kingdom will come and one must be prepared for it. Jewish wedding customs of the first century are not known in detail. Preparations for a wedding required a betrothal for a year. Arrangements were made by the fathers. At the betrothal mutual promises were made before witnesses at the girl's home. The prospective bridegroom made a payment to the girl's father and a present to her. He received a present from her parents. At the end of the year a day was set for the marriage feast which was held at night. There was no ceremony performed by a rabbi. The bridal procession led by the bridegroom marched with torches to the home of the bride to bring her to the feast in the bridegroom's home. Those who waited at his home went out to meet the procession as it came to the feast. The two processions joined and marched to the home where the entrance was closed except to those who had taken part in the procession.[5] Since there is no mention of the bride in the parable, except in lesser manuscripts, and since the bridegroom was delayed, it may be thought that the ten maidens were not bridesmaids who would have remained with the bride but village girls who were to welcome the bridegroom at his arrival from his distant home for his wedding and new home. The oil in small clay lamps was soon exhausted as the girls slept in the long wait for their guest. The wise maidens had brought additional oil and went with lighted lamps to the feast when the belated bridegroom finally arrived. The foolish girls lost their opportunity because they were not prepared. The refusal of the wise maidens to share their oil is not a statement of an ideal but of an incidental fact of the story since they had to maintain their responsibility to the guest. Jesus taught his disciples to be ready for the coming of the Kingdom. In addition to this main point Matthew has appended a saying about watchfulness because the day and the hour were unknown. This comment is valuable but in its present place it does not correspond with the action of all the girls who slept and whose part in the feast was determined by forehanded care rather than watchfulness. When Matthew wrote, Christians had begun to adapt the idea of God as the bridegroom of Israel (Hos. 2:16) to Christ as the bridegroom of the

---

[5] Oesterley, *The Gospel Parables*, 133–42.

church (II Cor. 11:2). He would come again unexpectedly even though he were delayed and his coming would separate the ready from the unready.

Matthew's parable of the talents has a parallel in Luke's parable of the pounds. It is sometimes thought that they are two different stories but more probably they are variant forms of the same story with some added allusions to a historical situation in Luke. Both stories teach the same point that a man, given responsibility, must face a reckoning. Luke places his story at the approach of Jesus to Jerusalem as an answer to speculations about the immediate coming of the Kingdom of God. The chief figure is a nobleman who distributed a pound, about twenty dollars, to each of ten servants before he left on a journey to receive a kingly power. His citizens protested his reign over them. This may be an allusion to the time that Herod Archelaus went to Rome (A.D. 4) to receive his appointment and the Jews sent an embassy of fifty to ask the emperor for relief from his impending rule.[6] On the return of the nobleman two servants reported gains of tenfold and fivefold but one who had hidden the money returned only the original sum. The nobleman rewarded the two servants with the supervision of cities but took the money from the wicked servant and gave it to the one who had prospered most. Then he punished his treasonable citizens.

In Matthew a wealthy man distributed large sums, graded to ability, to three servants. A talent is not an ability but money ($1,000). He gave ten talents to one, five to another and one to the third. Then he departed for a long time. The first two doubled their wealth. The third servant only hid his money in the ground. A temple or a clay jar hidden in the ground were the safe-deposit boxes of that day. At the reckoning with the owner he pleaded fear and falsely charged that the master was a hard man. The owner took his talent and gave it to the servant who had ten. Then he threw the worthless servant into darkness. This was punishment added to the loss of the talent. These parables, as Jesus told them, taught the important truth that men must use or lose their opportunities. Like the slave and the master, man belongs to God and his gifts must be used well with an accounting to God for all that man has or does. In Matthew's day there had grown up the expectation of the return of Christ and he records this story to illustrate not only its original truth but rewards, joy and punishments that would occur when Christ came. Luke,

---

[6] Josephus, *Ant.* XVII.2.1.

however, keeps the story, with its consequences of conduct, in relation to the coming of the Kingdom. In an earlier passage (12:47–48)
Luke reports a saying in which Jesus distinguished between the servant who received a heavy beating when he knew and ignored his
master's will and the servant who was given a light beating when he
did wrong in ignorance of his lord's will.

There is a question whether the description of the last judgment is
a parable or not. It is not named a parable and it has no parallel in
the other Gospels though there is a description of a judgment by the
Messiah in Enoch (62–63). But its sequence as a third story in Matthew indicates that he thought it illustrated the same general theme
of the future as the two preceding parables. Matthew has placed it
as a grand conclusion to his fifth and last large section of Jesus' teachings. Its rhythmic language, its far-ranging theme, its dramatic scenes,
its ethical emphasis and identification of Christ with his needy brethren combine to make it one of the most influential parts of the First
Gospel. This last judgment has had a powerful effect in literature
and art. "Christianity of the Graeco-Roman world as a whole responded to the expectation of a Christ about to descend from the
right hand of the Father 'to judge the quick and the dead.' Eighteen
centuries have scarcely dimmed it or relaxed the tension of its moral
spur." [7]

It is difficult to know exactly the anticipations of Jesus about the
future. His words follow the conventional forms of his day and yet
transcend them. He spoke often in figures of speech. The gospel
writers arrange his words in the light of considerable repetition and
interpretation. Jesus had a sublime confidence in God who would
triumph over evil. This triumph he depicted as a coming judgment
to correct the galling injustices of this world. A day of decision was
to come at the end of this present age. It would be administered by
an exalted Son of Man. Following judgment would come a Kingdom
of righteousness and truth in which the righteous would be rewarded
according to their good deeds. In the face of gathering darkness and
death Jesus felt sure that he would have a decisive part in the future
as he had had in his earlier work.

This judgment scene combines common Jewish expectations and
original ideas of Jesus with expert editorial arrangement. The entire
scene has extraordinary power, charm and penetration. In Jewish
thought the judgment had been portrayed as the triumph of Israel
over its enemies with God as judge. In Matthew's dramatic scene

---

[7] Bacon, *Studies in Matthew,* 428.

there are the judge, the people to be judged, the brethren and the verdicts. The judge is named Son of Man, King and Lord. The first Christians identified the risen Christ with the judge. The people to be judged are all the nations, who according to Matthaean usage may be the Gentiles. Their division into white sheep and black goats was symbolic of good and bad people since Ezekiel had prophesied a similar separation (34:17). The brethren of the judge are the followers of Jesus. The verdict for the righteous is to possess and enjoy the Kingdom which God had prepared for them from the beginning of the world. The basis for the verdict is that the righteous people had helped the king when he was hungry, thirsty, a stranger, naked, sick or a prisoner. To their happy surprise they had aided him whenever they had provided for the needs of any least one of his brethren. The verdict for the unrighteous is eternal fire, not prepared for them but for the devil and his messengers. They failed to meet the needs of the king and forfeited their inheritance in heaven. The final destiny of righteous and unrighteous was no arbitrary decision of the judge but it was determined by themselves by simple deeds of kindness or neglect of them. The mystic merging of Christ with humanity so that help for the suffering is help to him makes a radical, ethical, personal basis which determines the final future for any man.

35

Plans for Betrayal · The Anointing · The Last Supper · The Arrest

Mt. 26:1–56; Mk. 14:1–52; Lk. 22:1–53, 7:36–50 (231–240, 83)

MATTHEW CONCLUDES the teaching of Jesus with his fifth use of the formula that Jesus had finished all these sayings. Then he gives the repeated forecast of Jesus that the Son of Man was to be crucified. Mark states the time as two days before the Passover when a plot was made by chief priests and scribes to arrest and kill Jesus secretly but not during the feast lest the people riot. Matthew names the place of the plot as the formal meeting at the palace of the high priest, Caiaphas (A.D. 18–36). Their plans received unexpected aid when Judas appeared with an offer of betrayal which would make a quick, secret, easy way for the arrest. With gladness the conspirators promised him money which Matthew reports that they paid in thirty pieces of silver, probably shekels. Matthew's statement is patterned after the prophecy of Zechariah (11:13) who had told of a shepherd whose hire was weighed in thirty pieces of silver. Luke has the most complete report about Judas who met not only the chief priests but also with the Levite temple police. The motives which led Judas, a trusted disciple, to the betrayal remain dark. Luke explains that Satan entered him. The desire for money is evident though it alone hardly seems sufficient. It can be guessed that in addition to his greed, Judas was disappointed and resentful that Jesus did not set up an earthly, powerful, profitable kingdom. There is no evidence for the modern theory of DeQuincey that Judas expected to force Jesus to use his miraculous power, when arrested, to defeat his enemies and establish his Messiahship. There is no whitewash for selling out a friend like Jesus though Matthew later reports that the fatal move against Jesus led Judas to remorse and suicide. It may be that Judas did not expect a fatal outcome. It is to his credit that he did not appear as a witness against Jesus at the trial. There is also no validity in the arbitrary notion that Judas was destined to betray Jesus. He had the power of choice and the outcome cannot be read back into the purpose as if Judas were a puppet of fate though the betrayal was interpreted as a fulfillment of scripture, after the event was accomplished.

Between dark plans for Jesus' death and the traitor's offer Matthew and Mark have set the light of a beautiful deed. While his enemies plotted, Jesus received anointment at the hands of a nameless woman at a dinner in Bethany. Her motive is not stated. Matthew mentions Bethany as a place where Jesus lodged whereas Luke names Olivet (Mt. 21:17; Lk. 21:37). The crowds at Passover season were too great for them to remain in the city. Jesus' host is named as Simon, the leper. This must refer to his former illness since actual lepers were isolated by law. The costly perfumed ointment poured over Jesus' head aroused indignation because of its expensive waste. It was probably worth about sixty dollars. The ones who protested are unidentified in Mark but according to Matthew they were disciples who thought the money better spent on the poor. Jesus defended the woman because she had done a beautiful deed. She had done what she could. The poor were always on hand to be aided but he himself would soon pass. The woman had not known that Jesus would accept her generous gift as a preparation for his burial. The memory of her gracious act would spread wherever the good news was preached. This reference in Mark to the "gospel" preached to the whole world reads like a later reformulation of Jesus' words when the message of Christianity was on its way everywhere.

Luke does not relate this story of anointing at Bethany because he had written a somewhat similar narrative when Jesus was in Galilee. Luke composed a variant of the Marcan story or else he gives a different, independent event. Since there are many more differences than similarities, the latter alternative is preferable. The host was Simon, a Pharisee, and the woman was a sinner though her sin was not specified. There is no basis to name her Mary Magdalene as tradition centuries later asserted. She poured the ointment on Jesus' feet with tears and kisses. Guests usually reclined at meals with feet extended outward from the table. The Pharisee felt that if Jesus were a prophet he would have known the woman was a sinner. Jesus defended the woman with a story of two men, one forgiven an enormous debt and the other a small debt, and asked the Pharisee which would love the creditor more. The Pharisee answered correctly the one who had more forgiven. Then Jesus pointed out that the woman's actions were more hospitable than his host's. Guests were usually provided with water for hands and feet and with perfumed ointment and greeted with a kiss but the Pharisee had not shown these courtesies to Jesus. To the Pharisee Jesus said the woman was forgiven her many sins because "she loved much" and he repeated the assurance of forgiveness to the woman with the promise that, since her faith had saved her, she could go in peace. The woman, though a sinner, had done better than the pious Pharisee. The story of the debtors shows great love is the effect of great forgiveness. The words of forgiveness of many sins are the result of her love or faith. These two ideas lack a logical parallelism and indicate that Luke has used different sayings which disrupt the unity of thought in his story though both the sayings are important.

The chronology of Jesus' life involves great difficulties. Few scholars share the confidence of A. T. Olmstead, "We can even give the exact length of Jesus' ministry—475 days."[1] The difficulties about dates arise from the indifference and the divergences of the writers of the Gospels. They were not interested in chronology and their dates are incidental to their desire to give a faithful account of the life, the words and the character of Jesus. The divergences arise between the Synoptics and John. The Synoptists refer to one Passover and the public life of Jesus apparently covered a year. John with various references to annual festivals seems to reflect a three-year public ministry. Within this larger divergence is another one about the date of the Last Supper which occasions much controversy. Jesus died on the day before the Sabbath (Mk. 15:42) or Friday. He had a last meal with his disciples the night before. In Jewish reckoning each day began and ended at sunset. The last meal in the evening and the crucifixion came on the same day though on a modern calendar they come on Thursday evening and Friday afternoon respectively. According to John this day was the one before the Passover. There is no divergence on the fact that the day was Friday but whether Friday was the fourteenth or the fifteenth of the month Nisan is the problem. The Law specified that "on the fourteenth of the month [Nisan] is the Lord's Passover. And the fifteenth day of this shall be a feast: seven days shall unleavened bread be eaten" (Num. 28:16–17). John identifies the day as Nisan fourteen and the Synoptics as Nisan fifteen. Opinion is strongly divided between the two identifications. On the one hand, it is argued that the meal is the Passover because of the characteristic features required at a Passover celebration. They reclined at the table, ate from a dish before the bread was broken and

[1] *Jesus in the Light of History* (New York, 1942), 281; cf. G. Ogg, *The Chronology of the Public Ministry of Jesus* (Cambridge, 1940).

used red wine as its comparison with blood shows. As the food had symbolic and historical meanings in memory of the first Passover, so Jesus gave the bread and the wine special significance. They sang a hymn and went only as far as Gethsemane since Passover rules required that the night be spent in Jerusalem or its environs.[2] On the other hand, it is argued that the meal is not the Passover as John clearly stated. There is no mention of the important roast lamb nor of the bitter herbs nor of the four cups of wine nor is the bread called unleavened. On the holy festival day Jesus and his disciples would not have gone out of the city nor have carried arms. On the Passover the Sanhedrin would not have sat as a court nor have joined in a Roman trial of Jesus. There would be no execution nor would a man like Simon, who carried the cross, have been traveling from the field or the country. Linen could not be bought nor would the work of preparation of spices and ointment for the burial of the body have been done on the holy day. The Last Supper was a sanctification (Kiddush), a religious meal when blessings were invoked before a festival or a Sabbath. It was a custom for a circle of friends (chaburah) to gather for a common fellowship meal in which religious discussion prevailed.[3]

Many attempts have been made to explain the differences between the Synoptics and John. Possibly there was a calendar controversy between Pharisees and Sadducees which led to a concession to the Pharisees to begin the month one day earlier than the Sadducees. The division about the date was reflected in the controversy between the eastern and the western church. The eastern church followed John and insisted on celebration of the death of Jesus on Nisan fourteen or the Jewish Passover, no matter what day of the week it occurred. The western church selected Friday, irrespective of the day of the week on which Nisan fourteen chanced to fall and thus dropped any correlation with the exact day of the Jewish Passover. There is small chance of erasing the contradiction between the Synoptics and John. The written Gospels give evidence of variant traditions. The importance of a date about which memories differed needs to

[2] G. Dalman, *Jesus-Jeshua* (New York, 1929), 86–184; J. Jeremias, "The Last Supper," *Jour. Theol. Stud.* L (1929), 1–10.

[3] W. O. E. Oesterley, *Jewish Backgrounds of Christian Liturgy* (Oxford, 1925), 156–93; G. H. C. MacGregor, *Eucharistic Origins* (London, 1928), 32–49; A. W. F. Blunt, *Gospel of Mark* (Oxford, 1929), 249–52; H. Balmforth, *Gospel of Luke* (Oxford, 1930), 261–65; F. L. Cirlot, *The Early Eucharist* (London, 1939), 1–16; G. Dix, *The Shape of the Liturgy* (Westminster, 1943), 48–70; A. J. B. Higgins, *The Lord's Supper in the New Testament* (London, 1951), 9–63.

be distinguished from the events which took place. The Last Supper has a significance which transcends the question of its date.

Passover was an ancient annual festival with a prehistoric origin probably in some spring celebration. Historically it had been observed many centuries when Jesus and his disciples prepared for it in Jerusalem. The origin of the name was explained as due to the destroying angel of the Lord who passed over Hebrew homes but killed the first born in Egyptian homes. Moses had led Israel to freedom from bondage through the Lord's aid in destruction of the Egyptians (Exod. 12:1–30). Passover (Pesach) celebrated freedom. It had different meanings. (1) It referred to the actual meal when the lamb or goat was slaughtered, its blood smeared on the doorposts, its carcass roasted and eaten with bitter herbs, unleavened bread and wine. (2) It referred to the lamb itself which in Jesus' day was killed at a temple ceremony, the sacrificial parts burned and the rest roasted and eaten at evening within Jerusalem. (3) It referred to the seven-day period, to which an eighth had been added, when no bread made with yeast could be eaten, hence it was known as the feast of unleavened bread. After the Temple was destroyed (A.D. 70), the sacrifice of the lamb ended but the festival continued as a home meal and ceremony (Seder) with a much-developed story from Exodus.[4]

In Mark's record of the preparation for the Passover he wrote of the first day of unleavened bread when the lambs were sacrificed. From a strictly Jewish viewpoint the lambs were killed for the Passover and then the next day, which began at sunset, the feast of unleavened bread began. Mark may have written with the Roman day in mind or in accord with a Jewish tendency to refer to the festival as one though originally two parts had been distinguished. Luke agrees with Mark but Matthew in stricter Jewish fashion omits the reference to the sacrifice of the lambs. The directions for the Passover, which according to Luke Jesus gave his disciples, Peter and John, show he had made arrangements for the meal. The immense throngs, when the normal population of 25,000 quadrupled for the festival, required plans in order to have a place inside the city. Home owners in Jerusalem customarily provided rooms for the observance of Passover. Mark says nothing of prior plans and possibly intended to show Jesus had supernatural knowledge but a man carrying a water jar was unusual since women did such work and the inquiry for "my guest

[4] Danby, *The Mishnah,* 136–51; H. Schauss, *The Jewish Festivals* (Cincinnati, 1933), 38–85; J. Pederson, *Israel* (London, 1940), II, 384–415; I. Unterman, *The Jewish Holidays* (New York, 1950), 175–228; T. H. Gaster, *Passover* (New York, 1950), 9–94.

room" points to a previous arrangement. The two disciples prepared the food and the drink, tables and couches, for the Passover in a large upper room.

The brevity of the story of the Last Supper is in striking contrast to the extraordinary development and significance of the sacrament of Holy Communion in the centuries since Jesus. No other scene in Jesus' life, except the crucifixion, has been so often pictured in art. Every possible meaning has been read into the action and the words of Jesus. The early church called it the Eucharist or Thanksgiving; the Roman church named it the Mass; Protestants refer to it as Holy Communion or Lord's Supper. The important point is to attempt to discover what Jesus did, said and meant according to those who first knew him and wrote of him. It is important but difficult to see the Last Supper with the Synoptists when Paul and John also have early accounts and when the reader is influenced by the long history of the Lord's Supper and by a contemporary experience in a church rite which began with Jesus and his disciples. From the beginning the knowledge of Holy Communion has been transmitted by actions among Christians and by written records.[5]

The Synoptists name two important events at the Last Supper: (1) Jesus' warnings about betrayal; (2) his words and actions with bread and wine. From this point to the end of his book Luke has so many variations that it is suggested that he had a source of knowledge about these last days of Jesus that he valued more than Mark. At the Last Supper Luke adds that the disciples disputed about the greatest among them and that Jesus forecast Peter's denial and warned the disciples to get ready for the future. Jesus said the betrayer shared the same dish with him. It was customary for a family or a group to eat from a center dish where the flat baked bread served as a kind of spoon. Jesus deeply regretted the traitor's fate but he did not lighten the intense sorrow and surprise of the disciples by naming him. Jesus had a mission to fulfill as it was written but there is no quotation of scripture cited though it is usually thought that he had in mind the familiar lines from a Psalm (41:9) which describe the trusted table friend who turned against his host. The disciples questioned one another but could not identify the traitor.

In the midst of the meal Jesus took bread, blessed it, broke and distributed it to the Twelve and said, "Take, this is my body." He took

[5] MacGregor, op. cit., 50–110; Cirlot, op. cit., 145–70; W. Lowrie, The Lord's Supper and Liturgy (New York, 1943), 3–17; E. S. Freeman, The Lord's Supper in Protestantism (New York, 1945), 1–30; J. H. Srawley, Early History of Liturgy (Cambridge, 1947), 1–17.

a cup, gave thanks and gave it to them. They all drank of it and then he said, "This is my blood of the covenant poured out for many." Then he added that he would not drink wine until he drank it new in God's Kingdom. This action of Jesus followed Jewish custom in the blessing and the sharing of bread and wine but his words were new. His words enforce his actions which were symbolic of his death. Covenant blood was an ancient symbol. Moses had received the Law and sealed the pledge of the people to fulfill it as he sprinkled them with ox blood which was the "blood of the covenant" (Exod. 24:8). Zechariah (9:11) had promised God's freedom to Jewish prisoners because of their blood covenant with him. A covenant was a most solemn agreement, ratified in blood. It was a bond of union between God and Israel or between God and an individual. "Blood poured out for many" was reminiscent of the death of the suffering servant of the Lord (Isa. 53:11-12). The actions and the words of Jesus suggest that as the disciples partook of the bread and the wine they also shared the life of the giver. Table fellowship had great importance in Judaism. The Passover cemented the ties of friendship, loyalty and faith. The communion about the table in the upper room was deepened by partaking of bread and wine together in a simple significant, special action initiated by Jesus. The pieces of bread given and the single cup, when usually each Passover guest had his own cup, emphasized the unity. The closing words of Jesus look to the future. The Passover was a reminder of God's great deliverance in the past but it always directed the people to the future. God was expected to come with a second great deliverance to redeem his people. Often the hopes for a glorious future were pictured as an abundant Messianic banquet. Jesus knew that his last meal had come but he had confidence that he would share the new life in the coming Kingdom of God. Thus Mark's notably simple record of the bread and the wine has three eminent elements: (1) it pictured the coming death of Jesus; (2) it stressed the shared life of Jesus with his disciples; (3) it expressed a farewell and a confident hope of Jesus to participate in God's new and coming Kingdom beyond the bounds of death. Mark also has an outstanding omission which Matthew shares and a peculiarity. There is no reference to any repetition of the Supper. This omission causes various comments. Perhaps Jesus expected the end of the age so quickly that he did not command a future observance. Perhaps Mark took it for granted that every Christian knew the Supper was celebrated or perhaps he omitted any reference to repetition to avoid any possible attention of persecutors in Rome to the central ceremony of Christian worship. The peculiarity of Mark is that Jesus gave the explanation about the wine after the disciples had drunk it and gave no invitation to drink the wine. This may reflect the actual situation since drinking blood was forbidden in Judaism and his reference to blood stated that it was poured out.

Matthew enlarges Mark's record since Jesus said to eat the bread and to drink when he gave the cup and he added that all should share the wine and that his blood was poured out for forgiveness of sins. His promise to drink in the Father's Kingdom was an act to be shared with the disciples. These additions may mirror some of the meanings that the Supper gathered as it was observed. Eating the bread and drinking the wine were quickly regarded as commanded by Jesus. His death was not only for many but also like the Suffering Servant (Isa. 53) he bore their sins and his blood was a sign of a covenant that forgiveness was attainable. The joy of fellowship was not only at the Supper but was promised with disciples in the future Kingdom.

Luke's record of the bread and the wine has two important variations. First, his order of events is different and, second, his text (22: 19b, 20) is disputed. In the order of events Luke places first the words of Jesus about his future in the Kingdom and the giving of the cup precedes the bread. Jesus said he had earnestly desired this Passover with his disciples before his suffering. He had suspected his seizure might come before the festival but he would not eat again until the Passover was fulfilled in the Kingdom of God. Then he took the cup and told the disciples to divide it among themselves saying that he would not drink until the Kingdom came. This emphasis on the Kingdom puts it foremost as compared with the Passover. He omits any reference to the blood of the covenant or to forgiveness of sins. Then followed the distribution of the bread. Luke is like Mark in that he gives no invitation by Jesus to drink or to eat but he is unlike him in the words spoken about the cup when the disciples were told to take it and divide it. The order of cup-bread was observed in the early church as well as the bread-cup order because the Didache (9:2-3) has the former sequence. These variations show that the Gospels were written at an early time before a single standard order for the Lord's Supper had been established. Different traditions about the Supper were known in the many Christian communities.

Luke's second variation creates divided opinion. On the one hand, there are those who accept the longer text (22:19b-20) and, on the other hand, it is omitted because it is regarded as an addition to

Luke's manuscript from Paul's earlier account (I Cor. 11:23–25). There are remarkable similarities which can be explained as from Paul or as a repetition by Paul and Luke of earlier words of Jesus. The manuscripts are strongly in favor of the longer text but they are copies two hundred fifty years after Paul and Luke. Modern translations often follow the shorter text. If the longer text was originally part of Luke, then his account included two cups which meant a cup-bread-cup order. A comparative statement will illustrate the remarkable likeness between Paul and Luke.

Lk. 22:19b–20	I Cor. 11:23–25
which is given for you	which is broken for you
do this in remembrance of me	do this in remembrance of me
and likewise the cup after supper, saying	in the same way also the cup after supper, saying
This cup which is poured out for you	This cup
is the new covenant in my blood	is the new covenant in my blood

There is no agreement in sight about the longer or the shorter text (which omits Lk. 22:19b–20) but there are important ideas in the longer one. (1) It reports as the words of Jesus, "Do this in remembrance of me." The church had "breaking bread" from its earliest days and Paul claimed that he had received of the Lord his report of the bread and the cup. Both the observance and the description of it belong to the first circle of Christians who saw no incongruity between an early return of Christ and the constant observance of the Lord's Supper. (2) The bread and the wine constituted an act of remembrance. It is natural that Jesus desired remembrance by his friends for himself and his work. The whole Passover celebration was a remembrance and a renewal of sacred ties. The first Christians continued the historical recollection of Jesus whenever they celebrated communion and the passage of time enhanced this aspect. They moved from an annual festival like Passover to a daily or weekly remembrance of Jesus. (3) The new covenant was an advance beyond a blood covenant. It is quite possible that in the reference to the blood Jesus thought of a new covenant like Jeremiah (31:31–34) who believed that God would make a new agreement with his people which would surpass the one made with Moses. In this new covenant all men would know the Lord and find forgiveness. Jesus gave his life that men might enter into a new and living way with the Lord.

Conspectus of the bread and the cup

Mark	Matthew repeats Mark and *adds:*
1. "Take," "he gave"—fellowship between Jesus and disciples	1. "Eat," "drink"
2. "My body" "My blood of the covenant"— symbols of Jesus' death	2. "for forgiveness of sins"
3. "New in the Kingdom"—new life for Jesus, bread-cup	3. "with you in my Father's Kingdom"—bread-cup

Luke, shorter text	Luke, longer text, adds:
1. cup, "Take this and divide"	1. "Do this"
2. "until the Kingdom comes"	2. "In remembrance of me"
3. "my body"	3. "a new covenant"
cup-bread	cup-bread-cup

Luke reports some final words of Jesus to the disciples after supper as he spoke of betrayal, of the greatest among them, of Peter's denial and of their need to be prepared. This is an editorial arrangement by Luke. The first two topics have been discussed. The forecast about Peter's denial came at the Mount of Olives according to Mark and Matthew. The preparation of the disciples for dangers ahead is given in figurative language. In happier days Jesus had sent out his disciples without equipment, trusting hospitality. Now they had to take a purse and a bag and buy a sword as they faced hostility. Now Jesus' death was near as foretold about the Suffering Servant (Isa. 53:12). When the disciples replied that they had two swords, Jesus said, "It is enough." The disciples had taken Jesus' words literally but he stopped them with gentle irony. He did not counsel actual purses, bags and sword. It was a festival day when these things were not sold and later at night he forbade armed resistance. The future bulged with danger and Jesus wanted his disciples forewarned in mind rather than in money and might.

Sometime in the late evening Jesus and his disciples sang a hymn, probably one of the Psalms used to end the Passover (115–118). Then they went to the Mount of Olives. Jesus told his disciples that they would fall away, that their defection was verified in scriptural prediction and that he would go before them into Galilee after his resurrection. The citation from Zechariah (13:7) changes an imperative form, "Smite the shepherd," as given in the Hebrew Bible into a future intention, "I will smite the shepherd." This shows Luke used

a different text of scripture or else adapted it to illustrate his point.
The promises about defection and about Galilee were fulfilled in the
later experiences of the disciples. These experiences may have modified the present form of the forecast, both in the quotation from
Zechariah and in the exactness about Galilee. When Peter protested
violently about his fidelity, Jesus said that before the cock should
crow twice he would deny him thrice. Matthew and Luke refer to
one cockcrow. Peter avowed that he would risk death but not disown
Jesus and the other disciples joined him in his stand. When Peter
later became a prominent Christian, this incident gave him no credit
but Luke knew of an added conversation where Jesus had told Peter
of Satan's demand for him but Jesus prayed for him to maintain faith.
Peter was to turn and strengthen his brethren. These words anticipate
a rise in Peter's fidelity. Jesus was hopeful that in spite of temporary
failure Peter would fortify his fellow disciples.

Jesus went to pray at Gethsemane ("oil press") in an olive grove
on the lower slope of the Mount of Olives. Luke omits the name of
this enclosed place. In Mark this is the third and most candid view
of the occasions on which Jesus prayed. He asked the disciples to sit
while he prayed. Then he took the favored three, Peter, James and
John, as amazed awe and deep distress beset him. He told the three
he felt a deadly sorrow and asked them to wait and watch while he
went forward a stone's throw and fell to the ground and prayed that
he might escape his doom if possible. The agony of Jesus is reported
rather than explained but his terrific tension can be partly glimpsed.
The discouragement of a friend's desertion, the unknown future of
his disciples and work, the temptation to flee, the suspense before
seizure by ruthless enemies, the fearsome finality of suffering and
death for a young man drove him to his Father or Abba, the actual
Aramaic word given by Mark. In his prayer he asked God, to whom
all things were possible, to remove his cup but his final words were
not for his will but for God's will to be done. The Father's will, the
suffering and the will of the one who prayed had to be blended but
the effort was long as Jesus found not deliverance but strength for the
cross ahead. Jesus prayed the same prayer three times and between
his prayers he came to the three disciples who had fallen into sleep.
Luke, with his independent account, omits the scene with disciples
and tells of one time of prayer as Jesus knelt and an angel appeared
to strengthen him while he prayed and "his sweat became like great
drops of blood." These verses (22:43–44) are omitted in some of the
early manuscripts, a fact which still remains a puzzle. Luke reports

that before and after his prayer Jesus warned his disciples to pray that they might escape dangerous trials. In Mark and Matthew, after the first prayer, Jesus asked Peter if he could not watch one hour and urged the disciples to watch and pray lest they encounter temptation. The willing spirit wrestles with the frailty of flesh. After the second prayer the disciples could not answer Jesus. Mark explains that their eyes were heavy and Luke that they slept "for sorrow." They were not aware of the great need of Jesus nor of his danger. After the third prayer he roused them with the question, "Are you still sleeping?" Then came the startling summons; enough of sleep, the crisis has come, rise and be ready, the betrayal and the betrayer are near.

The crowd that arrested Jesus was probably temple police, well-armed and sent out by the Jewish leaders of Jerusalem. To assure the seizure of Jesus at night Judas had arranged the signal of a kiss, the customary greeting of a student to his teacher. When Judas said "Master" and kissed Jesus, the officers seized their victim. One of the bystanders in attempted defense struck with his sword at the slave of the high priest and cut off his ear. Jesus stoutly protested his secret capture like a bandit when he had been a teacher daily in the Temple. But he resigned himself that the scripture might be fulfilled. This reference to scripture may be an added interpretation of the early church which always sought to relate it to Jesus. With their leader taken, the disciples deserted him and fled though there is no indication that they were to be seized also.

Both Matthew and Luke have notable additions about the arrest. Matthew reports that the crowd was great and Luke that Judas was its leader. In Matthew Jesus still addressed Judas as a friend and asked why he came. In Luke he asked him if he would betray the Son of Man with a kiss but Luke avoids any mention that Judas actually kissed Jesus. He reports that the disciples asked permission to use their swords but that Jesus stopped the one who hit off the slave's ear and healed the ear. Matthew gives a longer response of Jesus when he ordered the sword into its place, "All who take the sword will perish by the sword." He rejected an armed defense because he trusted his Father who could send thousands of angels. How would the scriptures be fulfilled unless he accepted arrest? The fulfillment of scripture is one of Matthew's favorite themes which he sees in every crisis of Jesus' life. Luke records the rebuke of Jesus to the leaders themselves, rather than to the police, who had come to make the arrest. He recognized that they had their hour and power because they were backed by the black of night and by dark demonic forces. Luke has no account of the disciples' flight nor does he connect scriptures with the arrest. On this fateful night the Evangelists agree that Jesus was taken after he was identified by Judas, that the disciples made some resistance and that Jesus protested the way he was seized. They have differing traditions about who arrested Jesus, about Jesus' words to Judas and to the defending disciple and about the relation of scripture to the arrest. Mark has a postscript that has often been interpreted as his own autograph. A young man had followed Jesus but when he was grabbed, he escaped naked since he lost his linen garment to the police. "Naked" can mean both without clothes or in an undergarment only. There is little reason for the footnote unless it were a personal reminiscence of the one who made the escape. The unnamed young man will remain nameless though the speculation that he was Mark is interesting and can be expanded from the reports about Mark in Acts.

36

The Hearing before the Council ·
The Trial before Pilate

Mt. 26:57–27:31; Mk. 14:53–15:20; Lk. 22:54–23:25 (241–247)

DURING THE night and the early morning following his arrest Jesus was taken before a group of Jewish leaders, then to Pilate, then to Herod and back to Pilate. Only Luke records the appearance before Herod. Jesus was condemned and crucified in the midmorning. His trials occasion much discussion.[1] The night meetings, the speed of events, the absence of friends of Jesus and the lack of contemporary evidence on court procedures cause uncertainty about several points though there is no doubt about the main facts which are that Jesus had a hearing before Jewish leaders who held him on serious charges and took him to Pilate who turned him over to be crucified. Jewish and Roman authorities combined to end any possible rivalry from Jesus' leadership. It is not known how information reached the gospel writers from the hasty night Jewish hearing but the early morning trial before Pilate was open to the public. Peter was the only disciple who was near and he went no farther than the courtyard and the gateway of the high priest's house. It is not certain what powers over capital punishment the Sanhedrin possessed nor its rules for court procedures since the rules were written about three centuries after Jesus though they were based on earlier oral reports. It is claimed that there were two Sanhedrins, one religious, the other political, but it has been usually thought that there was but one. The Roman governor, Pilate, could order execution but how far he shared power with the Sanhedrin is disputed. The Sanhedrin had been the supreme ruling body in Judaism but the Romans took control through a governor or local ruler who used the Sanhedrin to help his rule. The earliest evidence in Acts (4–5) shows that the Sanhedrin could arrest, im-

---

[1] A. T. Innes, *The Trial of Jesus* (Edinburgh, 1899); R. W. Husband, *The Prosecution of Jesus* (Princeton, 1916); B. H. Branscomb, *The Gospel of Mark*, 271–291; Abrahams, *Studies in Pharisaism and the Gospels*, II 129–137; M. Radin, *The Trial of Jesus of Nazareth* (New York, 1931); S. Zeitlin, *Who Crucified Jesus?* (New York, 1947 2nd ed.), 144–179; F. G. Powell, *The Trial of Jesus Christ* (London, 1948).

prison and punish but the killing of Stephen (7:54–60) appears as an act of violence without judicial sentence. The writings of Josephus support the idea that the Sanhedrin could condemn Jews to death but that the Romans had some control over the execution.

Jesus was taken to the palace of the high priest, Caiaphas, where a group of Jewish leaders gathered. Their assembly cannot be called an official meeting of the Sanhedrin. According to the Mishnah the Sanhedrin sat in daylight in its own place of meeting. It did not meet on a holiday and a sentence was not executed until the following day. A quorum of twenty-three had to be present. A hasty unofficial gathering of the leaders with the high priest was understood by Mark to have taken official action and judged Jesus worthy of death. Witnesses were summoned since the Law required at least two witnesses for any offense (Dt. 19:15) but they did not agree. Finally some men testified that Jesus had said he would destroy the Temple and build another in three days. Matthew contains the charge that he said he was able to destroy and rebuild the Temple. This is a change from the threat in Mark to a statement of capability. The witnesses apparently had a garbled report of the forecast Jesus made to his disciples about the Temple. Though the testimony was not in agreement, the high priest asked Jesus to answer but he remained silent. Then the high priest turned to another possible accusation. He asked Jesus if he were the Messiah, the Son of the Blessed. Out of reverence Caiaphas avoided the use of the sacred name of God but Matthew who often observes this Jewish reverence for God's name gives the phrase as "the Son of God" and puts the question under the form of an oath. Mark alone reports the unequivocal claim of Jesus, "I am." In Matthew the meaning of Jesus' answer cannot be exactly determined. "You have said so" may be affirmative or noncommittal or ambiguous. The further claim of Jesus that his enemies would see the Son of Man sitting at the right hand of Power (God) and coming on the clouds is a figurative statement of his future vindication in the presence of God. This symbolic language is like the vision of the Son of Man in Daniel (7:13) which contained the promise of the Lord to exalt a ruler. This passage had been understood as Messianic in Jewish thought and this interpretation was continued among Christians though the original idea in Daniel meant that the Son of Man was a symbol for the "saints of the Most High."

The declaration by Jesus caused the high priest to tear his clothes, a sign of grief or horror, because he felt Jesus had committed blasphemy though Jesus had not reviled God's name. The Law required a blasphemer to be stoned to death (Lev. 24:16). The claim to be a Messiah was not blasphemy but the high priest may have believed that Jesus' claims of a future with divine honors and power were blasphemous. The council decided that he deserved death. Then some of the group covered his face, as was done with condemned criminals, spit on him and struck him, urging him to prophesy. Matthew omits the blindfold but explains that they slapped him and asked him to identify those who struck him. In Luke the assailants were the men who held Jesus and the mockery comes before the hearing which is placed at daybreak. No witnesses were summoned and the high priest's question was divided into two parts, one in which he asked Jesus if he were the Christ and the other if he were the Son of God. To the first Jesus refused to give a direct answer since his inquisitors would not believe and then he forecast the coming Son of Man. They declared his own words constituted the testimony but the council gave no decision about his death.

During the hearing before the Jewish authorities two of Jesus' disciples came to tragic experiences. Peter was the only disciple courageous enough to follow Jesus to the high priest's palace but he got no farther than the courtyard which was below the chamber where the examination was held. When Peter warmed himself at the fire with the guards, the light revealed him to one of the maids who named him as one seen with Jesus. Peter said that he did not know what she meant but he went out to the gateway where she again identified him as "one of them" but he denied it. He invoked a curse on himself if his word were not true and swore he did not know Jesus when a bystander challenged him a third time. But when a cock crew, Peter remembered the warning of Jesus and wept over his cowardice and denials. Luke places the denials before the hearing and notes that Peter was identified by three different people to whom he made replies which are essentially the same as in Mark. The curses of Peter are omitted. Since the examination had not begun, Jesus was within sight and at the dramatic moment of cockcrow he turned and looked at Peter. Both Luke and Matthew state that Peter wept bitterly.

Matthew relates the suicide of Judas who repented at the condemnation of Jesus. When he returned his silver to the leaders who had paid him, they refused it and he cast it into the Temple. They would not put the money into the temple treasury but bought a potter's field as a cemetery for strangers. This place became known as the "Field of Blood." Matthew regarded the incident as a fulfillment of prophecy which he credits to Jeremiah though there is no passage in Jeremiah parallel to it. Jeremiah had once bought a field in spite of a war threat and another time he went down to a potter's house (32:6–15; 18:2). Zechariah (11:13) had once taken his payment of thirty pieces of silver and at the Lord's command had cast it to the potter in the Temple. Matthew's quotation does not follow Zechariah closely and the Evangelist probably used a selection of scripture which had been adapted to match later events. This story of Judas explained the origin of the name for the potter's field and put the priests in a chill light as they scrupled to place the money in the Temple though they had no concern about Judas and his betrayal of an innocent life. Luke has another tradition about the death of Judas by a bloody accident (Acts 1:18–19). A field was named from it but it was not a cemetery. There is no mention of repentance. Judas had kept his money and bought the field which was the scene of the accident.

When morning came, Mark and Matthew report a second consultation by the Jewish leaders. Perhaps it was to validate in daylight their earlier decision against Jesus. They bound him and took him to Pilate, who had his capital at Caesarea, but came to Jerusalem for the Passover to forestall any revolt. He was known for inflexible, merciless rule and for disregard of the Jewish religious scruples, though the Gospels say little about him. He would have no dealings with the religious issues among the Jews but his first question to Jesus indicates that they had brought Jesus to him as a potentially dangerous leader. The idea of Messiahship was given a political meaning. When Pilate asked Jesus if he were the King of the Jews, Jesus answered, "You have said so." This answer like the one to the high priest has different meanings. The failure of Jesus to defend himself occasions wonder. The trial before Pilate was in daylight and it was public according to Roman justice. Perhaps Jesus felt it was no use to attempt to justify his position. He would not deny a leadership he had undertaken but could not explain it to a callous Roman pagan. He may have thought the case was already decided against him or that he had accepted his fate since his time of prayer in Gethsemane. The priests accused him of many things but he kept silent before them and Pilate's questions, to the wonder of Pilate who knew that Rome executed any rival kings to Caesar.

Luke lists three serious charges against Jesus before Pilate. He was misleading the nation as a political agitator. This was untrue though Jesus did have a popular following. The second charge that he obstructed the payment of taxes could be refuted because Jesus had said to pay Caesar his due. The third about his Messianic kingship could be taken by Pilate in a revolutionary sense but he would know nothing of a suffering, serving Messiah. He declared three times that he found no crime in Jesus. When Jesus was accused of stirring up the people from Galilee to Jerusalem, Pilate, upon discovery that he was a Galilean, sent him to Herod Antipas who as a native Jewish ruler was in Jerusalem for the Passover. Pilate probably did not send Jesus to Herod for disposition of the case which was in his jurisdiction but for advice and as a courtesy to a ruler whose subject was held as a prisoner. This courtesy changed Herod's enmity to friendship. Herod was full of curiosity which soon turned to contempt and mockery as Jesus made no answer to his many questions. After clothing Jesus in gorgeous robes to ridicule his alleged kingship, he finally returned him to Pilate. Then Pilate made his second declaration of the innocency of Jesus and offered to scourge him and let him go.

This suggestion was rejected by the Jews and a demand arose for the release of a prisoner named Barabbas. In Mark its origin was in a crowd who had come up to the governor for that purpose and who may not have known about the hasty trial of Jesus. The explanation for the release of Barabbas was that Pilate had a custom of releasing a prisoner at the holiday. Since no other evidence for this custom exists outside the Gospels and since it is an act more lenient than the usual methods in Roman administration, its historicity has been questioned. But the custom may have been entirely local and due to Pilate's desire to placate the Jews with whom he had much trouble. There is no adequate reason for the story of Barabbas if it were not a fact. Some of the manuscripts give his name as Jesus Barabbas. Jesus was a common name but its use for a man like Barabbas was distasteful to Christians and it was soon dropped from the Gospels. Barabbas meant "son of a father." This prisoner had been a revolutionary who was in prison among rebels who had rioted and committed murder. Luke infers that Barabbas also was in jail for murder. It is probable that the priests who urged the crowds to shout for Barabbas felt sympathy for him as an insurrectionist against Rome while they feared and envied the leadership of Jesus. When Pilate suggested release for Jesus, the crowd yelled for Barabbas. When Pilate asked what should be done with the King of the Jews, they cried, "Crucify him," and when Pilate asked what evil he had done, they shouted, "Crucify him." These three questions by Pilate in Mark, like the three declarations of Jesus' innocency in Luke and the dream of Pilate's wife and his washing of hands in Matthew, show that the gospel writers believed that the drive to kill Jesus was primarily the responsibility of the Jewish leaders together with a crowd of their countrymen though the execution was by Romans. This placement of blame on the Jewish people is heightened in Matthew by the account of Pilate's hand washing and his wife's dream. Both actions are possible but more probable as local traditions which were added to the main narrative and which lessen Pilate's responsibility. They reflect the period when Jews persecuted the Christians and when it was important for Christians to avoid Roman suspicion. It is hard to see in historic fact how Pilate's wife would have known about Jesus in the sudden trial or how Pilate, as governor, would claim no accountability when he had to make a final decision or how the Jewish crowd could look to their future with the ominous claim of a man's blood. Centuries of bad blood between Jews and Christians have found some rooting in misunderstanding of responsibility for the death of Jesus. The Jewish people did not kill Jesus. He was seized by leaders of the Jewish people, handed over to a Roman governor who had him crucified. The reason for Pilate's action, as given in Mark, is that he wished to satisfy the crowd. He gave no official sentence but released Barabbas and had Jesus scourged and handed over for crucifixion. Scourging was the usual brutal whipping that Romans gave to condemned criminals. The Gospels do well to omit the details. The holiday season was a time of high patriotic tensions and riots were frequent. Pilate desired to avoid trouble. He probably heard enough to realize Jesus was a leader of the people. He knew the potential danger of a leader in a nation whose religious zeal was fanatic. He could content the Jewish leaders, protect his own position and be rid of a possibly perilous leader. He had mingled the blood of Galileans with their sacrifices (Luke 13:1). One more Galilean mattered little nor could Pilate imagine his action would carve his name enduringly in the hall of infamy.

Matthew and Mark describe the rude horseplay of the soldiers with Jesus. Luke omits this second mockery and gives a second one by Herod and his soldiers. These Roman soldiers recruited in the provinces had known the difficulties of a soldier's life among rebellious Jews who hated them. They knew the charge against Jesus as King of the Jews and were acquainted with the ceremony which hailed an emperor. They took Jesus into the praetorium which was the headquarters and the residence of the governor. It may have been the Castle of Antonia beside the temple area or the Herodian palace on the southwest side of the city. The soldiers summoned their regiment for the ceremony. The wreath made from some thorny plant, the purple robe, the imperial "hail" mocked a kingship which they ridiculed as they struck, saluted and spat upon Jesus. Then they put his own clothes on him and led him out for execution.

37

The Crucifixion · The Burial

Mt. 27:32–66; Mk. 15:21–47; Lk. 23:26–56 (248–252)

THE CRUCIFIXION is the best-known fact in the life of Jesus. Christ crucified, as Paul wrote (I Cor. 1:23–24), was to the Jews a stumbling block and to the Gentiles foolishness but to the Christians, Jewish and Greek, Christ was the power and the wisdom of God. The gospel writers relate the crucifixion with brevity and reticence and with knowledge that the resurrection was yet to come. That their leader had been executed as a criminal was the most difficult and unavoidable fact that they had to face. They saw it as part of God's purpose which he had foretold in the scriptures. They had no desire to picture the gruesome details of death to readers who knew crucifixions by sight. After the fifth century when the horror of a cross had receded from common view and devotion began to cast its glamor, Christians started a long line of the innumerable pictures of Jesus' death. But the early Christians wanted decorative crosses no more than men today want religious ornaments of gallows or electric chair. The Romans adopted crucifixion from the Carthaginians but limited it to slaves and criminals and exempted Roman citizens from its torture. The condemned man usually carried the cross beam to the site of execution where he was stripped. A peg on the upright beam supported his body, hands were nailed and the feet nailed or tied. The victim lingered one or two days and died from pain, thirst, exposure and exhaustion.

A centurion, whom tradition later named Longinus or Petronius, and some soldiers took Jesus out for execution which in Roman custom followed soon after sentence. They compelled Simon of Cyrene who was coming into the city to carry the cross. His name indicates that he was a Jew from the city in north Africa. Perhaps he was a Passover pilgrim or one who had returned to the Holy Land to end his days. No reason is given for his impressment though it has been inferred that Jesus was not able to carry his cross the entire distance. Mark names Simon's two sons as if they were known and one of them, Rufus, may be the one Paul greeted (Rom. 16:13). Neither the way nor the place can be exactly determined. The Way of Sorrow, Via Dolorosa, with its famed Stations of the Cross had its beginnings in the thirteenth century. The place was named Golgotha or skull place. The name Calvary comes from the Vulgate. The idea of a hill is an inference from the place shaped like a skull. The traditional site of crucifixion and burial over which now stands the Church of the Holy Sepulchre cannot be identified beyond the fourth century. An early Christian wrote that Jesus suffered outside the gate (Heb. 13:12) and the mention of passersby has led to the idea of a near-by highway (Mk. 15:29). It was both Roman and Jewish custom to execute prisoners in public places as a warning against breaking the law.

On the basis of advice to give strong drink to those about to perish (Prov. 31:6), the women of Jerusalem prepared wine as an opiate and sent it to condemned men. Jesus refused some myrrhed wine, perhaps because he had promised at the Last Supper not to drink until in the Kingdom or he may have desired no drug before his death though wine and myrrh mixed for flavor was not an opiate. Matthew, influenced by a sufferer in a Psalm (69:21) who was given gall for food, wrote that the wine was mixed with gall. The garments of Jesus went by lot to the soldiers who probably brought their dice to while away the hours. Mark alone gives nine o'clock as the hour of crucifixion. The prisoner usually carried a sign swung round his neck with his name and crime and at execution it was placed above his head. The charge against Jesus was a grim warning to Jewish nationalists, "The King of the Jews." The exact reading varies according to each Gospel but they all agree on the charge of condemnation. Two robbers, one on either side, were crucified with Jesus. A third account of mockings is added to the earlier ones. At the cross passersby derided Jesus for his claim to destroy and to rebuild the Temple and for his inability to save himself from the cross. Matthew adds that they said, if he were the Son of God, he could come down. The leaders of the Jews mocked his claim as Christ and King of Israel. He could save others but not himself. If he came down, then they could believe. Matthew again enlarges the record. The robbers joined in the revilement. It is sometimes claimed that the Evangelists have adapted their reports to the familiar scriptures like those about the Suffering Servant in Isaiah (53) and the anguished Psalmist (22). This is possible since fulfillment of God's purposes revealed in the scriptures was a frequent theme of the first Christians. But the sadism aroused by the sight of suffering has always been one of the degradations of men.

From noon until three there was darkness over the whole land. It was seen as a supernatural prelude to the death of Jesus by his followers who knew of Amos who wrote of the day of the Lord's judgment when the sun would go down at noon (8:9). The actual occurrence may have been no more than an unusually dark cloudiness. Near death at midafternoon Jesus cried with a loud voice twice. The first time he spoke in Aramaic or Hebrew the first line of a Psalm (22:1). These are the only words of Jesus from the cross according to Mark and Matthew. Their meaning has been endlessly discussed but the mysterious question remains unanswered. Two main interpretations have appeared: (1) the cry is of temporary desolation at the doorway of death when Jesus felt the force of evil men overwhelm him; (2) the cry is an appeal to God in which Jesus quotes and shares the Psalmist's terrifying complaint and later assurance that God seemingly forsakes but will surely answer his desperate need in suffering. Matthew and Mark wrote to increase faith and they would not have reported the cry if they had thought God forsook Jesus. Luke may have omitted the cry because he thought it could be misunderstood. Some bystanders thought Jesus called on Elijah who was expected to bring aid to the distressed. One of them placed a spongeful of vinegar for Jesus to drink and waited to see if Elijah might help him down. But Jesus cried aloud a second time and died. Matthew shows the voluntary aspect of Jesus' death by writing that Jesus gave up his spirit. Two events witness to the passing of Jesus. (1) The temple curtain was rent. Various veils were used in the Temple but this portent probably referred to the one before the Holy of Holies. Later Christians saw the occurrence as a forecast of the coming destruction of the Temple and as a symbolic opening of a new way to God's presence through the death of Jesus. Matthew increases the portent with legendary additions which express the awe of his day but which increase incredibility for a critical reader. Earthquakes are known in Palestine but the resurrection of saints' bodies which appeared in Jerusalem after Jesus' resurrection is a rumor which Matthew repeated but one in which he had to safeguard the fact that Jesus was first in resurrection. This safeguard about a resurrection on the third day upsets the idea that the saints appeared at the time of Jesus' death. (2) According to Matthew the earthquake filled the centurion and the soldiers with awe and elicited their tribute, "Truly this was a Son of God." But Mark gives these words of the centurion alone facing Jesus as he breathed his last. Early Christian readers would regard the soldiers' words as the first confession of faith in Jesus after his death but the Roman officer expressed a thought well known among pagans. The emperor, following an ancient eastern idea, claimed divine sonship. In a supernatural sense he embodied the majesty and the power of Rome. On the cross a man had died uncommonly soon but he had some divinity in him and the centurion, to whom death was no stranger, admired his passing in words that would be an acknowledgment of an imperial idea. After listing the soldiers, Simon, the two robbers, the passersby, the religious leaders among those who came to Golgotha, Mark names three women and mentions others who came to Jerusalem with Jesus. They stood afar off and watched. Mark gives the names of the same women who were witnesses at the three crucial events of crucifixion, burial and the empty tomb. He gives no reports about these women earlier in his Gospel nor does he write anything of their fidelity or anguish.

Luke has his own account of the crucifixion. His sources cannot be ascertained beyond his own reliable claim that eyewitnesses delivered "these things" to him. Outside of the parallels with Mark, his own skillful composition and his actual sources cannot be separated with certainty. His narrative is less gloomy than Mark and gives some of the most prized words of Jesus. On the way to Golgotha Simon followed Jesus. Then came large crowds and last, women wailing for Jesus. To these women Jesus turned with an admonition that their tears should fall, not for him, but for themselves and their children when coming terrible days would make childlessness a blessing. Destruction was on its way when people would feel it better for mountains to fall on them rather than for them to fall into enemy hands (Hos. 10:8). At the crucifixion Jesus prayed, "Father, forgive them; for they know not what they do." The ones for whom he prayed may be the soldiers or all those responsible for his death. Since important manuscripts do not contain this prayer, there remains serious doubt whether the words have been added or omitted. But their sublime spirit of forgiveness overcomes evil with good and makes real the earlier command of Jesus to love enemies. The people stared and the soldiers jeered the king of the Jews. One of the most notable additions tells of the repentant criminal who rebuked his fellow victim for railing at Jesus whom he defended as innocent and then asked Jesus to remember him when he came in his Kingdom. He received more than he asked, for Jesus promised that he would share Paradise with him that day. Paradise, once the name of the Garden of Eden, meant the pleasant resting place in the world of the dead as they awaited resurrection. This promise of companionship arose from the criminal's recognition that God should be feared and that his own punishment came justly for evil deeds and from his confidence in Jesus as one who would aid him in Messianic power. The criminal had either heard of Jesus prior to their meeting on their crosses or Luke thinks of Jesus as able to impress him with future power even in the face of dire circumstances. Luke's reference to the sun's light failing might make his readers think of an eclipse which is impossible at the full moon of Passover season. In a final prayer Jesus committed himself with a loud cry into God's hands. Luke's three utterances of Jesus from the cross together with one in Mark and three in John constitute the seven last words of Jesus from the cross which the church has woven into a devotional pattern for Good Friday. The centurion praised God and declared Jesus an innocent man while the crowds who had gone out to see the sight turned homeward mourning.

Jesus died at midafternoon, sooner than expected at crucifixion. The Sabbath would begin at sunset and burial had to be completed quickly. The Law commanded that a man hanged on a tree must not remain overnight (Dt. 21:22–23) though Roman custom left the crucified on his cross. Final care for the body of Jesus was undertaken by Joseph of Arimathea. He bore the same name as the father of Jesus. His birthplace has not been accurately located. He was a man of standing since he belonged to the Sanhedrin. According to Mark he looked for the Kingdom of God. This does not necessarily mean he was a disciple of Jesus but rather that he was a loyal Jew, who held hopes for the realization of God's purposes. Luke explains that he was a good and righteous man who had not voted to condemn Jesus. Matthew declares that he was rich. This may be a fact or Matthew may see a fulfillment of the Servant in Isaiah (53:9) who made his death with the rich. Also he declares he was a disciple of Jesus and thus explains his concern for Jesus better than the suggestion that he was keeping the Law in respect to a corpse. He was a man of courage who went to Pilate to ask for Jesus' body which was granted to him when Pilate had the centurion's word that Jesus was dead. Joseph bought a linen cloth, took the body down, wrapped it, laid it in a rock-cut tomb and rolled a stone before the door. Sepulchres of this type hewn out of a rock cliff with shelves cut in the walls for the reception of bodies were owned by wealthy families of Jerusalem. They were guarded by a large circular stone, which was rolled upright to cover the entrance. Both Matthew and Luke write that the tomb was new, in keeping with the idea that newness meant sacredness. A later Jewish law forbade a criminal to be buried with his fathers. Matthew states that the tomb belonged to Joseph. According to Mark two women, each named Mary, saw the burial place. In Matthew they sat opposite the tomb. With Salome they brought spices for the preparation of the body after the Sabbath had passed. Luke states that an indefinite number of women who had come with Jesus from Galilee witnessed the burial. They then left and prepared spices and ointments, which they apparently had on hand, for the care of the body as soon as the Sabbath should pass.

The first followers of Jesus met slanders when they claimed the resurrection of Jesus. One slander was the Jewish assertion that the disciples stole the body of Jesus and then declared he had risen. Matthew related an incident in which he deflated this calumny. It is doubtful if the incident is any more historical than the slander. It is not probable that the priests and the Pharisees would go to Pilate on a Sabbath, nor have clear knowledge of Jesus' promise to rise after death, nor that Pilate would grant a Roman guard for Jewish leaders when he had a report that Jesus was dead.

38

The Empty Tomb · The Resurrection
Appearances

Mt. 28; Mk. 16; Lk. 24 (253)

THE RESURRECTION is the best-known belief about Jesus.[1] Its incomparable importance for Christians cannot be overestimated. It is the climax of the story of Jesus and the only sufficient reason for the rise and the spread of Christianity. It is the one explanation of the amazing change from fear and defeat into courage and life in the lives of the first Christians. It alone can account for their church, for their Sunday, for their New Testament and for their absolute confidence in the life after death. *That* God raised Jesus from the dead became the unanimous, most assured faith of his followers; *how* he was raised they never explained nor did they give identical testimonies about their experiences. A unique, unparalleled event, it was the greatest miracle in the entire story of Jesus and the surest evidence of the power and the purpose of God.

The earliest record in Mark shows that on the first day of the week, soon after sunrise three women, Mary Magdalene, Mary and Salome, came to the tomb to prepare the body of Jesus properly for burial. It was customary to bury on the day of death but the Sabbath had prevented the usual care for the body. Since the stone was too great for the women to roll, they wondered who would move it for them. The tomb was situated so that they looked up and saw it open. They entered and saw a young man in a white robe. He had supernatural

[1] K. Lake, *The Resurrection of Jesus* (London, 1907), 44–124, 166–279; J. Orr, *The Resurrection of Jesus* (London, 1908), 57–202; C. R. Bowen, *The Resurrection in the New Testament* (New York, 1911), 150–373; J. M. Shaw, *The Resurrection of Christ* (Edinburgh, 1920), 44–94, 123–207; P. Gardner-Smith, *The Narratives of the Resurrection* (London, 1926), ix–xxvii, 24–49, 61–80, 114–90; S. V. McCasland, *The Resurrection of Jesus Christ* (New York, 1932), 15–74, 169–98; M. J. Lagrange, *The Gospel of Jesus Christ* (London, 1938), II, 282–305; A. Lunn, *The Empty Tomb* (New York, 1945), 69–95; A. M. Ramsey, *The Resurrection of Christ* (London, 1945), 7–81, 115–23; S. M. Zwemer, *The Glory of the Empty Tomb* (New York, 1947), 38–62; Scroggie, *A Guide to the Gospels,* 602–22. H. E. W. Turner, *Jesus, Master and Lord* (London, 1953), 345–73.

knowledge of their situation such as an angel might possess. He calmed their amazement, told them they sought Jesus who had risen and showed them the empty place. The women were to go and tell the disciples and Peter that Jesus was going to Galilee as he had promised (Mk. 14:28). There they would see him. In trembling and astonishment they fled from the tomb and told no one through fear. Mark's Gospel ends abruptly with no report of the appearance to fulfill the forecasts given by Jesus to disciples or the promise of the angel. There is no way to settle the question about the ending of Mark. It may be complete or incomplete. Since Mark knew of the resurrection, it is argued that his climax would contain an account of the appearance of Jesus. But Mark may have thought his previous promises of the resurrection were sufficient and that the right result of the tremendous truth of resurrection was an amazed reverence. His report establishes the fact of the empty tomb with the promise Jesus would be seen in Galilee.

Matthew combines the two important elements in the post-resurrection period: the empty tomb and the appearances of Jesus both in Jerusalem and in Galilee. The two women went at dawn to the tomb but there is no statement of their intent to prepare the body. A great earthquake like the one at the death of Jesus and an awesome descending angel rolled back the stone and the guards fell unconscious. The message to the women was the same as in Mark except that they were urged to go quickly to tell the disciples but there is no mention of Peter which is unusual in the Gospel which exalts him. The women ran with fear and great joy to tell the disciples. On their way Jesus met and greeted them. As they worshiped him, he quieted their fear and repeated the message for the disciples to see him in Galilee. Matthew then gives the report of the guards to the priests, who bribed them to say that the disciples stole the body as they slept and who promised to safeguard them with Pilate. The reference "to this day" shows the lapse of time and the spread of rumor rather than fact.

With the Great Commission Matthew completes his Gospel. This second appearance of Jesus is at a mountain in Galilee where his disciples both worshiped and doubted him. The final words of the risen One constitute a great summary of the message of Christianity. Historically they establish the faith of the church in its mission and its relationship to Christ. They combine the actual confidence of Jesus in his work with his followers with the ensuing experience and practice of the church. During his life Jesus had ministered to fellow Jews and had nowhere commanded baptism nor given a formula of triple names to use with it. But he had sent disciples out on missions, had taught them and had lived in fellowship with them. It is a supreme marvel of history that his Jewish followers, beginning three days after his death, achieved within a few decades an unwavering assurance: (1) that Jesus had received universal authority from God; (2) that he had commissioned them to convert all nations, baptizing in the name of the Trinity and teaching them all of his commandments; (3) that his unseen but real presence remained with them to the end of the age.

Luke is at his best with his carefully constructed, entrancing narratives of the resurrection. He has a longer, more complete account, which includes the empty tomb, but the appearances of Jesus are in or near Jerusalem and not at the tomb, with none in Galilee. One half of his report is given to the matchless Emmaus story. He is interested in showing the kind of body Jesus possessed and that he continued teaching and that he appeared to a number of people. There are three women named at the tomb with others unnamed. They did not find the body nor see Jesus. The two angels in dazzling clothing did not announce the resurrection though many manuscripts contain the announcement. The question by angels, "Why do you seek the living among the dead?" assumes that Jesus had risen. Instead of the promise to see Jesus in Galilee the angels recall to the women the words of Jesus in Galilee about betrayal, crucifixion and resurrection. The women reported these words, not only to the Eleven but to the others, but their story seemed nonsense and was not believed.

The two to whom Jesus appeared on the way to Emmaus are not known apart from this story. Probably they did not belong to the Twelve since only one, Cleopas, was named. Their failure to recognize Jesus as he drew near was due to some unusual inability which is stated but not explained. Their puzzlement over the death of Jesus and the strange report of the women gave opportunity for the Stranger to question them. Their report about Jesus claimed him as a prophet, popular with the people and as the hoped-for Messiah to his disciples. "To redeem Israel" meant to deliver the Jewish people both from evil and from foreign domination. The experience of the women at the tomb was described as a vision of angels who reported that Jesus was alive and that his body was gone. Then the Stranger taught them how to interpret the scriptures which dealt with the suffering of Christ. The climax of the story came in the home in the evening at table when the two recognized Jesus as he took bread, blessed and gave it to them. The recognition of Christ present in the breaking of bread became one of the most certain assurances to the Christians that death did not hold him. But his vanishment showed a different kind of existence from their earlier knowledge of him. The two recalled their burning hearts as they had listened to Christ as he interpreted the scriptures. They went back to Jerusalem at once and found the Eleven and others who reported that the Lord had risen and appeared to Simon. There is no description of this second appearance. The third appearance came while they talked and Jesus suddenly stood among them. He allayed their fright of him as a possible ghost, quieted their troubled, questioning hearts and encouraged them to feel and see him, especially his hands and feet, and to watch him eat a piece of broiled fish. Then he gave them some final words somewhat like the Great Commission in Matthew. First, everything in the scriptures, the Law of Moses, the prophets and the Psalms, had to be fulfilled, especially about his death and resurrection. Repentance and forgiveness had to be preached to all peoples beginning at Jerusalem. The disciples were witnesses who had to stay in the city until God's promise of power should clothe them. This is a forecast of the coming of the Holy Spirit as Luke later described it in Acts (2:1-4). Finally, Jesus led them to Bethany, blessed them and left them. They returned to the city with great joy and worshiped in the Temple.

These reports by Luke pass by any appearance of Jesus at the tomb. All appearances are near or in Jerusalem and the disciples receive a command to stay in the city. Others, like the women and some companions of the disciples, share the appearances. This wider circle of those who experienced the resurrection is in keeping with Luke's universalism. The story of the appearances mingles disbelief and joy. Luke stressed both the evidence to the heart and the mind, an inner recognition, and the outer evidences of the physical senses. The fulfillment of scripture, especially about suffering, is stronger than in Matthew who usually places greatest emphasis on the relation between the Old Testament and Christ. Luke alone reports an appearance to Simon which probably indicates the time of restoration of Peter after his denial. Luke alone reports a promise of "power from on high" for the disciples. He gives a brief narrative of the Ascension. All these experiences occur on the day of resurrection. The sequence of time as the two returned from Emmaus, a two-hour walk after the evening meal, the appearance, the instruction to the Eleven and others and the two-mile walk to Bethany would place the Ascension after nightfall but Luke's interest is not in chronology but in the assurances and the teaching of Christ as he appeared to his friends. A more complete story of the Ascension is told by Luke in Acts (1:6–11) at the close of a forty-day period, which ended any further physical manifestations of the risen Christ. Luke's story of the Ascension moves in a different direction from Matthew where the final promise of Jesus is to be with his followers always. Two complementary thoughts continued among Christians. According to one, Jesus ascended to the right hand of God to a position of divine authority; according to the other, he remained as a spiritual companion to all his disciples who obeyed his commandments.

There is an ending in Mark (16:9–20) which is canonical scripture though not written by Mark and is later than Matthew and Luke. It differs in thought and style from Mark. It contains no report of an appearance of Jesus at the empty tomb or in Galilee. The first appearance was to Mary Magdalene alone who reported to those who had been with him that she had seen Jesus. The second appearance was to two, walking in the country. This is based on Luke's story of the walk to Emmaus. The third appearance was to the Eleven. This is similar to Luke's report. In each of these appearances the followers of Jesus did not believe. This appendix to Mark is a short teaching which condemns unbelief, encourages belief and enumerates the resurrection appearances. Jesus not only rebuked the disciples for unbelief but he commanded them to preach the gospel to the whole creation. This is based on the Great Commission given in Matthew. The disciples were promised miraculous power to cast out demons, to speak in new tongues, to be able to handle serpents, to drink deadly potions without hurt and to heal the sick. Finally the Ascension of Jesus and his place at God's right hand are mentioned. The disciples went out and preached everywhere and the Lord walked with them so that their message was verified by signs.

This conclusion provides important historical perspectives upon the half-century period following the resurrection though it does not present any new information about the resurrection. It is a composition which reflects beliefs and practices of early Christians rather than the immediate situation at the resurrection. It is distinctive because it contains the only gospel reference to the Lord as seated at God's right hand, because of its stress on signs or miracles to validate preaching, because of a strong statement that belief and baptism assure salvation and because it shows Christianity spreading everywhere.

The resurrection of Jesus has not only profoundly influenced the life of his followers but it has also called forth innumerable studies.

A survey of the resurrection in the Synoptics requires that certain points be distinguished: (1) the event itself; (2) the experience of the event by friends of Jesus; (3) the written record of the event by Gospel writers; (4) the interpretations of the records. (1) The writers of the Gospels never claimed that any man saw the resurrection of Jesus nor do they attempt to describe it imaginatively. They state that Jesus was buried late on the day before the Sabbath, that none of his followers did anything on the Sabbath, that the first day of the week the tomb was empty and that Jesus appeared alive to some of his friends. The actual event of resurrection remained unseen and mysterious. They believed it to be a new creative act of God, beyond the reach of human evidence. (2) The experiences connected with the resurrection antedate the written records by two decades at least. Something happened to the friends of Jesus which worked tremendous changes in them. They shared and spread their experiences with an ever-widening circle of believers. These actual transforming experiences in the hearts of men and women remain beyond the reach of the historian except as they are reflected in the brief vital deposits in the New Testament. (3) The Synoptic accounts have been summarized in the immediately foregoing paragraphs. (4) The interpretations of these narratives must begin with the fact that Paul (I Cor. 15) and John (20–21) also give accounts of the resurrection and that the entire New Testament is permeated with the thought of it. The stories of the resurrection are a unity in diversity. There is agreement that there was an empty tomb and that Jesus had risen to appear to his disciples. These are the basic points of agreement in the records. There are numerous lesser points where divergence appears in each writer as he adds his own special reports. These divergences cannot be arranged into one single consistent narrative of time and place, of words and appearances any more than the differing accounts of Jesus' earlier life can be eased into an unvarying harmony. Some of the reports have varying legendary details. Either one or two angels rolled back the stone and smote fear into the guards. All the reports are saturated with a faith which saw the facts transformed by divine significance. The friends of Jesus were filled with wonder, fear, unbelief, belief and joy. They had not expected the resurrection in spite of the four predictions of it by Jesus.

The women found the empty tomb. Though they said nothing, as Mark states, it is probable they soon talked as Matthew and Luke relate. The empty tomb is a negative witness and it does not appear in Paul's chapter in which he gives the earliest and longest list of six appearances. Paul had no reason to give all details even if he had known them. What became of the physical body of Jesus which Joseph of Arimathea put in the tomb? The traditional answer is that God raised it and transformed it into a new form of existence. There are also the ancient canards that the disciples stole it or that Joseph put it away or that the Romans got rid of it or that the gardener disposed of it or that Jesus recovered consciousness. There is also the theory that the Galilean women, strangers in Jerusalem, went to the wrong tomb. It is sometimes said that the empty tomb was a later inference from the appearances of Jesus. That the women came to an empty tomb may well be true while the mystery remains. How did it become empty?

The appearances of Jesus established the truth of his resurrection. In Matthew he appeared: (1) to the two Marys at the tomb at dawn; (2) to the Eleven in Galilee sometime later; in Luke he appeared (3) to two disciples on the Emmaus road; (4) to Simon; (5) to the Eleven and their companions in Jerusalem. In Mark there was the promise of Jesus' appearance in Galilee and in the later appendix he appeared to Mary Magdalene, to two who were walking and to the Eleven. These appearances combine aspects which indicate a change which made Jesus unrecognizable and able to move at will among the disciples who thought they saw a spirit. On the other hand, he appeared unchanged as he walked, talked, referred to his flesh and bones and ate with the disciples who saw him and identified him as the one they had known before his death.

Various interpretations of these appearances have been suggested. (1) These apparitions can be accepted as divine mysteries beyond all human knowledge like the devout claim that Jesus first appeared to his mother though there is no record of it in the New Testament. It can be stated, not explained, that God gave Jesus the supernatural kind of body that could appear with both physical and spiritual capacities. It is probable that since Jewish beliefs in resurrection expected some reanimation or divine transformation of the body that most of the first followers of Jesus could realize the reality of the resurrection only by evidence which included physical features. This is notable in Luke whose reports of bodily aspects soon cease. They last no longer than the Ascension forty days after resurrection. (2) Others, like Paul, said flesh and blood could not inherit the Kingdom of God. When he reminded the Corinthians of the gospel he had preached to them, he showed that according to the scriptures Christ died "for our sins," was buried and raised the third day. He appeared to Cephas, to the Twelve, to five hundred brethren, to James, to all the apostles and to Paul. While Paul may have known reports of a physical resurrection, he declared God revealed his Son *in* him (Gal. 1:16). He made no claim about an empty tomb. The consequence is that there have always been those who find the reality of Christ's resurrection in an inner spiritual revelation, accessible to all faithful believers.

There are difficulties in thought in either the traditional belief in bodily resurrection or the alternate belief in a spiritual resurrection. On the one hand, this traditional view which insists on the resurrection of the body modifies the physical form of Jesus by miraculous capacities which increase the difficulty of belief because his body was like no other bodies. On the other hand, an acceptance of a spiritual resurrection faces the question of the disposal of the physical body and also the difficulty of recognition of Jesus if he had no bodily form of existence. There remain some unsolvable mysteries in either conception of the resurrection.

There are other explanations which have commanded less support. (1) Originally there was only the single statement that the Lord had risen and appeared to Simon and from this germinal experience of Peter there developed all the narratives of the resurrection as a cult story which answered the needs of a growing Christian movement. (2) The resurrection was only a hallucination, generated in the high emotional tensions of the women or the disciples. (3) It was a real vision imparted by God to help the hopeless disciples. (4) It is a construction based on Old Testament ideas, like those of Hosea (6:2) who promised that God would raise his people on the third day. (5) The appearances were like the spirits which some investigators of psychical research claim can be summoned after death.

The Gospels make clear that there is no single understanding of the resurrection. An extraordinary event produced extraordinary impressions. The appearances of Jesus took place at different times and places and to different people. The order of the appearances varies. Some were on the first day, others late enough for disciples to travel to Galilee but none continue long. Luke ends them with the Ascension in forty days (Acts 1:3). One or two angels announce the resurrection. These variations witness to a multiplicity of experiences. Some aspects are temporary, others have had continuing real influence among Christians in all ages. The temporary aspects had their weight for the first believers but they soon lost their immediate significance and remain important only as parts of a past event. Jesus did not continue to walk and to eat with his disciples nor invite them to "handle" him. Angels did not remain at the tomb and tell faithful women what to do. There was no repetition of the "parting" at Bethany. As time passed even the location of the tomb was lost.

It is evident that some events of the past have great importance as history but religion has its greatest influence and sense of reality as real life in the present. The first reports of the resurrection mixed almost inextricably both the past and the present experiences of the followers of Jesus. History and religion merge and are not easily or sharply separable. But the importance of the resurrection of Jesus, which is anchored in the past as a unique event, stands in its continuing reality in the lives of believers. The most influential interpretations center in those aspects of the resurrection which all Christians can share in common everywhere and at all times. It is historical fact that the first followers of Jesus had certain experiences related to the resurrection but the validity of those experiences can never be established by historical criticism alone. The understanding of these experiences rests not only upon historical study but upon basic religious assumptions, which are the framework for reference and interpretations and which can be tested not only by thought but by emotion and action. The resurrection can be interpreted according to the following points which have a lasting significance. (1) God raised Jesus from the dead. It is surprising in the Synoptic reports of the resurrection to find that there are only five mentions of God, all of which are incidental to the past or the future. Nowhere is the resurrection claimed as an act of God. This fact stands in contrast to the Acts and the Epistles which strongly assert that God raised Jesus from the dead. That assurance was the spearhead in the Christian message. But the Synoptists wisely do not undertake to relate what occurred. They largely assumed that the events of Jesus' life were evidence of the power and the life of God. (2) The resurrection was part of the purpose of God as shown from the scriptures. Those who trusted God could discern his will made known in the Old Testament and more clearly fulfilled in Jesus whose suffering, death and continued life exhibit the divine will. (3) The resurrection gave to Jesus, not only life beyond death, but a unique position, leadership, authority and accessibility for all men. (4) The resurrection laid responsibilities upon those who knew it. They had a mission as witnesses for the resurrection to all men. They had to preach repentance and forgiveness, to make disciples, to teach all that Jesus commanded. They were not beyond fear or doubt but the outcome when they worshiped God was power and great joy as they found assurance that Jesus lived. (5) The resurrection appearances were the beginning of an endless spiritual fellowship with him. This kind of invisible divine companionship far transcends any historical analysis or theological explanation. The resurrection of Jesus let him loose among all his faithful believers, who find in him a living Presence, who energizes the inner life and makes hearts burn and who leads into an enlarging circle of brotherhood, worship and spiritual service with all men of like faith.

The Synoptic accounts of the resurrection stand as an early all-important stage in Christian belief. They do not cover all the later developments of thought about Jesus. They do not deal with the fate of Jesus in the world of the dead in the time between death and resurrection. Other writers taught that he preached to the "spirits in prison" (I Pet. 3:19). This idea was later incorporated into the Apostles' Creed as "he descended into hell" or Hades. There is no development of the resurrection of believers such as Paul portrayed in his great Corinthian Chapter (I Cor. 15). There is no use of the phrase "life eternal" which surges through the pages of John's Gospel. There is no celestial city with streets of gold and gates of pearl where God would dwell with his people and death would cease as the seer of Patmos saw in his visions (Rev. 21:1–22:5). Faced with the vast mysteries of life and death, the Synoptic writers believed they had a sure answer in the resurrection of Jesus to a question that Paul asked before Agrippa, "Why is it thought incredible by any of you that God raises the dead?" (Acts 26:8).

39

The Nativity Narratives

Mt. 1–2; Lk. 1–2, 3:23–38

THE STORIES of Jesus' birth do not belong to his public life which was first known and proclaimed by his followers. In a historical study these stories stand by themselves as they deal with private family affairs which acquired significance because the public life of Jesus first established itself as amazingly important. When Matthew and Luke relate the rest of the story of Jesus, they do not refer back to the birth accounts. These accounts belong to the secondary strata in the records of Jesus. They were not part of the first preaching about Jesus nor do Mark and John use them in their Gospels nor do the rest of the New Testament writers refer to them. Chronologically the birth stories stand first in the life of Jesus but in historical and theological development they are later than the first experiences of the disciples with Jesus. The disciples knew Jesus himself, his teachings, miracles, death and resurrection before they knew about his birth. They found in him the life and the will of God. They accepted him with the most exalted beliefs that could be accorded to anyone. They could not understand him in human terms alone and they were sure that God alone could account for him. They established a belief in both the humanity and the divinity of Jesus. Then, as often happens with earth's most famous sons, some of his friends undertook to investigate his origins since it would help to understand his unique person and position. Thus the birth stories can be more understandingly studied after the narratives of Jesus' public life. Once the Virgin Birth became known, it was widely and quickly accepted by Christians as an article of faith. It became part of the second-century form of the Apostles' Creed.

The infancy narratives have had many commentators who have written mostly to support the belief in the Virgin Birth or occasionally to question it or to attempt a historical investigation.[1] Matthew

[1] P. Lobstein, *The Virgin Birth of Christ* (London, 1903), 33–112; J. W. Orr, *The Virgin Birth of Christ* (New York, 1903), 30–90; L. M. Sweet, *Birth and Infancy of Jesus Christ* (Philadelphia, 1906), 193–238; G. H. Box, *The Virgin Birth of Jesus* (Milwaukee, 1916), 1–120; L. Prestige, *The Virgin Birth of our Lord* (London,

and Luke have independent accounts of the birth. There is no satisfactory evidence that either writer knew the other's story. They present a cycle of traditions which form complete sections with no cross
references to Jesus' later life. The sources of the narratives cannot be
determined accurately. There are traditional suggestions that Joseph
was responsible for Matthew's story and that Mary is the source for
Luke because he twice reported that she kept all these things in her
heart (2:19, 51). These are inferences only, based on the prominence
of Joseph in Matthew and of Mary in Luke. There are critical suggestions that Luke composed his own story from oral reports or that
he translated some Aramaic or Hebrew documents or that he incorporated some Jewish-Christian narratives. Matthew combined information about Jesus with Old Testament prophecies and a genealogy
from I Chronicles. He appears to have had several main interests. He
wished: (1) to trace Jesus' descent from Abraham and David; (2) to
establish the view that the conception of Jesus was an act of the Holy
Spirit; (3) to show that wise Gentiles honored Jesus soon after his
birth; (4) that he escaped Herod's destruction; (5) that everything
had been divinely ordered in dreams; (6) that there were five fulfillments of the scriptures. Luke has a wider range of events in an account almost four times as long as Matthew's. In stories of perfect
simplicity and in charming poetry he pictured the wonderful gifts of
God to good and faithful people. Angels in messages and songs announce these gifts to people who receive the marvels of the Holy
Spirit five times. The gifts of God are two sons, one born to an el-
derly couple and the other to a betrothed virgin. The angels' promises
and then the births of these two sons lead to the praise of God in
prayer and songs which exalt the sons and God's great blessings
through them. The naming of the sons and the recognition that a
great destiny awaited them point to the favor of God upon them and
for the people that God would lead through them. Luke maintains a
parallelism for John and Jesus in their annunciation, births, naming,
mission and growth, though his pictures of Jesus are more ample.

1918), 1–31; V. Taylor, *The Historical Evidence of the Virgin Birth* (Oxford, 1920),
115–33; W. K. L. Clarke, *New Testament Problems* (London, 1929), 1–17; J. G.
Machen, *The Virgin Birth of Christ* (New York, 1930), 210–35, 380–97; E. Wor-
cester, *Studies in the Birth of our Lord* (New York, 1932), 1–56, 94–132, 270–94;
T. Walker, *Is Not This the Son of Joseph?* (London, 1937); M. S. Enslin, "The
Christian Stories of the Nativity," *Jour. Bib. Lit.* LIX (1940), 317–38; D. A. Edwards,
The Virgin Birth in Faith and History (London, 1943), 199–236; C. K. Barrett, *The
Holy Spirit and Gospel Tradition* (London, 1947), 5–24; A. Graham, *The Christ of
Catholicism* (London, 1947), 22–30, 174–201, 275–92; C. J. Cadoux, *Life of Jesus*
(West Drayton, 1948), 27–40.

Finally he shows Jesus in a single unforgettable vignette as a twelve-year-old boy on a visit to the Temple in Jerusalem.

Matthew and Luke found different traditions about the birth of Jesus but they have some points in common. *They agree* that he was born at Bethlehem in Herod's reign, that his conception was due to the Holy Spirit, that his mother was a virgin, that the names of his parents were Joseph and Mary, that the family lived at Nazareth, that there were supernatural signs and that angels forecast events and selected the name of Jesus before his birth. *They differ* in the place where Joseph lived at the time of Jesus' birth. In Matthew his house was in Bethlehem, whence he later went to Nazareth. In Luke he lived in Nazareth but traveled on a visit to Bethlehem for a census. In Matthew the visitors are wisemen, in Luke shepherds. The circumstances of birth are related in Luke but not in Matthew. The two narratives cannot be woven into one consistent story. When such a traditional attempt is made, Luke's story is placed first with the birth on December 25 and then the visit of the wisemen follows on January 6. But each narrative is better studied for its own content, without devout embroideries of names, ages, places, people and events which apocryphal gospels soon began to imagine.

Matthew begins his book with a genealogy which lists forty-six names from Abraham to Jesus. This record established the legal descent of Jesus from two famous ancestors. Abraham was the first Hebrew who had been promised that in him all the families of the earth would be blessed (Gen. 3:12) and David was the greatest king from whose lineage the Messiah would come. Matthew arranges his official document into three sections of fourteen generations each. He adapts the list from I Chronicles (2:1–19) and departs from the normal Jewish genealogy when he names five women. The selection of these particular women is even more unusual. Three of them, Tamar, Rahab and Bathsheba, are tainted with sexual irregularities and one, Ruth, was a foreigner. Mary, the last, was the mother of Jesus and it is probable that these ancestral women were chosen to help meet Jewish slanders which charged that Jesus was the illegitimate offspring of a Roman soldier and a Jewish maiden. Luke also had a genealogy which has some names from Abraham to David in common with Matthew but many others are unknown and they represent a different record. Even the name of Joseph's father is not the same in each genealogy. Luke traces the ancestry from Jesus to Adam with a total of seventy-seven names while Matthew proceeds from Abraham to Jesus. Since Luke traced the genealogy to Adam, the son of God, he was interested not only to show that Jesus was a son of Abraham but related to the whole human race and also to God. Luke has no interest in national Jewish heroes or chronology and he places his genealogy not in relation to the birth but to the baptism and the beginning of Jesus' public ministry when he was about thirty years of age. Both genealogies trace Jesus' ancestry through Joseph and may well have been intended mainly to support his mission as the Messiah when the composers of the genealogies originally had no knowledge of his sonship to Mary alone. They have been adapted by Matthew and Luke though they present Jesus with an ancestry through Joseph which did not logically agree with the Virgin Birth.

Luke begins his story with Zechariah and Elizabeth who were older godly people who had no son. Barrenness was a great misfortune among Jews, for it meant the end of a family line and no hope that the Messiah could come from it. Zechariah served as priest at the Temple. There were many priests who were divided into twenty-four groups so that each man was on duty for a week twice a year and at the great festivals. Incense, the symbol of prayer, was offered in the morning and the evening. The people prostrated themselves when they saw the smoke arise and they waited until the priests came out on the steps as evidence that the incense had protected them from the awful majesty of God. Then the priests gave the beautiful benediction that the Lord would bless and help the people, shine upon them and be gracious to them (Num. 6:24–26). The vision of an angel came to Zechariah. Gabriel quieted his fear and assured him of a son, John, whose coming would bring joy and whose dedication to God and a mighty mission for God would be like the spirit and the power of Elijah as he prepared his people for the Lord. These promises follow the cadences of Hebrew poetry. When Zechariah naturally asked how a son could come in old age, the angel replied that he was a messenger from God's presence and that Zechariah would be dumb until events proved these promises. This experience reflects some of the beliefs of a religious faith that God had purposes for his people and power to complete them and that worthy people could receive assurances about God's will. Among the ways in which God's will was made known were angels and dreams and both of these are prominent in Matthew. Angels and dreams are interpreted by people today with a different significance as the former became symbols of divine providence and the latter become the happy hunting ground of psychoanalysts. When Elizabeth conceived at an advanced age, her condition was accepted as due to God's limitless power.

Parallel to the announcement to Zechariah, Gabriel came from God to Nazareth to the Virgin Mary with his greeting, "Hail, favored one, the Lord is with you." The angel quieted her fear and promised her a son, Jesus, whose name had special meaning. It is usually interpreted as God is salvation or is gracious. Jesus would be great, the Son of the Most High and the Messiah with an endless kingdom. At Mary's wonder, since she had no husband, the angel promised that the Holy Spirit would overshadow her and the child would be the holy Son of God. Mary's words, "I know not a man," an inquiry which prepares the way for the promise of the Holy Spirit, have been weighted by theologians, Orthodox, Roman Catholic and Protestant, to mean that Mary made a vow of perpetual virginity. This does not accord historically with Judaism which knew no such vow when a girl was betrothed nor with the fact that Jesus had brothers and sisters. The sign given to Mary, like one also given to Zechariah, was that her kinswoman, Elizabeth, formerly barren, would have a son. Mary's answer illustrates the perfect trust of one who serves the Lord and accepts his word.

Mary's visit to Elizabeth involved a journey of eighty miles. Elizabeth by inspiration of the Holy Spirit recognized Mary as thrice blessed for her pre-eminent position among women, for her motherhood of the Lord and for her belief in God's promise. Even Elizabeth's unborn child leaped when she heard Mary's voice. The Song of Mary is the first of four Lukan poems, known for centuries in the western world by Latin titles: Magnificat (1:46–55), Benedictus (1:67–79), Gloria in Excelsis (2:14) and Nunc Dimittis (2:29–32). These canticles are poetic mosaics, mostly from prophets and psalms which proclaim ardent thanks that the Lord has visited and redeemed his people in the coming of Christ. Their poetic beauty and warm trust may be the devoted work of Luke himself or a translation of some earlier compositions which were appropriately credited to the original circle of those who knew about the wonderful birth and babe. The Magnificat devotes one third of its lines to the joy and the personal gratitude of Mary and the rest to the mercy and the power of God as he helps Israel. He puts down the proud, the mighty and the rich and exalts the humble and the hungry. It is notable that God is the Savior in Mary's song and the same title is given to Jesus in the message of the angels. This is the only place in the Synoptics where Jesus is called a Savior, a title which became widely used in later New Testament writings.

The birth of John caused Elizabeth to rejoice and to remember God's mercy. Usually a child was named at birth, frequently after his grandfather, but John was named on the eighth day at circumcision, through a remarkable agreement between his father and his mother. Zechariah was released from his dumbness as neighbors and relatives wondered what the child would become. Zechariah focused their thanks to God in the Benedictus because the Lord had undertaken to save his people from their enemies and had chosen John to be a prophet. The horn of salvation is a symbol of the strength that God provided in his Messiah. John was to prepare God's ways with salvation, forgiveness, light and peace for his people. John's boyhood was quickly passed as he grew strong and dwelt in the desert until the hour of his mission.

The perfect story of Jesus' birth can never be appropriately scanned in the cold light of historical criticism alone. Its atmosphere is the mystery of birth in a humble place with joy and awe in the hearts of Mary, Joseph and the shepherds while overhead the dark sky grew luminous with a divine glory and angelic voices proclaimed the coming of the Lord and their songs glorified God for peace and good will. The momentous, date-dividing coming of Christ whose birth was God's purpose, deed and revelation "to all the people" appears in the fields of earthly history but it exceeds historical boundaries. However, the details of time and place and particular people and events cannot be ignored. Luke gives a general dating of a census ordered in the reign of Caesar Augustus and the governorship of Quirinius in Syria. He does not give the year, the month or the day for the birth of Jesus. The familiar date of December 25 appears to have been known from the fourth century. The year is estimated usually between 8 b.c. and 4 b.c. Augustus ruled from 31 b.c. to a.d. 14 but there is no evidence outside of Luke of an empire-wide census ordered by Augustus near the time of Jesus' birth. Quirinius was governor of Syria a.d. 6-9. This date occasions difficulty because it is too late for the birth date of Jesus. Saturninus Varus was governor of Syria 9-4 b.c. Luke's accuracy in dating has been defended by the suggestion that Quirinius had a position of military authority in Syria together with Varus as governor during 10-7 b.c. An inscription, found in 1912, which named Quirinius as duumvir or chief magistrate of Antioch was dated by Ramsay 10-7 b.c. Thus Quirinius was ruling a *second* time in Syria A.D. 6–9.[2] But Josephus wrote of a property census which led to a revolt in A.D. 6 when Quirinius was governor and Judea was made a part of Syria.[3] Since Herod was the native Jewish ruler in Judea until 4 B.C., it is a question whether Rome would have ordered a census in his dominions though the emperor was supreme over all of his local appointed rulers. Conditions changed politically in A.D. 6 when Judea came under the direct rule of a Roman governor who replaced Archelaus, son of Herod. Possibly the census named by Luke was to secure a pledge of loyalty and for enumeration rather than for money. A Roman census with a tax based upon property was usually taken at a man's residence. This required travelers to return home though not necessarily to an ancestral place. Possibly Luke had heard of a local census in Judea which enrolled a man in his native town. But there still remain two viewpoints about Luke's date: (1) that the tradition which he followed was mistaken in the date of the census under Quirinius; (2) that Luke's date is accurate, that the census is the first one during the first governorship of Quirinius, that the Jewish manner of census could be used by the Romans and that Augustus had the sovereignty essential to order an enrollment even in Herod's territory.

That Jesus was born in Bethlehem has been established from the time of Luke and Matthew. There is no question about the fact as long as the Evangelists are held to be infallibly accurate in all details. But modern biographers have asserted that Jesus was born in Nazareth. They cite the fact that he grew up in Nazareth, an obscure town with no Messianic connections; that Matthew and Luke have legendary elements in the nativity stories; that the story of the birth in Bethlehem was due to the common belief that Jesus was the Messiah and the Messiah had been foretold in scripture to come from Bethlehem; that there is no other evidence of birth at Bethlehem; that a betrothed woman would live with her parents and would not travel a hundred miles from them, alone with her betrothed. However, these reasons at most establish only some probability; they do not constitute proof. The familiar acceptance of Bethlehem, a humble village, six miles south of Jerusalem, will continue to hold its position in the minds of men as the birthplace of Jesus.

Luke does not locate exactly the place of birth in Bethlehem. There was no space at the "inn" but this time honored translation is uncer-

---

[2] W. M. Ramsay, *Was Jesus Born at Bethlehem?* (London, 1898), 241–47, and *The Bearing of Recent Discoveries on the Trustworthiness of the New Testament* (London, 1915), 222–300.

[3] *Ant.* XVIII.13.5; XVIII.1.1; cf. Acts 5:37.

tain because the "inn" is the same kind of room or chamber in which
the Last Supper was eaten. What or where this crowded room was
cannot now be known. For the baby that was soon to be born the
situation was aptly described when Jesus in his later wandering said
that the Son of Man had nowhere to lay his head (Lk. 9:58). Since
the baby was laid in a "manger," the imagination of readers has often
constructed a stable or a part of a Palestinian house used for animals.
But Luke has no mention of a dwelling. The manger was a feeding
trough or pen and the birth of Jesus can well have occurred in the
open air with the sky for a roof in a spot easily accessible to shepherds whose flocks were out in the field near Bethlehem.[4] Second-
century tradition centered on a cave as the birth spot but this
suggestion did not come from Matthew or Luke. It did lead to a
fourth-century building of the Church of the Nativity which was replaced in the sixth century by another church which has become one
of the oldest churches of Christendom. It has its altar above the traditional grotto with its Latin inscription in silver to mark the holy
site.

The angels announced to the shepherds the great significance which
Jesus would attain. He was given three titles, Savior, Christ and Lord.
The two latter names have been discussed in preceding chapters.
Savior is a rare term for Jesus in the Gospels. This is the only use of
Savior for Jesus in the Synoptics. In Hebrew scriptures the word bore
the thought that God would enable his people to escape their enemies, oppressors and their sins. For Luke's Gentile readers it meant
a royal exaltation given to emperors who used the title. The well-
known "Gloria" of the heavenly host has two translations. There is a
glory given to God about which there is no question. Christ's coming
was an occasion to honor God but the peace may be either to men of
good will or good will to men. In the latter case it means God's favor
to men and in the former man's good will conditions the coming of
God's favor.

The naming of Jesus, like John's, came at the time of circumcision.
Forty days after the birth of a male child the parents presented sacrifices to the priest for a burnt offering and for a sin offering (Lev. 12:
6–8) and the ritual uncleanness of the woman, due to childbirth, was
removed. The first born belonged to the Lord and he was presented
to the Lord and then redeemed with a gift of money (Exod. 13:2, 15).
At the time of these ceremonies at the Temple in Jerusalem, two aged
saints, Simeon and Anna, who had waited for the coming of the Mes-

[4] Cadbury, *The Making of Luke-Acts,* 250.

siah to redeem Israel, recognized Jesus through the guidance of the Holy Spirit. Simeon took the child in his arms and blessed God and the parents. In this psalm Simeon felt ready to depart from this world because he had seen and held the one who was to be a light to all peoples both Gentile and Jewish. To Mary Simeon spoke words of warning that Jesus would test both belief and unbelief in Israel while his mother would be pierced as by a great sword.

The godliness of the parents appears as they did everything according to the Law of the Lord. On return to Nazareth the child grew strong and wise with God's favor. These unknown years left no record. It can be assumed that a humble home, godly parents, several brothers and sisters, worship in the synagogue, teaching of the scriptures, labor in the shop, the daily village life and the great world of nature matured the child as he grew in favor with God and man. Nazareth was small but its highways led quickly to larger cities and to historic places.

The one story of Jesus' boyhood at twelve portrays living scenes. His parents at Jerusalem, after the week of Passover, started home to Nazareth and supposed Jesus was in the caravan. When they missed him at the end of the day's journey and hastened back to Jerusalem, they located him in the Temple with the learned men, listening and asking questions. Jewish teachers usually questioned their pupils who answered with replies or further questions. In his answers Jesus amazed the teachers. At the rebuke of his mother he wondered at his parents' quest and asked if they would not know that he would be in his Father's house. Since there is no noun in the Greek, it can also be translated as his Father's business. This leads to a sense of vocation rather than the Temple and the scriptures as the things in which he expected his parents to find him. These were the Father's things which had occupied him while his relatives had started homeward. Their lack of understanding of his words did not prevent him from a return to Nazareth to the obedient life of a worthy son. The reticence of the Gospels about the early life of Jesus has been overbalanced by the wild marvels of the apocryphal gospels. The Gospel of Thomas reports boyhood activities of Jesus which make the reader glad that they are not true. The marvelous child would make twelve clay sparrows fly away or could curse his teacher or a playmate so that they died at once.[5]

A study of Matthew's nativity narrative shows five fulfillments of prophecy and reports of five dreams which are the means by which

[5] M. R. James, *The Apocryphal New Testament*, 49–50.

the purpose of God was carried out. The evil figure of Herod stands
as a foil to these divine purposes. It is Joseph who received directions
from an angel about the miraculous conception. Though a girl lived
with her parents during the year before marriage, her betrothal was
as legal as marriage. The reference to Joseph as husband and to Mary
as wife reflects this situation. The betrothal, if broken, was dissolved
only by legal action in the presence of two witnesses with a written
statement of divorce. This is the action Joseph contemplated when
Mary was found pregnant. The message from the angel of the Lord
stopped Joseph from his plan. The child was forecast to be named
Jesus because of his mission to save people from their sins. There is
a play in meaning on the Hebrew name of Jesus and from the
promise that he *shall save* from sin. He was named by Joseph at
birth. The conception of the child was an act of the Holy Spirit. In
earlier Hebrew history the Holy Spirit meant the creative power of
God which had been known in two main ways: (1) in the creation
of the world and (2) in the redemption of Israel. In later Jewish history the Spirit enabled a man to prophesy. The proof of the child's
coming according to God's power and purpose was a quotation from
Isaiah (7:14) in which Matthew used the Septuagint. A son was to
be born of a virgin and was to be called Immanuel, which meant
"with us is God." The Septuagint, for some unknown reason, translated the Hebrew word for young woman by the word "virgin."
Thus it provided a most valuable proof text for Matthew who could
establish the thought of a son born of a virgin though Isaiah's original prophecy had no such idea.

The visit of the wisemen introduces the Messiah as the King of
the Jews, identifies Bethlehem as his birthplace in fulfillment of
Micah's prophecy (5:2), shows gifts brought by Gentiles to him (Isa.
60:6) and proves that God's good purposes prevail over Herod's evil
desires and actions. The wisemen from the east were probably astrol-
ogers or priestly seers. How long after Jesus' birth they came is not
stated. They are not called kings, neither is their number known.
Later legends, influenced by scriptural prophecy (Isa. 60:3), called
them kings and named them Melchior from Persia, Casper from
India and Balthazar from Arabia. Their number is an inference from
the mention of three gifts, gold, frankincense and myrrh. Though
the interest of their story is religious truth rather than factual knowledge, there is but one element which is historically improbable if it
be meant literally. The star may be a poetic means to express divine
guidance. There is little purpose in the attempt to find astronomical

verification in a comet or a meteor or some unusual conjunction of the planets, Saturn and Jupiter. Whether Matthew meant the star literally or allegorically, he had no difficulty in thinking that it could guide the wisemen on the short distance from Jerusalem to Bethlehem. Their joy, worship and gifts are tributes to a Child destined to rule the world. Herod was a capable ruler but cruel and crafty. In his later days he was ridden by jealousy and fear of conspiracies against him even in his own family. He did not hesitate to execute wife and sons. In a play on similar Greek words Augustus said he would rather be Herod's sow than his son. When some Pharisees foretold that by God's decree he and his descendants faced an end to their rule, he slew the Pharisees and the members of his own household who had consented to the forecast.[6] There is no evidence outside Matthew of any slaughter of babies in Bethlehem but Matthew saw it as a forecast of Jeremiah when he pictured Rachel, wife of the Hebrew patriarch Jacob, weeping for the Jews when they passed in calamitous captivity to Babylon in 586 B.C. (Jer. 31:15). When an angel in a dream warned Joseph, he fled to Egypt with wife and child and remained there until Herod's death, when again in a dream he was directed to return to Palestine to live in Nazareth in Galilee. The reference to Jesus as a Nazarene is not known in the prophets and the derivation of Nazarene from Nazareth is an unsolved puzzle. The escape from Herod, the Egyptian sojourn and the return to the Holy Land parallel the exciting story of Moses, Israel's greatest son, whose birth also was marked by murder of babies and whose escape from Pharaoh's wrath enabled him to lead Israel to a new life in Canaan. Matthew saw Jesus as a second and greater Moses who had foretold of a prophet like himself.

The stories of Jesus' birth contain historical elements and aside from a guiding star, the angels and the supernatural conception there is little that exceeds historical probability. The stories, like classic poetry or drama, have historical settings but range far beyond the prose of history. In charming, chaste narratives, interspersed with poetry, they deal with the mystery of conception, of motherhood, of fatherly protection, of high hopes for children and their amazing future when dedicated to God, of love's long glory, of Holy Scriptures, of glowing Messianic dreams, of the wonder of worship, of royal plans, rage and murders with ensuing grief, of far journeys and of new homes. Over all these vital human affairs is an open

[6] Josephus, *Ant.* XVII.2.4.

heaven of divine intent which swings low to pour into devout and receptive hearts the joy and the endless wonder of God's coming to earth. The recurrence of Christmas is an annual tribute to the perennial beauty and the religious significance of these stories which unfold many truths. It is a mistake to read these stories with the whole attention limited to one point, the miraculous conception. Though it has central significance, there are very few verses out of the one hundred eighty total which deal with the birth. But the theological superstructure erected upon the brief verses in order to deal with the Virgin Birth requires some listing of the attitudes of the builders. (1) The Virgin Birth is not mentioned in the New Testament outside the few verses in the first two chapters each of Matthew and Luke. It was known probably only in some Palestinian Christian circles or homes of the first century. In the second century it became widely believed and later was incorporated in the Apostles' Creed and ever since it has remained one of the orthodox beliefs of Christianity. It was assumed that the family of Jesus provided the information and that the Virgin Birth was a fitting mode in which the Son of God came to earth. It involved a mysterious, creative nonmaterial act of the Holy Spirit which provided for mankind a new Man, the promised Messiah and Son in whom God's life and power came to save men from sin. The coming of God in Jesus became known as the Incarnation. The beginning of this human life was in a supernatural conception. Later thought exalted the mother of Jesus who was given the title, Mother of God, and eventually Mother of the Church, Mother of men and Co-redemptrix with her redeemer Son. Celibacy was elevated to a plane superior to marriage and Mary's perpetual virginity was proclaimed. In the Roman church her own conception was eventually declared immaculate so that the stain of original sin from Adam onward was broken and the sinlessness of Jesus supported. At death her virginal body was raised in immediate Assumption to heaven where she receives prayers like the "Hail Mary" and extends her gracious aid to all believers.[7]

Unsatisfied with the traditional ideas about the Virgin Birth there are those who have sought further explanations of the story. (2) There are suggestions that these stories have a basis in important truths but not in literal facts. The Hellenistic world with its myths of divine paternity has been searched for parallels. But these alleged parallels have no connection with Matthew and Luke because the pagan myths are low in moral tone, there is no stress on the virginity

[7] I. Giordani, *Mary of Nazareth* (New York, 1947), 1–120.

of the mothers, the gods act like men in a physical manner or even in nonhuman material forms such as a snake. But the Gospels know only a creative, nonmaterial action of the Holy Spirit.[8] They abound in Hebraic, not Hellenistic, forms of thought and words. Parallels from the Old Testament and Jewish writers have been sought. But the miraculous births to barren and aged women like Sarah lack any parallels to the idea of virginity. It has been thought that the story of Jesus' birth was originally understood in all Jewish homes not only as an ordinary birth but also as due to the creative presence of the Lord. Then this Semitic thought of the sacredness of conception as a human act in which the Holy One was also a creator was misunderstood and adopted by Greek Christians who never got free from their earlier notions that the body was the seat of evil for the soul.[9] It has been thought that Luke originally had no mention of the Virgin Birth, that the short verses which refer to it (1:34-35) are a later interpolation, and that Matthew knew Luke and developed his narrative from Luke's reference to a virgin who was betrothed, a statement which was a normal one for any maiden who entered a marriage contract.[10] Others have thought that the real manhood of Jesus depended upon a normal conception and birth and that his sinlessness was not related to his manner of birth but to his own decisions to do God's will. Faith in the divinity of Jesus was due not to a miraculous conception. He never made it the basis for following or believing in him. Faith came by personal relationships to Jesus himself and by acceptance of God's presence known especially in his words, deeds, death and resurrection.

Between these two general views there are some sharp distinctions. The first view maintains that the Virgin Birth is essential to belief in the Incarnation or that God was in Christ and that there is a final decisive choice between the facts of the Gospels and their possible errors. In this view the errors cannot be granted. The silence of the rest of the New Testament is not due to lack of knowledge but to the delicate reserve essential to the private nature of the experience of Mary lest it be ridiculed by the Jews or ruined by the gross taste of the Greeks. There can be but one conclusion. The Virgin Birth is a new act of God, with no parallel in Greek or Jewish sources, and the records of Matthew and Luke give the essential and true points for faith about the beginnings of Jesus' life. The second view insists

[8] Barrett, *op. cit.*, 5-24.
[9] Walker, *op. cit.*, 3-34.
[10] Worcester, *op. cit.*, 270-89.

that belief in the Incarnation preceded knowledge of the Birth and that belief in the latter is elective rather than essential. It holds that the decision about belief in the Birth will not rest upon factual historical evidence because that base is too slender. The final testimony about the conception could only be given by Mary. There is not adequate historical proof that she gave the evidence. The evidence of Matthew and Luke in their stories reached far beyond the one point of miraculous conception. The belief in the Virgin Birth can be reached on a religious basis of faith, not in a few verses, but in God revealed in Jesus Christ. The belief in the Incarnation is cardinal for all Christians but some will accept the great ideals in the nativity narratives as the true purposes of God and yet reserve final judgment on the one point of virginal conception as possible but not proved.

PART V

The Fourth Gospel

40

Introduction

FROM THE days of Jerome in the fourth century the eagle has been known as the symbol of the Fourth Gospel to indicate its soaring spiritual significance. Jerome found his symbol in Revelation (4:7) and in Ezekiel (1:10) where the eagle was one of the four living creatures who dwelt in the presence of the Eternal One to praise him or moved like mysterious lightning wherever the Almighty directed. Since Clement of Alexandria in the second century John has been called the spiritual Gospel. It is a profound book written in childlike language. It is an independent book about Jesus since 90 per cent of it is new in comparison with the Synoptics. It is a book of devotion, meditation and mystical insight. It is a book of simplicity, directness and depth. It is a divine drama, with vivid narratives, dialogues of dispute and symbolic discourses. It is good tidings which arise from God's eternal purposes, made known in the man Jesus, and intended to reach everyone in the world with the aid of the universal Spirit.

The contents of the Gospel have been outlined in many ways. Usually the outlines have been based on the regions Jesus visited or on the ideas which he taught. The Gospel alternates teachings and narratives. After the Prologue the record of the public work of Jesus does not lend itself to analysis but the main plan of the Gospel is clear.

1. Prologue: The Word   1:1–18
2. Public Ministry of Jesus in Galilee, Samaria, Judea   1:19–12:50
3. Private Teachings for the Twelve   13:1–17:26
4. Final Events in Jerusalem   18:1–20:31
5. Epilogue: Last Appearance of Jesus   21:1–25

There is a Johannine problem which is much further from solution than the Synoptic one. This problem extends to all aspects of the Gospel but it arises because John is different from the Synoptics and because the first century after this Gospel does not provide satisfactory proof about the needed historical facts. An earlier section in this study summarized the external evidence about the Gospel in the first Church Fathers. The Gospel was in use in the Church in the second century and since its latter part the Fathers like Irenaeus, Origen, Clement of Alexandria and Tertullian quote it and testify that John the Apostle is the author. This traditional answer to the problem of authorship has always had defenders.[1] There was no other suitable candidate put forward. The internal evidence is inadequate. The book itself does not identify author, date or place nor does it explain why its characteristics, plan, order of contents and style differ markedly from the Synoptics. The Gospel states its religious purpose which is that its readers may believe that Jesus is the Son of God and find life in him (20:31). There is personal witness about the author in three passages. "The Word became flesh and dwelt among us" (1:14). "He who saw it [the piercing of Jesus] has borne witness" (19:35). "This is the disciple who is bearing witness to these things" (21:24). This witness was a Palestinian Jew who wrote in Hebraic style, who quoted Old Testament, argued in rabbinical form, knew Palestinian topography, explained Jewish customs and thought and knew the time, the people and the circumstances of Jesus' life. The name of John, the disciple, one of the Twelve, does not appear in the book but there are five references to a disciple whom Jesus loved (13:23; 19:26; 20:2; 21:7, 20). He is usually identified as John.

If it be accepted that the author is the Apostle John, it soon appears that there is not much known about him because the interest of the Evangelists is in Jesus. In the Synoptics John, son of Zebedee, was a fisherman in Galilee who with his brother, James, came to Jesus as a disciple. Soon Jesus selected him as one of the Twelve. He was one of the inner circle with Peter and James present at the healing of Peter's mother-in-law, at the raising of Jairus' daughter, at the Transfiguration, at the questioning of Jesus about the future and at Gethsemane. With Peter he prepared the Last Supper. He was an impetuous friend and "Son of Thunder" ready in defense of Jesus and intolerant of others not of his own group. He was ambitious for a first place in the Kingdom. In Acts in the early days of the church he is named among the Eleven and he was with Peter at the cure of the lame man. He shared imprisonment with Peter when they were

[1] A. Plummer, *St. John* (Cambridge, 1887), 9–58; B. F. Westcott, *The Gospel according to St. John* (London, 1908), ix–clxxviii; J. A. McClymont, *St. John* (Edinburgh, 1922), 3–52; C. F. Nolloth, *The Fourth Gospel* (London, 1925), 37–82; J. E. Steinmueller, *Companion to Scripture* (New York, 1944), III, 129–69; J. Chapman, *The Four Gospels* (London, 1944), 47–64; W. G. Scroggie, *A Guide to the Gospels* (London, 1948), 398–466.

described as bold but uneducated, common men. He went with Peter on a mission to Samaria and when Herod beheaded James, John was listed as his brother. Paul in his Galatian letter named him with James and Cephas as "pillars" in the church. There was a John who wrote Revelation but he did not name himself as an Apostle. There is one mention of the sons of Zebedee in the Fourth Gospel (21:2). Though John is not named, he is a follower of Jesus and if he was the beloved disciple, then he was with Jesus at the Last Supper, at the trial where he brought Peter into the courtyard of the high priest whom he knew, at the cross where he received the mother of Jesus into his care, at the tomb where he outran Peter and at the Sea of Tiberias where he recognized the risen Lord on the seashore. He was the disciple about whom rumor developed that he would not die. Later tradition assumed that he went to Asia Minor where he became the leader of churches, perhaps after Jerusalem was destroyed. Stories grew up that he was banished for a time to the Isle of Patmos, that he escaped death at Rome though plunged into boiling oil and that he drank poison unharmed. Other legends tell of risks he took to convert a robber, of the dead he raised, of how he relaxed tension by playing with a tame partridge and of the way he wearied his hearers by repetition of the words, "Little children, love one another." He sped out of a public bath in Ephesus when he found Cerinthus, the heretic, there lest the building fall upon that enemy of truth. He was inspired to write the beginning of his Gospel at the request of Ephesian elders.[2]

For two hundred years but especially during the last fifty years questions have been widely raised about the traditional position of John. The results have been exceedingly complex.[3] The early church

[2] H. L. Jackson, The Problem of the Fourth Gospel (Cambridge, 1918), 160–62.

[3] J. Drummond, Character and Authorship of the Fourth Gospel (London, 1903), 1–71; E. F. Scott, The Fourth Gospel (Edinburgh, 1906), 353–76; A. E. Garvie, The Beloved Disciple (London, 1922), 202–58; W. Manson, The Incarnate Glory (London, 1923), 13–54; B. H. Streeter, The Four Gospels (New York, 1924), 363–481; B. W. Robinson, Gospel of John (New York, 1925), 11–56; J. E. Carpenter, The Johannine Writings (London, 1927), 191–289; G. H. C. MacGregor, The Gospel of John (New York, 1928), ix–lxvii; J. H. Bernard, The Gospel according to St. John (Edinburgh, 1928), I, xxxiv–clxxxviii; B. W. Bacon, The Gospel of the Hellenists (New York 1933), 3–51; F. C. Grant, The Growth of the Gospels (New York, 1933), 200–219; E. C. Colwell, John Defends the Gospel (Chicago, 1936), 1–14; 127–51; F. V. Filson, The Origins of the Gospels (New York, 1938), 178–212; E. B. Redlich, Introduction to the Fourth Gospel (London, 1939), 3–148; E. C. Hoskyns and F. N. Davey, The Fourth Gospel (London, 1940), 3–126; R. H. Strachan, The Fourth Gospel (London, 1941), 1–96; W. F. Howard, The Fourth Gospel in Recent Criticism (3rd ed. London, 1945), 33–105; E. R. Goodenough, "John, a Primitive Gospel," Jour. Bib. Lit. (1945), 145–82; V. Taylor, The Gospels (5th ed. London, 1945), 84–109; C. W.

placed the Synoptics and John together. There was one gospel according to four different men. The Gospels are alike in that they deal with Jesus from a religious interest. They combine fact and interpretation. They all know about John the Baptist, the Twelve, miracles, the public teaching of Jesus in Galilee, opposition to him and especially in the last days in Jerusalem the entry, the Last Supper, the arrest, trials, crucifixion and resurrection. Concerning Jesus himself they all felt his authority, his leadership, his sense of a divine mission and his special relationship to God. But anyone who comes to John from the Synoptics finds omissions and additions as well as differences in the order of events, in style and ideas and in the portraiture of people, especially Jesus.

There is an independence of method and of content in John which has caused most scholars to abandon the traditional effort to correlate and harmonize the Synoptics and John. John omits the baptism of Jesus, the temptation, the transfiguration, the agony in Gethsemane and the ascension. There are no parables, no exorcisms, no Aramaic words and no special words and actions with bread and wine at the Last Supper. John differs from the Synoptics in time, place and order of events. In John the mention of three Passovers (2:13; 6:4; 12:1) indicates that Jesus had a three-year public ministry in which he alternates between brief visits to Galilee and longer ones in Judea. In the Synoptics there is one Passover and Jesus' public work was in Galilee with one final week in Jerusalem. The cleansing of the Temple is placed by John at the beginning of Jesus' work. In the Synoptics it is in the last week where it precipitated a crisis and a plan to destroy Jesus. In John this plot was occasioned by the raising of Lazarus. The Last Supper in John is not Passover and the date for it and for the crucifixion is identified as Nisan fourteen instead of Nisan fifteen as in the Synoptics. John has seven miracles only, three of which are nature miracles and two are in John alone (2:1–11; 4:46–54; 5:1–9; 6:1–14, 16–21; 9:1–7; 11:1–44). They are called signs instead of mighty

Quimby, *John, The Universal Gospel* (New York, 1947), 14–78; B. K. Rattey, *St. John* (Oxford, 1947), 5–22; T. W. Manson, "The Fourth Gospel," *Bull. J. Rylands Lib.* 30 (1947), 313–29; A. C. Headlam, *The Fourth Gospel as History* (London, 1950), 2–106; C. J. Wright, *Jesus the Revelation of God* (London, 1950), 13–96; R. M. Grant, "The Origin of the Fourth Gospel," *Jour. Bib. Lit.* (1950), 305–22; A. M. Hunter, *Interpreting the New Testament* (Philadelphia, 1951), 78–92; T. Henshaw, *New Testament Literature* (London, 1952), 145–81; W. F. Howard in *The Interpreter's Bible* (New York, 1952), vol. 8, 437–63; H. P. V. Nunn, *The Authorship of the Fourth Gospel* (Oxford, 1952), 3–93; C. H. Dodd, *The Interpretation of the Fourth Gospel* (Cambridge, 1953), 3–9, 444–53; A. H. McNeile, *An Introduction to the Study of the New Testament* (2d ed. Oxford, 1953), 267–300.

works as in the Synoptics. The people in John appear in a different light. John the Baptist is never called the Baptist and he is a witness to Jesus rather than a prophet of repentance and righteousness. His subordination to Jesus is marked. The Sadducees disappear entirely and the Pharisees appear much less as the opponents of Jesus and the Jews take their places. New characters like Nicodemus and the woman of Samaria have long interviews with Jesus and Lazarus is the center of an extensive teaching and miracle. In the presentation of Jesus outstanding aspects are emphasized. There is no secret Messiahship in John. From Jesus' first appearance there is a full-grown recognition by various people like John, Andrew or Philip or the Samaritan woman to whom Jesus declared himself the Messiah. The human side of Jesus which could be misinterpreted is played down and his exalted divinity is played up. There is no lowly birth, no temptation, no agony before arrest, no cry of desolation from the cross. From the beginning to the end of the Gospel Jesus stands on the same sublime level with no growth or development suggested. He determined his own time and destiny and even his acceptance of death. He knew all that was in men and read their thoughts and actions with divine prescience. His relationship with God is increasingly magnified in its Father-Son aspect. In addition to the many names and titles bestowed on Jesus in the Synoptics John has his own symbolic designations such as Word (Logos) of God, Light, Bread, Only Begotten, Way, Truth, Life, Vine, Door and Resurrection.

John's style is known for its simple words, repetition of key ideas, short independent sentences, dramatic antitheses and Hebrew poetic parallelism. There are long discourses, veiled in figurative language which reveal spiritual meanings. Know, believe, see, witness, world, life, love, father, truly, judge, glory, light, truth are plain words with profound meanings. There are sharp contrasts expressed in life and death, love and hate, light and darkness, truth and lies. Jesus uses allegories rather than parables and abstractions rather than concrete pictorial terms. Instead of brief anecdotes and pithy sayings there are short narratives with extended discourses based on them. A large section (ch. 13–17) contains special teaching addressed only to the disciples on the night of the arrest. It is unlike the Sermon on the Mount in setting, content and style. The great theme of the coming Kingdom in the Synoptics becomes present eternal life. Anticipation of the end of the age and of judgment to come give way largely to spiritual knowledge and a present sifting of people according to their belief. The words of Jesus center much more in himself with great prominence of the pronoun "I." The discourses follow patterns of controversy. An event occurs, questions follow, misunderstanding or opposition arises and a lengthy explanation clears the situation.

These omissions and differences between John and the Synoptics find some readers who attempt to harmonize and minimize them and others who admit that there are different, even contradictory, interpretations of Jesus. Since John wrote the last Gospel, it has been thought that he wrote: (1) to supplement the Synoptics; (2) to explain them; (3) to supplant them; (4) or with no knowledge of them. That John wrote to take the place of the Synoptics or that he wrote independently of them is not generally accepted though the latter view has had able support.[4]

John's book shows other purposes besides the one he stated even as Luke had interests beyond certainty for Theophilus in his Christian instruction. John the Baptist left followers who rivaled the first Christians. The Fourth Gospel shows that John was a witness who willingly stated that he must decrease while Jesus increased. The evidence about John the Baptist places him always as subordinate to Jesus. Another purpose arose from the deep feelings and the bad blood between Judaism and Christianity. The writer of the Fourth Gospel knew about this opposition and perhaps had suffered from the antagonism of mother-Judaism against this new, weaker daughter-religion. He showed how Jesus battled throughout his Gospel. He has been accused of anti-Semitism but his attitude to Judaism is not best described by that term. One of his purposes was to show how Jesus fulfilled scripture. Salvation was from the Jews though they had opposed Jesus and John felt he had to show that they were wrong. The Jews who were opponents of Jesus were mostly Judeans, not Galileans. Another purpose was to keep the historical humanity of Jesus from evaporation into ideas and unreal appearance. John's narratives present Jesus in human reality. The actual earthly scope of his existence is the backbone of the book. There are small touches which prove that "the Word became flesh." Jesus was weary at the well at Sychar, he wept at the death of his friend Lazarus, he carried his own cross and he thirsted before death. An early heresy taught that Jesus only seemed a real person (Docetism) and John felt its beginning danger. In the opposite direction John intended to adapt the story and the meaning of Jesus' life and teaching to his own age which was possibly seventy-five years distant from Jesus and which

[4] P. Gardner-Smith, *St. John and the Synoptics* (Cambridge, 1938); H. E. Dana, *The Ephesian Tradition* (Kansas City, 1940).

was Hellenistic in language and thought. Though the roots of Christianity were Jewish and Palestinian, it was growing in a Greek world. John had known some decades of Christian fellowship and meditation on the inner significance of Jesus in relation to God and man. He wrote about Jesus from a Jewish historical background but enlarged his ideas into Greek Christian universalized truths. The atmosphere of the book is a blend of a Palestinian dawn with the light and the heat of a Hellenistic forenoon. Knowledge, life, light and word (Logos) were words often heard in Greek philosophy and theology. As John fitted the gospel into current Greek language and thought, he unfolded and crystallized certain aspects of Jesus, his teachings, his miracles, his death and his resurrection. The love of God, made known in Christ, was given to anyone who believed but disbelief brought judgment. John sometimes used the Jewish title, Son of Man, for Jesus but the common human terms like way, water, bread, life, light, truth, shepherd and vine opened a wider door for understanding him. Another purpose of John revolved around his fellow Christians. He does not name the church and the sacraments but a vine and its branches, a shepherd and his flock, water and bread shared or an act of foot washing by Jesus portray the life, the love, the unity and the service of Christians. Most of all this fellowship was instructed, guided and united to God and Christ by the Spirit which after the death of Jesus was his divine gift to his followers. They could be born again through the Spirit. John deeply desired his readers to enter into life, remembering Jesus in an actual historical existence, knowing a spiritual continuance of his presence and finding the eternal love of God revealed in Christ, in the Christian community and in each individual heart. John proposed to keep faith with the historical Jesus but he also modernized and spiritualized the gospel for his own day with an effectiveness and attractiveness exceeding any of his endless successors.

The form and the order of contents of John's book require consideration. It is a Gospel which means that it does not fall in any particular class since it is of its own kind. It has been described as a spiritual biography, a selection of sermons, a book of devotion, an inspired meditation, a dramatic dialogue, a theological treatise and a Hellenistic religious mystery-drama. Since the book has been all things to all men, it cannot be contained in any common classification. It stands as a unique Gospel with historical narratives which are sometimes of the same substance and importance as the Synoptics and with discourses which inextricably blend the truths that Jesus taught with the living reflections of the writer. The fabric of thought is of one piece throughout with little difference in the style of the various speakers.

The order of contents has been thought to show some dislocations and many attempts have been made to restore an imagined original order.[5] It is possible that separate sheets of the original Gospel may have been disarranged before they were united into a roll or codex or perhaps an editor may have changed the first order. It is generally thought that the story of the adulterous woman (7:53–8:11) was not a part of the book at its beginning. It is missing in the earliest manuscripts, omitted in many later ones and sometimes appears in the manuscripts of Luke. It interrupts the order of John and differs from him in style and thought. It probably is an authentic story but it does not belong in John. The next point concerns the final chapter. At the end of chapter 20 it appears that the book is complete since John had stated his reason for writing. The language and the style of chapter 21 are like the rest of the book and it may be an addition by John to explain certain ideas about Peter and the disciples Jesus loved. However, there are some words, expressions and purposes in this chapter which have led to the thought that it was written by an editor who knew John well enough to add to his Gospel. There is no agreement about the authorship of chapter 21 but it is probable that the last two verses (21:24–25) are separate comments added to the book. The first one verifies the witness of the disciple who wrote the book. "We know his witness is true." The second verse is by an individual who wrote "I suppose" the world would not contain the books which could be written about Jesus. There have been efforts to discover various authors and sources in John but his book is best viewed as a unity except for the story of the woman taken in adultery and the two final verses. One man's thought, style and purpose appear in the Gospel though he may have written over a considerable span of time. However, as the book stands there are some possible rearrangements which might make a better sequence of ideas and actions. The fact that the present order has been read for centuries without disturbance to the readers indicates that possible dislocations have no great importance except to the experts who come to no agreement in their judgments. But among several possibilities two can be illustrated.

---

[5] F. W. Lewis, *Disarrangements in the Fourth Gospel* (Cambridge, 1910); J. Moffatt, *Introduction to the New Testament* (New York, 1911), 550–63; Howard, *The Fourth Gospel in Recent Criticism*, 125–41, 258–63; F. R. Hoare, *Original Order and Chapters of St. John's Gospel* (London, 1944).

Chapters 4, 5, 6 show Jesus in Galilee, in Jerusalem and on the other side of the Sea of Galilee respectively. Geographically the last reference (6:1) reads as if Jesus had gone to the other side of the sea from Galilee, not from Jerusalem. Therefore, it is suggested that the order, 4, 6, 5, for the chapters is preferable with the content remaining undisturbed. Another possibility, illustrated in Moffatt's translation, is to place chapters 15 and 16 at 13:31. The order of reading them then appears as 13:31; 15:1–16:33; 13:31–38; 14:1–31; 17:1–26. In the present order the last verse of chapter 14 contains the words of Jesus, "Arise, let us be going," yet there is no departure until three chapters later (18:1). Moffatt's order brings these words closer to the actual departure. However, such guesses at dislocation do not command the assent of many scholars.[6] These words may be an editorial device to divide the long discourse.

Date, place and author remain subjects of debate because the Fourth Gospel does not state them. The range of years, A.D. 50–125, covers the possibilities on the date. Agreement is quite general that the Gospel was written near the end of the first century, A.D. 95–105. This conclusion is based upon the maturity of thought in the Gospel, upon the possibility that John knew Paul's writings, Mark and Luke and that the last chapter (21:19) refers to Peter's martyrdom. John is earlier than the Church Fathers of the second century who reflect some of his ideas. The place is commonly thought to be Ephesus, the great capital of the province of Asia, owing to a statement by Irenaeus (c.180) that John, "the disciple of the Lord . . . gave out" the gospel at Ephesus.[7] Irenaeus as a boy "in lower Asia" had heard Polycarp who had known John though proof is lacking that Polycarp had told Irenaeus that John was the author.[8] The book has been called "the Ephesian Gospel" but the more inclusive term, "the Gospel of the Hellenists," is nearer the mark. Ephesus has not won universal consent as the place of origin for the Gospel. Alexandria has been suggested because early writers in Alexandria quote the Gospel and because some recent papyri discoveries from Egypt are dated about A.D. 150. A Rylands papyrus contains part of the Gospel (18:31–33, 37–38) and an Egerton papyrus gives fragments of a work much like the Gospel.[9] It has been held that the Gospel originated in Antioch in Syria because it is claimed that it was written in Aramaic

---

[6] C. C. Torrey, *Our Translated Gospels* (New York, 1936), 138–40; C. H. Dodd, *The Interpretation of the Fourth Gospel* (Cambridge, 1953), 407, 410.

[7] *Adv. Haer.* III.1.1.

[8] Eusebius, *Eccles. Hist.* V.20.5–7.

[9] J. N. Sanders, *The Fourth Gospel in the Early Church* (Cambridge, 1943), 85–87.

and shows much knowledge of Palestine and of Jewish customs and ideas.[10] But the view that the Gospel was written in Greek in Ephesus remains the dominant one.

Date and place are bound up with authorship which is an unsolved riddle owing to the lack of early evidence and to conflicts in the evidence. The appendix of the Gospel declares that a beloved disciple wrote it but the difficulty is to identify this disciple. He has been variously identified. (1) The apostle John. This is the traditional view which is largely based on the statements of Irenaeus. (2) The Elder John which is due to mention of two Johns in Papias. (3) An unknown disciple from Jerusalem. (4) An unknown Greek Christian. (5) An ideal, unhistorical figure. The three latter suggestions remain in the field of conjecture. The name of John was common and eventually the church assigned five of the New Testament writings to the Apostle John. There are the Gospel, three Epistles and Revelation. The outstanding differences between Revelation and the other four documents have led to the modern conclusion that one man could not have written both Revelation and the other four. It has been generally thought that the Gospel and the Epistles have the same author. The Epistles, II John and III John, name their author the Elder but do not call him John nor do they give a place or a date. But it is possible that the Elder is not the writer of the Gospel but rather his disciple who was like him in ideas and language but also different in style and lacking the Semitic element and developed theological outlook of the Fourth Gospel.[11] Consequently there may be three authors of the five Johannine writings rather than one.

There are questions about the Apostle John as author: (1) because of his advanced age by the end of the century when it is thought the Gospel was written; (2) because of two Johns mentioned by Papias; (3) because of two tombs, each for a John, at Ephesus; (4) because of a fifth-century tradition of Philip of Side who repeated Papias who reported that John was killed by the Jews; (5) because Ignatius wrote to Ephesians (12:2) and mentioned Paul but omitted any reference to John; (6) because there is no evidence for almost a century which ascribes the Gospel to John; (7) because there was opposition to the Fourth Gospel by orthodox Christians about A.D. 180; (8) because John in modesty would probably not call himself the beloved

[10] C. F. Burney, *The Aramaic Origin of the Fourth Gospel* (Oxford, 1922), 126–31; M. Black, *The Aramaic Approach to the Gospels and Acts* (Oxford, 1946), 1–12, 206–12.

[11] C. H. Dodd, *The Johannine Epistles* (New York, 1946), xlvii–lvi.

disciple; (9) because the Gospel does not bear his name. When the appendix was added which asserted that the beloved disciple was the author, why was he not named?

There are questions about the elder John because he is a shadowy influence rather than a historically established person. Papias mentioned an elder John who was a disciple of the Lord who may or may not be the elder who wrote the two Johannine epistles. He does not state that he lived in Ephesus. Evidence is lacking to identify the elder with the Apostle John though this has been done. It is possible that two men, named John, both disciples of the Lord, could cause confusion about authorship of the Gospel. It may be granted that an elder John existed but that he is the author of the Fourth Gospel is another question which has not been satisfactorily answered.

The identification of the beloved disciple with the author is found only in the appendix and it is probable that the statement is a later editorial one to support a certain view about the author. Without the appendix no one would think that the beloved disciple is the author since he appears in the third person. Streeter thinks the identification of the beloved disciple with the author is mistaken. "We are almost compelled to the conclusion that the Gospel was written, not by the beloved disciple but by someone to whom that disciple was an object of reverent admiration." [12] The appearances of the disciple, late in the Gospel, at the Last Supper, at the examination of Jesus before the high priest, at the cross, at the grave and at the Sea of Galilee after the resurrection of Jesus, give no hint about authorship. Since the Gospel contains claims about an eyewitness (1:14; 19:35; 21:24), the actual writing of the Gospel has been variously explained. (1) The Apostle John wrote from his own participation in events with Jesus. (2) The Apostle John or an unnamed disciple, not one of the Twelve, related the contents of the Gospel to the Evangelist who wrote the Gospel. (3) The claims of an eyewitness are to be understood symbolically as those of a Jewish Christian in a Hellenistic environment who knew some early traditions about Jesus and adapted them and added his own interpretations. The authorship can be narrowed to two choices: (1) the traditional Apostle John satisfies some readers who desire certainty and accept authority from the church and its scholars who adjust uncertainties and differences in the evidence so that they weigh less than the supporting proof in favor of John, the son of Zebedee; (2) the authorship is unknown and probably never will be known. Those who accept this view admit

[12] Streeter, op. cit., 432.

it is unsatisfactory to leave the riddle unsolved. They think there are probabilities rather than proof because the existing evidence seems inadequate for historical certainty. They console themselves with the thought that the time-transcending religious value of the book remains though its author is undetermined.

Some estimate of the value of the Fourth Gospel is inevitable. Any thoughtful reader of this illuminating book forms some opinions which are tempered by the assumptions found in every mind. Archbishop William Temple called it "the profoundest of all writings." "I have more love for St. John's Gospel than for any other book." [13] Its appeal eludes complete analysis because its genius becomes all things to all men.

The Fourth Gospel offers a unique fusion of history with philosophy, of realistic character portrayal with presentation of religious experience. Here is both truth and poetry, both simplicity of narration and conscious manipulation of means to artistic ends. Here is realism side by side with symbolism, humanity bodying forth abstraction. Here is fusion of the life story of Jesus with the religious experience of the author of the writing, which defies at this date a sure and complete analysis into the component parts which made it up. The secret of true understanding of the Gospel lies here, in the recognition that, as a literary work it is a unique blend of history with religious experience, an unusual fusion of fact with poetry. [14]

"The starting point for any profitable study of the Fourth Gospel is the recognition of the author as a mystic—perhaps the greatest of all mystics [and] an inspired prophet. [15]

The Fourth Gospel is historically valuable because it is the actual record of a superlative first-century Christian, a thinker, a seer, a poet-prophet, a spiritual genius in his understanding of Jesus. His book is historical fact, a transcript of his own experience and the reflection of the life of his time.

Within 100 years of the crucifixion the Christians had come to see in Christ, the incarnation of the eternal Word of God; they had come to believe that he and the Father were one; to see in him the agent of creation and the revealer of God through the ages; they had learned to revere him as the light of the world, the source of all true life, their Lord and their God. These are facts of greatest significance. [16]

[13] Readings in St. John's Gospel, First Series (London, 1939), v, ix.
[14] M. E. Lyman, The Fourth Gospel and the Life of Today (New York, 1931), 44.
[15] Streeter, op. cit., 366, 368.
[16] P. Gardner-Smith, The Christ of the Gospels (Cambridge, 1938), 54.

This Gospel in its narratives supplements the Synoptics and in its discourses enters the mind of Christ to portray the surpassing importance of his person, his mysterious relationship to God and his boundless significance for both believer and disbeliever. In words that are like a veil that reveals, the author explores the mystery of life, of love, of spirit, of Christ and of God. With one hand he directs the sight of his readers to simple earthly scenes and events and with the other he lifts their vision to discern the sublime Person whose splendor suffuses the scenes and the events with the ineffable wonder of eternal life. It is a historical fact that, since this Gospel was first read, it has had an immense widening influence. The wise action of the church which selected not one but four Gospels is evidence that the essential truths of this Gospel were in accord with a living faith in Christ. The religious values of the Fourth Gospel lie beyond the historical level. They can scarcely be determined by a contemptuous Pilate who asks, "What is truth?" but rather by those who experiment with the words and the spirit of Jesus which lead to freedom from the power of evil and to knowledge of God.

41

The Prologue · The Word

JOHN OPENS his Gospel with a hymn whose theme is the Word or Logos. There are three stanzas: (1) the Word and God (1–5); (2) the Word and the world (6–13); (3) the Word made flesh or human in Jesus (14–18). There are two prose parenthetical passages (7, 8, 15), which interrupt the rhythm of the poetry though they give information about John the Baptist. This Prologue stands apart from the rest of the Gospel as do the birth narratives of Matthew and Luke. John does not use the "Word" in the rest of the Gospel. Opinion is divided as to whether the Prologue was written as a prelude to the book or as a summary after it was done. John composed the poem or possibly adapted an earlier Jewish hymn in praise of wisdom or possibly he transformed a Gnostic poem about John the Baptist so it became a tribute to Jesus. This Prologue summons the highest insights of Hebrew thought, Greek philosophy and Christian experience to Jesus as the Word. Each of these sources requires a brief discussion.

"In the beginning was the Word." This opening statement echoes the first verse of Genesis. The Word of God in Hebrew scriptures had power to create the world. "By the word of the Lord were the heavens made" (Ps. 33:6). It was the means by which God spoke to prophets who heard it and declared God's will for his people. In the Wisdom literature and in the Apocryphal books God's wisdom, by poetic personification, became largely identified with his power to create and with the Torah (Instruction) which God spoke. The Torah was thought to be created before the world was made and since it was first born, it brought life and light to men. Its main form was given through Moses. These important ideas about God and his word and the world were well known and John found in them one of the roots of his thought about God and the Word in Jesus.

The Logos had been known for centuries in Greek philosophy. Its first important expounder was Heraclitus (c.535–475 B.C.). It became a dominant conception because Greek philosophers believed the world was rational, an orderly whole, subject to thought. The Logos was divine reason. For the Stoics the material and the spiritual were different aspects of the same thing, an ethereal fire. God and the world were one in an organic unity with an indwelling Logos. The Logos was the universal reason shown in the orderly working of nature, in the unitive power and the growth of life in plants and in animals. In men it appeared as the power to reason. The Logos was an eternal, pervading principle in the universe and in man. John found in Greek philosophy one of the elements for his claim that the Logos was God though this aspect of Greek thought had been Judaized.

Philo (c.20 B.C.–A.D. 41) was an Alexandrian Jew who built a bridge composed of Jewish theology and of Greek philosophy. He knew the Bible in its Greek translation and he fused in allegory his Hebrew scriptures with Hellenistic speculation. Logos was one of his frequent terms. He thought of it as eternal, as next to God, the eldest-born image of God, as the agent of creation and as a cosmic principle by which God's power and guidance were expressed in the world. It was the link between the timeless and time, between God and the universe. It was an outward expresssion of God's utterance and the inward reality of his thought. For Philo the Logos was not personalized. John gives no evidence of study of Philo but he knew of the Hellenistic-Jewish thought of which Philo was the outstanding example. There had been four centuries of mingling Greek and Jewish thought before the time of John.

Christian experience was a deep root for John's idea of the Word. For three quarters of a century the meaning of Jesus for Christian faith had been explored. The great creative affirmation of John was that "the Word became flesh." Paul's letters had described Christ as the image or the manifestation of the invisible God, as the first born of all creation, as the one through whom all things were created and in him all things consisted (Col. 1:15–17). He dwelt in believers and formed himself within them. "Christ liveth in me" (Gal. 2:20). Paul did not use the term "Logos" but he had many ideas which were like John's Word. Similar ideas were written in the epistle to the Hebrews where God's Son is the very stamp of his nature, the reflection of his glory, the heir of all things, through whom he made the worlds and who sits at God's right hand now that he had made purification for sin (Heb. 1:1–3). It was inevitable that, by the time John wrote, Christians who had found God's life and power in Jesus as he lived among them and who had witnessed their continuance in his resurrection should attempt to extend their thought about Christ upward and backward beyond their historical knowledge of Jesus and their present experience of his spiritual presence among them. That which they had known in time they believed had existed in eternity and that which had appeared in history came from beyond history. Things too deep for prosaic words John fashioned into a sublime hymn which sparkled with insights from his ancestral religion, from Hellenistic-Jewish thought and from the transforming sight and knowledge of the Word who "dwelt among us."

The Prologue may be studied with the two prose references to John the Baptist left as a postscript. The first stanza sings of the Word and God. There was a beginning in creation as recorded in Genesis in which God had spoken light and life and all things into existence. At the beginning of creation the Word rather than the Torah existed. The Word is eternal, with God, active, creative, living, lighting men and opposing darkness. The Word is divine, related to God yet distinguishable from him. All things were made through the Word in the beginning and ever since creation. As there was light from God's command at creation, so the Word is light and life for men. His light shines in darkness but there is conflict. The important point is that the light is manifested and it is here for men. "The double significance of the Greek verb—to grasp with the mind and so to comprehend and to grasp with the hand and so to overcome or destroy—must be given full weight in the interpretation." [1] The darkness does not comprehend or overcome the light. Both light and dark are given an ethical significance as areas of good and evil respectively. Light goes forth, it reveals and is the condition for life to flourish. John states the darkness exists as the light shines though he does not attempt to explain why it is so. This dramatic contrast of light and dark is a major theme in the Gospel which reaches its climax in the death of Jesus.

The second stanza turns to the Word and the world. The "world" is one of John's words with multiple meanings. He refers to the world about 100 times. Sometimes it means the physical planet where men live and sometimes all men in general and sometimes the social ways of men in darkness apart from God. The Word is a genuine light and also a divine light coming into the world to enlighten every man. Or it may be translated to mean that the light enlightens every man who comes into the world. John is confident that a light shines to all men. There are two responses to the light, rejection or acceptance. The light is the personal Word. He came to his own home but

[1] Hoskyns and Davey, *op. cit.*, I, 139.

his own people did not welcome him. He was in the world which was made through him yet the world did not know him as he really was. "To know" is another expression in John with more than one meaning. To know is to recognize. To know God was a familiar thought in the scriptures. This knowledge was shown to men in God's activity in the affairs of men and in the world. To know God, in the prophets' words, meant obedience and righteous living. To know God in John is an active acceptance of his life and will revealed in Christ. This acceptance was open to all who believed in his name. This belief meant, not acceptance in mind alone, but moral discernment, obedience, loyalty and service. It is like faith in other New Testament writings though John never uses the noun "faith" but stresses greatly the verb "to believe" which he uses about 100 times. To all who receive and believe the Word he gives power to become children of God. John sees believers who are begotten of God. This means they are like him. God is the source of life for the Word and for those who accept the Word. Their birth, as children of God, is not of blood, which was thought to generate life, nor of human desire, nor man's will. Their privilege to become God's children is beyond human or natural powers.

The third stanza begins with one of the most important affirmations of Christianity: the Word became man. "This is the cornerstone on which the whole structure of Johannine thought is erected." [2] This statement is John's great contribution about the Word, an idea which was not in Hebrew, Hellenic or Philonic views of the Word. He relates the Word to Jesus as a historic person. The Word became a man and lived among those who knew him and saw his glory. John liked the term "glory" because it was a many-sided word which had a long history of association with God in the Old Testament. It was used to express "the power, character, radiance and physical accessibility" of God. [3] These characteristics of God came to a climax in Jesus Christ who possessed a glory as a unique son of God, full of grace and truth. When John wrote that the Word "dwelt [tabernacled] among us," his thought reminded his readers of the presence or Shekinah of God which dwelt in the tabernacle in the Wilderness as Moses led the people toward Canaan. John believed that the invisible presence of God was made visible in Jesus who was the Son whereas other people were the children of God. This Sonship is de-

---

[2] E. K. Lee, *The Religious Thought of St. John* (London, 1950), 135.
[3] A. M. Ramsey, *The Glory of God and the Transfiguration of Christ* (London, 1949), 82.

scribed as "only begotten" from God the Father. Since God's care was known throughout the scriptures, "begotten" is a metaphor to indicate his affection (Ps. 2:7). Abraham had an "only begotten" son, Isaac. This term in the Prologue indicated love, a divine relationship and uniqueness. It appears again during the talk between Jesus and Nicodemus (3:16, 18). The Son was unique, the only one of his kind. The Word was full of grace and truth and out of his fullness or totality of divine life all believers received grace added to grace. The grace that was in him was for them. The Law was given by Moses but grace and truth came by Jesus Christ who was in the bosom of the Father and had made him known. Moses had asked to see the glory of God but God said, "Thou canst not see my face; for man shall not see me and live" (Exod. 33:18, 20). But the Son who came from the Father brought grace and truth from God and revealed him to man. Grace and truth are John's words for the familiar Old Testament idea of a God of mercy and truth. There is little about grace in the Gospels but much in Paul. John writes of grace only in the Prologue. Grace has the twofold meaning of attractiveness and divine favor or kindness.[4] Grace meant all of God's good will and gifts freely and pre-eminently offered in Christ to undeserving men who are free to accept or reject them. Truth meant the reality and the faithfulness of God himself who expressed his will in the person, the teaching, the death and the resurrection of Jesus. Truth is the nature of God and exists in perfection apart from men but they enter into life as they accept the truth manifested in Christ.

John the Baptist has no title in the Fourth Gospel but he came from God to give his testimony to the light in which all men might believe through his evidence concerning it. He was not the light but he came to bear witness to it. The testimony of John is paradoxical because he spoke of one who comes "after me" but is "before me" (1:27, 30). He acknowledged that there was one who came after him in time in this world but who stood ahead of him because he (the Son) actually existed from the beginning with God before he appeared on earth. His authority was superior to John's. The Fourth Gospel often assumes a knowledge of ideas on the part of its readers which establishes some truth but the ideas do not follow a historical sequence. How much John the Baptist knew of the eternal divine Word at his first contact with Jesus is not known. This Gospel makes much of witnesses. They established the truth about Jesus with strong evidence which was essential for Christians who faced controversy

---

[4] J. Moffatt, *Grace in the New Testament* (New York, 1932), 6.

with Jewish opponents and questions from Greek thinkers. The Christians were distant enough from Jesus in both time and place so that they needed proof about him. These witnesses were people like John the Baptist and the Samaritan woman (4:39); the crowd at the raising of Lazarus (12:17); the Twelve (15:27); and the Beloved Disciple (21:24). Or they were the Works of Jesus (5:36); the Father (5:37); the scriptures (5:39); Jesus himself (8:14) and the Spirit (15:26). Jesus never used the Logos as a title for evidence about himself. The term sounds strange to modern ears unacquainted with John's Gospel or Greek philosophy. But the Word was a term which helped convey the profound conviction of Christians that there was an eternal life of God which came into earthly existence in Jesus. That which is beyond time, the divine life and light, became known within time among men. In simple words whose meanings have proved inexhaustible the Prologue puts into the poetry of faith the Christian confidence about God, the Word, the world and man. "The Gospel is a record of a life which expresses the eternal thought of God, the meaning of the universe." [5]

---

[5] Dodd, *op. cit.*, 284.

42

The Witness of John · The First Disciples

1:19-51

THE AUTHOR of the Fourth Gospel leaves the soaring interpretations of the Prologue and turns to an account of four days of associations with John at the beginning of Jesus' public life. "On the morrow" marks a transition from one scene to another rather than a note of actual time. The first interest of the author is to continue the subordination of John the Baptist to Jesus. "This treatment of the figure and function of the Baptist is one of the clearest examples of the transformation of tradition to serve a polemical purpose." [1] The Baptist had founded his own group, had baptized Jesus and never followed him and questioned him as Messiah. The Fourth Gospel had to defend Jesus against attacks of inferiority to John who had preceded Jesus in time and work and had baptized him. The function of the Fourth Gospel is largely to be a witness for Jesus.

On the first day the Jews, who are later identified as Pharisees, sent priests and Levites to John to inquire about Jesus. John's testimony was a triple negative. He himself was not the Christ, nor Elijah, nor the prophet promised in Deuteronomy to be like Moses (18:15). John was only a voice, not the Word, in the wilderness proclaiming the way of the Lord as Isaiah foretold (40:3). Asked why he baptized, John replied that his baptism was in water but one was coming for whom he was unworthy even to untie his sandals, the menial task of a slave. The reference to the water is repeated twice on the second day where it leads to the significant contrast with the greater baptism of the Spirit by Jesus. John baptized outwardly with water. Jesus baptized with the Holy Spirit which was an inner permanent spiritual endowment. There is no mention of the baptism with fire, the symbol of judgment, as in the Synoptics. It is assumed that the Holy Spirit was known to the readers since many experiences with the Spirit which began at Pentecost were familiar to Christians. Later in this book, on the night before his death, Jesus promised the Spirit to his disciples and described his functions. In this Gospel there is no

[1] Colwell, *op. cit.*, 38.

370

baptism of Jesus, nor repentance at John's preaching and no personal description of John. His function, when he saw Jesus, was to declare him the Lamb of God who takes away the sin of the world, whose coming it was John's work to make plain to Israel as he gave his testimony that Jesus was the Son of God. At first John did not recognize Jesus but the One who sent him to baptize said to him that he would see the Spirit descend and remain on Jesus and thus he would know him.

John's testimony about Jesus exalts what he does and what he is. He takes away the sin of the world and he baptizes with the Holy Spirit. He is the Lamb of God and the Son of God in whom God's Spirit remains. He is the man in whom the eternal Word dwelt. The Fourth Gospel abounds in titles and symbolic names for Jesus which is evidence of his immeasurable importance and of the passage of time and experience which had explored his possibilities for faith. The death of Jesus was inevitably associated with the sacrifice of the lambs at the Passover season, with the daily sacrifice of lambs at the Temple, with the Suffering Servant who went to his death as a lamb to the slaughter (Isa. 53:7) and with the painful experience of Jeremiah as his enemies plotted against him (Jer. 11:19). Paul had written of Christ as "our paschal lamb" which had been sacrificed (I Cor. 5:7) and the Seer in Revelation often called Christ the lamb. The death of Jesus was unlimited in its effect. It was to remove the sin of the world, hence forgiveness was for all who accepted it. This is part of the universalism of the Fourth Gospel which appears everywhere in its pages. In John Son of God means both the Messiah and the Revealer of God, who sent his Son with authority, judgment and life-giving powers.

The third day Jesus gained his first disciples when John directed two of his followers to the Lamb of God. They called Jesus "Rabbi," he invited them to come with him, they followed to see where he was living and stayed with him since it was four o'clock in the afternoon. One of the disciples was Andrew who told his brother, Peter, that they had found the Messiah. Then he brought him to Jesus who changed his name from Simon to Cephas or Peter. There are overtones in this simple story. John's followers leave him for Jesus. This continues the willing subordination of John to Jesus. The disciples discover their teacher and Messiah. They see, they inquire, they follow, they remain with him and they bring others to him. All of these statements suggest religious meanings in addition to their factual meanings. To see is inward discernment, to inquire is spiritual seek-

ing, to follow is discipleship, to remain is fellowship and to bring
others is conversion or missionary effort. A new name meant a new
relationship to the Lord and a new nature. When Jesus gazed at
Simon, he saw that he would be a Rockman. The titles for Jesus,
"Rabbi" and "Messiah," both translated by the Evangelist for his
Greek readers, are notably different from the Synoptics. "Rabbi" appears in John nine times (1:38, 49; 3:2, 26; 4:31; 6:25; 9:2; 11:8; 20:
16) which equal the total in Matthew and Mark together while Luke
does not use it. The Fourth Gospel uses "Rabbi" usually when a question was addressed to Jesus and there was need for teaching or information. It was a comparatively new title in the time of Jesus and
John had to explain it. Since John wrote to induce belief in Jesus as
the Christ, his book has more references to the Christ than any other
Gospel. He uses Christ, like the Synoptics, not as a proper name but
as a title. From the beginning in John there is an open recognition
and discussion of Jesus as Christ. He is aware of his vocation throughout his life. This view of Jesus as Christ contrasts with the Synoptics
where the Messiahship is not public nor discussed until shortly before
Jesus started for Jerusalem.

The fourth day Jesus decided to go to Galilee where he found
Philip and invited him to follow him. Philip found Nathanael and
thus two more disciples were gained. Both of these men discover an
exalted significance in Jesus which is the main purpose of the narrative but the story also reflects the historical fact that Jesus gained early
disciples in Galilee and that greater opportunities for him lay ahead.
Philip is known in the Synoptics only as a name but he stands out in
the Fourth Gospel. He was responsible for Nathanael's belief in Jesus,
he helped feed the 5,000, the Greeks in Jerusalem came to Jesus
through his assistance and on the last night with Jesus he asked for
proof about the Father (1:43-45; 6:5, 7; 12:21-22; 14:8-9). To Nathanael Philip identified Jesus in threefold fashion as one of whom
Moses and the prophets wrote (the Messiah), as a man from Nazareth and as a son of Joseph. Nathanael, who lived in neighboring
Cana, was skeptical about what could come from Nazareth, least of
all the Messiah. Philip did not argue but invited him to come and
see Jesus. When Jesus saw him, he commended him as an Israelite
free from guile. To Nathanael's surprise Jesus had seen him under a
fig tree, a shady spot, which may mean at his own home or in peace
and comfort (Mic. 4:4) or a place favored by Rabbis for study. That
Jesus had such unexpected knowledge of him led Nathanael to acknowledge him as Rabbi, Son of God and King of Israel. These high

titles exalt Jesus as Master and Messiah. A well-known Psalm (2:6–7) had been understood as a forecast of the Messiah where he was both King and Son. No higher honor could be found for Jesus than as one related to God and ruler of his people. Jesus promised more things for Nathanael than this unusual recognition. Little is known about him beyond this incident. He does not appear in the Synoptics. Any identification with Bartholomew is precarious. His name meant "gift of God." Since he had believed in Jesus, he was to see heaven opened and angels of God ascending and descending on the Son of Man. This promise, introduced by the impressive double formula, "Truly, truly I say to you," appears only in John. "Truly, truly" is used twenty-five times to indicate special authority in the words of Jesus which follow the formula. The angels ascending and descending a ladder which reached to heaven refer to a part of a famous dream of Jacob in which he received a promise of the Lord of abundant blessings (Gen. 28:12). So the Son of Man who was like a ladder linking earth with heaven would reveal greater things ahead. As angels were messengers between the Lord and Jacob so the Son of Man would be on earth with men but he would lead them to realize the promises and the power of God from an opened heaven. Jesus used the "Son of Man" for the first time in this promise. John has this enigmatic name about one half as often as it appears in each of the Synoptics (1:51; 3:13–14; 5:27; 6:27, 53, 62; 8:28; 12:23, 34; 13:31) but as in them the term appears mainly on the lips of Jesus. It meant many things but in this story the Son of Man is like a mediator between man and God. Later references indicate that the Son of Man descended from heaven and had authority to execute judgment and to give eternal life to those who believed in him. The Son of Man was to be lifted up (crucified) and glorified (exalted after death). This favorite self-designation of Jesus eludes definition. It conveyed the mystery of one who came from God and unveiled the wonder of God as a man among men whose death released divine purposes for all men. In an ideal aspect the Son of Man embodied in himself the true life of man so that he stood forth, not only in perfect union with God, but also in perfect human relationship with all believing mankind who are united to him like branches to a vine.

43

First Works of Jesus at a Wedding
and at the Temple

2:1–25

THE FIRST deeds of Jesus are linked by John to the two areas of Jesus' ministry, in Galilee at a wedding at Cana near his home and at the national shrine at a Passover in Jerusalem. John selected seven stupendous miracles of Jesus which are usually called signs and sometimes works. A sign is a real event which contains a deeper meaning. Two of them, the water turned to wine and the raising of Lazarus, are in John alone. It is difficult to see why the Synoptics omitted them if they knew them. In four of them, the sick son, the impotent man, the blind man and Lazarus, the miracle affects people. In three, the water into wine, feeding the 5,000 and walking on the sea, the miracle occurs in things. There are no cures of maladies of the mind like demon possession. John calls these miracles "signs" because he regards them as a display of the divine glory in Christ, because they lead to important teachings or controversies which developed from the signs and because these exhibitions of divine power result in belief. However, the signs do not convert opponents and Jesus also had to rebuke those whose belief depended on signs (4:47–48; 6:26). John's signs are mosaics of meanings. There is an over-all statement that Jesus did many signs (20:30) but his whole life, his teachings and deeds were signs to show that he was the Messiah and the Son of God. The reports of the actual historical events are penetrated with superhistorical meanings. Each deed had to be understood with an inner divine significance. These signs have been regarded as allegories in which John made no attempt to give actual events. Or they have been read as simple reports of historical occurrences. Neither allegory nor history alone will suffice for John's signs. The narratives are plain and realistic but they do not stand as mere records of events. In and through them there are gleams of divine glory and deep symbolical truths. As an artist sees beauty rising out of a rocky seacoast or as a musician hears more than the physical sound of a violin, as a lover visions more than gold in a wedding ring, so John sees the sign of Jesus' deeds to meet human needs but the facts were but stones which he could freely arrange as a foundation for a temple of truth. John did not differ essentially from the Synoptics in his view of miracles. Such events belonged in the record of a man of God. He expected them to be believed both as events and as religious truth. What John joined together cannot easily or wisely be sundered. The scalpels of criticism are indispensable for the perplexed reader but they must be operated, mindful of the Life, elusive of any instrument, that activated John and that he intended for participation with his readers.

In Mark Jesus was baptized by John, tempted by Satan and after John was jailed, began his public ministry when he came preaching the gospel of God, called disciples, cast out demons and healed disease. In the Fourth Gospel Jesus was hailed by John the Baptist as the Lamb of God, found followers when John directed disciples to him and while the Baptist was still free and active, Jesus began his public ministry by two notable deeds at a village wedding and at the Temple. These deeds demonstrated, locally and nationally, that something divinely new had come into the world.

Cana was a village a few miles north of Nazareth where the family of Jesus and his disciples were guests at a wedding. Usually a wedding was celebrated several days. The mother of Jesus appears in this story and at the cross but it is curious that John alone of the Gospel writers does not name her though he twice calls Jesus the son of Joseph (1:45; 6:42). When the wine failed at the wedding, Mary appealed to Jesus and directed servants to obey him. When he called his mother "woman" both in this story and when he commended her to the care of the beloved disciple at the cross, the word in Greek carried no disrespect but this word and his question show his independence of maternal authority. "My hour" or "his hour" are terms which carry double significance. They indicate time but especially the time of his death and exaltation. In this instance his hour for a sign was his decision, not his mother's. In similar fashion he refused to let his brothers tell him when to show himself to the world (7:3). In each case he did act as requested by his family but at his own choice of time. Jesus acted by the will of God, not by the will of man. The six big stone jars, each holding about twenty gallons, provided water for washing hands and dishes during the marriage according to Jewish religious ceremonies. When they were brim-filled at Jesus' command and the water taken to the head waiter (steward) of the feast, he found it such good wine that he asked the bridegroom why it was not served first as was the custom. He apparently knew of no miracle and only the disciples believed in Jesus as a consequence of this sign which displayed his glory.

Modern explanations which infer that Jesus and the steward play-acted with water as if it were wine in order to save a social embarrassment have no place in the original account. John relates the story because it showed a divine life and power in Jesus and because it led the disciples to believe. Not the wine but Jesus is the center of interest. There are symbolic overtones to the story that Jesus attended a marriage and helped in its joyful celebration but this human act of Jesus is important. A marriage was often the symbol for the Kingdom. Jesus determined his own time for activity in the Kingdom. The water, used usually in Jewish rites of purification, at Jesus' direction, became wine that was better than that known earlier at the wedding. Thus Jesus transformed Judaism into something better just as sparkling wine was better than stagnant water. He also provided a great abundance. The Word *became* flesh and the water *became* wine. John spent no time in explanation of a divine creative act in which reality was to be experienced, not analyzed. Tasting wine preceded talking about it. Jesus changed things but more important he changed men. The theme of water is a favorite one in John. John the Baptist baptized in water only, while Jesus baptized in the Holy Spirit. The woman of Sychar had to discover Jesus' gift of living water that sprang up to eternal life (4:13). This living water, which was the Spirit, Jesus offered to all at the Feast of Tabernacles (7:37). The blind man had to wash in the pool of Siloam (9:7). At his last meal Jesus washed the feet of his disciples (13:5). In this story of water which became wine Jesus took one of the commonest elements of the world to teach his transforming power but after this first sign he did not stop for teachings about it as he did later in the Gospel. John follows this narrative with a brief historical note that Jesus, his mother, brothers and disciples went down from Cana to Capernaum, about twenty miles eastward, for a short stay. But there is no report that his family shared his mission and work.

John mentions three Passovers. The Synoptics name one Passover near the end of Jesus' ministry when he went to Jerusalem and while there cleansed the Temple. Since the Passover is an annual festival, the two records differ in the length of Jesus' work. John tells of Jesus' visit to Jerusalem and the cleansing of the Temple at the beginning of his public life. This variation in time is not best resolved by the supposition of two cleansings. Either the time in John or in the Synoptics must be chosen as more probable. The Synoptics generally remain closer to the historical order and setting of Jesus' life and are less concerned to show symbolic meanings though their interest in Jesus and his significance is greater than concern for chronology or for a mere record of events. The Synoptics show that Jesus was charged before Jewish authorities with intent to destroy the Temple. This is more probable if he had recently cleansed it than if the cleansing were three years past.

John places the beginning of Jesus' public activity at the Temple which was the center of Jewish religious life where God's presence dwelt. There is first the attack by Jesus and the contrasting reactions of disciples and Jews. He attacked the sellers of sacrifices and the money-changers. With a small whip of cords he drove out sheep and oxen, turned over the tables of the money-changers and ordered deal-ers in doves to take them away. The reason for the attack was that they made "my Father's house" a place of business. "The action is not merely that of a Jewish reformer; it is a sign that the end of an-imal sacrifices is at hand." [1] John differs from the Synoptics in the mention of the whip and in the reason that Jesus gave for his action. In the Synoptics he protested that the Temple had become a den of thieves but in John it had been used as a place to make money. Either one obstructed its true function of worship. The results were differ-ent. In the Synoptics the people hung on Jesus' words in astonished admiration while the priests planned to destroy him. In John the dis-ciples remembered a Psalm (69:9) which foretold the Messiah's zeal would wear him out, and after his resurrection they recalled that he had spoken of the destruction of the Temple which symbolized his body and therefore they believed both the scriptures and the words of Jesus. By contrast the Jews asked Jesus for a sign or evidence about his action. His answer carried different levels of meaning. "Destroy this temple and in three days I will raise it up." Jesus meant that the temple was his body and his resurrection would be the sign the Jews requested. But throughout John's Gospel there are many misunder-standings when questioners take Jesus' words literally when they should see symbolical meanings. The Jews thought only of the stone Temple which had been forty-six years in building. They thought of the Temple destroyed while Jesus thought about the end of his life; they scoffed at the erection of a structure in three days but he talked of his resurrection. It is notable that in John the opponents of Jesus

---

[1] Hoskyns and Davey, op. cit., I, 203.

are the Jews while in the Synoptics definite groups are named like
Pharisees, scribes, Herodians or Sadducees. The author of the Fourth
Gospel was a Jew. He explains Jewish names and customs; he knows
Palestine, the home of Jews, and he is familiar with the Old Testament and with the Jewish methods of argument and with Jewish
thought. He believed salvation came from the Jews (4:22) but he felt
the deep antagonism of Jesus' own people against him. John knew
both that the Jews refused to believe that Jesus was from God and
that they plotted and accomplished his death. He saw Jesus apart
and above the Jews rather than as one of them. His mission was to
the world rather than to his own people. "The pagan who approached
Christianity through the pages of the Fourth Gospel would not suppose for a moment that Christianity was a Jewish movement." [2]

John closes his narrative about the early visit of Jesus to Jerusalem
with the report that many believed in him when they saw his signs.
Their sight may have been physical vision or mental contemplation
since John often refers to those who "see." Their belief was not stable
since Jesus did not trust himself to them nor did he need their witness because he knew with marvelous insight the motives of men.
This supernatural divine knowledge of Jesus is fundamental
throughout this Gospel: (1) Jesus knew his hour as he knew everything beforehand; (2) he knew all things in heaven and earth; (3)
he knew all that was in man; (4) his knowledge was derived from
the Father.[3] People believed in Jesus when they saw his signs but
the signs are not named or described and belief based on them appears to be insufficient in this incident.

[2] Colwell, op. cit., 43.
[3] H. Odeberg, The Fourth Gospel (Stockholm, 1929), 43–44.

44

First Discourse with Nicodemus · The Second Witness of John

3:1–4:3

THE SECTION about Nicodemus contains much more than appears on the surface. (1) It is the first of three stories which set forth the universal appeal of Jesus to different kinds of people. The first is to a Jewish Pharisaic ruler, the second is to a Samaritan woman of dubious character and the third is to an unnamed government official. (2) It is the first of the discourses in this Gospel which comprise one half of the book. The discourses are given as the words of Jesus but they are cast in a Johannine mold. In them it is difficult to know when the words of Jesus end and those of John begin. The thought of the discourses is pictorial, dramatic and intuitive rather than logical and analytical. The thought is practical and intended to cause belief rather than speculation. It revolves around striking contrasts rather than orderly argument. It blends the historical aspects of an event with spiritual reflection on its inner import. John writes with creative memory. "Every scene he depicts, every discourse he relates—whencesoever originally derived—is the distilled essence of something that has been pondered upon and lived out in actual life until it has become of the very texture of his soul." [1] (3) This discourse contains the most famous verse in the Gospel (3:16) which is the core of John's thought about God's nature, his gift and his purpose. This section also introduces far-ranging truths which reappear in other discourses.

Nicodemus was a Pharisee and a member of the Sanhedrin, a man of some wealth and a teacher in Israel. These points can be gathered from the story and the two brief mentions about him later in the Gospel (7:50; 19:39). In the first of these references he cautions about the use of legal procedures in the judgment about Jesus and in the latter his interest in Jesus reappears with his help and his costly gift at his burial. Nicodemus is not known in the other Gospels. But in

[1] Streeter, *op. cit.*, 383.

this chapter he is little more than a foil whose misunderstanding of questions gives Jesus the opportunity for his teaching while the questioner fades out before the discourse is done. The important point is the teaching of eternal truths and not information about the responses of Nicodemus. These exalted themes reverberate throughout the Gospel and through the centuries since it was written. They shine in every direction like the revolving beams from an island lighthouse. They lighted the mind of Nicodemus on a dark night and their inexhaustible radiance still directs men to meditate on: (1) the new birth that gives new life; (2) Jesus; (3) God; (4) beliefs and works; (5) judgment.

Whether Nicodemus came at night because it was the custom for rabbis to teach after the day's work or because he was timid or because he desired a quiet private interview cannot be decided. Like the crowds who believed in Jesus because of his signs, Nicodemus acknowledged him as a teacher from God. Signs were evidence of God's favor and aid. But Jesus did not deal in signs with Nicodemus. He said a man must be born anew to see the Kingdom of God. Birth meant new life from God. The new birth may mean to be born again or from above. "The Kingdom of God" was a phrase of vast meanings in Judaism. It was the main theme of Jesus' preaching in the Synoptics but John makes few references to it. In this passage rebirth enabled one to see or to enter the Kingdom of God. In another reference (18:36) Jesus told Pilate, "My Kingdom is not of this world." In John the Kingdom is replaced by eternal life (3:15-16, 36; 4:14, 36; 5:24, 39; 6:27, 40, 47, 54, 68; 10:28; 12:25, 50; 17:2, 3). For a Jewish term which had both political and religious significance he substituted a more general Hellenistic expression devoid of political meaning. Thus he avoided any suspicion of Roman authorities about the leader of the Christians as a possible rival to the emperor.

Nicodemus misunderstood about physical rebirth but rightly thought of its impossibility by human action. The new life in man was given by God from above. Man must be born of the Spirit, not of the flesh, though one is also born of water, known in Christian baptism. This rite developed greater significance after Jesus' death. Water was a symbol of cleansing but it was also essential to maintain physical life and it became a symbol of eternal life. God gives new life but it is as real, unseen and mysterious as the wind whose origin and destination were unknown. The "wind" in both Hebrew and Greek meant the actual air in motion and also the spirit in God and man. But Nicodemus still wanted to know how one could be born of the spirit. Jesus wondered that he, a teacher, did not know. His answer in its plural form has aroused the commentators. The things "we" have spoken about, known and witnessed may refer to the experiences of John the Baptist and of the disciples and to the forecasts of prophets which reinforced Jesus. Or the plural form may show that the writer of the Fourth Gospel felt that he wrote in the spirit of Christ which was continued in the members of his church. If Nicodemus had taken too literal a view of earthly things like birth, water and wind, how could he understand about things beyond physical observation?

The discourse moves from the words of Jesus to teachings about him (3:13). Two thoughts about the Son of Man declare: (1) that he alone both descended from heaven and ascended; (2) that he must be lifted up so that men who believe in him may have eternal life. There are references to the birth, the death and the resurrection of Jesus. When the Israelites were bitten by poisonous snakes, Moses had saved them from death by erecting a brazen snake in the wilderness for them to look at and live (Num. 21:8–9). The Son of Man must likewise be lifted up. This suggested not only the height of crucifixion but the exaltation that his death brought to him. All men could view his death and believe in its power to give life. The belief in him that led to eternal life was first acceptance of him as Christ and as Son of God and then personal faith in him which is the gift of God. Eternal life is to know God and Jesus Christ (17:3). This eternal life is not quantitative length of existence for the future but a present qualitative possession, shared with all believers who receive it from God.

God's nature is love, active, giving, seeking only good for others; its object is the world of mankind; his gift to the world is his only Son; his purpose is eternal life for all who believe in him. God's purpose in sending his Son was not to judge the world but to save it. Salvation is the result of the life-giving power of God made personal in the Son to those who act in faith to receive it. It is deliverance from death to life. Belief in God's gift of his Son frees one from a future judgment because the believer has eternal life now. Judgment, according to John, is here and now and depends upon man's choice about Christ. This is one of John's most characteristic ideas. As light shines for guidance but can also cast shadows, so light from God in Christ causes some men to choose darkness lest they face reproof for their evil deeds. Those who do evil want no exposure to the light. John has a curious expression about those who "do the truth" and who know that their works can stand scrutiny because they are done in the sight of God and according to his will. Truth is not something only to be believed or spoken but to be done in trustworthy fashion. But John also looks to a future judgment when the words of Christ will be the means of judgment at the last day (12:48). However, the main stress in John is that present good or evil deeds lead to belief or disbelief in Christ as the supreme test which determines life or death. The Son came not only to save the world but to execute judgment (5:27). This later thought stands in logical contrast to the earlier declaration that Jesus came, not to judge the world but to save it (3:17), but John saw in the many-sided mission of Jesus too much to be compressed into one formal statement. The term "judgment" has the threefold sense of sifting, of a verdict and of condemnation.[2] In this discourse John has crowded his main majestic themes which will appear again and again throughout his Gospel.

The author turns again to the witness of John the Baptist. He states that Jesus went out into Judea with his disciples and baptized while John was still baptizing people. These concurrent baptisms by John and Jesus are not known in the Synoptics. It has been supposed that the Fourth Gospel is reporting an earlier ministry of Jesus before his activity in Galilee. But it appears more probable that the writer of the Fourth Gospel has placed these events in their order to support certain ideas about John and Jesus. A later statement asserts that Jesus did not baptize (4:2). John's words are cited as his final evidence about the superiority of Jesus. The washings of John and of the Jews and of Jesus stand in a kind of competitive line and Jesus, who was baptized with the Spirit, had been given from heaven the evidence which settled all controversy in his favor. The last witness from John the Baptist arose from a dispute over some point in ceremonial washings or his insistence on baptism. When John's disciples jealously reported that Jesus was baptizing and that all people flocked to him, John spoke in generous support of him as one whose work was a gift from God. He repeated his denial that he himself was the Christ and affirmed his position as one sent before Jesus. John was like the friend of the bridegroom who arranged the details of the marriage and presided at the feast and rejoiced greatly when he heard the bridegroom's voice. The bride was not named but the idea was familiar because Israel had been the Lord's bride (Hos. 2:19) and later the church was declared the bride of Christ (II Cor. 11:2). The

2 Odeburg, op. cit., 147.

final words of John exhibit the generous loyalty of a friend who welcomed the growing importance of Jesus with a frank recognition of his own waning.

There is a brief meditation (3:31–36) which contains the comparison of John with Jesus and enlarges upon Jesus as the Son. Some scholars think that it fits logically at the close of the discourse with Nicodemus (3:21) but its present position is not out of place. Since John was a son of earth, he spoke of earthly things but there is one who came from heaven and is above all, yet even his testimony was not accepted. Whoever accepts it authenticates the truth of God, who sent his Son to speak the words of God, who gives his Spirit without stint, who loves his Son and who has given all things into his hands. This is a complete confidence in Christ, in his relationship with God and in his teaching and authority. All things and all power necessary for man's life with God had been claimed by Jesus both before and after his death (Mt. 11:27; 28:18). Whoever believes in this Son possesses eternal life but whoever disobeys the Son shall not see life because the wrath of God remains on him. John's distinctive thought and style appear in this statement which is also given in another form which states that the action of disobedience rather than disbelief leads to disaster (3:18). To see life means the same as to have it. Of the Evangelists only John writes of the "wrath of God." He thinks of God as an active Holy One, who inevitably stands in ceaseless opposition to those who are disobedient. In this single passage life and the wrath of God stand in antithesis. The wrath of God was well known to Paul who shared the idea with Jewish writers who pictured the future or repeated Old Testament passages which vividly set forth God's judgments upon evildoers.

45

Jesus and Samaritans

4:1–42

THE LATER Gospels use "Lord" for Jesus almost three times as frequently as Mark. Sometimes it is a vocative like "Sir"; sometimes it is a divine title for Jesus similar to its use for God in the Old Testament or its reference to the Emperor's divinity in the pagan world; sometimes it is uncertain whether the title means simple respect or special reverence when used by Jesus' disciples and friends. When the "Lord" knew that the Pharisees heard of his increase of disciples, even exceeding John's, he left Judea for Galilee to avoid their antagonism. He had to pass through Samaria which lay between Judea and Galilee. This visit at the village of Sychar was the first time that Jesus dealt with other than his fellow Jews. The story is told in two conversations between Jesus and a Samaritan woman, then between him and his disciples, followed by a summary about the Samaritans who believed in him. The homely subjects of water, food and work become the transparent symbols of eternal truths in the inimitable blend of everyday life and its transcendent significance that only John achieved in his record of Jesus.

Wearied one day during his journey, Jesus sat down at Jacob's well while his disciples went one half mile to the village of Sychar to buy some food. The well is not known in the Old Testament but it was in the area which Jacob, the Hebrew patriarch, had bought many centuries earlier (Gen. 33:18-19). Tourists still peer into its narrow dark seventy-five-foot depths surrounded by the ruins of Byzantine, Crusader and modern churches. It is called both a spring (4:6, 14) and a well (4:11-12) by John. When Jesus asked for a drink, the woman of Samaria questioned how he could ask her, a Samaritan woman, for water. She had an unsavory reputation, the Samaritans and the Jews had no dealings and a Jewish man did not talk to a woman in public, not even with his own wife. Samaritans and Jews had separated 450 years earlier and subsequent clashes in religion and politics had embittered them. The Samaritans had their own law of

Moses and worshiped at a temple on Mount Gerizim, not at Jerusalem. This temple had been destroyed by the Jewish monarch, John Hyrcanus (129 B.C.). The Jews scorned their Samaritan neighbors and usually avoided travel in their territory. Jesus in his answer reversed the customary situation. The woman should ask him for living water if she knew God's gift and the one who talked to her. God's gift was the water of Jesus' teaching which gave men both knowledge of life and of the source of life in men. As usual in John's narratives, the woman took a literal physical view and had to be enlightened. She doubted that Jesus could draw living water since he had no skin bucket to drop into the deep well. Was he greater than their forefather Jacob? Then Jesus told her of water which could quench inner thirst forever and also become a fountain within to spring up to eternal life. The thought of the Lord as a fountain of living waters was known to the Psalmist (36:9) and Isaiah had written of water from the wells of salvation (12:3). To the sage the Law was a fountain of life (Prov. 13:14; Ecclus. 15:3) and in a vision of the new Jerusalem John, the Seer, had seen a crystal clear river of water which flowed from the throne of God and of the Lamb (Rev. 22:1).

When the woman desired this living water, Jesus spoke of her five husbands and of the man she had then who was not her husband. The woman recognized his insight as a prophet and turned from husbands to the controversial subject of worship about which Jews and Samaritans quarreled. Jesus pointed beyond the disputed places for worship, Mount Gerizim or Jerusalem, though he defended Jewish worship which led to the knowledge of God better than the part-pagan worship of the Samaritans. True worship of God the Father was not in some place or by some race but in spirit and in truth because God is spirit. This essential nature of God has its counterpart in the spiritual essence of man and it is the basis of worship. The hour of this worship was now come. The woman turned to the hopes of the coming Messiah who would teach the needed truths. Little is known about the Samaritan beliefs about the Messiah at this time though they probably had some of the same expectations as the Jews. The woman's Messianic hopes met a momentous declaration by Jesus, "I who speak to you am he." This identification of Jesus as the long-awaited Christ is but one of the affirmations of this belief which appear throughout this Gospel. In the brief conversation with the woman Jesus had taught her of life-giving water, reminded her of her dubious marital relations, announced the arrival of the true worship of God and asserted that he was the Christ.

In John there is an extraordinary use by Jesus of the expression "I am" (4:26; 6:35; 8:12; 10:7, 11, 36; 11:25; 14:6; 15:1). This use, which far exceeds anything similar in the Synoptics, exalts the person of Jesus. In the Synoptics Jesus has a life with God and a mission from God which exceed analysis but in John the "I-style" of speech might lead to the conclusion that even the greatness of Jesus was tainted by egoism. This style is due to John and it has been suggested that the use of the pronoun "he" in place of "I" would convey the sense of the claims about Jesus more accurately though less traditionally. The use of "I am" can be understood as a means for the presentation, recognition, identification and qualifications of Jesus. In Jewish and Christian thought "I am" was familiar in the affirmations of divinity. Moses at the burning bush learned that the Lord was named "I am that I am" (Exod. 3:14) and he was the one who miraculously healed his people (15:26). The Psalmist heard the promise of the Lord, "I am thy salvation" (35:3). Isaiah proclaimed the word of the Lord from birth to death, "I am he" (46:4), "the first and the last," no other God exists. The seer on Patmos heard the words of God, "I am Alpha and Omega" (Rev. 1:8). The use of the first person in utterances by gods or goddesses was in widespread use in pagan cults outside Judaism and Christianity.[1]

When the disciples came, they wondered at Jesus' talk with the woman. She hastened to invite the men of the city to come and see a man who told her all she ever did. "Can this be the Christ?" The disciples offered Jesus food but he had food of which they did not know. As in John's usual device they thought of literal food but Jesus taught them that his food was to do God's will. He lived by the work he had to do. That work had just been partly begun with the Samaritan woman. But there was a harvest now ripe for reaping. This harvest would yield wages of eternal life for the worker as well as joy with the ones who sowed. This spiritual harvest had been prepared by Jesus with the woman who spread the good news. Also other earlier prophets, like John the Baptist, had labored and their labors were completed by their successors.

John swiftly summarizes the climax. Many Samaritans believed first because of the woman's extravagant testimony that Jesus told all she ever did. But when Jesus stayed two days, at the request of the Samaritans, many more believed because of Jesus' own words. This was evidence better than the woman's words because they themselves

---

[1] A. Deissmann, *Light from the Ancient East* (New York, 1927), 136-43.

heard directly. They knew Jesus was the Savior of the world. This is the only time that this title is given to Jesus but it shows that he was more than the Messiah of Samaritans and Jews. He was meant for everyone. This universalism characterizes the Fourth Gospel. As water was needed and used by everyone so Jesus provided the water of life for all who believed. Historically it is doubtful if the Samaritans recognized in Jesus all that the later thought of John found in him as the Savior of the world. As John saw Jesus tell Nicodemus of a new birth, so that a new religious life replaced the old faith of Judaism, so Jesus taught the Samaritan woman of the living water of spiritual worship to take the place of the older ceremonial life and worship of both Samaritan and Jew. These teachings amplify the thought which appears repeatedly in the first four chapters of John. There is new grace and truth in the Word. There is new wine, a new temple, a new birth and new water of life.

46

Two Healings and Their Teachings ·
The Nobleman's Son · The Impotent Man

4:43–5:47

JESUS MOVED northward into Galilee. He said a prophet had no honor in his own country. Since these statements stand in sequence and since neither Judea nor Samaria was home country for Jesus and since he was welcomed in Galilee, it has been thought that the saying is misplaced or else inserted because mention of Galilee led John to repeat a saying which Jesus had spoken in Nazareth. Or it has been guessed that Jerusalem was his home symbolically as for every Jew. Or John may have thought that as Jesus came to his home area, he would not receive the enlarging publicity which led to Pharisaic suspicion. But the Galileans, who had been to the feast in Jerusalem and had seen what Jesus had done there, were ready to welcome him on his return, contrary to his expectation.

The second sign and the first acts of healing had their beginning in Cana where an unnamed official, perhaps one of Herod's courtiers who had heard of Jesus' arrival, begged him to come to Capernaum, twenty miles distant from Cana, where his son lay sick and near death. The reply of Jesus is difficult because he uses the plural "you" but it seems to be a rebuke of those who want belief to be established by miracles. But the official repeated his request for Jesus to come before his child died. With great faith the father accepted the word of Jesus that his son would live. His faith was met next day when the servants reported that his son's fever left at one o'clock, the time when Jesus had spoken. The father and his household became believers. Since John sees this event as a sign, it is evident that he meant to teach some truths by his report. It is a story that proved that Jesus could heal at a distance and that he would help a man of high station in his desperate need as readily as at a marriage celebration. But the repetition of two thoughts points to an emphasis on belief and on life. In the brief account both belief and the son's life are stressed three times. Jesus deprecated a belief based on miracles but the man believed his word and went his way. John uses the verb "to believe" 100 times but he does not use the noun "faith." It is likely that when John wrote, faith meant a fixed deposit of truth but he used the verb which "stands for an active exercise of higher judgment, with a certain moral force, in so far as it involves taking up a personal attitude to Christ." [1] Faith meant belief or credence and it also meant confidence to act and personal trust. For John this trust was in Jesus who was sent by God. The result of belief in the words of Jesus addressed to the distraught father was life for his child. "Your son lives" resounds through the narrative. It was the promise of Jesus, reaffirmed by the servants and remembered by the father. "In him was life" and this life reached out to heal a fevered child.

This miracle has some aspects parallel to the healing of the centurion's servant (Mt. 8:5; Lk. 7:2). In both the Synoptics and in John the cure takes place in Capernaum, it is wrought at a distance and strong faith is shown but the discrepancies are obvious and numerous. The same incident may lie at the base of the two narratives or they may refer to independent events. John had his own interests and does not show dependence on the Synoptics.

John related two signs without discussion about them but his third miracle is followed by a report of criticism and teaching five times as long as the story of the cure. In the first four chapters Jesus had dealt largely with individuals without much opposition but in chapters 5–12 his work and teaching deal more with crowds at the festivals in Jerusalem with the results of rapidly rising controversy and enmity from the Jews. Throughout this section the discourses outweigh the events.

Jesus went up to Jerusalem for a feast which is not identified. It might have been Purim in March, the Passover in April or Pentecost in May, Tabernacles in October or Dedication in December. Both the name of the pool, Bethzatha, and its location by the sheepgate are uncertain. It was a pool whose waters stirred at times, perhaps from an intermittent spring or by the wind so that it was believed to have healing qualities which were explained in a late addition to the story as due to an angel (5:4). Around the pool lay a crowd of infirm folks. Among them was a man who had been afflicted for thirty-eight years with some weakness. Perhaps he was a paralytic or a cripple. Jesus saw him and knew about him. This knowledge aroused the man who desired health but lacked help to reach it in the pool which

[1] W. F. Howard, *Christianity according to St. John* (London, 1943), 155.

he believed would heal him if he were first to enter it after it bubbled. But Jesus gave no recognition to the water as a curative agent. He commanded a triple action, "Rise, lift your mat and walk" and the man obeyed at once.

In this rapid narrative the result was not wonder at the cure but controversy because the man was healed on a Sabbath. The Jews who were opponents of Jesus in the Fourth Gospel were mostly Jerusalemites or Judeans. When they saw the man carry his mattress, they objected because it was labor on the holy day, a serious offense which could be punished by death. The man defended himself with the command of the one who had healed him whose name he did not know until he met him again in the Temple when Jesus warned him to sin no more lest he fall into a worse condition. There is no explanation given about the man's former sin or why he told Jesus' name to the Jews. But they began their first persecution of Jesus because he had violated Sabbath laws by a cure when life and death were not involved and by a command to carry his bed. The defense of Jesus about the Sabbath is different from similar controversies in the Synoptics where Jesus had asked about doing good or showing mercy on the Sabbath or had appealed to necessity as proved by the scriptures. In this incident Jesus made a claim which put him on a level with God in freedom of activity. "My Father is working still and I am working." While God had rested to establish the Sabbath after the creation of the world, he was believed to be refreshed and to continue his activities (Exod. 31:17). How God maintained the universe on the Sabbath was much debated. It was thought that God kept the Sabbath in regard to physical work but always maintained his works of judgment. The consequence of Jesus' claim was that the Jews sought to kill him not only for Sabbath breaking but for blasphemy in making himself equal to God. Blasphemy required the death penalty (Lev. 24:16). This charge of equality with God was made by Jesus' opponents but it was not claimed by Jesus himself. Such equality meant independence of God or usurpation of God's authority. The relationship of Jesus with God is one of the constant themes of the Fourth Gospel and it is the great issue between Jesus and his opponents. It is stressed by Jesus' reference to God as "My Father." Jesus does not use "Our Father" as in the Synoptics and it is the Fourth Gospel which has popularized the name of Father for God since it appears 119 times.

The long discourse, by which Jesus met the attack of his foes, explains: (1) the Father-Son situation and (2) the witness for Jesus.

The deeds of Jesus and the judgment given into his hands illustrate the Father-Son relationship. The Son is dependent on God. Whatever he sees God is doing the Son does also. Since God loves the Son, he shows him all things that he does and will show him greater works than the cure of the impotent man which will make his enemies wonder. Two works committed to the Son are to give life and to judge. Since God awakened the dead and gave them life, so the Son can give life to whom he will. This quickening of the dead is amplified later when Lazarus was raised (11:1–44). The next work of the Son is to judge. This is not a contradiction of the earlier claim (3:17) that the Son came to save not to judge. John presents different aspects of Jesus' work with different purposes. The Son came to save men but his light inevitably became a standard against which darkness was revealed. In order that the Son may be honored God gave to him all power to judge and whoever refuses to honor the Son refuses to honor God who sent him. Whoever listens to the word of the Son and believes in God who sent him possesses eternal life. He will not come to judgment because he has passed from death to life. Judgment and life stand in contrast. The time is here for those spiritually dead to listen to the voice of the Son of God who has life in himself, granted him from God who has life in himself. He gave the Son of Man authority to execute judgment. The time is coming for those physically dead to hear his voice also and their fate depends upon what they have done of good or evil. Their deeds determine their resurrection to life or to judgment. Life has two aspects. (1) It is a present imperishable possession, a spiritual fellowship with Father and Son. It is knowledge of God revealed in Christ here and now. It is a gift to those who believe that the Son is life for the world. This is John's special thought. (2) Life is for the future. It is agelong and related to a future resurrection and a final hour. This is the traditional idea of the Day of Judgment for those in their graves which John shares with others of this time. Thus the Son makes men alive both in their present existence and at the final hour. Judgment also has two aspects. (1) It is a present crisis in which men must make a decision about the revelation of God in the Son. In Jewish thought God's judgment dealt to men both justice and mercy. Men were responsible for their actions which brought bane or blessing. The Son of Man in his words and works presents a test for men to take now. (2) But there is future completion of their present decision when the wicked face a last condemnation and a final disposition.

It is notable that John did not use the word "gospel" which Mark favored in the noun form and Luke in the verb form and which rings everywhere in Paul's letters. The Johannine equivalent is "witness." [2] As in all the thought of John, witness also bears a higher and a lower meaning. (1) Witness "is the Divine life itself in relation to the world." [3] It is the divine-spiritual reality which descends upon man and also the self-expression of that reality in man which ascends from him in response to God. The Son possesses the witness which he received from the Father and gives to the world. (2) Witness has also the common normal meaning of evidence or proof. In order to establish the truth about Jesus, John presents a discourse about witness in which Jesus supports his claims in the face of attack. Jesus rejects his self-witness and summons the witness of God, of John the Baptist, of his own works and of the scriptures. The arguments follow the methods and the evidence that were customary in the time of Jesus. Self-testimony was inacceptable. According to the Law two witnesses established a fact (Dt. 19:15; Mt. 18:16). That Jesus came with the authority of Another is clear from his twenty-six references to "him that sent me." God is his first, true, continuous witness. But his witness is not externally audible or visible. His word was not in the hearts of the Jerusalemites because they had not believed in the one God sent. This is an appeal to the thought that spiritual life is discerned only by those who, in some measure, possess it. Only life can recognize life. John the Baptist's witness was past and Jesus' appeal to him was not for himself but that his hearers might be saved. They had rejoiced in John for a time as in a burning, shining lamp though he was not the final Light but a witness to the truth. There is a witness greater than John in the present works which Jesus was doing. They were evidence from God. The works were not the miracles alone but all the activities of Jesus which God gave him to do. Last, there is the witness of scripture in which the Jews searched diligently for eternal life though they refused to come to Jesus for life. The search for eternal life in the scriptures was based on the confidence that "he who has gained for himself the words of the Law has gained for himself life in the world to come." [4] The indictment of the foes of Jesus is that they lack the love of God and do not really believe the scriptures or seek the glory of the only God. They do not accept the Son who came in the Father's name but do accept another who came in his own name. This other one cannot be identified be-

---

[2] Howard, op. cit., 20.

[3] Odeberg, op. cit., 217.

[4] Pirke Aboth 2:7; Danby, The Mishnah (London, 1933), 448.

yond some vague meaning about a false Messiah. There is an accuser before God. He is Moses who was the hope of the Jews. In the scrip tures he wrote of the Messiah. No passage is named though John had quoted from the books of Moses in an earlier reference to the brazen serpent (3:14) and he refers to Abraham's joy in the day of Christ (8:56; Dt. 18:18). If Moses' writings about Christ were not believed, how could Jesus' words be accepted? In this discourse John has given an extension of the controversies Jesus arouses about himself and his activities as they were pondered and fought over between Christians and Jews at the end of the first century.

47

Two Signs and Their Teachings · Feeding 5,000 · Walking on the Sea

6:1-71

THE FOURTH and fifth miracles stand in striking contrast. The feeding of the 5,000 is told with considerable lifelike details; it is called a sign and there is an extensive discourse on the bread of life. The walking on the sea is briefly told with no added comment about it. Perhaps the difference is due to the fact that there was the recurrent need of food for all men and the sacrament with the bread was a most significant continuing action in the church while the story of the sea did not involve any repetitive act in the common life of the church. John undertook to show the true meanings of the feeding because it had an immediate bearing in the experience of his readers. The setting of the miracle is at the Sea of Galilee which John alone calls the Sea of Tiberias. The water had been called Chinnereth in older days (Num. 34:11) and Luke and Josephus knew it as Sea of Gennesaret or Gennesar. When Herod Antipas built the city of Tiberias on the west shore in honor of his emperor Tiberius, the name was also transferred to the sea.

If John knew the Synoptic accounts of the feeding of the 5,000, he still felt free to give his own report. His general outline is the same as theirs but he knew interesting details not found in the others. The great crowd followed Jesus because of the signs (miracles) which he did for the sick. The place was in the hills, east of the sea. It was the Passover season. Jesus took the initiative to help the hungry people and knew what he would do. He tested Philip about buying bread and Andrew discovered the only food on hand. A lad, not the disciples, provided five barley loaves and two fish. Jesus himself distributed the food. He commanded the collection of the remaining fragments so that nothing would be lost. When the people saw this sign, they declared him to be the long-awaited prophet that God had promised would be like Moses (Dt. 18:18). The people wanted to force Jesus to be their king but he went away into the hills alone. There is no mention of private prayers in John as in the Synoptics. Some of these details read like reminiscences of an eyewitness. The mention of the Passover seems to be only a dating. The fragments left over indicate the plentiful supply of food and the need of care for the bread. Jesus was competent to handle everything but his motives are not given. The results depict the highest tribute possible in recognition of his religious and potential political leadership. He did not refuse the title of king bestowed by Nathanael (1:49) and at his entry into Jerusalem (12:13) but the plan of the crowds to make him king portended the danger of revolution against Rome and he withdrew from it at once.

The next miracle is also told in Matthew and Mark. The night, the wind, the absence of Jesus, the hard four-mile row and the fear of the disciples are all facts but they are also symbolic of conditions which Jesus alone could relieve. The disciples lost their fear when he came with words of assurance and they reached their long-sought goal at once. John does not call this incident a sign. The immediate arrival at land may indicate that Jesus was walking *by* the sea or *at* it (6:21) rather than *on* it even as he did in his final appearance *by* the sea (21:1). The fear of the disciples may have been due to uncertainty about what they saw in the dark. They were willing to take Jesus into the boat but John does not state that he entered it. Therefore, it is possible to claim that "in John there is no miracle whatever." [1] But this claim is improbable in view of John's interest in Jesus as one able to work signs of the greatest kind with divine ease. The fear of the disciples implied an event beyond their understanding. When Jesus later spoke to the crowd, he referred to signs which indicates more than the one feeding (6:26). There is even the suggestion of a second miracle in the immediacy with which the boat arrived at land. For John this story meant that Jesus had actual power to walk on the sea, that he could quiet fear by his presence with his disciples and that he could enable them to attain their desired goal.

When the crowd the next day saw that the boat was gone, they got in some boats which had crossed from Tiberias and came to Capernaum where they asked Jesus how he got there. Jesus did not answer their question directly but pointed out that their interest was not in signs of spiritual truths but in food to fill their stomachs. Then follows the long discourse in the synagogue which is interrupted by the question and the misunderstanding of the people. This lengthy

---

[1] Bernard, *op. cit.*, I, 185.

section has three parts: (1) the bread of life (6:27–50); (2) the necessity to eat the bread (6:51–59); (3) the effects of teaching on disciples (6:59–71). One question about this discourse arouses debate. Did John substitute a view of the Lord's Supper that was different from the usual Christian one? John has no account of Jesus' actions and words with bread and wine at the Last Supper. This omission may be due to John's attitude to the sacraments by which he wished, within Christian circles, to safeguard them against undue emphasis or infiltration by pagan sacramentalism or misunderstanding by his readers, recently pagan. Or perhaps he desired to stop nonbelievers from false attacks upon the sacred Christian meal. Hence he gave them no ammunition against the sacred words of the sacrament. One view holds that John had his own special understanding of the sacrament which he related to the feeding of the 5,000 and he intended to emphasize the life of believers shared with Christ as living rather than with the materials of bread and wine as related to his death. This places a strong emphasis on the spiritual aspect of John's thought and leads to the suggestion that John, in figurative language, rejected the usual views about the sacrament. But another view, more commonly followed, is that John shared the general Christian view of the Lord's Supper but wished to develop certain truths about it since he saw a close connection between the meal with the 5,000 and the last one with the Twelve. He maintained a belief that eternal life was related to both the material and the spiritual aspects of man's existence and that God's activity was everywhere manifested to believers. It was not localized in one place or time or in particular elements of bread and wine but in the Son of Man. There is no mention of wine for the 5,000 or at the Last Supper. How much the later church read into John's view about the sacrament is illustrated by the symbols by which Peter is pictured with keys, Paul with his sword and John with his cup. Yet John has no cup in his Gospel.

The discourse of Jesus follows the plan found in his talks with Nicodemus and with the Samaritan woman where birth and water were vehicles for spiritual truths about a birth from above and living water. This discourse concerns enduring food for which Jesus urged the people to work since the Son of Man gave it. He was certified by God, by baptism, by scriptures and by miracles and teachings. The people asked what they must do as God's work and Jesus answered that the work of God was to believe in the one God sent. This places faith ahead of deeds. They inquired what Jesus was doing as a proof about himself. Then he cited one of Moses' greatest deeds which provided manna or bread from heaven for the Hebrews during their forty years of wandering in the wilderness. Jesus corrected them by the answer that it was not Moses who gave but God who gives true celestial bread which provides life. Like the woman at the well, the people asked for this bread always. In a claim repeated four times (6:35, 41, 48, 51) Jesus affirmed, "I am the bread of life" or the "living bread" or "from heaven." Yet though they had seen, they did not believe him though he came down from heaven to do God's will which was to give life to all who believed. These believers are God's gift to his Son who will receive them and will raise them up at the last day. The fourfold reference to the last day (6:39, 40, 44, 54) is a special term in John which is equivalent to the Day of Judgment. Present eternal life comes to anyone who sees and believes in the Son but this life will continue into the future. John "regards the 'rising at the last day' as only the fulfillment and confirmation of something already effected, not as the real beginning of a new state of being." [2] When the Jews objected, he repeated his claim as the bread of life, which meant that he both is life and gives life. They saw him only as an earthly son of his parents and asked how he came down from heaven. Jesus did not discuss his descent but the need for his hearers to be taught of God as the scriptures stated (Isa. 54:13). Learning is essential beyond mere hearing. The Father who sent Jesus stands in contrast to Joseph, the earthly father, whom the Jews knew. They could not understand how the Son came down from heaven. Only the Son had seen the Father but the Son is accessible to all who believe. Life comes only from life and Jesus is the life-giver since he came from God who is the eternal source of life. The manna in the wilderness had sustained the life of forefathers for a time but a man could eat of the living bread and never die. This life from the Son made a man independent of physical death through a real, invisible, personal sharing of life with the Son. This is a contrast between physical death and spiritual life which exists within but also beyond the material body of man. The bread which Jesus will give for the life of the world is his flesh. This is an allusion to his coming death and it is typical of John's thought which symbolically reminds the reader of the important issues concerning Jesus. John the Baptist had seen Jesus as the Lamb of God which suggested his coming sacrifice according to the first witness about Jesus.

On this theme the second part of the discourse moves to a different concept. "The thought passes from what Christ is to what he gives." [3] In the first section he is the living bread, in the second this bread is

[2] Scott, *op. cit.,* 249.
[3] MacGregor, *op. cit.,* 152.

his flesh for food together with his blood for drink. This incredible idea, taken literally, rouses the Jews to dispute among themselves. "How can he give us his flesh to eat?" The symbolic language of eating and drinking flesh and blood rests upon the idea that as physical life is sustained by food and drink so spiritual life is united with, and absorbed from, Christ who lives because a living Father sent him to give life. Judaism taught that the "blood is the life" (Dt. 12:23) and that life is sacred because only God created it. Therefore, the Jew obeyed the commandment, "You shall not eat the blood" (Dt. 12:16). "This language must have contributed to widen the gulf in the second century between the synagogue and the church." [4] Judaism knew its sacrifices at the Temple when blood was poured out daily in abundance but it did not allow worshipers to eat bloody meat as did some of the pagan mystery religions. The Fourth Gospel, as it presents Jesus' answer to the Jews who disputed about eating his flesh, is interpreting the rite of Holy Communion. "He who eats" is repeated four times (6:54, 56, 57, 58) and the symbols of flesh and blood contain certain promises of eternal life and of the Son who abides in the participant. The repetition suggests the frequency of the Holy Communion and the indwelling mystical life which the communicant receives as imperishable food and as the seed of immortality.[5]

The third part of the discourse shows both a negative and a positive effect upon the disciples, some of whom murmured at his offensive teaching and left Jesus. But Peter, spokesman for the Twelve, declared that they had no other leader and that Jesus alone had the words which had power to produce the belief which the Twelve had reached that Jesus was the Holy One of God. This is another title, given once only in John, to re-emphasize the thought that the Twelve already had known Jesus as the Messiah (1:41) and that Jesus had an essential relationship to God whose holiness had always marked him apart from sinful man. This affirmation is the Johannine parallel to Peter's momentous declaration at Caesarea Philippi that Jesus was the Christ (Mk. 8:27-30). This loyalty stands in dramatic contrast on the one hand to the faithless departing disciples and on the other to the traitor Judas. Jesus knew with superhuman insight the attitudes of the disloyal ones who would not believe and the one who would betray him. Only those whom God had given to the Son were loyal. He countered the murmurers with a question about their possible

[4] Carpenter, *op. cit.*, 435 (note)

[5] Rigg, *op. cit.*, 81–116; Dodd, *op. cit.*, 333–40, 140–50.

sight of the ascent of the Son of Man to his former place. This is a reference to the idea that Christ came down from heaven to the world and that his ascension would mark his return to heaven. This spiritual origin was known only to those who live in the spiritual world. Angels were believed to ascend and descend (1:51). The Messiah was sent from God and would return to him. But the spirit gives life while the flesh is of no use. The words of the Son are spirit and life. The hard teaching that the disciples rejected had to be understood spiritually because Jesus' words were not merely literal but possessed creative power as a part of himself or they were like God's words. Though Peter had spoken the belief of the Twelve about Jesus and his words yet the reply of Jesus was a blunt disclosure that one of the chosen Twelve was a devil. John assumes that the Twelve were known to his readers for he had not told about their selection by Jesus. John sees the Twelve as men who had staked their lives on what Jesus said and what he was. They are the beginning church which later is described as a flock (10:3) or as branches of a vine (15:5). Yet within this chosen group was a traitor. John shows by this double identification of Judas both as devil and traitor the strong antipathy he felt toward Judas whose father, Simon Iscariot, he alone mentions. John may have meant that both Judas and his father came from the village of Kerioth and that Simon Peter stood loyally in contrast to Judas, son of another Simon, but a betrayer.

This discourse illustrates clearly the spiral nature of the teaching of Jesus as recorded by the Fourth Evangelist. The thought is stated, it mounts and is repeated, the same thought is clothed in slightly different words, intricate skeins of ideas stretch out in profusion, key phrases occur and reoccur, dramatic contrasts appear and significant ideas cross the trail of others at angles so that there is apparent contradiction. When there is stress on flesh (51–58), how can it profit nothing (63)? These antitheses are the evidence of a great thinker moving not in a field of logic but in actual religious life where memory and meaning, events and actions, divinity and humanity, popular thought and his own advancing insights exceed the confinement of words. "There is no evidence that the author of the Fourth Gospel has in mind a contrast between a spiritual religion of the Word and a material sacramental religion. Everything points in an opposite direction. Christianity is the spiritual religion not because it is divorced from the physical world but because the Flesh has been submitted to the Spirit and thereby vivified." [6]

[6] Hoskyns and Davey, *op. cit.*, I, 344.

48

Teaching · Opinions · Opposition at the Feast of Tabernacles · The Adulterous Woman

7:1–8:59

A NOTE of deadly opposition to Jesus appeared in Judea since the Jews sought to kill him, hence he went about in Galilee. The Feast of Tabernacles came in the fall and lasted eight days (Dt. 16:13). It was a harvest festival and was also linked historically with the wilderness days when the Hebrews dwelt in tents on the journey from Egypt (Lev. 23:33–35; 39–43). Its observance was a time of joy, of offerings, of suspension of work, of living in booths and for holy convocation. It stood next to the Passover among the significant feasts of the Jews.

The sign-minded, unbelieving brothers of Jesus suggested that Jesus go to Judea to display his works for the benefit of disciples since he had lost many by his hard teachings. He should show himself to the world for public recognition. When his brothers said, "If you do these things," there is no certainty whether they were skeptical about the deeds or assumed that he should go because of his works. But he did not take his brothers' advice since he felt his opportune time had not come. Neither his brothers nor his mother (2:4) but God determined the time of his actions.

John has numerous references to his "hour" which point to his death but to his brothers Jesus spoke of his "time" as the appointed period when he had his work to do. The nature of time has aroused endless speculations. The symbol of time in Judaism and in early Christianity is an upward sloping line, not a circle as in Hellenism.[1] Time is a reality which includes eternity, which is not Greek timelessness but an unlimited succession of ages and also limited time such as is marked by creation and the end of the present age or a beginning and a goal. God controls the line of time and at his will he enters history. He selects the "D"-day. In John's thought this action of God is the Word. When Jesus told his brothers their time was

[1] O. Cullmann, *Christ and Time* (Philadelphia, 1950), 51.

ready, their travel to Jerusalem had no special relation to God's plan as his journey did. They did not face the hate of the world as he did for rebuking its evil. When Jesus decided to go to Jerusalem after he told his brothers that he was not going, it is not intended as a contradiction and still less a falsehood but as his own decision after a three-day wait though he did not go publicly but privately as he followed God's will. This decision to go is important since it marks the end of his public life in Galilee and it is the introduction to a complex of teachings and events in Jerusalem which continue through chapter ten.

The first section (7:10–52) contains a series of opinions about Jesus which include his brief conversations with those who question him or reports concerning him. The first opinions are divided as the people muttered much about him. Some held that he was good, others that he misled the people. When he taught in the Temple, the Jews marveled that he had learning without formal study. This reference to learning has been thought to refer to the capacity of Jesus to read or to teach without professional training like a disciple's with a rabbi. The latter is more probable. Jesus defended his teaching as from God which could be tested and known by anyone who did his will and also by his own unselfish, honest motives. By contrast his opponents had the Mosaic Law but did not keep it since they sought to kill him. The people thought him out of his mind. But Jesus reminded them of one deed when he cured the impotent man (5:19) and incurred the danger of death. Then he showed that their custom of circumcision on the Sabbath, which technically broke the Sabbath, was carried out because a greater law took precedence over a lesser one. Jesus believed that the cure of the man likewise was defensible.

The next opinions came from Jerusalemites who wondered that Jesus was allowed to teach and they questioned if the authorities really knew that he was Christ. But they decided that it was incredible because they knew where Jesus came from although they did not know the real One who sent him. Their lack of knowledge of God disqualified them to judge Jesus. In contrast to their ignorance of God is the claim of Jesus, "I know him," which is made four times (7:29; 8:55; 10:15; 17:25). He came from God and was sent by him. Knowledge that is eternal life is one of John's important themes. There is knowledge of God by Jesus and also by men who come to know God through belief in Christ and who become obedient. Such knowledge always has an ethical and a personal aspect. It arises from the activity of God in man. Jesus claimed a knowledge not about

God but of God himself. This knowledge is plainer in John's Greek than it is in English since John used a verb which emphasizes the absolute all-inclusive idea of knowledge whereas, for the enemies of Jesus who claimed to know God, he used a verb which meant an acquired but less complete knowledge. Though there were areas of knowledge between Jesus and his Father that were never fully explored, John most strongly affirms that Jesus knew God. But "Jesus' relation to God is never expressed in terms of faith." [2] Men *believe* in Jesus and come to *know* God. The relation of Jesus to God is an ideal for man. Belief or faith involves a venture of will and of trust; knowledge reflects an attainment which is the result of faith. Usually knowledge follows faith but John, with his strong interest in "knowledge," presented Jesus in prayer in which he recalled that his disciples knew that he came from the Father and believed that he sent his Son (17:8). In this instance knowledge led to faith. As Jesus taught in the Temple, the authorities wished to arrest him but John indicates that his seizure was delayed because his hour was determined by divine purpose. But many believed on him because they said that even the Christ who was expected to work miracles would not do more signs than Jesus had done. There was an unusual joining of high priests and Pharisees as they sent officers to take him. The high priests were mostly Sadducees though John nowhere mentions Sadducees by name. They did not usually co-operate with Pharisees. When Jesus spoke of his soon-coming departure to the One who sent him, the Jews misunderstood his reference to his death and thought he referred to a journey among the Jews dispersed outside Palestine where he would teach the Greeks. His words puzzled them since they could not see why they would neither find him nor could they come where he was.

On the last great day of the feast Jesus stood up and invited any thirsty one to come to him and drink. Anyone who believed in him would find, as the scripture said, within himself a fountain flowing with living water. This is the same promise of thirst quenched and of a spring of the water of life that Jesus made to the Samaritan woman. There is no exact scriptural identification for the promise of living water within a man but the idea of abundant water for thirsty folks as a symbol of God's spirit was a favorite of Isaiah. "With joy shall ye draw water out of the wells of salvation" (12:3); "I will pour water upon him that is thirsty" (44:3). It is possible that Jesus' words about water reflect customs of the Feast of Tabernacles which are

[2] Lee, *op. cit.*, 235.

found in rabbinical references. During the feast each morning a priest went to the Pool of Siloam and filled a golden pitcher. On his return there was the trumpet blast as the water was poured out as a libation at the Temple.[3] This ritual, coming in the fall near the beginning of the seasonal rains, was a symbolic action to induce abundant rain which would insure crops and fill the cisterns for use in the rainless season. John explains that the words of Jesus about water refer to the Spirit. Believers would receive the Spirit after Jesus was glorified. John interprets the death of Jesus as his glorification or exaltation into a new life. In a similar form he later gives Jesus' teachings about his death (12:23; 13:31) and in his last teaching to the Twelve the Spirit's nature and functions are described and promised to them (15:26–16:15). The words of Jesus to the Jerusalemites resulted in varied opinions. Some said he was the awaited prophet, the successor to Moses (Dt. 18:18) or they may have meant Elijah, the expected predecessor to the Messiah (Mal. 4:5). Others thought he was the Christ and others doubted because the Christ was to come from Bethlehem and Jesus came from Galilee. If John knew about the birthplace of Jesus, he makes no use of the narrative. Still others wanted to arrest Jesus but they made no move to seize him.

The final opinions about Jesus came from the temple police who returned to the priests and the Pharisees without Jesus and said, "No man ever spoke like this man." The Pharisees scoffed at their report, warned them not to be misled by Jesus who had not won any believers among the authorities or the Pharisees though they did grant that among the crowds, for whom they had only contempt because of their ignorance of the Law, were some who believed on Jesus. When Nicodemus, also a Pharisee, protested that a man must be judged according to the Law in his own defense by knowledge of what he had done, the others silenced him with the scornful assertion that no prophet came from Galilee. This was an extreme assertion since Jonah had come from Galilee.

The story of the woman taken in adultery is an authentic story of Jesus though it is not an original part of John's Gospel. It interrupts the sequence, it is not in the style and the thought of John, it is not in the earliest manuscripts and it sometimes was placed after Luke 21:38. However, it is canonical scripture and was placed in John: (1) to illustrate the superiority of Jesus in controversy with the Pharisees; (2) to set forth his merciful action and summons to sin no more; (3) to introduce the section in which Jesus said, "I judge no man" (8:15).

[3] *Sukkah* 4.9; Danby, *op. cit.*, 179.

As Jesus sat teaching in the Temple, the scribes and the Pharisees brought the woman to gain an opinion from Jesus on the Mosaic Law which might be turned against him. The Law required adulterers to be stoned (Dt. 22:22) and the death penalty is repeated in Leviticus (20:10) where the means of execution is not stated. Later rabbinical orders required strangulation. As he sat, Jesus wrote on the ground with his finger. This is the only mention of writing by Jesus in the Gospels and it is the act of one who scribbles as he waits. What he wrote is unknown but some ancient writers, as shown in late manuscripts, asserted that he wrote the sins of the accusers. When pressed for an answer, he deftly turned the attack from himself and the woman to the questioners. This moved them to look at their own moral conduct rather than at a point of law. Then he wrote again as the attackers slipped away one by one. With the same words he used for his mother he asked the accused if anyone had condemned her. Her only words, "No one, Lord," led Jesus to say that he did not condemn her. He did not condone her sin nor speak of forgiveness but he commanded her to "go and sin no more."

The rest of the discourse continues with briefer interruptions and questions from Pharisees and Jews. In the flood of ideas three waves can be distinguished: (1) the light and its witness; (2) "Who are you?" (3) freedom by the truth. When Jesus finished the first topic, he was still left free of arrest. At the second many believed, at the third he was threatened with stones. Jesus said, "I am the light of the world." In the Synoptics the disciples were the light of the world. Perhaps the symbol of light was suggested by the ceremony on the first day of the Feast of Tabernacles when four golden candelabra were lighted in the Court of Women in the Temple as a reminder of the miraculous pillar of fire which guided the Hebrews through their wilderness wanderings. But light is a familiar figure of speech in the scriptures where the light of the Lord's countenance is his approval of his people (Ps. 4:6) or the Lord himself is a light (Ps. 27:1; Isa. 60:19) or a good man walks in light (Prov. 4:18). It was a familiar thought in Judaism that the Law was light or the Messiah was to be a light. Paul saw Christians as "saints in light" (Col. 1:12). John had set forth the light in his Prologue and he repeatedly used the thought. The light which came to the followers of Christ was divine spiritual reality. They shared this life and light with Christ and guided their lives by his light. When the Pharisees objected to the self-witness of Jesus as the light, he affirmed its truth though in an earlier passage he had refused self-witness (5:31). This contrast may be deliberately intended to arouse the reader or it may be the paradoxical aspect of a larger truth. His witness was true because he knew his origin and destiny and because God had sent him and bore witness to him. This is an affirmation of the eternal divine knowledge and relationship possessed by Christ. When the Pharisees asked, "Where is your Father?" he told them that they lacked the knowledge both of God and of him. Their ignorance was not of his life in Nazareth but of his divine inward life.

When Jesus spoke of his departure where his hearers could not come because of their sin, they mistakenly thought that Jesus was talking of suicide. Jesus declared that they were of this world and their death in their sins would be due to their failure to believe in Christ. They asked, "Who are you?" The answer is obscure and may mean what he had told them from the beginning of his ministry or it may be a question in which he wonders why he should talk to them at all. He proceeded to tell them that he had many things to say and judge about them, which he had heard from the One who sent him, but they failed to realize that he spoke of God. The best evidence could come when they had lifted him up. This may be a reference to the crucifixion or to any exaltation of Christ. God had sent him, taught him and was with him because he did everything to please him.

To those who believed Jesus spoke of freedom contrasted with slavery to sin. They had to make his words their home; they had to know the spiritual reality of truth and it would free them from sin. This truth is a tremendous concept in this Gospel. Truth is all that God is and all that he reveals to men. Its effect is not an abstract idea about liberty but an actual freedom from slavery to sin. The Jews thought of their descent from Abraham as God's people who had his Law, which they believed made them free. But no one is free who sins. The Son sets men free but his words found no response in his hearers though he spoke from a knowledge of his Father. This statement neglects the fact that his auditors were believing Jews (8:31). It indicates John has returned to the frequent opposition of Jews to Jesus and that while the setting is in historical Jerusalem the issues discussed are the sharp-edged controversies between Judaism and Christianity, which had increased in the decades since the death of Jesus. The argument continues as the Jews reaffirm that they are sons of Abraham and also of God. The counterargument is that they seek to kill Jesus and therefore do not act like Abraham's children nor recognize that Jesus was sent from God since they would not hear his words. Their father is the devil whose will they do because he was a murderer from the first and the father of lies. His is the kingdom of falsehood. The devil was regarded as responsible for death which came into the world when in the guise of a serpent he tempted Adam and Eve. The foes of Jesus would not believe the truth when told to them because they did not belong to God. They gave no answer when challenged to convict Jesus of sin. This is one way in which the sinlessness of Jesus is affirmed by John. The acrid argument proceeded as the Jews charged that Jesus was a demon-possessed Samaritan, one of the half-breeds of Hebrew and Gentile descent. Jesus said nothing about the Samaritans, perhaps because he already had believers among them, but he denied the demon since he who sought not his own selfish interests was honored by the Father who would be the final judge. Then by his usual double affirmation to emphasize its truth Jesus declared that if a man kept his word he would not die. Eternal life is the great theme of the Fourth Evangelist and its present possession is attained by a complete confidence in Christ. To keep the word of Christ is one of John's phrases for the knowledge and the practice of the teachings of Christ whose word was a living part of himself who kept the word of God. As Jesus kept the word of God, so the believer was to keep Christ's word. As usual the Jews did not understand the references to death and thought not of those who kept Jesus' words but of himself. He answered that it was his Father who exalted him and whom he knew. Their father Abraham had rejoiced to see "my day." This is a reference to the idea that Abraham, who lived in the heavenly world, could see and be glad at the day of Christ's appearance in this world. The Jews misconstrued the thought and asked if Jesus, who was not yet fifty, had seen Abraham in this world. This incredible question received a more mysterious answer, "Before Abraham was, I am." Abraham came into existence but Christ had existed always. "In the beginning was the Word." The divine name for God, "I am that I am," is echoed in this claim for the ever-existence of Christ. Jesus spoke in the language of divinity and was held to be a blasphemer. The reference of the Jews to the fact that he was not yet fifty years old is not a statement about the actual age of Jesus at the time but a round number to show that he was still active and not old when compared with the centuries which spanned the time to Abraham. The Levites, the temple attendants, retired from active duty at the age of fifty (Num. 8:24-25).

The preceding chapters (7, 8) present the alternation of events and teachings, characteristic of John, but they also have some distinct aspects. (1) There is no long discourse by Jesus. The multitude, the Jews and the Pharisees interrupt him with questions and disputes. (2) There are several references to conflict, danger, death and departure. These are the prelude to the cross and the resurrection. (3) There are decisive results when Jesus comes and teaches. Among his hearers many believe, some question about him but his enemies persistently plot his destruction.

49

Sight for the Blind Man · Discourse on Sheep and Shepherd

9:1–10:42

WHEN JESUS left the Temple, he saw a man blind from birth. John's account of this sixth sign follows his usual pattern. Jesus restored the man's sight and a considerable controversy ensued in which knowledge which comes from sight in a spiritual sense is contrasted with unbelieving blindness. The story is the "result of a very complicated and complete fusion into one narrative of the experience of conversion to Christianity, of the controversy with the Jews which was caused by the success of the Christian mission and of the traditional accounts of the healing of blind men by Jesus." [1] The allusive character of John's writing is nowhere better illustrated. The story starts trends of thought in many directions besides its main teachings. The lifelike story is longer, with more people in it, with more conversation by Jesus and with more symbolic suggestions than any Synoptic record of a cure of the blind. It is a parallel to the cure of the impotent man. It deals with the cause of blindness, the light of the world, the effect of light in judgment, the method of curing blindness, the Sabbath and with true sight and beliefs. The disciples assumed that the man's blindness was due to sin, either his own or his parents'. There was a current speculation in Judaism both about prenatal sin and sin in a pre-existent state before the soul descended into the body. One view declared for goodness. "Being good I came into a body undefiled" (Wisd. of Sol. 8:20). Punishment of children for parents' sins was a well-known, ancient idea but it was questioned from the standpoint both of justice and of flattery of those who seemed free from punishment. Jesus rejected both suggestions of his disciples and declared that the blindness was to let God's power be seen in the man. Human penetration into God's designs is limited but the statement is not to be read that the man was blind in order to show God's

[1] Hoskyns and Davey, *op. cit.*, II, 418.

works but rather that the works of God might be manifest in him. His blindness was the occasion for Jesus to do something. "The primary task of Christian men is to remove, by all the means God has given, the known causes of suffering: neither to solve the mystery of pain, nor curiously to speculate about it." "Pain would be no more tolerable even if we could explain it." [2] Jesus had the work of God to do before night came, which is not only darkness at the end of day or in the tomb but in the condition of those whose minds reject spiritual light. When Jesus said, "I am the light of the world," he was speaking figuratively to all men who could receive light or sight as the blind man did. Saliva was thought to possess healing power and clay made with it would have curative potency. When Jesus sent the man with clay on his eyes to the pool of Siloam, John gives the meaning of the name of the place, "Sent," perhaps simply as a geographical remembrance that the water of the pool in the valley of the Kidron was sent or discharged by a tunnel from the Virgin's Spring. But he may also suggest that there was the one who had been sent by the Father to be a light for the blind who receive not restored but new sight. The meaning of the sign is that Jesus came for the sightless to see and for the seeing to become blind. These are the moral results, not purposes, which depend on the way that men answer to Jesus.

When the man's cure became known, the Pharisees objected because it was the Sabbath when the work to make clay and to heal with saliva was forbidden. They thought Jesus a sinner, not a man from God. They doubted that the man had been born blind until his parents established the fact. They called the man a second time and reviled him as a disciple of Jesus whose origin was unknown compared with Moses to whom God had spoken. Intolerantly they threw the man out of the synagogue. This was an act of temporary expulsion but not of excommunication which only the Sanhedrin could enforce. Finally they asked Jesus if they were blind and he answered that if they really were blind, they would not be in sin but since they claimed to see and yet denied the light before them, they remained morally blind. In dramatic contrast to the unseeing Pharisees stands the blind man who received sight. Questioned by his neighbors, he answered that a *man* called Jesus anointed his eyes with clay and when he obeyed his command to wash, he declared, "I received sight." Next asked by the Pharisees he repeated his story and said, "I see," and gave his opinion about Jesus, "He is a *prophet*." His parents,

[2] Strachan, *op. cit.,* 218.

afraid to speak because anyone who confessed Christ would be ex-
communicated, shifted all responsibility upon their son. Pressed by
the Pharisees, he could give no explanation but "one thing I know
. . . now I see." Then his testimony, given in plural form as self-
evident and to counterbalance the knowledge of the Pharisees, was
that "this man" is *"from God"* who answers prayers of the worshiper
who does his will. "This man opened my eyes." Last, after Jesus
found him, he now saw him whom he had heard and obeyed when
blind. When Jesus identified himself, he declared his full belief in
him as the *Son of Man* and worshiped him. The eyes of faith were
wide open.

Jesus continued his conversation with the Pharisees in figurative
language about sheep which have a fold and a shepherd. Then he
explained that for the fold he is the door of the sheep and for the
flock he is the good shepherd. Since Palestine was a pastoral land,
the scriptures had many allusions to sheep and shepherds both true
and false. There was an intimate homelike relationship between
shepherd and sheep. The Lord is the shepherd of his flock Israel
(Ps. 80:1) or he will set up shepherds for his people (Jer. 23:4) or
the shepherd is David (Ezek. 34:23). The Synoptics had written that
Jesus had compassion as a shepherd for his sheep. John develops the
figure by a contrast of Jesus with thieves and robbers and by his life
given for his sheep. He first describes the situation in the sheepfold
or courtyard which had a wall and a door. Brigands climbed the wall
but the shepherd used the door and the sheep followed his familiar
voice. Since the Pharisees did not understand this figure of speech,
Jesus declared that he was the door for salvation. The statement that
all who came before him were thieves and robbers whom the sheep
did not hear is a difficult one because it sounds like a condemnation
of all predecessors of Jesus. But Jesus viewed the righteous men of
the past as spokesmen for God. "Salvation is of the Jews" (4:22).
The predecessors need to be limited to those whom "the sheep did
not heed" who may be the thieving leaders of the day or the false
prophets of the past. The thief destroys life but Jesus came so that
men might have life to the full.

This life, paradoxically, comes through the death of the good
shepherd who voluntarily gives his life for his sheep. The sheep will
know the good shepherd as Christ knows the Father. A hireling, who
does not own the sheep, flees at the approach of a wolf who seizes
and scatters the sheep. In the future there would be other sheep who
must be brought and joined into one flock with one shepherd. This

is an allegorical indication that Christianity would expand to include Gentiles with Jews in a united church. John emphasizes the inclusive aspect of Jesus' teaching which had been realized as time progressed. The life which Jesus laid down of his own free will and which he could take again was due to power given of God. This independence of Jesus with his life, which he gave in order that he might rise, is based on a commandment from God but John stresses the authority of Jesus over both his death and his resurrection though always subordinate to the Father. The result of these figurative words was division of opinion among the Jews. Some held he was mad and others, more friendly, that a demon-possessed man could not make the blind see.

The eight-day Feast of Dedication or Lights came in mid-December and commemorated the consecration of a new altar by Judas Maccabeus (165 B.C.) after the Syrian ruler, Antiochus IV, had desecrated the Temple with the sacrifice of swine on an altar to Zeus (I Macc. 4:59). There is a lapse of two months between the preceding Feast of Tabernacles and the Feast of Dedication but John's interest is in the continuing controversy rather than in chronology. Winter had come as Jesus walked in the eastern cloister of the Temple while Jews gathered round him. This is a realistic setting of time and place and people which John often inserts into his discourses. It recalls historical facts but in John's drama there is the play of emotion and tightening of tension in and through the facts. "Jesus, the fulfillment of the hope of Judaism, stands in the most sacred place of Jewish religion, compassed about by its leaders who are intent upon his destruction. It was winter indeed." [3]

The leaders wanted a plain answer from Jesus if he were the Christ. His reply is the witness of his works in his Father's name, the good works from the Father and the "works of my Father" (10: 25, 32, 37). This is an answer somewhat like the one given by Jesus to the messengers of John the Baptist (Mt. 11:4–6; Lk. 7:22–23). Though Jesus was known as Messiah to Nathanael, to the Samaritan woman and to the blind man, he reserves any verbal claim about Messiahship before enemies who could misinterpret it. His deeds verified him as Christ. His hearers at the Temple did not belong to his flock and hence did not recognize him. His followers hear and follow him and he knows them and gives them eternal life. They cannot be snatched out of his hand because their final security is in

3 Hoskyns and Davey, op. cit., II, 448.

the Father who gave them to Christ. "I and the Father are one." The response to this famous utterance was a preparation to stone him for blasphemy, the usual penalty for making oneself God (Lev. 24:16). The reply of Jesus is a typical scriptural one in which a quotation "Ye are gods" (Ps. 82:6) was spoken by God to the judges of the Hebrews. Since scripture could not be set at naught, then why was there blasphemy when God consecrated and sent the Son of God into the world? If Hebrew judges were gods, how much more may a greater one be God's son? This method of proof was sound in Jewish scholarship at the time of Jesus though modern argument would point out that gods and Son of God were not quite the same in meaning. Jesus made a final appeal to believe, if not in him, then in his works so that the Jews might know that the Father was in him and he in the Father. John does not try to explain or define fully the mystery of the unity of God and Jesus. He thought of Jesus as one who lived the truth rather than defined it. Ever since John wrote, men have attempted to do more than John did as they explored the oneness of the Father and the Son in mystical, metaphysical, ethical or trinitarian terms. When John wrote of the encounter between Jesus and the Jerusalem Jews during the feast, he constantly emphasized the Father, the works and Jesus. The good deeds and the teachings of Jesus were the clear evidence that God dwelt in him and he in God. He believed the opposition to Jesus to be utterly mistaken in religious insight and action.

John ends this section with his last reference to John the Baptist. Jesus went for a time eastward across the Jordan where he had first appeared (1:28). There in contrast to the unbelief in Jerusalem believing crowds came to him. They had heard John who was less than Jesus because he worked no signs but all his witness to Jesus was true and had helped to win believers to Jesus. Since many came to Jesus in the place where John had first baptized, this is the final evidence of the subordination of the Baptist and his followers to Jesus.

50

Raising of Lazarus · Plots against Jesus · Anointing at Bethany

11:1–12:11

THE LAST and greatest sign in John is the raising of Lazarus. This stupendous event and its attendant teachings not only exalted Jesus whose life could defeat death but since it resulted in many believers, the high priests and the Pharisees plotted his death. Though there had been earlier attempts to kill him for breaking the Sabbath or to arrest him or to stone him for blasphemy, this miracle precipitated the plans by the authorities, which in the Synoptics had resulted from his cleansing of the Temple. In contrast to the deadly conspiracy against Jesus John sets the generous devotion of Mary at the supper in Bethany where her perfume became an unintended preparation of Jesus for burial.

The story of the miracle about Lazarus abounds in difficulties as well as in devotional riches. Why was this impressive sign omitted by the Synoptics? Why did Jesus delay when Lazarus was sick? How can a man dead four days live again? What elements are historical and what are symbolical? What happened to Lazarus after his resurrection? The story is a supreme illustration of John's thought about Jesus. "In him was life." It is the account of a miracle in which its teaching is tightly interwoven with the events. It is not easy to disentangle any sources from its well-balanced unity. Its four scenes move with dramatic realism. First the news was brought to Jesus about the fatal illness of Lazarus, his loved friend. Then at Bethany Jesus talked first with Martha and then with Mary, then at the tomb the dead man is summoned to life. Last the death plots are formed against Jesus.

Lazarus does not appear in the Synoptics though Luke tells of a visit of Jesus to Mary and Martha (10:38). Their home in Bethany was two miles east of Jerusalem. There are few mentions in the other Gospels of Jesus' affection for individuals but John several times reports his love for people including this family at Bethany. The sisters sent news of Lazarus' illness to Jesus while he was still beyond the Jordan. The comment and the action of Jesus on receipt of the news require interpretation. Lazarus' illness was fatal physically but it was not to end in death because he was to be raised to life. Mention of Jesus' delay was not so much intended to record a historical fact as it was to indicate that his loved friends, like his mother at Cana and his disciples at the Feast of Tabernacles, tried to hurry him to action. But while in each case Jesus eventually fulfilled their requests, he acted at his own decision. He declared that the illness of Lazarus would be for the glory of God and his Son. There was glory for God because his divine power over death was to be displayed and for the Son because soon after the miracle many believed. "Twelve hours in the day" suggests there was still time for Jesus to do his work. The light of the world is the sun which can symbolize the spiritual light which frees a man from a benighted condition when there is no light of God within him. The disciples misunderstood Jesus' statement that Lazarus had fallen asleep. They thought of natural sleep but Jesus meant the sleep of death from which he would awaken. This resurrection could cause the disciples to believe. But when Jesus started to Jerusalem, Thomas, whose name, Twin, only John mentions, felt the danger of death ahead. He was the doubter who looked on the dark side of life (1:45; 20:24) but he stayed with Jesus in spite of his doubts. He later was thought important enough so that an apocryphal book, the Acts of Thomas, was named for him in the second century.[1]

The second scene took place at Bethany where Lazarus had already been buried four days. This time is mentioned to establish the fact that Lazarus was really dead because the soul was thought to hover three days over the body. The talks with the bereaved sisters heighten the suspense but they are not literary devices so much as teachings which establish the importance of belief as the essence of the miracle. The sisters act differently. Martha, controlled in her grief, went out to meet Jesus. Mary sat at home, nursing her sorrow. Martha reminded Jesus that his presence would have saved Lazarus but that God would still grant any of his prayers. Jesus promised that Lazarus would rise but Martha thought that this meant the future general hope of resurrection. Then came the all-important declaration of Jesus, "I am the resurrection and the life." Anyone who believes in him never dies spiritually even though he may die physically. Jesus offers, not a distant hope for life and resurrection but an assurance

---

[1] James, *The Apocryphal New Testament* 364–438.

of life here and now in all its reality, and its immediate power was soon to be applied to Lazarus. This statement had meaning both for the dead brother and for anyone who believed. "He is the Resurrection and therefore the believer in him, though he die, yet shall live again. He is the Life and therefore the believer in him, who has been 'raised from the dead' and is spiritually alive, shall never die." [2] This thought establishes the central truth of the sign before the miracle was wrought. Its timeless truth soars above any single incident for one family in Bethany. Through Christ the believer finds true life with God which never dies even though the body has its end. The answer of Martha shows the confession of faith which can appropriate this truth. Like Peter at Caesarea Philippi (Mt. 16:16) she accepted Jesus as Christ, the Son of God. Martha felt that she had to share Jesus and his assurance with Mary who came quickly at her call. At sight of Jesus she fell at his feet in wailing grief and repeated Martha's thought that he could have prevented Lazarus' death.

There was no more time to talk. Jesus' message had been given to Martha and his action would stay Mary's anguish. In this third scene Jesus' love struggles in sorrow for Lazarus. Jesus had been called the man of sorrows (Isa. 53:3) but there are only two occasions reported in the Gospels when he wept. He sorrowed over Jerusalem (Lk. 19:42) and at the death of Lazarus. His shuddering groans portray his real humanity and caused some of the onlooking Jews to speak of his love for Lazarus. Others wondered as they recalled that he had made the blind to see if he could not have saved Lazarus from death. Jesus asked where Lazarus was laid and at the tomb he was still deeply moved. This repetition of his inner disturbance points to a real emotion though it is not easy to see its relationship to the preceding comments of the Jews unless it might be indignation at their criticism as they saw him advancing to the tomb in tears. The commentators through the centuries have woven many patterns of thought about the feelings of Jesus in this scene. The repeated references to his emotions can be understood to mean: (1) that Jesus was genuinely human; (2) that he was indignant perhaps at criticism or at the devastation wrought by death; (3) that he was full of grief. "The groaning, the troubling, the tears have all the same cause: the contagious sympathy with sorrow." [3] Jesus ordered the stone before the tomb to be removed. When Martha protested because she feared decay had come to the body, Jesus reminded her of her earlier belief.

[2] Bernard, *op. cit.*, II, 388.
[3] Prat, *Jesus Christ*, II, 143.

When the stone was taken away, Jesus' prayer was remarkable. He looked up and thanked God that he had been heard. This confidence in an answer already given was based on the fact that he always did the will of the Father and therefore God always heard him. Not all prayers are in accord with the will of God but John presents the prayers of Jesus as uniquely in accord because the life of Father and Son were one. The last part of the prayer may be taken as an affirmation to lead to belief that God has sent Jesus. When he summoned Lazarus with a loud voice, the man who had been dead came out in his bandages with his face wrapped in a cloth. Then Jesus ordered him freed to go. This was like his practical advice to give Jairus' daughter something to eat (Mk. 5:43). Life and freedom lay before Lazarus.

The last scene pictures the divided effects of the sign. Many believed in Jesus. Some went to tell the Pharisees what he had done and the shadow of death falls across this story of life restored. The enemies of Jesus in John's Gospel often contribute to his praise in words and acts which mean more than their original intent. When the chief priests and the Pharisees gathered in council, they feared that all men might believe in Jesus. If they let his leadership continue to grow, a Messianic rebellion might lead to Roman suppression and the "place" or Temple and the nation would be lost. Caiaphas was a high priest from A.D. 18–36. A high priest was supposed to remain in office for life according to Hebrew custom but his political and religious prominence caused the Romans to appoint at their pleasure those who would lead the Jewish nation according to the plans of Rome. The office had many occupants during the last century of its existence which ended with the Roman war in A.D. 70. "That year" (11:49, 51; 18:13) is in the remembrance of John the fateful year of Jesus' death when Caiaphas in rough rude language rebuked the know-nothing council who should have been able to see that one man had better die for the people than that the whole nation should be destroyed. John interpreted these words as an unintended but divinely inspired utterance of the high priest. Caiaphas, probably a strong Sadducee, spoke for political reasons but in Jewish thought the office of high priest conferred on its occupant not only power to inquire of the Lord and to direct the movements of Israel (Num. 27:21) but to foretell the future.[4] He spoke far better than he knew because Jesus was to die not for Jews alone but to gather into one flock God's scattered children (10:16). This prophecy looked ahead to the union of

4 Josephus, *Wars*, III.8.3.

all believers, Jew and Gentile, that would come through Jesus' death, which the council proceeded to plan.

This long story of Lazarus, like any great work in writing, allows no single, simple explanation. There are those who prefer to read it as an allegory throughout in which one thing must be replaced by another to discern the meaning. Lazarus, then, is a man created by imagination. His sisters are symbols of sorrow or of Jews and Gentiles. Death is sleep. The tomb is sin. Life is spiritual reawakening. Another view accepts the historicity of everything about Jesus and about his friends and foes. Their words are literally spoken and their actions done exactly as written. The past becomes the only touchstone of reality. The presence of the Evangelist as the writer of the story is ignored. But John's story is neither allegory alone nor history alone. It is both and much more. It is a masterpiece of literary and religious art, of historical reminiscence and symbolism, of fact and truth, of act and meditation, of past event and present theological wonder. Death and life are inescapable facts faced by all humanity but with mysterious meanings as old as the human race. John knew One whose earthly life was also an eternal life. To know him was to share his life and God's, not in some far future but immediately and actually. When the mortality of man meets "most kind and gentle death," as Francis of Assisi called it, Paul declared that it "must put on immortality" (I Cor. 15:53). John saw this truth best in his story of Jesus and his dear friends in Bethany. Out of the death of Lazarus came life for him and also for all who believe and out of Lazarus' life came death for Jesus which in turn came to life eternal for him and for all who enter into the power of his resurrection.

Jesus withdrew with his disciples for a time to Ephraim, northward from Jerusalem about fifteen miles. This place in the wilderness is one of many topographical mentions in John though its modern location is uncertain. As Passover drew near, the pilgrims crowding into Jerusalem wondered if Jesus would come to the feast since the authorities were hunting him. Six days before the Passover Jesus came to Bethany to a supper with his friends. John's account, when read with the Synoptic stories of anointings (Mk. 14:3–9; Mt. 26:6–13; Lk. 7:36–50), shows his independence though it is usually assumed that John knew Mark and Luke. But his sources may be common oral tradition rather than the Synoptics. John has his own special emphases. He has a different date and the place for the supper and the ones who gave it are not identified. Martha served, Lazarus was at table and Mary anointed Jesus. The amount of perfume, one pound, was large and its fragrance filled the house. Judas Iscariot objected because he wanted money at his disposal for the poor but he really was a thief who carried the money box and "lifted" its contents for himself. The answer of Jesus is difficult but it is taken to mean: (1) that Mary still had some perfume left and would use it for his burial; or (2) that she had saved this whole amount for his burial but had used it beforehand. John puts Mary's generosity in contrast to Judas' cupidity and her devotion in contrast to the deadly plotting of the priests. The poor could be helped at any time but Jesus' time with friends was soon to end. Later interpreters, influenced by Synoptic stories, made Lazarus a leper and Mary identical with the sinning woman in Luke and Mary Magdalene in Mark but there is no historical basis for these famed but unfounded assumptions. The results of the story, as John shows, are widespread publicity and many believers in Jesus but the priests even thought to kill Lazarus as well as Jesus since his restoration of life to Lazarus had led many to believe.

John's story of this anointing of Jesus contains some difficult points though the purposes of the narrative are discernible. These difficulties are notable: (1) the relation of John's account to the actual event; (2) the surprising action by Mary. Of the four reports of the anointing it appears that Mark and Matthew are quite similar, while Luke and John are mainly independent. The actual event seems to be that Jesus was anointed by a woman but when, where, how and by whom are questions answered by varying traditions. Like Mark, John locates the event at Bethany, and declares that the ointment was expensive and that Jesus defended her action with a reference to his burial. Like Luke, John states the ointment was poured on Jesus' feet and the woman wiped his feet with her hair. But John alone names the woman, Mary, sister of Martha and Lazarus. He alone gives the name of Judas, the thieving objector to the waste of the perfume. But John is unlike Mark, who states the nard was poured on Jesus' head, and unlike Luke, who locates the event at the home of a Pharisee in Galilee early in Jesus' ministry. Luke alone mentions that the woman was a sinner and he puts no price on the ointment. The incredible part of John's story is the action of Mary in wiping Jesus' feet with her hair because a modest woman would not unbind her hair at a public dinner. There is no evidence that Mary of Bethany was immodest. Either John copied an independent tradition which he felt obligated to follow or intent on certain purposes, he adapted his narrative to express his special interests. One main purpose is evident in the sequence of the anointing after the raising of Lazarus. Mary could only give an extravagant expression to Jesus for the restoration of her brother to life. This special act by Mary is anticipated (11:2) by John unless this verse is an editorial gloss. Other purposes in John's account include the forecast of Jesus' death and the tremendous public interest, friendly and deadly, which Lazarus had aroused.

51

Jesus Enters Jerusalem and Teaches

12:12–50

ON THE next day a great crowd, hearing that Jesus was coming to Jerusalem, took palm branches and went out to meet him. Palm branches were symbols of victory waved to honor a triumphant leader (I Macc. 13:51) or to celebrate a festival like the Feast of Tabernacles (Lev. 23:40). The greeting of the people was a well-known verse from the Psalms (118:25–26) which priests used to bless the procession of worshipers who entered the Temple. Hosanna means "save now." Twice Jesus is referred to as king, first by the people and then by a prophetic quotation from Zechariah (9:9). Jesus' peaceful mission is symbolized by the ass which he rode. This brief report stresses the palms of victory from which the church later developed Palm Sunday. The twofold mention of "king" implies the Messiahship of Jesus which was a peaceful, not a royal, mission to Jerusalem, daughter of Zion. John follows the event with an interpretation which exceeds the narrative in length. There are three effects of the entry of Jesus into Jerusalem. The disciples did not understand at first. After the crucifixion and the resurrection they remembered the prophecy and the event. They had time to reflect on the situation in the light of their later experiences with Jesus. The event therefore acquired significance both in the foregoing scripture and in the following exaltation of Jesus. The second effect concerns the crowd. Their action arose from their interest in Lazarus because they had seen the resurrection and they greeted Jesus at his entry with palms and shouts because of what he had done for Lazarus. The third effect was upon the Pharisees who paid Jesus an honor which they did not intend. Among themselves they felt ineffective in their opposition as though they could accomplish nothing. They said, "The world is gone after him." It was an unwilling description of what they had seen and John gives it as a pointer to a glorious future.

A sample of world interest is shown by the Greek proselytes who came for the feast but sought to see Jesus also. Their inquiry was

addressed to Philip, who bore a Greek name, and he relayed their
question to Andrew. Then the two told Jesus. Andrew appears as
the man who solved difficulties (6:8) and won followers for Jesus
(1:43-46). John was not interested in completing the story from the
standpoint of the Greeks. His interest lay in the significant teaching
in which Jesus declared that he, when lifted up, would draw all men
to himself. The narrative serves only as an introduction to truths
which illuminate the death of Jesus. Previously his hour had not yet
come (7:30; 8:20) but now (12:23; 13:1; 17:1) the hour had come
for the Son of Man to be glorified by death even as wheat sown in
the earth produces a rich harvest or by physical life lost to gain eternal life. The one who serves the Son must follow him, remain with
him in service and receive honor from the Father. These paradoxes
illustrate life, sacrifice, danger, service and fellowship. John has no
story of agony in Gethsemane. His nearest approach is the troubled
soul of Jesus when he knew not what to say. Should he ask the Father
to save him from the hour for which he had come into the world?
His words have also been read as a prayer rather than as a question.
This prayer, "Father, glorify thy name," is John's form for "Hallowed
be thy name, thy will be done." The name of God meant God himself and to glorify his name meant to fulfill his purposes even in the
death to which Jesus became obedient. Jesus did not pray to glorify
himself and the voice from heaven which was God's answer assured
him that his prayer had been answered in the past and would be
answered again in the future. The crowd heard something but failed
to understand anything. Some called it thunder which was often
taken by Hebrews as the voice of God. Others thought an angel had
spoken to Jesus but he explained that the voice was for their benefit.
They had not understood any words though there had been a sound.
The answer to prayer reaches those who are ready to receive it. Jesus
felt certain that God spoke to him but the crowd had need to listen
to God also. The time had come for judgment, a judgment not so
much of Jesus as of the people who condemned him to death. The
prince of this world (14:30; 16:11) was a Jewish name for the devil
who was believed to hold his earthly place by the permission of God.
But he was to be cast out at once when Jesus would draw all men to
himself. When he is "lifted up" meant both his position on the cross
and his heavenly exaltation with God. His drawing power is a spiritual magnet for all men. As usual the crowd mistook his words about
the elevation of the Son of Man, though they believed the coming
Messiah would remain forever, and they asked who he was. The an-

swer of Jesus, as often in John, is not direct but figurative. "Light" is used five times to teach that it was here for a time for people to walk by it, to believe in it and to become closely related to it. "Sons of light" was a Hebrew expression for those who knew and lived by the light of God.

Jesus left the crowds and hid himself. The results of his teaching were twofold. First, many disbelieved in spite of his signs and John cites the scripture to explain this lack of belief. Isaiah had spoken of the situation. The questions in the Servant passage (Isa. 53:1) John understood as a reference to the teachings ("report") and deeds ("arm of the Lord") of Jesus which were not accepted. In Isaiah's vision and call (Isa. 6:9-10) he had been warned of failure in his work as a prophet. In John's understanding of Isaiah he assumed that the prophet's vision of God had included sight of the divine eternal glory of Christ. He repeats the view of the prophet to whom the results of his work were known and who therefore states the results as if they had been purposes. Whatever happened had been taken as God's intent. But neither Isaiah nor John taught that man had no choice though this passage, taken alone, might be so understood. The responses of men came from their own free wills though they were always under the sovereign purposes of God. Spiritual blindness was the result of unbelief. Judgment came inevitably if men turned from the light but what God had foreseen was not inevitable as long as men could choose. John felt that since men would not believe they came to the place where they could not believe. Yet as the second result he wrote of many who believed even among the rulers though they were fainthearted because they feared the Pharisees would expel them from the synagogue. They loved man's approval more than God's. This belief of the many counterbalances the earlier unbelief. It is one of the numerous references in John to the successful response which Jesus created by his signs and words.

John closes the public work of Jesus by a summary of some of the leading ideas of his Gospel. Jesus "cried out" his great truths. Belief in him is belief in the Father. He is the light of the world. He who believes in him is out of darkness. He came not to judge but to save the world. Anyone who rejects belief is judged by God and by the words of Jesus. The Father gave the commandment for him to speak. The commandment of God is eternal life.

52

The Last Supper · Teachings to Disciples · Prayer of Consecration

13:1–17:26

ONE OF John's most notable contributions is a section, without parallel in the Synoptics, in which Jesus' final hours with his disciples are presented in remarkable fullness: (1) Jesus washed the disciples' feet and explained his action; (2) he identified the traitor, Judas, who quickly departed; (3) two long discourses prepared the disciples for the departure of Jesus by a special interpretation of the new commandment to love and by the new coming of the Holy Spirit, with several other ideas like peace, joy and life; (4) a prayer of consecration fortified Jesus for his fate. All this teaching is directed to the inner life of fellowship among believers. Their unity of life with Jesus, with one another, with the Father and Christ through the spirit, their coming situation when Jesus would be gone, their opposition by the world, their instruction in prayer and their part in Jesus' prayer constitute an interwoven fabric of devotion which shines like a resplendent altar cloth in a hushed sanctuary. A humble deed, far-ranging teachings, a holy prayer reveal the depths in this part of John's Gospel which an entire book can explore and not exhaust.[1] Or the final prayer of Jesus can lead to an even larger volume of meditation.[2] Certain words and phrases occur and reoccur. This is the part of John which made love famous in the teaching of Jesus. Love is taught in five chapters (12–17), five times more frequently than in chapters 1–12 where the leading ideas are life and light. The disciple that Jesus loved appears here for the first time (13:23). "These things," seven times repeated, were spoken for the instruction and the inspiration of his friends yet they still misunderstood. "My commandments," five times referred to, are to be kept. The disciples are to ask in prayer, six times repeated, and to receive their requests when sought in the name of Christ. They will have the constant aid and direction

[1] W. J. McGarry, *Unto the End* (New York, 1941), 328 pp.
[2] M. Rainsford, *Our Lord Prays for His Own* (Chicago, 1950), 476 pp.

423

of the Holy Spirit who is named seven times. The world is mentioned five times in two verses (15:18–19). But the one word which echoes almost in every line and which undergirds all that is said and done, the supreme word which sustains all that Jesus and his disciples can be or do is "Father." Fifty times in three chapters this name for God appears because in him, through him, to him and for him everything is known and done that Jesus reveals in truth and action to his friends.

John begins his account of the last night of Jesus with his disciples with a reference to time and an explanation of the momentous hour. The time is before the Passover. The date is confirmed by later references to the feast (13:29; 18:28) and its "Preparation" (19:14, 31). John dates the Last Supper on the day before the Passover and places Jesus' death at the same time that the paschal lambs were being killed. He differs from the Synoptists who report that the Supper was celebrated as the Passover. John has his own original account of the meal for which he gives a remarkable interpretation. He omits much that is found in the Synoptics such as the place and the institution of the bread and the wine but he adds much more to the total scene. On this last night Jesus knew that his hour had come and that he would return to the Father. He had loved his disciples and his affection continued not simply to the end of his life but to the uttermost limit of love. He knew that though Judas would betray him, that God had given all things to him and that he had come from God and would return to him. These great affirmations set the tone for the rest of the section. They show that Jesus acted freely and lovingly and in accord with his divine destiny.

When guests arrived, foot washing was a slave's service which was performed by pouring water over the feet. Oriental custom differed from western ways in that the washing was done not by placing the feet in a basin nor by repeated use of the same water kept within a utensil. Cleanliness required pouring.[3] John mingles eyewitness details with subtle meanings. When Peter objected to Jesus' humble service to him, Jesus told him that he would understand later. Still Peter objected, only to be informed that washing was an essential to be shared with Jesus. When Peter offered hands and head, he learned that only the feet needed to be washed. The disciples were clean yet not all clean because Judas was present. This conversation with Peter required "understanding later." It can be read with literal meaning

[3] Bernard, op. cit., II, 460–61.

but it also carries deeper thoughts about cleansing. This cleansing a disciple must receive from Christ at his direction and for his service.

The need for foot cleansing as compared with a whole bath may symbolize the idea that baptism, like a bath, once given was sufficient while the washing of the feet meant frequent cleansing from trivial stains which were like dust. When James asked the disciples what he, whom they called Lord and Teacher, had done to them, he enforced the lesson of humble service, one for another, because they had to do what he had done. He added a beatitude upon them for knowing and doing these things. This blessing led, as early as the fourth century, to the custom of foot washing as a ceremonial duty for the newly baptized and then later to liturgical observance of the custom in which the clergy of the Eastern Orthodox Church play the part of Christ and his disciples as may be observed at the Church of the Holy Sepulchre in Jerusalem. In the Western Church prelates and popes formerly washed the feet of twelve poor men on Thursday of Holy Week. Mennonites made the act a part of their church ritual. Maundy Thursday received its Latin name from the new commandment (mandatum [13:34]).

But not all the disciples received the cleansing, humble service of Jesus. Therefore, the scripture was held to be fulfilled which had foretold the enmity which kicked in contempt against the hospitality of a shared meal (Ps. 41:9). This forecast would be verified in the future and then the disciples would believe who Jesus was since this fulfillment provided evidence. Then with troubled emotion over his traitorous friend Jesus startled his disciples as he declared one of them would betray him. The beloved disciple reclined next to Jesus. This unnamed man holds a special place of intimacy with Jesus in his last day, his death and resurrection. At Peter's prompting he asked who the traitor was. Jesus replied in word and action. The morsel of food he gave Judas pointed him out yet he was not disclosed to the disciples even when Jesus urged him to do quickly what he had to do. When he left, the others thought he had an errand to do for the Passover feast or for charity. The Fourth Evangelist clearly identifies Judas at the supper as the traitor yet he was not known at the time to the disciples. Satan entered Judas and it was night when he went out but the darkness was in him as well as around him. That Jesus tried to save Judas with a final gesture of shared food is possible but John more probably thought Jesus made known to Judas that he was aware of his treason. The faithful friends could not receive intimate truths until the traitor was purged. At the supper there was the cleansing both of the feet and of the traitor. The dark deed of Judas had been forecast three times (13:2, 11, 18).

When Judas left, the first discourse for the loyal disciples began. It concerned the Son of Man who was to be glorified of God at once as God was glorified in him. This glory came from the departure of Jesus which meant his death and resurrection but the disciples could not foresee it. Jesus gave famous answers to four of them who asked about it. Peter queried, "Where are you going?" (13:36); Thomas asked, "How can we know the way?" (14:5); Philip requested, "Show us the Father" (14:8); Judas, not Iscariot, inquired, "How is it you will manifest yourself to us?" (14:22). Each of these disciples is a living device by which John develops some life-giving truths from Jesus. Before the questions began, Jesus gave a new commandment which shone like an island of light in an ocean of dark hate. The old commandment was to love but the new commandment was for his "little children" to love one another as he had loved them. That was the supremely exalted standard of their affection for one another which would cause all men to know they were his disciples. Other references to "my commandment" make plain that obedience to Christ is evidence of love. The new commandment had its perfect example in Jesus who always did God's will and his love for his friends is the measureless ideal by which his disciples were to love one another. This love was to create a new community of affection for God, Jesus and one another. This is John's equivalent to the "covenant" which appears in the Synoptics. "It is noteworthy that in the Johannine writings there is no command to love God or Christ." [4] John assumes that the love for God or for Jesus is an inevitable part of spiritual life with them and that love of fellow believers could flow from the example of Jesus. The whole of Christian conduct is in the ideal of love. God loved and gave his Son who loved enough to lay down his life and, therefore, his disciples would keep his new commandment to love one another. To share this divine activity meant newness of life in the beloved community.

Peter, as the first inquirer, turned back to Jesus' statement that he was going where his disciples could not come. Peter's question, known by the Latin of the Vulgate as *Domine, quo vadis?* was asked again of Jesus in the legend of Peter's flight from Rome before his martyrdom. [5] Jesus assured Peter at the supper table that he would follow afterward. This is a veiled allusion to the death by which

[4] Lee, *op. cit.,* 248.
[5] *Acts of Peter,* 35; James, *op. cit.,* 333.

Peter eventually entered upon his road to immortality. But he mistook Jesus' answer and wished to follow at once thinking as one willing to risk his life that he should go with Jesus anywhere. But Jesus warned him of his three denials before dawn. Then he quieted the troubled hearts of the disciples with faith. "Believe in God, believe also in me" may be either imperative or declarative. Belief in Jesus assured his friends of a many-chambered home with God to which he would go to prepare a place for them and would return to receive them and to remain with them. These are assurances that veil and reveal the death, the return and the eternal fellowship of Christ.

But Thomas wanted practical information which the disciples lacked about both the goal and the road. The famed declaration of Jesus reveals the Father as the goal and he himself as the way, the truth and the life. To know Jesus is to know the Father. This union of goal and road gives the disciples the great ideal of this Gospel. Jesus is the way which guides men to himself and to God and which unites man and God. He is the truth which knows God and reveals him to men with living power. He is the life which gives life because in him is the life of God. The God of Jesus is the Father to him and to those who believe in him. But Philip felt that Jesus should reveal the Father who alone is satisfying to men searching for some sight of God. Jesus gave a longer answer to Philip. He wondered if Philip really knew him though he had been long with him. "I am in the Father and the Father is in me." This insight came from belief not eyesight. The words of Jesus are from the Father for it is by him that he did his works. Believe in the oneness of Father and Son or else believe in the deeds themselves. It is better to believe in his acts than in nothing. The mystery of the divine relationship of God and Jesus may exceed understanding but there is the available evidence of an acting belief which starts with Jesus and moves on to do as he did. Even greater works were promised for the disciples to do since Jesus was going to the Father. This extraordinary statement implies the coming of the Spirit at Jesus' departure. These greater deeds are not defined but they are to continue what Jesus did and then expand through the whole world. Then Jesus turned to promises about prayer. Anything asked "in my name" he promised to answer so that God may be glorified in the Son. "In my name" meant in the mind and the reality of Jesus. Oneness with him, who is also one with God, would make possible the answers to prayer. This promise that Jesus will do what is asked in his name is linked to the Father who is to be exalted by such prayer. Other references to prayer advance the thought that whatever is asked of God in Christ's name he will give (15:16). The disciples had not asked before in Christ's name but now God will grant any requests in the spirit of Christ (16:23-24). Those who love Jesus will keep his commandments and then his prayers to the Father will be added so that God will send a Counselor, the Spirit of Truth, to remain forever with the disciples since they would know this Helper as he dwelt within them. The departure of Jesus would really mean his return. He will disappear for a time but his disciples would see him again. "Because I live, you will live also." On that day of resurrection the disciples will know the inner oneness of Father, Son and believer. This oneness has its sure foundation in Jesus' commandments which are kept by those who love him. God will love those who love Jesus and Jesus will love them and make himself known to them. This answer to Philip assured him: (1) that seeing the Son was seeing the Father; (2) that the deeds of Jesus merit belief; (3) that similar and greater deeds will be done by believers; (4) that prayer in Jesus' name will be answered; (5) that God will send a divine Helper; (6) that Jesus will rise and return to believers; (7) that love will be shared mutually by Father, Son and disciples.

The newer elements in these promises are the coming of the Holy Spirit and the divine love. There are five sayings which deal with the Holy Spirit (14:15-17, 25-26; 15:26-27; 16:5-11, 13-15). The Paraclete is variously translated as Comforter, Convincer, Helper, Counselor or Advocate. It means one who is called to the side of another. John also names the Paraclete the Spirit of Truth and the Holy Spirit. He is the Helper who comes from the Father when Jesus must leave this world. As the Spirit of Truth he is an inward presence like Jesus who is the truth. He is to be "with you" collectively and "in you" individually forever. His function is to teach the disciples all things and to remind them of all that Jesus taught. He will come from the Father to bear testimony concerning Jesus. He will come invisibly as Jesus physically leaves his disciples. He will bring conviction to the world about sin, righteousness and judgment. In John's thought sin is unbelief in Jesus; righteousness is shown by Jesus' return to the Father; judgment falls on the devil. The Spirit of Truth will guide into all truth which will not be his own new contribution but a deeper understanding of truth already given. His declarations will deal with things of the Father. The Spirit has power to predict but "things to come" may refer to events immediately at hand or in the future which in Jewish thought looked to some final close of worldly affairs. John has references to "that day," which is an echo of Jewish apocalypticism, but he is more concerned with the eternal here and now. These noted teachings about the Spirit constitute a fortification for the disciples against a dubious future when Jesus would be gone but in which they would possess the divine Counselor whose coming meant peace and joy and victory over the world.

When Judas asked how Jesus would show himself to disciples and not to the unbelieving world, Jesus replied that love was an avenue by which the Father and he would come to live in the one who observed his teachings. Peace will come and the disquieted heart will no longer fear but rejoice that though Jesus was going away, it was but a prelude to his joyful coming again. Love for him will be glad that he could go to the Father whose greatness undergirds even Jesus so that the devil had no power over him as he taught the world that he loved his Father. This is the only reference to Jesus' love for the Father though the Father's love for him appears repeatedly.

The close of the questions by the disciples is marked by the words "Arise and let us go hence." Since a long discourse and prayer follow before Jesus went across the Kidron (18:1), his words have led to speculation about the dislocation of chapters or to the idea that the discourse and the prayer were spoken on the way to the Kidron. Another suggestion is that John used the sentence as a literary pause before the next section or that he gave an allegorical meaning of going from death to life. Perhaps the simplest explanation is that a slight Aramaic correction would lead to a declarative reference to the future by Jesus, "I will arise and go hence." [6]

The second discourse covers two chapters (15-16) in which the disciples say nothing until near its end when they ask two questions and declare their belief (16:17-18, 29-30). The discourse contains the following topics which partly repeat thoughts from the preceding one: (1) the vine and the branches; (2) love one another; (3) the hate of the world; (4) the future of the disciples in persecution, in the departure of Jesus, in the coming of the Counselor and in the "little while"; (5) their belief. Commentators like to think that Jesus spoke of the vine because of a meal where the "fruit of the vine," wine, was used. But John's supper has no cup nor wine and the main point of the vine is that it is a good organic analogy for God's care and for the life of Jesus with his disciples. The vine was a well-known symbol for Israel though the nation was not a satisfactory one to the Lord as its planter (Hos. 10:1; Isa. 5:1; Jer. 2:21). Any hillside in

6 Torrey, op. cit., 135, 138-40.

Palestine provided the natural setting for Jesus' teaching. In allegorical style the Father is the vine dresser, Jesus is the true vine, the disciples are branches and their actions are the grapes. The Father does away with fruitless branches and prunes the fruit bearing ones which must remain united to the vine in order to live and bear much fruit. The good harvest of grapes honors God and proves discipleship to Jesus.

God's love is the kind of love with which Jesus loved his disciples who remain in his love as they keep his commandments. As his followers do what Jesus commanded, they remain in his love as he did God's will and retained his love. This leads to fullness of joy. The new commandment of Jesus is to love one another as he had loved them. The disciples are not ignorant slaves but friends of Jesus for whom he gives his life so that they might do his will as he made known to them all things from the Father. "The Lord divested himself of life so that he might invest them with the apostolate to the world. He set aside his life and set them to their work." [7] This appointment for a fruitful mission is also an appointment to prayer which will be granted by God when asked in true harmony with Jesus. It was the initiative of Jesus which had led to their work and fellowship in prayer. Again he commanded them to love one another.

Friendship with Jesus incurred hatred from the world which had hated him who chose his disciples out of the world. The servant receives the same treatment as his master. The reason for persecution was ignorance of God. This ignorance is sin because the coming of Jesus had brought both words and works which should have been accepted but actually had resulted in hatred of him and God. This hatred was a fulfillment of scripture since a Psalmist had written of his numberless enemies who hated him without a cause (Ps. 69:4). John believed that God has foreseen and planned the future.

The disciples might stumble at coming persecution as Jesus foretold their expulsion from the synagogue or their death at the hands of those who thought they could thus serve God though they ought to have known better. Jesus told these things to forearm his friends at this crisis as he had not done at the beginning. He had many things yet to teach them in which the Holy Spirit would instruct them. To their great sorrow Jesus was now to leave them to go to the one who had sent him. "The withdrawal of Jesus from bodily fellowship with his intimate circle is the necessary condition of his

[7] Hoskyns and Davey, op. cit., II, 565.

spiritual fellowship with the church universal." [8] When Jesus spoke of the "little while" in which they would not see him and they would see him again, the disciples missed the point about the span of time and about his departure to the Father. He did not directly explain the "little while" which meant his death on the morrow and the brief interval until his resurrection and continued spiritual presence. He spoke of their sorrow while the enemy world rejoiced but short sorrow would turn to lasting joy even as anguish in childbirth precedes joy. The time was coming when they would see him again and they would regain a permanent joy which would be complete as they prayed the Father, who would give them anything in the name of Jesus.

Jesus had used figurative language in the past about his coming death. The time had come when to fulfill his life mission, he would speak plainly of the Father. Since his life on earth was near its end, it may be that this teaching about the future is a reference to the things which the Spirit would bring to their remembrance after his death. Or it may mean that after the resurrection his invisible presence would illuminate their minds and hearts about the Father. At that time they would have Jesus' prayers for them since God would love them because of their love of Jesus and their belief that had come from him. Then the paradox of the heavenly-earthly life of Jesus is summarized. His pre-existence is *with* the Father, his life is *in* the world, his death takes him *from* the world and his ascension returns him *to* the Father. It is remarkable that the admiring disciples affirm these statements as plain speaking. Their affirmation is a bridge which leads to their confidence that Jesus knew all things and that they believed he came from God. But their faith, Jesus pointed out, was to be short lived for they would scatter to their homes and leave him alone, yet not alone since the Father was ever faithful to him. But Jesus had spoken these things that they might have peace in him, though they had trouble in the world. In the face of his seeming failure they could take courage because he had conquered the world. His defeat was become his victory.

The brief prayers of Jesus in the Synoptics stand both in contrast and in some similarity to the long stately consecration prayer in John. It stands as the summit of Jesus' last hours and long discourses with his friends. It is a farewell prayer, a prayer of dedication, of intercession and of outpourings rather than of petitions. It repeats many of the ideas of the Fourth Gospel. Its simple words have varied mean-

[8] MacGregor, *op. cit.*, 296.

ings. It combines teaching and persuasion with prayer. It contains one declaration that affirms faith about Jesus rather than the exact prayers of Jesus (17:3). It unites Jesus' trust in God and his concern for his disciples in his last hours with worship by his followers, a union superbly prepared by the interpretative genius of John. Its simple cadences and profound thought alternate between the trust of Jesus in the Father and his sense of mission on earth. "Thou didst send me" is repeated six times. The prayer divides into three sections in which the address to God moves from "Father" to "Holy Father" to "Righteous Father." Its thought expands into three enlarging circles. It begins most briefly with prayer for the Son (17:1–5), then for those God had given him (17:6–19) and last for those who believe through their word (17:20–26).

This prayer begins, as the Lord's Prayer did, with the invocation of God as Father. The crisis of Jesus' death and resurrection was at hand. Let the Son be exalted not for himself but for God's honor since he had been given authority over all men to give them eternal life as God had given them to him. The definition of eternal life reads like an explanation by John. It consists of knowledge both of one true God and of Jesus Christ whom he had sent. This simple yet tremendous definition of eternal life requires the entire Gospel for its explanation. As the Son honored God by completing his work so now may the Father honor him in his own presence with the glory he had before the world was made (1:1). This final eternal glory is the resumption of an earlier position in heaven and the reward for his work completed on earth.

"Jesus prays for his apostles and urges the four reasons most apt to touch the heart of God. The apostles are his own; they have glorified him; they will soon find themselves alone; they will be exposed to the hatred of the world." [9] To these reasons a fifth must be added; namely, that the disciples may be consecrated in the truth. The disciples were the gift of God to his Son. To them he revealed the truth of God as they believed and obeyed God's word. They had knowledge that the things they had learned were from God through Jesus. They had received the words of Jesus and most of all they had believed God sent him. On his last night Jesus prays not for the world but for these believers who were the gifts of God. They belong to God and also to Jesus. God is to keep them united in him and in Jesus who had kept and guarded them in God's name while he was

[9] Prat, *op. cit.*, II, 301.

with them. Only one perished, Judas, the son of perdition. The coming of Jesus to the Father will bring to the disciples a fulfillment of joy, creative and complete. God was not to take them from the world but to keep them from the evil one though they remained in the world. He is to consecrate them in truth because his word is truth. Jesus consecrated himself on behalf of his disciples to the service of God and also as a holy sacrifice in death. "The consecration of the disciples depends therefore upon the consecration of the Son of God. But the similarity of consecration rests upon great dissimilarity: they are consecrated, he consecrated himself; and his consecration precedes theirs." [10]

The third section of the prayer concerns the church or "those who are to believe in me" through the word of the disciples. Jesus' prayer is for the oneness of all believers and for their entrance into a vital union with the Father and the Son and for a world convinced of the Son's divine mission. The importance of this perfect spiritual unity which is an act of God is indicated by the repetition of these requests with two additional desires: (1) that believers who had already received the earthly glory of Jesus' life among them would also see his eternal glory which God gave him before the foundation of the world; (2) that the world would know not only that God had sent his Son but that God has loved those who believe even as he has loved his Son. This part of the prayer looks to the future when all Christian disciples might be with Christ to behold him as he is in heaven. The final thoughts of the prayer to the Righteous Father summarize the amazing past, present and future knowledge and mission of Jesus: "I have known thee," "I made known to them thy name," "I will make it known." He had a unique knowledge of God, he imparts this knowledge to faithful believers and he will continue spiritually to enable men to know God. "The end and crown of all Christ's revelation of God's nature and purpose is to make men worthy to be loved even as the Father loved the Son." [11] The last prayerful word of Jesus is that he may be "in them."

A retrospective look at these chapters (13–17) reveals their main thought and the relation between the teachings of Jesus and his prayer. C. H. Dodd has observed these farewell discourses turn upon the one central theme of union with Christ, which is treated in a kaleidoscopic variety of aspects. Friends of Christ are united with him in the love which is mutual indwelling and in which knowledge

---

[10] Hoskyns and Davey, *op. cit.*, II, 598.
[11] MacGregor, *op. cit.*, 323.

of God, vision of God and eternal life are given to men. But prior to the union of the eternal Son with his friends is the union of the Son with the Father. Therefore, the prayer represents in human terms the inward reality of the relation between Jesus and God. The disciples are given the incomparable opportunity of sharing the divine life and love of the Son and of the Father. Immediately prior to the prayer Jesus assured his disciples of peace and courage in the face of their coming desertion of him. "It is part of the character and genius of the church that its foundation members were discredited men; it owed its existence not to their faith, courage or virtue, but to what Christ had done with them; and this they could never forget." [12]

[12] *The Interpretation of the Fourth Gospel*, 416.

53

The Arrest · Jesus before Jewish Authorities and before Pilate

18:1–19:16

JOHN'S NARRATIVE of the last events in Jesus' life is singularly independent. He knew the same tradition which had produced the Synoptics but he did not depend on them. He appeared to have had firsthand information so that he could write his own report, which is authentic both in general plan and in lifelike details. But these momentous hours also conveyed divine purposes, which arouse the reader to wonder how far the plainest statement of fact is freighted with religious import.

Concerning the arrest John reports that Jesus and his disciples went forth, whether from the house or from the city is not stated. They crossed the Kidron (dark) valley which lies between Jerusalem and the Mount of Olives and entered a garden. It is not named and it may refer to a private place but since a garden is also the site of resurrection (19:41) it could suggest that a disaster turned into a new beginning of life for Jesus. Judas came not only with some temple police but with a Roman captain and his band (cohort). Since a cohort numbered 600 to 1,000 men, it is uncertain whether John meant the whole company came or part of them. But Jesus knew all that was to come to him and he voluntarily took command of the situation as he went forth to meet the crowd and identified himself with the majestic "I am" which resounds throughout the Gospel. It is an identification and also a divine claim. Its effect is indicated as the company were "floored" by his assertion. It can be said that some of them stumbled and fell or that the statement is not "they" but "he" (Judas) fell but the awesome effect of the fall of all of them appears to be John's meaning. Again Jesus identified himself and stipulated that if the men sought him, they should let the disciples go. This fulfilled the words of his prayer (17:12) that he had lost no one of the Eleven. Peter drew his sword in defense and struck off the ear of Malchus, a

slave, but Jesus stopped his attack and declared his willing acceptance
of the cup the Father had given him. This similarity of words about
the cup is reminiscent of his prayer in the agony described in the
Synoptics. The independence of John in this short account can be
seen when it is noted that he alone mentions the Kidron ravine, the
garden, Jesus' visits there, the soldiers, the torches, the commanding
conversation of Jesus, the fall of the company, the safeguard for disciples, Peter as an attacker and the name of Malchus. Finally, Judas
never nears Jesus.

John has a brief examination of Jesus before Jewish authorities and
a much longer one before Pilate. John and the Synoptics agree that
Jesus had hearings before Jewish leaders and the Roman governor
and that the Romans crucified him. But there are variations within
John and also in comparison with the Synoptics which require discussion. The soldiers and the police seized Jesus, bound him and
took him to Annas, father-in-law of Caiaphas, the high priest. But
Annas is also called the high priest (18:15, 19, 22). This may be
understood as a loose reference to Annas because he had formerly
been high priest (A.D. 6–15) though Caiaphas actually held the office
when Jesus was arrested. Annas asked Jesus about his teaching and
his disciples. Jesus made considerable defense of his teachings openly
given to all. He had no secrets and his hearers could be questioned
about what he had said. When unjustly slapped by an officer for supposed insolence in his reply, Jesus asked him to prove that he had
done any wrong. This examination dealt with questions different
from the Synoptic report in which Jesus was charged with destruction of the Temple and with blasphemy. In John there is no decision
to condemn Jesus at the time of the examination but when he was
brought before Pilate (19:7), the Judeans declared that he ought to
die because he made himself the Son of God. Blasphemy was pun-
ishable by stoning to death and Jesus had been charged with blasphemy on earlier occasions (5:18; 10:33). Since John reported no
hearing or charges against Jesus when he was before Caiaphas and
Matthew places the examination before Caiaphas, not Annas, it is
sometimes thought that the sequence of Annas-Caiaphas should be
reversed but John's order cannot be correlated with the Synoptics. He
knew of a hearing before Annas whose former high priesthood and
close relationship with Caiaphas entitled him to take the lead against
Jesus. Matthew and John both knew that Caiaphas had dealt with
Jesus but John assigns the role of questioner to Annas, Matthew to
Caiaphas, as they tell of the hasty night hearings which were obscure

to the disciples because in the Synoptics none of them were present whereas in John "another disciple" went into the high priest's court along with Jesus.

While the examination before Annas was in progress, John interweaves the story of Peter's denials. The "other disciple" cannot be identified. He has usually been thought to be the loved disciple who is traditionally identified as John, one of the Twelve, but it is doubtful that a Galilean fisherman would be known to the high priest. This disciple, perhaps from a priestly family of Jerusalem, was courageous enough to stay with Jesus. It has been guessed that as another unknown young man on the night of arrest in Mark (14:52) may have written Mark so this disciple may be the author of the Fourth Gospel. But this suggestion remains in the realm of the possible rather than the historical. Peter's entrance had been secured by this disciple when he spoke to the maid who kept the door into the high priest's courtyard. Peter was questioned about his discipleship with Jesus first by the maid and then by one of the group of slaves and officers as he warmed himself at the charcoal fire needed on spring nights in Jerusalem with its altitude of 2,500 feet. Last a kinsman of Malchus asked if he had not seen him in the garden but each time Peter denied his discipleship. Then as the cock crew, the warning of Jesus was verified (13:38).

The trial before Pilate is highly dramatic as the questions and the answers of Pilate, of the Jewish leaders and of Jesus mount to a dreadful climax. The time is early in the morning, the place is the praetorium, the governor's official residence. The action alternates as Pilate three times moves outside to the Jews and enters to question Jesus within the building. The decisive issue is Jesus as a king. To the Judeans he was a leader to be charged as an earthly king who was liable to execution as a political rival to Rome. But as a king in his own thought Jesus had a kingdom not of this world but of truth. As a king he was to Pilate an object of scorn, wonder, mockery, even of superstitious fear and of unfathomable words. As a king he was to be ridiculed by the soldiers with a crown of thorns and a purple robe. Three times Pilate declared Jesus innocent of any crime. He tried to release him according to a Passover custom which freed a prisoner. He had Jesus scourged as a substitute punishment. But the Judeans balked all his efforts. They wanted Barabbas, not Jesus, released. They were implacable as they yelled for Jesus' death. The chief priests wanted no king but Caesar. Pilate was both fearful and cowardly as he faced the final charge that he was not Caesar's friend if he let Jesus go. Pilate could not tolerate the possibility that he had let live a rival king to Caesar. He took his position formally on the judgment seat at a place which had both a Greek and an Aramaic name. The Greek probably meant a mosaic pavement and the Aramaic indicated an elevation, perhaps like a dais. It may refer to Roman pavement on higher ground which constituted the court of the Tower of Antonia, adjacent to the Temple. Then he handed Jesus over for crucifixion.

The issues of the trial can be more sharply sketched by an abbreviation of the triangular talk between Pilate, the Jews and Jesus.

Pilate: What accusation?   Jews: an evildoer
       Judge him   not lawful

Pilate: Are you king of Jews?   Jesus: This ... of your own accord
                                         or others?
       What have you done?   My kingdom not of this
                                         world
       So you are a king?   I . . . witness to truth
       What is truth?

Pilate: I find no crime   Jews:
       Release for you the king?   Barabbas

             Jesus scourged and mocked

Pilate: I find no crime   Jews:
       Here is the man   Crucify him
       Take him, yourselves
       I find no crime   He ought to die
                                         He made himself Son
                                           of God

Pilate: Where are you from?   Jesus:
       You will not speak?
         I have power   No power unless given

           Pilate sought to release him

                          Jews: If you release,
                                 You are not Caesar's
                                 friend

          Jesus brought out for judgment
          Noon, Day of Preparation for Passover

Pilate: Here is your king   Jews: Crucify him
       Shall I crucify your king?   We have no king but
                                    Caesar

Jesus handed over for crucifixion

John's account of the trial before Pilate is notable in several ways. (1) It contains considerable conversation. Jesus gave four answers to Pilate whereas in the Synoptics he was almost entirely silent. Pilate was voluble with fourteen utterances, questions or declarations to Jews and to Jesus. (2) John sets the hour of crucifixion at noon whereas Mark gives it as 9:00 A.M. The day is Friday in both reports but in John it is the day of preparation for the Passover, while in Mark it is the Passover. These differences about hour and day have been much debated but no harmony has been satisfactorily established. They represent the kind of variations found whenever testimony is taken from witnesses about an important event. (3) John's effective use of contrast appears in the irony about the Jewish leaders who would not enter the pagan praetorium lest they be ceremonially defiled so that they could not keep the Passover for a month (Num. 9:11) but who had no hesitation by words and actions to compass the death of their own countryman. Jesus was a king but his kingdom had no political meaning for this world. An earthly king had his officers to fight but Jesus permitted no use of the sword in his behalf. (4) Two questions by Pilate had no answers from Jesus. "What is truth?" could have been answered "I am the truth" (14:6) but it would probably have been meaningless to Pilate. "Where are you from?" brought no reply because the Son sent from the Father meant nothing to Pilate. Under the mockery of a crown of thorns and a purple robe Pilate could see only a man. But his words have been transformed by wonder and admiration in the later Latin form, *"Ecce homo"* (Behold the man!). (5) John has interests beyond a historical account but some questions remain about certain of his points. When the Jews claimed it was not lawful for them to put any man to death, John interpreted this reply as fulfillment of the words of Jesus that his crucifixion was coming. The Jewish law did not sanction crucifixion though the death penalty was well known as in the case of stoning for blasphemy. After A.D. 70 the Jews lost their power to execute but the extent of their authority is uncertain under Roman governors who began to rule in A.D. 6. In general Rome allowed its subject nations to exercise their own religious customs. For the Jews this meant control over life and death for religious offenses.

However, the governor also had the power of life and death. It is probable that the Sanhedrin did not execute without the governor's confirmation. Since Rome punished sedition by crucifixion and since the charge against Jesus was kingship, the Jewish leaders shifted the responsibility for execution upon Pilate. Another question concerns the conduct of Pilate. He was reluctant to execute a prisoner of whose guilt he was not assured. But that he was "more afraid" when he heard the Jews state that Jesus made himself Son of God appears as an interpretative Christian explanation. Pilate feared for his position since he had had much trouble to hold it and he acceded to the pressure that he was not a friend of the emperor if he set Jesus free. John thought Pilate superstitious enough to fear a suggestion that Jesus was more than a mere man but a powerful pagan governor would not look at Jesus through Christian eyes. Throughout the trial John makes clear that the death of Jesus is not due to any conviction of Pilate about Jesus as a seditious king but that he was pushed by the murderous activity of the priestly leaders. A final question revolves around the declaration of the Jews that they had no king but Caesar. Legally their claim was true. The emperor tolerated no rivals. But Jewish patriotism never forgot its former kings and independence and John gave the declaration not just as a clincher in the argument with Pilate but as a final rejection of their own crucified king.

54

The Crucifixion · The Burial

19:17–42

JOHN DIVIDES the crucifixion into five scenes, each of which contains
a unique contribution: (1) the all-important theme, the King of the
Jews, continues in the dispute over the title on the cross; (2) the incident of the seamless robe fulfills scripture; (3) Jesus provided for
his mother's care; (4) he uttered his final words before death; (5)
the soldiers certified his death when one of them pierced his side as
scripture foretold.

Who took Jesus to the crucifixion is indefinite in John. "They"
might mean the chief priests but more probably it means the soldiers
who later crucified him. He carried his own cross. John saw Jesus as
sufficient for all things to the bitter end. Why Golgotha was the place
of a skull is not known. Possibly it was due to the shape of the place
or to the ancient unreliable tradition that Adam's skull was buried
there. It was near the city but its exact location is not given. Pilate
wrote the title which carried the name of the condemned man and
his offense, written in Hebrew, Latin and Greek. "Jesus of Nazareth,
the King of the Jews," when read by many Jews, caused the chief
priests to object to Pilate. They wanted it changed to show that the
title was not a fact but a sheer claim by Jesus. But Pilate, for once,
held obstinately to his action. He may have felt a grim irony in the
mockery of a crucified king for the troublesome Jews. The title, with
its information for all men, was an unconscious tribute to the universal rule that Jesus was destined to attain.

John shows that four soldiers shared the garments of Jesus. These
would include an outer and an inner robe, a waistband, turban and
sandals. It was customary for the executioners to take the clothing of
criminals. The soldiers found that the inner robe was seamless and
John reports their words as they decided to cast lots rather than to
tear the tunic. John knew the scriptures well and as he looked back,
he referred four times (19:24, 28, 36–37) to them to help his readers
to understand the tragedy which had taken place under the over-

441

ruling will of God. The soldiers who gambled for the garment had unwittingly fulfilled the words of the Psalmist who lamented his illness, his enemies and his possible death (Ps. 22:18). Since the high priest wore a seamless garment (Exod. 28:32), John may have had the symbolic thought of Jesus as a priest at sacrifice, or the seamless robe may be a symbol of unity of all believers associated with Christ, as the church later affirmed about itself.

John reports that some women and the beloved disciple stood near the cross. First among the women was the mother of Jesus. Whether there were two or three other women is obscure. Tradition affirmed that there were three Marys at the cross but it is more probable that four women are meant because "his mother's sister" is not apt to be in apposition to "Mary, wife of Clopas" since that equation would mean that two sisters, Mary mother of Jesus and Mary wife of Clopas, had the same name. Nothing is known of Clopas. He is probably not the man, Cleopas, in Luke (24:18). An early tradition cited by Eusebius from Hegesippus (c.180) states that Clopas was a brother of Joseph.[1] Mary Magdalene, whom the Synoptics mention, appears at the cross for the first time in John who reports her prominently connected with the resurrection. John's concern is with the mother of Jesus and the beloved disciple since he bade them look upon each other as mother and son. This provision for his mother is usually read as a literal-loving concern of Jesus to provide a home for his mother after his death. Symbolically the mother has been taken to signify that the older faith of Judaism (Mary) is committed to the new care of Christianity (the disciple).

The complete mastery of Jesus over affairs even in the face of his death is shown by his knowledge during his last hours. He knew when his hour had come (13:1) and all that was to befall him (18:4) and at his end on the cross he knew that all was now finished (19:28). The terrible pangs of thirst tormented him on the cross. When he said, "I thirst," they met his need by a sponge dipped into a bowl of sour wine which was the drink of common soldiers. The sponge, full of drink, was put on hyssop and held to his mouth. Since the hyssop, if it has been correctly identified, is a low grassy wall plant without long stems, it is conjectured that the sponge was placed upon a spear which in Greek is spelled nearly the same as hyssop. Bunches of hyssop were used for sprinkling blood on the lintels of the door at Passover (Exod. 12:22). Moses used hyssop to sprinkle blood on the book of the covenant and upon the people (Heb. 9:19).

---

[1] *Eccles. Hist.* III.11.2; IV.22.4.

The thirst of Jesus was reported by John as a fulfillment of scripture since a suffering Psalmist had been given vinegar to aggravate his thirst (Ps. 69:21). But it is probable that Jesus received the wine as a relief for his parched mouth. His last words, "It is finished," carry multiple meanings since they refer not only to the end of his physical existence. John placed these last words as the appropriate ending of the mission of Jesus on earth. He had accomplished his Father's will. He died as a victor because his work was done. He had power to lay down his life (10:18) and when the end came, he did not simply die, he bowed his head and voluntarily handed over his spirit.

The final scene at the cross has for its background a second request from the Jews to Pilate. Roman custom left the bodies of criminals on the cross but Jewish law required that the body of a man hanged on a tree had to be taken down before sunset (Dt. 21:22–23). The coming night was the beginning not only of Sabbath when burial could not be performed, but also of the first day of Passover or the great day. To hasten death and the removal of the bodies the Jews asked that the legs of the crucified men be broken. This was usually done by blows with a heavy mallet. The soldiers dispatched the two who had been crucified with Jesus. John does not name their offense. Jesus had died before the soldiers came to break his legs but one of them pierced his side with a spear. Blood and water issued at once. This condition has aroused much theological and medical comment. There is not enough evidence for a satisfactory physiological explanation of blood and water flowing from a corpse. John may have intended only to report a physical fact which helped to verify the real death of Jesus. Many interpreters have dealt with the significance of the blood and the water as symbols. It is possible that they indicate the two sacraments of Eucharist and baptism though their order is reversed. Or the blood may suggest life which is a favorite theme of the Gospel while the water recalls the thought that Jesus taught of the water of eternal life. Or the water and the blood may lead to the idea of a covenant because they were used for sprinkling when a sacred agreement was established (Heb. 9:19). But the incident is important to John because he states that it is supported by the witness and by the scriptures. The purpose of the witness was to aid belief. The witness was probably the beloved disciple who saw the incident and gave true testimony about it. "He knows that he tells the truth" may be understood to mean the witness or the gospel writer or even Christ. There is a similar appeal at the end of the book (21:24) to the disciple who gave witness by his true testimony about "these things." John supported the report about the blood and the water by two quotations of scripture. The lamb slain at Passover was a sacrifice of which the Israelites were commanded not to break a bone (Exod. 12:46; Num. 9:12). Since Jesus died at the same time as the Paschal lambs were sacrificed at the Temple, John interpreted the action of the soldiers as a fulfillment of scripture though his citation appears to be a free adaptation of the scriptures to Jesus. The early Christians regarded Jesus as the Paschal lamb who had been sacrificed (I Cor. 5:7). The other quotation, "They shall look on him whom they have pierced," came from Zechariah (12:10) who had told of a day of the Lord when the dwellers in Jerusalem would look with bitter lament upon some unknown martyr whom they had stabbed. John found this passage to be a fitting forecast about the people who had slain Jesus.

John identifies Joseph of Arimathea as a secret disciple of Jesus who went to Pilate like the other Jews with a request about the body of Jesus. Pilate granted him the disposal of the body. Joseph came to Golgotha and took Jesus away. He was joined by Nicodemus who once came to Jesus by night but who now acted before nightfall. He brought a costly one-hundred-pound mixture of myrrh and aloes for use in the preparation of the body for burial. "The myrrh was a sweet smelling gum which was mixed with the powdered aromatic wood of aloes." [2] John explains that Joseph and Nicodemus bound the body with linen cloths and spices according to Jewish custom. This was different from Egyptian embalmment or Hellenistic cremation. Then they placed their dead one in a new tomb in a garden near Golgotha. Since it was the "Preparation" or Friday, they had to complete their task quickly before the Sabbath and the Passover which began at sunset. Even in the brief rapid story of burial John provides special information as he alone tells of Nicodemus, his rich spicery, the linen cloths, the preparation of the body, the garden twice named and its tomb in the place where Jesus was crucified.

[2] Bernard, *op. cit.*, II, 654.

55

The Resurrection Appearances

20:1–31

THERE ARE three post-resurrection appearances of Jesus in the Fourth Gospel to which should be added a fourth from the appendix (21:1). The three are located near Jerusalem, the fourth is in Galilee. Jesus appeared to Mary Magdalene near the tomb on the first day of the week. That evening he appeared to ten disciples and after eight days to the Eleven. The longest account deals with Mary Magdalene in which Peter and the beloved disciple were also involved. Each appearance has its climax in an important declaration by the risen Lord. In each appearance Jesus is known as "the Lord" or "my Lord" to his uncertain, sorrowful, fearful and unbelieving followers who became confident, joyful, believing and Spirit-endowed. John's interest in the resurrection is to create what has later been known as the Easter faith. The resurrection stories of John and Luke have most decisively influenced Christian beliefs in the resurrection.

The first appearance established the belief of the beloved disciple and of Mary Magdalene. Mary went early on Sunday to the tomb and found it open. With unforgettable realism the story swiftly unfolds with details which can easily be ascribed to an eyewitness. Mary ran to tell Peter and the beloved disciple. Someone had taken the Lord and "we do not know where they have laid him." The plural "we" includes the two disciples or the other women who had been at the cross. Peter and his companion came out and went toward the tomb on the run. The other disciple was the faster runner but arrived first at the tomb, he only looked in and saw the linen cloths. Why he did not enter is not known. Peter arrived, soon entered the tomb and saw not only the cloths but the napkin which had been used to wrap the head, rolled up in a place by itself. This mention of cloths precluded Mary's surmise that Jesus had been taken elsewhere. Then the other disciple went into the tomb and saw and believed. He was the first to accept the resurrection. His belief is in keeping with his prominence in the Gospel. He appears with Peter but excels him at the Last Supper, at the trial, at the cross and at the tomb. It is his witness which is claimed for "these things" about death and resurrection (19:35; 21:24) though Peter's certified the empty tomb also. Neither of the disciples was expectant of the resurrection since John comments that they did not yet know the scripture which forecast the rising from the dead. The scripture is not named but it is usually identified as from a Psalm (16:10). John shares the early Christian view that the scriptures were the foregoing record of God's eternal purposes which were actualized in Jesus and the events of his life. "It is an axiom of this Evangelist that only after the resurrection do the scriptures illuminate the historical facts concerning Jesus." [1]

Though the disciples returned home, Mary remained at the tomb weeping. When she peeped into the tomb, she saw two angels in white. The idea of angels as heavenly messengers is clear but the actuality of conversation with them eludes a reader of today. John is sparing in his references to angels (1:52; 12:29). They asked Mary why she wept. She replied in the same words in which she had reported to the two disciples. When she turned and saw Jesus, who also asked why she wept, she mistook him for the gardener who had stolen away the body and for the third time her anguish sought an answer. "Where" was Jesus? Glad recognition came when Mary heard her name spoken by Jesus and she answered in Aramaic, "Rabboni," my teacher. His two commands to Mary required that she not cling to him and that she tell his brethren of his going up. This is the first time that the disciples are called "brethren." She was not to hold him because he had not yet ascended to the Father. Her report to the disciples was to inform them that he was ascending. John seems to think of an immediate ascent to God but not the formal action forty days later, recorded in Acts (1:9) which became known as the Ascension. The first important news for his brethren was not that he had risen from the dead but that he was returning to God. His unique relationship to his Father is distinguished from theirs by the use of "my God" and "your God." In John Jesus is the Son while other men are children of God. His going to God completed his mission on earth and made possible the coming of the Counselor (16:7) and became the starting point for his following appearances to his brethren. But his appearances to his disciples were not from death but from the Father so that he could give them the Holy Spirit and assure them that he was the one they had known by human sight. "Blessed are those who have not seen and yet believe."

[1] Strachan, op. cit., 325.

Mary Magdalene carried out the commands and gave her confident testimony, "I have seen the Lord." She was the first to behold him. Her belief came both by ear and eye and the beloved disciple believed without audible words and physical sight of Christ which soon ended for all witnesses.

Ten disciples gathered on the evening of the first day of the week in some secret place, perhaps for fear of the Jews. Though the doors were shut, Jesus came and stood among them. John does not attempt to tell how Jesus arose nor how he could enter a closed room. His greeting was the usual Jewish salutation, "Peace," but their fearful hearts needed it as his repetition of the greeting indicated. He gave to them his peace as a sublime encouragement to free them from fear as he had assured them on the eve of his departure from them (14:27). His first act was to show them his hands and his side, the evidence of his identity as the one who had been upon the cross. The disciples rejoiced when they saw the Lord though it was sight not touch which led to their joy. His next words constituted a commission for his disciples as he sent them forth as the Father had sent him. He breathed on them or "inspirited" them and said, "Receive the Holy Spirit." This fulfilled the important promises he had made three days earlier (15:26). His act of breathing recalled the creative power of God who breathed into Adam the breath of life (Gen. 2:7). In John's thought the day of resurrection brought the empty tomb, the ascent of Jesus to the Father, his return to his followers, his commission of duty for them and the descent of the Holy Spirit to the ten disciples as a gift from the Father and himself. This reception of the Holy Spirit is earlier and quite different from the coming of the Spirit that Luke has famously described at Pentecost (Acts 2:1-4). When the ten disciples accepted the Holy Spirit, they were empowered to remit or to retain sins. This is the only mention of forgiveness of sins in the Gospel. Much controversy has swirled around this power to forgive or to retain sins and many inferences have been drawn from it which is as notable for its omissions as for its commission. Nothing is said about this power over sins for anyone beyond the ten nor about individual exercise of the power nor about punishment for sins nor about the free will of sinners. An immensely important power is bestowed upon the few disciples. When they had received the Holy Spirit, that had been promised to guide them into all truth (16:13), they received power to pass judgment on the sins of anyone. As the Spirit indwelt them, they were to continue Christ's work with a divine responsibility in which they determined who should be forgiven or held for sin.

But Thomas had not been present at the first appearance to the disciples. His doubt was in keeping with his foreboding and misunderstanding on two previous occasions (11:16; 14:5). He would not accept the testimony of the ten whose experience like Mary's was, "We have seen the Lord." Hearsay could not help him. His belief would come only at the evidence to his own senses as he saw the nailprints and touched the lance-thrust side. The following week Jesus came again though the doors were shut and stood among the Eleven and gave his greeting, "Peace." With miraculous knowledge about Thomas he offered the test the disciple had required for his faith. "See my hands and put out your hand. . . . do not be faithless but believing." There is no report that Thomas acted on the offer. The words of Jesus and the sight of him were sufficient to lead Thomas to the highest declaration of personal belief. "My Lord and my God." John ends his Gospel as he began it with a supreme affirmation about Jesus. "The Word was God" (1:1). This declaration by Thomas arose out of his living contact with the risen Christ. The double title expressed the faith in Jesus which developed to a higher level after the resurrection. During his historic life John prefers to call Jesus the Son, Son of God, Son of Man or the Messiah since he is always subordinate to the Father but when he thinks of his divine pre-existence, he uses Logos and after his resurrection John especially calls him Lord which was a divine title as well as a respectful form of address. Lord and God are terms frequently used for deity in the Old Testament. These words were claimed by the pagan emperor Domitian as a divine honor for himself. He ruled near the time that John wrote but there is no certainty that John intended to exalt Jesus with the emperor's lofty claim. The words of Thomas express the plainest and strongest belief in the divinity of Jesus to be found in John's Gospel but the term "my God" is unique among the twenty-five titles which also must be considered in any understanding of its meaning. It expressed an equality of Christ with God but concurrent with this thought John maintains his much-repeated subordination of the Son to the Father. The words of Thomas are not the final ones because his faith had been established by sight. The last words belong to Jesus who questions Thomas about his triumphant belief based on sight and sound so that he will not think it is the ultimate level for religious life. The highest blessing comes to those who, like the beloved disciple, possess an insight which surpasses the senses. A spiritual faith exceeds a sensory impression. "Blessed are those who have not seen and yet believe." All these never see Jesus after his resurrection but they enter into life as they climb the ladder of faith to God revealed in Christ.

John closes his book with a frank statement of his definite purpose. He knew Jesus had done many other signs which he did not report. These "signs" refer both to the miracles and to all Jesus had done. But John had written about the ones which would lead to the belief that Jesus was the Christ and the Son of God. That belief meant a personal relationship with Jesus which, historically and spiritually, would assure the believer of eternal life. "In him was life" (1:4). "No one of the Synoptics, however true to the actual events, could compare with this book of John in compelling and converting power among the readers in the first centuries."[2] Its power to create living faith prevails over all centuries and whoever reads in hearty accord with the author's purpose will best appreciate how much all Christians everywhere owe to the eyesight and the insight of a genius whose great book surpasses explanation as surely as his devotion to Jesus urged him to write about him. His Gospel is "the personal testimony of a profound religious spirit, expressing in the language of a given time the truths which must ever be vital to the Christian faith."[3] To see the historic Jesus visible for a few years and with spiritual vision to interpret him as an abiding divine Christ, supremely creative of faith and life for all men who believe in him, is a lasting achievement of the Fourth Evangelist.

[2] Bowen, op. cit., 398.
[3] Scott, op. cit., 372.

56

Epilogue · The Appearance
at the Sea of Tiberias

21:1–25

WHETHER JOHN or another wrote the Epilogue cannot be finally determined. Traditionally this supplementary chapter is taken as the work of John because no manuscripts exist without it. The narrative is like the language, the thought and the structure of the rest of the book. It contains intimate references to the people and the events known in the remainder of the Gospel. It is like an afterthought which was needed to clear up some ideas which had developed in the post-resurrection period. On the other hand, it is evident that the original Gospel ended with chapter 20. The epilogue also has variations in language and style from the remainder of the book. Its report on the resurrection has a different setting in Galilee instead of in Jerusalem. If it were by the same author, it might have been incorporated before the close of the Gospel. While the question remains unsettled whether John or an editor, who knew him well, wrote the last chapter, the more important question about the purposes of the Epilogue requires consideration. It is intended: (1) as a record of a third appearance of Jesus to the disciples; (2) it re-established Peter's loyalties and duties and forecast his death; (3) it corrected the mistaken idea that the beloved disciple would die.

Jesus showed himself to seven disciples at the Sea of Tiberias. Three are named, Peter, Thomas and Nathanael. The sons of Zebedee are mentioned for the first time in this Gospel as the writer takes for granted that their names were known. The "two others" cannot be identified. Peter had said, "I am off to fish," and others had joined him. But they had no luck during a night of work until Jesus directed them. This story, like others in the Gospel, has remarkably lifelike details: the net cast on the right side of the boat, Peter's donning his jacket before he jumped into the water to wade ashore, the 100-yard distance of the boat from the shore, the 153 fish in an unbroken net, the charcoal fire and the breakfast of broiled fish and bread. But there is another mysterious side to the actual events which makes them symbolical. The beloved disciple was the first to recognize Jesus but there is no explanation about the failure of the disciples to know him at once. They did not dare to ask him, "Who are you?" How Jesus happened to be at the seaside or to have the fire and food prepared or whether he ate anything is not stated. Nothing is related about Peter's haste to get ashore though when Jesus asked for fish, Peter dragged the net intact and full of big fish which numbered 153. Conjectures about identifiable meanings abound but there are only possibilities about these figurative ideas. The disciples accomplished nothing apart from Jesus. The right side is auspicious for a good venture in obedience to the directions from Jesus. Peter put on his garment of repentance or reverence. The fish may represent those to be gathered into the Christian group. The exact number in the catch equals the number of all species known at that time and it may have symbolized the idea that all people should be enclosed in the net of the gospel handled by the disciples and brought to Jesus. The net unbroken may point to the power of the gospel or of the church to hold everyone in it. The breakfast indicates that it is the risen Lord who feeds his disciples and who is ever ready with the bread of life, especially for those weary from work in his cause. There is some obscure relation to the story in Luke (5:1-11) where first the disciples went fishing and caught nothing and then had a great catch at the command of Jesus. But it is not clear whether either of the Gospel writers knew the other or whether each drew from a tradition which in varied form connected the story with the beginning of discipleship or to the beginning of the post-resurrection period. In John it is clear that this appearance of Jesus is the third time that Jesus manifested himself to his disciples.

Following the morning meal Jesus asked Peter if he loved him "more than these." Peter had been the leader in fishing and in getting ashore though the beloved disciple had been the first to recognize Jesus. "These" may refer to the other disciples or to these things, like fishing. The question, repeated three times, parallels Peter's threefold denial. Probably there is no special significance in the different words used for love or in the variations between feeding or tending sheep or lambs. The main point is that Peter three times affirmed a love for Jesus which resulted in a special direction from his risen Lord to care for the people under his leadership as a shepherd looks after his flock. The contrast of his condition when old with his youth is taken as a forecast of his death. "You will stretch out your hands" and be bound and carried against your will. The words "Follow me" foreshadowed his death by crucifixion. The explanation that this was to show "by what death" he was to glorify God is almost identical with the references to Jesus' death earlier in the Gospel (12:33; 18:32). A third-century tradition relates that Peter was crucified at Rome.[1] It is probable that John wrote of Peter's death which may have occurred a quarter century before he wrote his Gospel. However, there is no statement about death in the words of Jesus to Peter. The reference to his age has also been understood to mean the increasing disabilities of age which lead to death.

When Jesus directed Peter to follow him, Peter saw the beloved disciple was also following. He had come after Christ without the command. Since Jesus had spoken of Peter's future, he later asked, "Lord, what about this man?" The answer of Jesus was ambiguous and it was incorrectly taken by "the brethren" or the Christian community to mean that the beloved disciple would not die. But Jesus had stated conditionally that if it were his will, the disciple might remain until he came but that it was not Peter's concern. He was summoned to follow Jesus, not to speculate on the unknown future of his fellow disciple whose destiny was an open question, dependent upon the will of Jesus. The second command of Jesus for Peter to follow him stresses his obligation to continue in the footsteps of Jesus in all things. The other disciple, who was to remain at the will of Jesus, might stay in a literal sense or continue in fellowship in a spiritual sense. "Until I come" refers to the hope of the Christians that after Jesus' death and resurrection he would come again. This hope had been aroused by the promises of Jesus, "I will come again" (14:3), and "I will come to you" (14:18, 28). There had been a partial completion of these hopes by the coming of Jesus in resurrection and by the immediate bestowal of the Holy Spirit but the disciples had also looked to the future when Christ would come in judgment on unbelievers and with eternal life for believers. John unites both the present and the future in the fellowship of believers with Christ.

The Gospel of John closes with two editorial verses which are testimony about the disciple who wrote the book and about "other things which Jesus did." The first verse (21:24) attributes the Gospel to the beloved disciple who was witnessing to "these things" and wrote them. It is possible that the author makes this statement in-

[1] *Acts of Peter*, 33–41; James *op. cit.*, 332–36.

directly about himself but the claim that "we know that his testimony is true" appears as evidence about the author. The whole verse may be understood as an authentication by those who knew the author or by leaders of the Christian community. The final verse (21:25) reads like a comment in another early editorial addition which with striking hyperbole reminded the reader that Jesus had done many things not recorded in this Gospel (20:30). The world itself would not have room for the books which could be written about the One whose life from God to man and from man to God is an inexhaustible theme.

Reference Index

OLD TESTAMENT

APOCRYPHA AND PSEUDEPIGRAPHA

RABBINICAL WRITINGS

NEW TESTAMENT

GREEK AND LATIN WRITERS

Topical Index

Topical bibliographies appear in relevant chapters